DOGWOOD

OSPREY
PUBLISHING

Dogwood is published in association with
The Center for the Study of the National Guard
at the University of Southern Mississippi

DOGWOOD

A NATIONAL GUARD UNIT'S
WAR IN IRAQ

ANDREW WIEST

OSPREY PUBLISHING
Bloomsbury Publishing Plc
Kemp House, Chawley Park, Cumnor Hill, Oxford OX2 9PH, UK
Bloomsbury Publishing Ireland Limited,
29 Earlsfort Terrace, Dublin 2, D02 AY28, Ireland
1385 Broadway, 5th Floor, New York, NY 10018, USA
E-mail: info@ospreypublishing.com

www.ospreypublishing.com

OSPREY is a trademark of Osprey Publishing Ltd

First published in Great Britain in 2025

A catalog record for this book is available from the British Library.

ISBN: HB 9781472863188; PB 9781472863195; eBook 9781472863201; ePDF 9781472863218;
XML 9781472863225; Audio 9781472863232

25 26 27 28 29   10 9 8 7 6 5 4 3 2 1

Maps by www.bounford.com
Index by Alan Rutter

Typeset by Deanta Global Publishing Services, Chennai, India

Printed and bound in Great Britain by Clays Ltd, Elcograf S.p.A.

Osprey Publishing supports the Woodland Trust, the UK's leading woodland conservation charity.

To find out more about our authors and books visit www.ospreypublishing.com. Here you will find
extracts, author interviews, details of forthcoming events and the option to sign up for our newsletter.

For product safety related questions contact productsafety@bloomsbury.com

Contents

List of Illustrations

SFC Norris Galatas. (Janis Galatas collection)
1LT Thomas Howell and 1LT Eric Kimbrough. (Thomas Howell collection)
LTC Roz Morris. (Paul Lyon collection)
SPC Terrance Lee. (Paul Lyon collection)
Stephanie Lee, wife of Terrance Lee. (Photo by Gary Miller/FilmMagic/Getty Images)
Iraqi interpreter Assim and CPT Paul Lyon. (Paul Lyon collection)
Iraqi interpreter Joseph. (Paul Lyon collection)
Bravo Company soldiers searching a vehicle. (Paul Lyon collection)
Charlie Company soldiers. (Chris Thomas collection)
LTC Roy Robinson at a combined planning session with the Iraqi Army. (Paul Lyon collection)
Platoon leader Richard Rowland. (Paul Lyon collection)
Alpha Company and the construction of Bottom Line. (Thomas Howell collection)
Alpha Company soldiers. (Thomas Howell collection)
SGT Chad Dauzat. (Greg Fernandez collection)
Greg Fernandez. (Chris Thomas collection)
The three sheiks who came to meet with the leadership of the 150th. (Paul Lyon collection)
A MEDCAP mission in Owesat. (Paul Lyon collection)
Medic Joe Smith. (Paul Lyon collection)
1LT Jay Standley. (Paul Lyon collection)
SPC Chang Wong. (Photo by Myung J. Chun/Los Angeles Times via Getty Images)
Alicia McElroy (now Alicia Thornton) and Dane McElroy. (Alicia Thornton collection)

List of Maps

Prologue

The roaring fire in the hearth at Buckman's Tavern popped and crackled, battling in vain with the predawn cold of a spring morning that seeped in through the doors and windows. Slowly exhaling a cloud of pipe tobacco that mingled in the air with a growing cacophony of heated discussion regarding Britain's duplicity and the coming of battle, Ensign Robert Munroe felt every one of his 63 years. As men shouted, and some gave speeches, Munroe's eyes were fixed and staring. Seeing and unseeing at the same time. A deep draw on his pipe sent Munroe further into thought and memory.

Like all the other 80 men at Buckman's and on the nearby Lexington Green, Munroe was rough-hewn. There were, of course, a few of the local gentry in the growing crowd, but most of those who were milling about were stout farmers and tradesmen who occupied civilization's edge in a new world. Their lives were defined by hard work, a delicate balance between success and ruin, peace and war. The British colonies had long struggled to survive against both European and native foes, meaning that these men of the frontier were soldiers. Not professional soldiers like the British who threatened their freedoms now, but militiamen. Armed citizens who answered their community's martial call in time of need. And of those militiamen, Robert Munroe was among the most celebrated. He had served in several campaigns, even carrying the standard at the fabled capture of Louisburg in 1758 during the French and Indian War.

It was due to both his military prowess and his sterling reputation in the community that Munroe had been chosen ensign of the Lexington militia. John Parker was the unit's commander, but Munroe was its heart and soul. It had been Munroe who greeted a breathless Paul Revere as he arrived deep in the night to warn of the coming of British soldiers. Startled by the galloping figure in the night's stillness, Munroe asked Revere to not make so much noise. Revere retorted, "You'll have noise before long. The British regulars are coming out!" After delivering his warning, Revere rode on to carry the dire news further into the countryside, leaving Parker and Munroe to face the grim reality of battle with the British.

By morning, the decision had been made. The citizen soldiers of Lexington would form on the common outside of Buckman's when the British ranks neared the village. All hoped that there would be no bloodshed; that the British would somehow relent. As the discussions in Buckman's had continued through the hours of darkness, Parker had even ordered that the men under his command were not to fire, but rather to disperse if the British proved unreasonable. As the first rays of sunlight gleamed in the tavern's windows, heralding a brisk dawn, though, Munroe pulled on his pipe one final time and wondered. He knew battle. He knew men in battle. And he knew that battles and warriors have minds of their own. He feared that the morning might be a bloody one, no matter Parker's hopes.

As word arrived that the British were fast approaching, the militiamen began to make their way out of Buckman's and onto the village green to face the unknown. Knowing that it was his task to organize and galvanize those men, Munroe tapped the embers from his pipe, and turned to pat his seatmates at the table on their backs and to wish them well. Those seatmates were Ebenezer and John Munroe, the ensign's own sons. As Munroe got to his feet, he fully understood the danger of what loomed before him. But he would be there amidst that danger with his sons, and, come what may, all would be well.

FORWARD OPERATING BASE DOGWOOD, ANBAR PROVINCE, IRAQ, FEBRUARY 2005

Larry Arnold wasn't smoking as he sat on the edge of his cot in a tumbledown building that had been thoroughly looted by the Iraqis.

Cracking his neck side to side in a moment of peace, Arnold's gaze passed over the young men working around him. It was a beehive of activity. The forward operating base that his National Guard unit had landed on in Iraq wasn't really a base at all. It was more a scratch of dirt in the middle of the desert. A couple of busted old buildings, a few tents, lots of sand, and an unknown number of locals who were going to try to kill them. But the soldiers around him approached their new situation with gusto. Improbably, someone had scrounged up some lumber and the guys were building rooms, lofts, double-decker bunks. You name it. The National Guard – the modern militia – had come to town and was settling in.

The fellas were talking and employing dark humor as soldiers do amidst the unknown. And it was all music to Arnold's ears. At 46, he was the grandpa of the unit, and these men were all his boys. Having grown up on a small farm in the hardscrabble Ozark Mountains of Missouri, Arnold had the sun-worn look of a true soldier. He had joined the Army in high school, serving through the 1980s, and then shifted to the National Guard. All those busy young guys working around him knew that Arnold was a soldier through and through. But they knew him even better as the best mechanic in the unit, even though he wasn't technically a mechanic. Arnold was a true gearhead, his property stateside covered in classic cars that he was busily restoring. He was famous for finding cars in the oddest places – old barns, junkyards, cotton fields. He would wheel and deal for the cars and then lovingly resurrect them. The guys came from all around back home to watch him work, especially on his beloved 1967 Mustang.

Arnold shivered a bit as a gust of cold night air blew through the hole in the wall where the door should have been. No doubt the guys would have a door up soon. But weren't deserts supposed to be hot? This one was wet and windy, at least in February. Shaking his head, Arnold knew better than to wish for heat. That would come, and it would be relentless. After the terror attacks of 9/11, Arnold had known that he would be sent to war. It was part of being a soldier after all, and he had kind of looked forward to it. America had been attacked, and he was determined to do his part. In 2003 his National Guard unit had been mobilized and sent to Iraq as part of Operation *Iraqi Freedom*. Although he had done his part, a medical condition had resulted in Arnold being evacuated home, unable to see out his entire tour of duty, leaving him frustrated as the end of his military career neared.

A grin flashed across his face as Arnold remembered his good luck. The very next year another nearby Guard unit was notified of its mobilization for Iraq. Arnold wasn't even in the unit. He certainly didn't have to go. Even trying to go would mean calling in the many favors he had built up over a long career. But Larry Arnold was determined to go. So, he called in those favors, transferred units, and was now sitting on a bunk in Iraq once again. He did have to admit that the fact that his unit had landed slap in the middle of the "Triangle of Death" in Iraq was a bit off-putting. He had already talked to one of the old sergeants from the cavalry unit that had held the base before the Guard's arrival and knew that there were strikes by improvised explosive devices, mortars, and rockets almost daily. He knew also that some of the men around him would not survive to return home. Knowing that it was his task to organize and galvanize those men, Arnold turned on his cot to pat his neighbor on the back and to wish him well. That neighbor was his son Robert Arnold. As Larry got to his feet to ready for his first patrol into the desert vastness, he fully understood the danger of what loomed before him. But he would be there amidst that danger with his son, and, come what may, all would be well.

Introduction: What Was the Guard?

Every Man therefore that wishes to secure his own Freedom and thinks it his Duty to defend that of his Country, should, as he prides himself in being a Free Citizen, think it his truest Honour to be a Soldier Citizen.
EXERCISE FOR THE MILITIA OF THE PROVINCE OF THE MASSACHUSETTS BAY, BOSTON, 1758[*]

By keeping up in Peace "a well regulated, and disciplined Militia," we shall take the fairest and best method to preserve, for a long time to come, the happiness, dignity and Independence of our country.
GEORGE WASHINGTON, SENTIMENTS ON A PEACE ESTABLISHMENT, 1783[†]

THE MILITIA TRADITION

The militia that stood against British tyranny on Lexington Green and the National Guard that served in Iraq in 2005 were separated by more than 200 years of martial history, but they were very much the same thing. Militia forces are the foundation of the American way to fight wars: a way like no other in the world. To understand America's way of war, one must first understand the place of the militia in

---

[*]Michael Doubler, *I Am the Guard: A History of the Army National Guard, 1636–2000* (Washington, DC: Army National Guard, 2001), 14.
[†]Doubler, *I Am the Guard*, 43.

American society and how that militia transformed into the modern National Guard.

The United States military system was a product of its British colonial forbearers, and in Britain, at that time, the trained, full-time soldiers of the Regular Army were often mistrusted and held in uniquely low esteem. At least since the dawning of the Tudor era, all too often the fighting and dying in English wars fell to the dregs of society. Relying on impressment to force the unlucky to fight, the English Army preyed on the lowest and most vulnerable, especially in terms of overseas military service. Even in the famed Elizabethan military, English military critic Barnaby Rich observed, "In England, when service happens, we disburden the prisons of thieves, we rob the taverns and alehouses of tosspots and ruffians, we scour both town and country of rogues and vagabonds." The situation indeed got so bad that in the 1560s the English Army impressed the entire population of Newgate Prison, which was reserved for only the most hardened of criminals, while in 1597 when the army needed new recruits it simply rounded up 700 vagrants from the streets of Piccadilly in London and sent them to war.[*]

While the great unwashed masses were fine as cannon fodder in wars abroad, home defense in England was quite another matter. Toward this end, the government of Queen Elizabeth I developed the idea of forming the more stalwart local citizens of England into "trainbands" tasked with local defense and with keeping public order. These trainbands were made up of armed, loyal local citizens and were officered by dependable men of the upper classes of society. Thus, England developed a two-tiered military: regular forces impressed from the lowest ranks of society mainly for use in overseas campaigns since they could not be trusted at home, and the trainbands that consisted of stout, dependable sons of England for home service.

The tradition of armed, upstanding local citizenry forming the true centerpiece of England's power found fertile soil in the newfound American colonies. By 1631 Massachusetts had set up the first American trainbands, then known as militia, with armed local males in each town setting up defense forces that consisted of every male

[*]Kyle Zelner, *A Rabble in Arms: Massachusetts Towns and Militiamen during King Phillip's War* (New York: New York University Press, 2010), 20, 26.

between the ages of 16 and 50. By 1672 the situation had become less chaotic, with local militias answering to a sergeant major general for the Massachusetts Colony. Town militia companies were established at a strength of 64 men who answered to a locally chosen captain who was assisted by a lieutenant. The men were directed to drill and be inspected six days out of every year, with military duty falling to all able-bodied men, at the risk of a five shilling fine. If militiamen were habitually absent, they could be sentenced to the stock, "riding the wooden horse," or even prison.[*]

The militia system of Massachusetts flourished and became the centerpiece of the new American way of making war across the length and breadth of the colonies. The military system tied communities and the military together with unbreakable bonds of kinship and camaraderie, with Parker's unit at Lexington standing as a sterling example since the nearly 80 men in the company included eight pairs of fathers and sons, and nearly one quarter of the men were Parker's own blood relatives or in-laws. The "army as community" was initially looked down on by many of the British regular officers who fought alongside and often commanded colonial militia units in Britain's many colonial wars in the New World, but the martial capacity of these local citizen soldiers soon became clear, with one British commander remarking, "Whoever looks upon them as an irregular mob, will find himself very much mistaken. They have men amongst them who know very well what they are about."[†] However, there were downsides to having the local young men of every town gather on occasion to train. During King Phillip's War (1675–76), one of Massachusetts' leading colonial generals complained that the men of many militias engaged in "the shameful and scandalous sin of excessive drinking, tippling, and company keeping in taverns," and later fumed that some of the men were in "loose and sinfull costume and going riding from toune to toune and that often times men and women were together ... to merely drink and revell in ordinarys and taverns, which itself is scandalous, and ... a notable means to debauch our youth and hazard chastity."[‡]

[*]Zelner, *Rabble in Arms*, 29–31.
[†]Doubler, *I Am the Guard*, 43.
[‡]Zelner, *Rabble in Arms*, 171.

It was the healthy suspicion of Britain's Regular Army, coupled with rising taxes and British moves to lessen colonial autonomy, that led to the American Revolution. The first battles of that revolution were militia affairs, including the famous stand at Bunker Hill. Only in 1775 did the Second Continental Congress act to create the Continental Army, the first standing Regular Army in the nascent country. To construct his new army, General George Washington was escorted by a mounted militia unit – the First Troop, Philadelphia City Cavalry. This first ever unit of Washington's army still exists today as Troop A, 104th Cavalry of the Pennsylvania National Guard.[*] For the entire American Revolution the Continental Army, much of which was composed of ex-militia members, fought alongside militia units in campaigns up and down the Atlantic seaboard.

FORMING AN AMERICAN WAY OF WAR

After independence, the United States remained skeptical of the threat posed to democracy by a Regular Army. As would become American military tradition, in 1783, only six months after the Peace of Paris, all troops of the Continental Army were discharged, and by the next year the Regular Army consisted of 80 Revolutionary War veterans who guarded the military stores at West Point and Fort Pitt.[†] American reliance on the "citizen soldier" had begun. Instead of a national army, the United States chose to depend on an armed citizenry organized into local militia units that could be federalized and brought together to form a true national army only in time of great need. Once the need for a national army had passed, control of the soldiers would return to the states and localities that they served. It was Thomas Jefferson who put America's peculiar reliance on citizen soldiers over regular soldiers into words, stating that the militia formed "one of the essential principles of our government" and supported "the supremacy of the civil over the military authority," reasoning that "a well-regulated militia [stands as] our best reliance in peace and for the first months of war, till Regulars

[*]Doubler, *I Am the Guard*, 51
[†]Doubler, *I Am the Guard*, 70.

may relieve them."* America's citizen soldier concept and reliance on the militia was codified in the Militia Act of 1792, which maintained the militia as the chief source of martial manpower for the new country.

In America's ensuing conflicts, criticism of militia ineptitude in battle often ran in tandem with calls at the national level for a stronger Regular Army. As a result, in conflicts as diverse as the Whiskey Rebellion (1791–94), through the War of 1812, and even the American Civil War (1861–65), the militia was sometimes questioned in its ability, leading to larger iterations of a Regular Army. But in each of these conflicts it was militiamen that formed the leading edge of America's armed force, whether it be incursions into Canada in 1812, or the pivotal Battle of Buena Vista (1847) in the Mexican–American War, where 90 percent of the soldiers engaged on the US side were volunteers, or the Battle of Bull Run in 1861. Whether the militia performed well or sometimes haphazardly in these conflicts, it was largely the militiamen who fought, until the Regular Army found its way. And after the wars' cessations, the Regular Army once again evaporated in favor of the continued reliance on militias. Moreover, in the wake of the Civil War, the reliance on militias only grew. There were grave concerns over the Regular Army's role in policing the South during Reconstruction. If the Army could be utilized to rule and reshape the South, what was to stop it in the future perhaps extending its rule on the home front? To many it brought back unhappy memories of the British Army being used as a tool of tyranny over the colonies. As a result, Congress passed the Posse Comitatus Act of 1878, prohibiting the Regular Army from a civil role unless so ordered by the President in time of great need. Thus, aspects of civil order, from storm relief to calming political disturbances, would fall to the local militias.

The Spanish–American War saw the emergence of the United States into the troubled waters of world affairs. The militia once again performed admirably, and, of the 194 militia units that served in the conflict, the much-ballyhooed heroes of the war quickly became Teddy Roosevelt and his "Rough Riders," which included New Mexico and Arizona militiamen. There were, however, also massive problems of supply, enlistment issues, training problems, and tactical gaffes that

*Doubler, *I Am the Guard*, 78.

demonstrated that the American militia system of citizen soldiers needed a marked upgrade as global events threatened to draw America into further wars. Following a campaign to reform the militia led in part by Elihu Root, in 1903 Congress passed the Militia Act (often known as the Dick Act after its chief congressional champion) that converted the hodgepodge of trained and semi-trained state and local militias into the National Guard. Guard units remained under the command of their state's governors, but the Guard was also proclaimed the chief reserve force of the Regular Army, and America's first national line of defense in the advent of war. Called to national service by the President, the Guard was meant to check the advance of any enemy force until a Regular Army could be raised, equipped, trained, and deployed. The Dick Act required Guardsmen to attend 24 drill periods a year, supplemented by five days of summer camp, all overseen by Regular Army trainers.[*]

THE NATIONAL GUARD AND WAR

The true test of the Dick Act was quick in coming, with the outbreak of World War I in 1914. The government of President Woodrow Wilson was able to avoid becoming enmeshed in the conflict until 1917, giving it nearly three years to prepare for what many considered to be an inevitability. Even with that time, though, America's reliance on its National Guard was clear. In 1917, as American entry into the conflict loomed in part due to the submarine war in the Atlantic, the Regular Army numbered only 133,000 men, while President Wilson called over 400,000 Guardsmen to national service.[†] Controversy quickly ensued as many Guard units were broken up and pieced out to form parts of new Regular Army units. Guard units also had their unit numbers and heraldry stripped as they were cannibalized. And Guard officers were often relieved of duty in favor of Regular Army officers. Eventually, of the 43 American divisions sent to France, 18 of them, nearly 40 percent of the entire American force, were National Guard. And Guard units suffered a total of 103,721 killed and wounded,

---

[*]Doubler, *I Am the Guard*, 117, 128.
[†]Brian Neumann, ed., *The U.S. Army in the World War I Era* (Washington, DC: Center of Military History, 2017), 5.

nearly 43 percent of America's total casualty numbers. By the end of the conflict, even the notoriously hard-headed and demanding General John Pershing understood the value of the Guard, and recognized its shabby treatment. He stated, "The National Guard never received the wholehearted support of the Regular Army during the World War. There was always more or less a prejudice against them."[*]

After World War I the Regular Army was again dismantled in a controversial process of demobilization. Amidst the economic turmoil of the 1920s and 1930s, the Regular Army languished in size, usually hovering at just under 200,000 men. It once again fell to the Guard to augment America's dwindling military might. Toward that end the National Defense Act of 1920 authorized 435,800 Guardsmen, but congressional funding consistently fell short of supporting that number. In a resultant effort to enhance Guard recruiting, states all over the nation decided to place Guard armories, used for training and for storage of equipment, in as many communities as possible. The ensuing armory-building boom brought the presence of the Guard to hundreds of new communities large and small across the country. As America lurched toward depression even as war clouds began to gather again, the new National Guard armories became erstwhile community centers, providing havens of certainty in an increasingly uncertain world. Many provided meals to the needy, others provided entertainment, ranging from concerts to parades, and all were comfortable gathering places where Guardsmen and civilians alike could seek camaraderie and solace amidst instability. The Guard building boom was transformative. The militia had always been part of the fabric of America, but it had now become intertwined with the nation at a much deeper level than ever before. Entire towns turned to the Guard for rescue and remain Guard havens to this day.

In World War II the Guard did what it had always done, with its service admirably summed up by Secretary of War Robert P. Patterson:

The National Guard took to the field 18 infantry divisions, 300,000 men. Those State troops doubled the strength of the Army at once, and their presence in the field gave the country a sense that it had

[*]Doubler, *I Am the Guard*, 162, 165.

passed the lowest ebb of its weakness... Nine of those divisions crossed the Atlantic to Europe and Africa and nine went to the far reaches of the Pacific. The soldiers of the Guard fought in every action in which the Army participated from Bataan to Okinawa. They made a brilliant record on every fighting front. They proved once more the value of the trained citizen-soldier.[*]

While the Guard's service in World War II was heralded, and its place in the community was secure, a yawning gulf grew between the Guard and the Regular Army. In the new world of the Cold War, America could no longer afford to completely dismantle its Regular Army's strength after 1945. In its new role as the world's policeman, ready to militarily counter the Soviets at a moment's notice, the Regular Army now had to remain in permanent readiness. The Guard was still there, standing as America's military reserve, but the Guard took an ever-receding second place to the Regular Army.

The conflicts of the Cold War era were carefully managed, lest they spiral into a catastrophic nuclear world war. And full mobilization of the Guard could have been interpreted as a provocative escalation by the Soviet Union. In Korea, only select Guard units were mobilized either to take part in the war or to replenish American strength in Europe. A complex reorganization of the Guard in 1952 resulted in a renaissance of Guard training but was followed with the decision not to call the Guard to service in the Vietnam War.[†] Instead, the Guard was perceived to be a place where those with connections could avoid exposure to combat. After Vietnam, the Guard retained its connection to community, and maintained its reputation on the home front in everything from storm rescues to efforts in support of school integration. However, in a military sense the reputation of the Guard sank to its lowest level, with many within the Regular Army seeing the Guard as "weekend warriors" who did the bare minimum of training and had a penchant for being overweight and enjoying beer and barbeque over any real military endeavor.

[*] Doubler, *I Am the Guard*, 187.
[†] The idea that no Guard soldiers served in Vietnam is not quite accurate. By the end of the war circumstances had required roughly 3,000 Guardsmen to serve in Vietnam, but the Guard was never a part of major combat operations.

A RADICAL CHANGE

Even as the Guard's public military reputation ebbed, a radical change in how America would fight its wars took place. After the failure in Vietnam, everything was on the table as the military rethought how it would approach future wars. From recruitment, to training, to education, to a reliance on technology and maneuver, the American way of making war was restructured during the 1970s and 1980s. And one of the bedrock changes was the disappearance of the draft. Public support of the selective service process had cratered after 1968, and the draft itself was gone by 1973, and most in the military realized that it was likely never to return. Without the prospect of a draft to fill the ranks in case of war, the role of the Guard was perhaps more important than ever. Barring a conflict on par with one of the world wars bringing a forced return to the draft, the Regular Army and the National Guard, fleshed out by the Reserve, would have to suffice in wars both large and small.

Many within the military who were tasked with assessing Vietnam concluded that not calling up the National Guard had been one of the most glaring mistakes of the war. America's resolve had failed in Vietnam, they argued, in large part due to a public disconnection with the conflict. These planners pointed to the National Guard – its myriad local connections, its armories as community focal points, its soldiers as citizens – as the most important aspect of connecting the military to the people. And not calling up the National Guard in Vietnam had severed that critical connection. Such a severance could not be allowed in future conflicts if the United States hoped to emerge victorious.

Facing a military world without a draft and needing to maintain the military's connection to the people, planners developed the Total Force Policy. Although the tactical elements of implementing the policy have altered since its inception, the fundamental goals of the policy remain in place as a part of American war planning to this day. In essence, the Regular Army and the National Guard were to be merged. The Guard, while it retained its home front duties of disaster relief, community connection, and as a deterrent against civil disturbance, was also slated to train to a constant state of readiness that put it on par with the Regular Army. In addition, Guard units were affiliated with, trained alongside, and tasked with "rounding out" Regular Army units in time of war. Initially this meant that a Regular Army division would contain only two brigades, but it would train and work with a "round-out" National Guard brigade. In the event of war, the Regular Army brigades and the National Guard round-out brigade would join together to deploy overseas.

The shift to the Total Force Policy was a fundamental rewrite of how America approached conflict. The militia that had defined America at war was gone. That being said, the new Guard did retain much of its local connection. Its armories remained the focus of life in small communities across the country. Those same communities sent their sons and now daughters to serve in their local unit, in something that resembled a British "Pals Battalion" in World War I. The tradition of Lexington continued. Brothers, cousins, friends, local football heroes – all of whom had grown up together, played sports together, gone to church together – formed the local Guard unit. These units retained their role in disaster relief and in community service. However, these units were also now a much more integral part of the American warfighting machine. How this process was to be negotiated; how the Guard was to be much more kinetic in nature, facing potentially constant wartime deployment, yet was to retain its local character, is where our story begins.

THE GUARD IN MISSISSIPPI

The centerpiece of this book is the 150th Combat Engineer Battalion of the Mississippi National Guard. Under its present structure, the Mississippi National Guard hosts one of the Guard's five armored brigade combat teams, the basic deployable unit of the U.S. Army. The parent unit, the 155th Brigade Combat Team, has its headquarters in the north of the state in Tupelo, and its subsidiary commands are based in communities across the state. Its cavalry, 1st Squadron, 98th Cavalry, is headquartered in Amory; its infantry, 1st Battalion, 155th Infantry, is based in McComb; its armor, 2nd Battalion, 198th Armor, is based in Senatobia; its artillery, 2/114th Field Artillery Battalion, is based in Starkville; its support, 106th Brigade Support Battalion, is based in Hattiesburg, and its combat engineers battalion, the 150th Engineers, is based in Meridian, while other support, sustainment, maintenance, and aviation elements are headquartered at other sites.

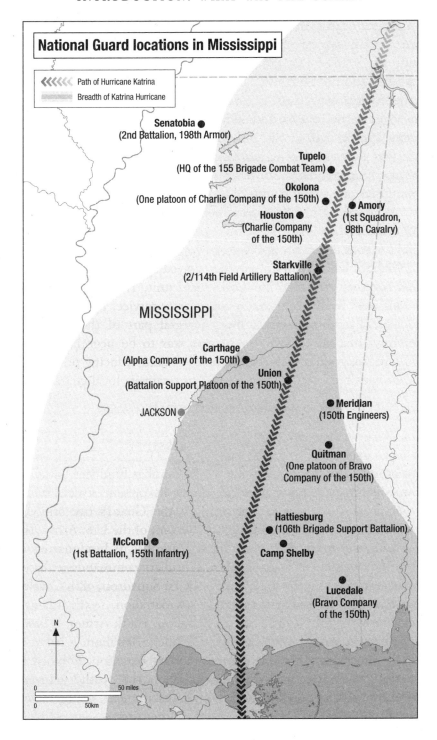

National Guard locations in Mississippi

◀◀◀◀◀ Path of Hurricane Katrina

▨▨▨▨▨ Breadth of Katrina Hurricane

Senatobia ●
(2nd Battalion, 198th Armor)

Tupelo
(HQ of the 155 Brigade Combat Team) ●

Okolona
(One platoon of Charlie Company of the 150th) ●

● **Amory**
(1st Squadron, 98th Cavalry)

Houston ●
(Charlie Company of the 150th)

Starkville
(2/114th Field Artillery Battalion) ●

MISSISSIPPI

Carthage
(Alpha Company of the 150th) ●

Union
(Battalion Support Platoon of the 150th) ●

● **Meridian**
(150th Engineers)

JACKSON ●

● **Quitman**
(One platoon of Bravo Company of the 150th)

Hattiesburg
● (106th Brigade Support Battalion)

McComb ●
(1st Battalion, 155th Infantry)

● **Camp Shelby**

● **Lucedale**
(Bravo Company of the 150th)

N

0 ___ 50 miles
0 ___ 50km

Within the structure of the 155th, the 150th Combat Engineers are tasked with the typical jobs associated with combat engineers, namely the defense of friendly forces through creation of hardened emplacements and minefields and the breaching of enemy defensive fortifications through the destruction of minefields and emplacements, and the crossing of natural and manmade barriers. While the 150th has its headquarters in Meridian in the eastern part of Mississippi, the component companies within the 150th are located and train at armories in communities across the state. In 2005, the deployment that is the focal point of this study, Alpha Company of the 150th, was located in Carthage in the central part of the state, Bravo Company in Lucedale (with a platoon located in Quitman) in the southern part of the state, and Charlie Company in Houston (with a platoon in Okolona) in the northern part of the state. And there was a battalion support platoon located in Union. Companies undertook local training at their home armories but shifted to the major base at Camp Shelby near Hattiesburg for brigade training. The 150th can and did certainly act as a distinct infantry battalion of the 155th, but its expected role in 2005 was to serve as individual combat engineer companies assigned to elements of the 155th.

THE GUARD AND THE COMMUNITY

The armories of the 150th, many of which were founded during the armory construction boom of the 1930s and 1940s, had long served as the vibrant hubs of life in their communities. Certainly, they were sites of serious military training, but they were also social sites and even medical sites where citizens went to get their government-supported vaccinations. And the communities kept their local units packed with soldiers, and offered those soldiers support of all kinds. The armories were the community and the military as one. For many in these Guard communities, joining was an intensely personal and even transformative experience. One that was individual, yet somehow universal at the same time.

Stephanie Carter and Terrance Lee
Stephanie Carter was raised in the poor part of Lucedale. Her mom had her young and was focused on her own life – so she wasn't much of a mother at all. Stephanie knew who her father was, but that was about it. He lived in Mobile, but as an adult she didn't even have his phone

number. So, Stephanie was raised by her grandmother, whom she called "Muh," which was short for "Mother Dear," and her grandfather, whom she simply called "Daddy." Her grandparents were everything to her. They were busy raising a boatload of grandchildren, but Stephanie was always their favorite, and she knew it.

Life was tough, with the large family living very much from paycheck to paycheck. Most of the kids in the household were in a state of constant trouble, often mixing with the wrong crowds and getting told that they needed to get right with the Lord. But not Stephanie. Of all the kids, she was the one who was most determined to make something of herself. Life somewhat limited her goals, but she certainly had goals and knew what they were. Her goals weren't pie-in-the-sky dreams of being a model, or a scientist, or a star athlete. Stephanie was better grounded in the reality of her world than that. Her dreams were practical, real-life ambitions. She wanted a good stable job – the kind where she could work with her hands. She wanted enough money to keep a roof over her head and to pay the bills without having to worry. That was it; that was enough for Stephanie. And Muh and Daddy couldn't have been prouder.

It wasn't much of a shock when Stephanie got pregnant during high school; such was the norm in the community and in the family. Again, Stephanie was practical. She and the baby's father had agreed to marry, and all would be well. The couple would set down to the hard work of making sure that their child had a chance at a real future – perhaps one that extended beyond Stephanie's own practical dreams. As high school neared its end, Stephanie was too pregnant to attend senior prom, so the couple decided to go watch a movie and have dinner instead. But Stephanie's fiancé never showed up that night; he had taken another girl to the prom instead. Stephanie went to his house later and found the two together. Irate and heartbroken, Stephanie dumped him right then and there and concluded that she had been abandoned and forgotten for the last time in her life. She was now determined to take control and never have to rely on others.*

---

*As with most of the source material for this book, information regarding Stephanie Lee comes from oral interviews, in this case with her in-laws – the family of her husband Terrance Lee. However, information regarding Stephanie also comes from printed sources that chronicled her story, including Warren Kulo, "Stephanie Lee: A Story of Unspeakable Tragedy, Remarkable Courage, and Hope," Gulflive.com, January 2014.

Stephanie had her child, a daughter named Kamri, completed high school, and got a good paying job as a pipe fitter at Ingalls Shipyard. But Stephanie wasn't done; she felt that she needed more, so she joined the National Guard. She really wanted to be in the Guard. These were the folks who helped others in times of emergency. These were the folks on whom everyone relied. She looked forward to the extra pay and benefits that being in the Guard provided. The training and physical regimen of Guard life was kind of tough, but she knew that it was all teaching her more discipline and gave her a whole host of new friends. But still Muh and Daddy were everything to her. She got a small place near them, and they helped out a lot with Kamri. Sadly, Stephanie's National Guard career didn't last that long. During a training cycle a couple of years later she injured her back and received a medical discharge. The injury didn't affect her job at Ingalls, but her career in the National Guard had ended almost before it had really started.

Terrance Lee was from Moss Point. His mother, Dinah, was a high school junior who worked at McDonald's. His father, Dedrick Lee, was also in high school. Although the young couple did not marry, they were determined to take care of Terrance the best way they could, and the matriarch of the Lee family stepped in to help. Terrance moved in with his grandparents, Anice Lee and Robert E. Lee, where his father also lived while completing high school. It was almost like Terrance was Dedrick's much younger brother, and little Terrance soon ruled the roost. As he grew Terrance ran the neighborhood with a group of friends, with everyone sharing snacks and drinks with the boys. From the beginning Terrance was a fashion plate, always wanting the best clothes. And he was every bit a ladies' man.

By the time that he was in high school, Dinah and Dedrick's second son, Darius, had joined in living at the Lee family home. Although there were 13 years separating Terrance and Darius, the duo soon became close. After graduation, Terrance got a job at Ingalls, where he made enough to buy a car. It was a Chevy Avalanche, his pride and joy. Soon he had it tricked out with a set of rims, and he and Darius would ride through the neighborhood listening to Tupac and Master P loud enough for everyone to hear. By the time he was 20, Terrance and his girlfriend Stacey had begun to have their own children, welcoming Terrance Jr. and Raemone to the burgeoning Lee family. Anice could see the change that those children wrought in Terrance – he fairly doted on them and beamed with pride. And although his relationship with Stacey didn't last, it was clear to all that parenthood brought him immense joy, coupled with a new and mature approach to his future.

It was about this time that Terrance first saw Stephanie Carter, both eating lunch at the same time in the Ingalls factory cafeteria. She was beautiful, and plainly had her act together. All of Terrance's friends noticed his growing interest in her, something that they liked to poke fun about from time to time. And Stephanie certainly noticed that this young man was paying her attention. Stephanie noted how serious and mature Terrance was – she also couldn't help but notice his good looks. And he sure was a snappy dresser. So, it wasn't long before the couple started dating.

Things quickly became serious, and Terrance knew he wanted to provide a stable home for both his children and her daughter Kamri. One of the things that Stephanie loved about Terrance is that she could really talk to him – he would listen intently to anything she had to say. In 2004, though, when Terrance was 24 and Stephanie was 27, much in their lives changed. On a bright Sunday afternoon, Stephanie's beloved Muh and Daddy were on their way home from church on Highway 98 when they were struck head on by a driver who was high on meth. Muh and Daddy died at the scene of the accident. Stephanie had lost the only relatives who had really cared about her. She was adrift. And there through it all was Terrance – the only person to whom she could vent; the only shoulder she could cry on. In the wake of the life-altering disaster the couple decided to marry – to start a new chapter together.

Terrance knew just what he needed to do to make his marriage a success; he needed to join the National Guard. Both his father Dedrick and his uncle Douglas were in the Guard, which had provided them with a job, benefits, and a new outlook on life. The Guard could make Terrance a better man. The Guard would make it possible for him to be the husband and father he wanted to be. Grandmother Anice wasn't surprised that Terrance had opted to join, but it did worry her a bit. In 2004 it was plain that the Guard might well get called up to go to war in Iraq. She counseled Terrance on the possible dangers of joining, but he countered with a story. Just two weeks prior a thief had pulled a gun on him while he was stopped at a stoplight and threatened to kill him for his money. Terrance told Anice that Iraq might be dangerous, but he could just as easily get killed in Moss Point, and in Iraq he would be making a difference for America while also bettering his future. Anice knew that Terrance was determined and did not stand in the way of his enlistment. There was a surprise in store for Anice, though. She was going through Terrance's pockets one day getting his clothes ready to wash, and she found a paper that listed Terrance's wife Stephanie as his beneficiary for his military insurance. That was the first that Anice had heard about Terrance's marriage. He and Stephane had secretly visited the justice of the peace just before he shipped out to basic training. Anice folded the paper neatly and set it aside while slowly shaking her head and smiling. Stephanie was a fine young woman, and Anice's smile only grew as she daydreamed about the future that Terrance and Stephanie had together.

Sean Cooley and Laura Kehoe

Sean was born to Katherine and Jerry Cooley in 1969, the year that Hurricane Camille slammed into the Mississippi Gulf Coast. Jerry worked for a local chemical company and moved the family to a small village outside of Lucedale in 1971. Jerry kept his job at the chemical plant, but the family now also had a 160-acre farm complete with cattle, goats, and a fishing pond, which gave young Sean and his brother Patrick plenty of opportunity for chores to keep them busy. And the neighborhood was a family affair, with Sean's grandparents living right next door. Sean loved the outdoors above all else and was fearless. Katherine nearly screamed when toddler Sean opened the back door one sunny afternoon asking for a bottle to put his baby whales into so he could keep them alive as pets. Those baby whales, however, were baby snakes, and Katherine very much did not like snakes. It only got worse a couple of years later when Sean brought home a skunk as a pet, which failed spectacularly. And Katherine always made sure to give Sean's clothes a good shake before checking his pockets on laundry day. She had made the mistake once of reaching into one of his pants pockets and pulling out a live fish.

Sean was rather bored by school, but he loved to read. In the winter, when there was less outside fun to be had, Sean would often climb up into a deer stand. Not to hunt. He much preferred to just watch the beauty of the deer and really couldn't bring himself to shoot something so majestic. And when there weren't deer to watch, Sean would curl up in the deer stand and read for hours. It didn't matter what kind of book

– adventure books, science fiction, even nursing books. Katherine was a nurse, and her study books were all over the house. She knew where to look if one went missing. It was in the deer stand with Sean.

After he graduated high school Sean worked for a summer at the local sawmill. In all honesty Sean had never thought much about college or a career. But that one summer in the sawmill changed things. He wasn't cut out for that kind of work and never wanted to do it again. While he was gathering his thoughts about his future, Sean decided to join the Navy. Both of Sean's grandfathers had been in the Navy in World War II, so he had grown up with stories about their service. And he figured that it would give him time to sort out what he really wanted to be. Sean spent the first six years of the 1990s as a Seabee, and by the time he got out he did indeed know what he wanted to spend the rest of his life doing. He was going to become a nurse. So, Sean joined the National Guard, in part for the college benefits and in part because his time in the Navy had taught him a great deal about service. He very much wanted to do his part to keep his nation safe in an uncertain time. Sean also enrolled in his first nursing classes at a local junior college. After graduation, Sean worked at several local hospitals before winding up at Singing River Hospital in Ocean Springs where he worked as a trauma nurse.

Laura Kehoe had grown up in Ocean Springs and had tried computer science in college before moving into nursing. Bored with life in one place, Laura had served as a travel nurse, moving from town to town as the job demanded. But she had tired of eating alone and never quite knowing where she was, so she returned to Ocean Springs to work at Singing River. When she walked into the emergency room, there was Sean who smiled and said, "Hey. I remember you." For the life of her Laura couldn't remember meeting Sean, but it slowly dawned on her from Sean's conversation that they had both been in a nursing class together. Initially she worked the night shift and Sean the day shift, but one night there he was. Turned out that he had altered his schedule so they could work together. She knew that Sean was married, but she had also heard that the marriage was in trouble. But at this point Sean was just a friend. The night shift was a tight-knit group that often sat around talking about everything under the sun when there were lulls in the action, and they often socialized together. And through it all Sean and Laura kept getting closer and closer.

Laura was instantly attracted to Sean. Sure, he was good-looking. But Sean also had a serious nature and a deep kindness that somehow set him apart from other men. Slowly the night shift group conversations became more Laura and Sean conversations. And they talked about everything, from life goals, to whether each of them eventually wanted children, to the best way to raise children, to faith, to money. They talked about it all, long before they were in any kind of relationship. It all meant so much to Laura – having an honest-to-God confidante. She just felt like she could share anything with Sean, no matter what. And it enchanted her that, even during the most serious conversation, Sean remained mischievous with the joyous heart of a little boy. She could tell that something was coming when his face began to break into a smile. And what was coming was a prank. His favorite involved the head nurse of the night shift, who liked to leave her car keys on the counter. Sean would go and move her car multiple times a night, cracking up the staff and leaving the head nurse with a perpetual, but good-natured scowl. Most importantly, though, Sean was incredibly giving. He would often stay long after the conclusion of his shift to sit and talk with a patient who was having trouble dealing with their trauma. He would hold their hand, pray, be a friend – whatever they needed, Sean did. Soon Laura Kehoe realized that she was in love with this nurse and Guardsman.

The National Guard was and is the heart of American military tradition, one that was undergoing great change at the dawn of a new century. Yet, throughout, the Guard retained its local character and connection, another throwback to America's deep past. The Guard *is* its local families, its men and women. It is Stephanie Carter, Terrance Lee, Sean Cooley, and Laura Kehoe.

Who Was the 150th?

I remember feeling a sense of anxiety because I'd never been deployed before. I've never even left the country before... Honestly, everything you see on TV, you kind of believe because that's the way society is. That's the way things are supposed to work. So initially, I thought I would be killed. I was afraid, but I knew that I had an obligation to fulfill. So I had a duty to go do, and I put everything aside, put my selfish feelings aside and did what I was trained to do.

TERRANCE BLOODSAW

JOINING THE GUARD

Some members of the 150th, like Sean Cooley, came to the National Guard only after stints in the Army or Navy, but for most the decision to join was an organic first step into the US military. Reasons for joining the Guard were, of course, intensely individualistic and were often tied to the community's close connection to the local unit. For some, joining the Guard was a ticket out of poverty in the poorest state in the union. Russell Griffith grew up on a farm in the countryside outside of Laurel, Mississippi. It was hard times for the local and national economy, and, even though everyone in the community tried to help each other out, the Griffith family could barely get by. Russell worked with his father picking peas on the family plot and selling them to locals, sometimes parking their pickup on the side of the road and hoping that customers would see their sign and stop. But it was barely enough to keep Russell in clothes for school, much less allow him to dream of anything like college. He did have dreams of maybe getting a degree in agricultural studies so that he could help his family, but instead he fell in with a bad crowd in high school and things looked even more bleak. For the Griffith family, serving in the Guard had long been an escape valve in life, with two of Russell's uncles and three of his siblings already serving once they became of age. Seeing little future for himself and knowing that he needed to get away from the negative influence of his friendship group, Griffith joined the Guard to restart his life.

Christopher Dueitt spent his childhood in the deep rural fastness of Greene County. Only 13,000 people lived in the entire county, and his tiny hometown of Clark numbered just over 100 residents. Christopher had nearly limitless energy, but there never seemed to be any outlet for his drive and passion; there seemed to be nothing for him but dead-end jobs or getting into trouble with his equally bored friends. His mom worked hard to keep Christopher on the straight and narrow, but somehow that didn't work, and by the time Christopher was halfway through high school he was using drugs heavily and had dropped out. His family didn't know what to do to help him, and he certainly didn't know what to do to help himself. There were a few people in the local communities who had "made it," though, and their way out had been the Guard, which had an armory in Lucedale, in neighboring George County. Fearing for his future, and taking his mom's advice, Christopher joined up, hoping to find something better.

Stacey Ford grew up the opposite direction from Lucedale in the village of Buzzard Roost, which boasted 75 residents. It was a town where everyone knew everyone, and they all sure knew the Ford family since Stacey's father, John Henry, was a local Pentecostal preacher. Stacey loved motorcycles, especially his Indian 75cc, and he got a decent job apprenticing as an iron worker after high school. But something along the way went wrong, with Stacey running into trouble with local law enforcement. It was made clear that he had two choices – doing time or joining the Guard. Didn't turn out to be a difficult choice at all. The Guard it was.

For Rickey Posey the choice was equally easy. His family lived in the sticks outside of Meridian, and his childhood playground was the woods where he and his family hunted pretty much anything they could. His father, a plumber, built their tiny house. As a young child

Rickey could even remember when the house was nothing but floors – no walls, roof, or anything. Rickey had five siblings, which meant that he and his three brothers all slept in the same bed with two at the bottom and two at the top. And, even though Dad was a plumber, there was no indoor bathroom. The family never went hungry, but Rickey knew that they were poor. Two of his older brothers had already joined the Guard by the time Rickey was in high school, so joining the Guard like they had seemed the natural order of things. To Rickey Posey the Guard seemed to be the best ticket to a better life.

GET THAT EDUCATION

Others in the 150th joined the Guard more specifically due to the educational benefits associated with Guard service. Sherman Hillhouse grew up in Okolona, where his father drove 18-wheelers cross country while his mom worked as a seamstress in a local factory. In high school Sherman played on the local football team, and he had a fairly standard middle-class life. But he really wasn't sure what he wanted for his future. His parents pushed him toward college, but he wasn't convinced that the college life was for him. Then career day rolled around at high school, and the presenter on National Guard opportunities wound up being someone that Sherman knew, so he paid more attention to him than the other speakers. The speaker talked about Guard life and training but spoke a lot about educational benefits. The Guard would pay for him to go to school. And, to top it all off, the local Guard unit at the time was a construction unit, and construction interested Sherman deeply. So, as it turned out, Sherman and about 14 of his buddies went to see the recruiter to join up, and Sherman also enrolled at the local community college to learn more about electrical systems. He hoped that the two, together, would forge him a future.

Dexter Thornton was raised in the Sunrise Community outside of Carthage, Mississippi. His father worked as an electrician, and his grandmother ran a small country store across the street from their house; a store that served as much as a community center as anything else. Dexter's parents had not been fortunate enough to attend college themselves, so they did their best to steer their children toward educational opportunity. Attending Leake Academy High School, Dexter took his parents' hopes to heart and graduated with honors, planning on making their college dreams for him come true. What came next was made much easier by the fact that Dexter's father had joined the local Guard unit himself before Dexter's graduation. So, for Dexter Thornton, joining the 150th meant going to college and getting a chance to serve with his father. It didn't take him long to make up his mind, and he joined during his senior year in high school.

Ken Cager was raised an old country boy and lived in the town of Carthage. His father Quentin worked offshore on the oil rigs, and his mom Janeese ran the local country store that served lunches to the workers at the nearby poultry plant. Neither parent had enjoyed much educational opportunity, so they pushed Ken and his two siblings toward excellence in school. And at school it seemed that nearly every male teacher or coach was a military veteran. Ken never believed much in his own academic ability but worked hard because it was what his parents wanted. He knew that he was going to college, but he had no idea whatsoever about how anyone in his family was going to be able to pay for it. But his dad knew exactly how he was going to pay for it: Ken was going into the Guard. One bright Sunday morning Quentin told Ken it was time to head down to the National Guard recruiter – no ifs, ands, or buts about it. So, the very next morning, Ken, aged 17, showed up at the recruiter's office. The recruiter introduced himself and Ken said, "My dad told me to come down here and sign up. So here I am." The recruiter responded, "Son, we can square you away." Ken couldn't help but think that he was the easiest recruit that the Guard had ever signed up.

Roy Robinson, who eventually commanded the 150th on its deployment to Iraq in 2005, grew up along with six siblings in Meridian, Mississippi. The family was by no means wealthy, but there was always a premium put on education, so for Roy there was never really a choice. He was going to college. Knowing his future, Roy started working at every job he could find to save money for his education. After high school he enrolled at the University of Southern Mississippi and discovered fraternity life. His first two years of study were "memorable," perhaps not in an academic sense but certainly in a social sense. Then his savings simply ran out, and it looked like his college education was over. But one of his fraternity buddies patted Roy on the shoulder and told him that he had a solution. "No problem. Come with me. We will go over and talk to the recruiter." His fraternity buddy was in the

National Guard, and Roy got into the passenger seat of his car and the duo headed to Camp Shelby just south of town.

Robinson told the recruiter his situation. His academic standing wasn't the best, he didn't have any money, and had no interest in going home to live with his parents again. The recruiter had an easy answer: "Hey, no problem. We'll put you in the Guard. The Guard will pay for your college. I know you're here, kind of in between semesters. If you'll work with me, I think we can have you on your way pretty quickly and have you back in time for the fall semester." So, Robinson signed up for the Guard on the split option, which meant that he could undertake basic training and then go back to school before Advanced Individual Training (AIT). Thus, in the summer between sophomore and junior year in college, Robinson was off to Fort Leonard Wood, Missouri, for basic training. For some reason he didn't think that they buzzed your hair any more in basic, but he was wrong there. All his nice hair was gone the next time he showed up to Southern Miss.

DELVING DEEPER

Norris Galatas

Connections to the Guard and reasons for joining ran deep across the 150th. Norris Galatas was born at Fort Meade, Maryland, where his father served in the Army. His mother was also in the military, and for a while things were good. The family grew quickly to include two sisters and four brothers. While Norris' father was in the service everyone was pretty well looked after, but things got bad quickly when he retired. The family moved to Slidell, Louisiana, where Dad could not come to terms with civilian life; it simply didn't suit him. He bounced from job to job, always thinking that he deserved more and always quitting. When he was between jobs, which was often, the situation was dire for the Galatas family. As Norris approached his teen years, the family all lived in a 1963 Chevrolet Impala Station Wagon. No water, hardly any clothes, barely enough to eat – and all eight crammed into a single car. The family was falling to pieces, and in desperation Norris' father turned to his own mother, Peggy. The broken-down Impala and its many passengers barely made it to Peggy's driveway in Jefferson, Louisiana. Norris' parents bluntly told Peggy that the choice was simple. Either she could take the children in, or they would have to go to foster care.

Wiping tears from her eyes, Peggy knew that it wasn't really a choice at all. All six children piled out of the car, hugged their parents, and moved into Peggy's trailer. With seven people living in a two-bedroom trailer, it was not a life of luxury, but there was food on the table and real beds to sleep in. The two sisters shared one room, all four boys crammed into the same bed in another room, and Grandma Peggy slept on a fold-out couch in the living room. Peggy could hardly believe the condition of her grandchildren, and immediately set about putting their lives in some kind of order. They had largely done what they liked while living with their parents, but Peggy demanded more. She never beat them, but she required accountability and a strict schedule. For some of the older kids it was just too much, and soon the eldest three moved out.

Norris, though, who was just entering eighth grade, thrived under the new regime. He needed and enjoyed the guidance that Peggy provided. Convinced that some of the friction that had beset the family had come from their cramped living arrangements, Peggy moved to a small house outside of Meridian, Mississippi, where the remaining siblings could have more room to live their lives. Norris enjoyed school, especially Mr. Flowers' science class. He attended Meridian High School and eventually became the only one of his siblings to receive a high school diploma. There had never been much talk of education in his family, although Norris was a good student, and certainly no talk of college. But Norris already knew what he wanted to do, so none of that mattered. He wanted to join the military – and to do better at both it and life than his father had. Toward that end, while he was in high school Norris took the Armed Services Vocational Aptitude Battery (ASVAB) test and scored well. He scored so well that the Navy wanted him to work in its nuclear reactor program. But Norris had no desire to work with reactors in the bowels of a giant ship or, worse yet, undersea on a submarine. Both filled him with a sense of claustrophobia. Instead, right after high school Norris chose to join his local National Guard unit.

Peggy was proud that Norris had graduated and had chosen to serve. Initially he worked as a movement specialist, issuing fuel and arranging for its transport to the unit that needed it. He also got a job working for a wholesale pharmaceutical company, starting off in packing but quickly moving his way up to driving a truck. The Guard pay, combined with the pay from his "regular" job, was enough for Norris to buy a small house on an open piece of property outside Meridian. And he had fallen in love and gotten married. Both he and his wife Janis shared a love of horses. After fighting so hard to get there, Norris could barely slow down enough to see how far he had come. A nice home, a horse paddock, and several horses that kept both him and Janis busy. He couldn't help but think that he was living the American dream.

Larry Arnold

Larry Arnold was born in Thayer, Missouri – the hardscrabble land of the Ozark Mountains. If anything, his parents were even harder than their surroundings. His father, Howard, a preacher, was very demanding in all aspects of Larry's life. There were difficult chores to do every day, and the family saw little need for schooling. Real men worked their way through life with their hands, so Larry dropped out of school to work and make money for the family. He worked at pretty much any job he could find, and as a result became something of a jack of all trades. He could build houses, run electricity, rebuild motors on cars, work with concrete, drive big rigs. If it meant working with your hands, Larry Arnold could do it. Through it all, though, Larry knew that there was more to life. He wanted something that stretched beyond his rural surroundings, but without much of a formal education any distant dreams seemed unreachable. But there was one way out. Larry's mom had long told him that you aren't a real man until you serve in the military. So, as soon as he was of age, Larry enlisted in the Army. Sure, it had basic training, orders, and hard work. But he was used to those kinds of things. The Army also had schools and travel to faraway lands: things that Larry could only dream of.

Before heading off to the military, Larry had met Melinda Burge on a blind date after the family moved to Ocean Springs, Mississippi, following Howard's job. The newly married couple set off on deployments across the nation and even in Germany, a deployment that Melinda dearly loved. Even though there were language difficulties, everything seemed so quaint, and family problems were so far away. Amidst the deployments, the Arnolds had three sons: Larry Jr., Robert, and James. Even though he enjoyed the military with its sense of honor and strict work regimen, the constant travel got to be too much for the burgeoning family. Larry knew that his children needed stability and roots, so in the mid-1980s he retired and moved the family back to Ocean Springs. Larry landed a pretty good job driving big rigs across the country, which bothered him a bit because it meant that he would often be away from home. Civilian life started out well enough, but friction with his father Howard caused Larry abruptly to move the family to Arkansas to allow for some breathing room.

Larry didn't make much money with his job, and often took on part-time work to help make ends meet. But he always made sure that his family wanted for nothing. It was only as adults that the Arnold children realized how hard their father worked to keep them from knowing that they were poor. The houses that Larry bought as the family made a few more moves were often a bit run down, but Larry would fix them up like new by hand. For Christmases Larry would head to thrift stores to buy toys, and then take them to his shop and make them sparkle. By the time the kids were older, he had moved on to cars. Larry would buy old junkers and get them running like they were fresh out of the factory. Through it all, including a move back to Mississippi, Larry had felt something was missing. The military had given him a prideful purpose. And the 1991 Gulf War had shown him that America still sorely needed its military – a military that he suspected would be called on again soon in an uncertain world. So, Larry joined the National Guard. The sense of purpose returned, the extra pay didn't hurt, and Larry knew that his many skills would be put to good use if his nation ever needed them.

WEEKEND WARRIORS

The National Guard that the men of the 150th were joining was in the beginnings of its transition to more of a fighting force, but, for many on the outside, the Guard retained its image as weekend warriors for whom beer and barbeques took precedence over training and military readiness. In general, Guard units undertook one weekend of training per month and during the summer underwent two weeks of annual training. For the 150th, annual training often took place at Camp Shelby – one of the National Guard's largest training facilities in the country. Even the term "annual training" was somewhat new. Brad Hollingsworth had grown up in Tupelo in the far north of Mississippi and had joined the Guard in 1999, in part because he thought it would be fun to fire the main gun of a tank. He had heard that training had once been called "summer camp." But that term conjured up images of Boy Scouts in tents around fires. And that is not what the Guard was doing. The Guard was preparing for war, thus the switch to "annual training." During the year, each Guard company would have three to four of its members on active (full-time) status to take care of the constant training and supply details associated with a military unit, especially in preparing the unit for its annual training.

The Guard of the late 1980s did retain some of its weekend warrior qualities. Stacey Ford recalled that it was common for the men of his unit to take their deuce-and-a-half cargo truck from Camp Shelby to nearby Hattiesburg after their annual training. The men would load up on beer and grilling supplies, ice the beer down, and head back to Camp Shelby for an end-of-training barbeque and beer bash. Another soldier saw the weekend warrior Guard from the other side of the fence. Although Richard Rowland would go on to join the Guard, in the 1980s he was in the Regular Army – the elite 82nd Airborne. The Beirut bombing of 1983 had pissed him off to the point he decided to join up. Military service ran in his family, with both his father and grandfather serving in the Navy. As Richard pondered his decision to join, his father made things easy for him. His dad said, "Boy, if you go in the Navy, I'm going to get you in my command. If you think living with me is hell, wait till you work for me." Richard knew what that meant. He wanted the farthest thing from the Navy as possible – and that was in the Army jumping out of airplanes. Part of his grueling training involved parachuting into Fort McClellan, Alabama. The plan was to jump in, then march and navigate to meet with the remainder of the unit in the wilds of the northern part of the state. It was brutally hot, the sun was relentless, and mosquitoes the size of birds dogged the unit's march. Then they rounded a corner and saw something Rowland couldn't believe. Sitting next to a five-ton truck was a National Guard soldier. Just sitting there breezy as you please perched atop his cooler. As Rowland and his men neared, the Guardsman said, "Hey man. How y'all? What unit you with?" Noticing the sweat dripping off the airborne troopers, the Guardsman thoughtfully continued, "Hey, y'all want a Coke?" Rowland and his men were sure thirsty, so they took the Guardsman up on his generous offer. As he was drinking his refreshing beverage, Rowland thought, "What the hell is this? We're out here humping in the heat for days. We have been doing the hard-core shit.

And this Guard guy is just sitting here chilling out on his cooler of Cokes? Man, if that's what the Guard is about, I don't want anything to do with it."

THE PERSIAN GULF WAR

Regardless of its lingering image as weekend warriors, the Guard in 1990 was at its height of readiness. Pushed by Senator Sonny Montgomery of Mississippi, the Guard had received new equipment, including the Abrams tank and the Bradley fighting vehicle, that had put it on par with the Regular Army for the first time in its history. Guard units had also undergone a modified training regimen that was intended to make them ready for war as the intended round-out forces for Army divisions. But, when the Persian Gulf War flared to life, the military was left with the decision of whether to call the round-out brigades to action as US forces rushed to Saudi Arabia, first to stem potential Iraqi aggression in Operation *Desert Shield*, and then in the liberation of Kuwait in Operation *Desert Storm*.

In the end, there was only a partial mobilization of the Guard. Many of its valuable logistic components were lifted from their commands and sent overseas, but the combat brigades intended to round out their assigned divisions were not. The Pentagon had a host of excuses, everything from questioning the Guard's readiness level to concerns about the length of federalized service time for Guardsmen, but in the end the Guard was overlooked in the Persian Gulf War. The Guard's supporters in Congress, including Sonny Montgomery and Les Aspin, applied pressure to the Pentagon, which resulted in a belated mobilization of several Guard brigades, including the 155th of Mississippi.

The Guardsmen and women reported to their home armories and then made their way to one of the national training centers so that the units could be certified ready for combat. For the 155th, that meant initial training at Camp Shelby before a journey to Fort Hood, Texas, for qualification and certification. But the unit was held in place in one of the longest certification periods in history and was not certified before the war had ended. Many in the Guard believed that the Army had never intended to certify Guard units – that the Army was there specifically to fail the Guard units so that they could say that the Guard couldn't hack the modern version of war. Tasks that were passed were marked as failed, passes were revoked, and there was "chickenshit" all around – and this was for a unit that had passed a National Training Center rotation just over a year before. But this time everything was different. The Guard soldiers believed that it was not a function of qualifications – indeed the Guard units functioned well and capably. Instead, they believed that the Army did not want the Guard in the front lines: a position that it jealously protected as its own purview. The situation got so bad that there were fistfights and knock-down brawls between members of the 155th and their evaluators at Fort Hood. What was clear by the conclusion of the Persian Gulf War, however, was that the round-out brigade concept had fallen far short of functionality, leaving the Persian Gulf War as the only major war in US history prosecuted without using a single National Guard ground maneuver unit.* The relationship between the Guard and the Regular Army, which was often tense, had reached a low point and needed to be reestablished.

While the main combat elements of the Guard were not called to duty, many of its logistic components were called and saw service in the Persian Gulf War, attached to Regular Army units, including the 786th Transportation Company, which was part of the 150th (which at that time was a quartermaster battalion). Many of the Guardsmen who served in the 150th after its reconfiguration into a combat engineer battalion in the wake of the Persian Gulf War saw service in Kuwait and Iraq in these logistic efforts, which provided the 150th with a veteran presence when it returned to Kuwait just over a decade later.

For the men and women of the 786th the Gulf War was a rushed job. There had been some individual mental preparation on the part of the individual soldiers when it became clear that war was imminent. But reality hit fast. Notice went out on November 17, 1990. After a couple of days to get their family affairs in order, it was off to Fort Stewart, Georgia, for final checks and linking up with equipment. By January 15, the 786th had touched down in Saudi Arabia. Once on the ground, the unit headed off to a staging area to ready for their part of the invasion of Kuwait and Iraq. If there was one thing that everyone had heard of in the unit it was the threat of Iraqi SCUD missiles, possibly armed with chemical or biological payloads. Once on site, the unit bedded down in

*Doubler, *I Am the Guard*, 285.

an old Saudi canning facility with a tin roof. One night, what they all feared was a possibility actually happened. The SCUD alarms went off, and a nearby Patriot missile defense battery sprang to violent life. First came the mechanical squeal of the missiles being activated, followed by a massive report and the shockwave of launch. For Jamie Davis it was like nothing he had ever heard before, and he hoped never to hear it again. The next sound was perhaps even more frightening, as the metal building shook from impact and the metal walls and roof clanged as shrapnel from the crippled missiles rained down. Davis could only pray, "Lord, don't let the next round come through the roof." It was a long night, and the news the next morning made everything even more grim. Just across the compound on the same night a building had taken a direct hit from a SCUD, resulting in 28 deaths in another unit.

The SCUD threat remained a constant worry for the Mississippians. Lucedale native Larry Mergenschroer, who had joined the Guard for its educational benefits, was the Nuclear/Chemical/Biological NCO of the unit, meaning it was his task to suit up and make certain that all was clear of chemical or biological threats in case of an Iraqi attack. And nobody knew for sure whether the next SCUD would have chemical or biological weaponry or not. When the next SCUD alarm went off, his buddies fairly tossed Mergenschroer into his gear and shoved him out the door to check for the all clear. Mergenschroer had to hold them at bay, saying, "Whoa, whoa! Wait a minute! Don't shove me out the door yet! It ain't even hit the ground. Wait till the damn thing hits the ground! It's still up in the air!" About a minute later came the telltale sounds of shrapnel impacting the metal building. Then his buddies did, indeed, shove him out the door, closing it behind him. Everyone was in their chemical gear, but it was only Mergenschroer who was outside with his testing kit. It was going to take almost 20 lonely minutes for the test to be complete, so Mergenschroer went to rest under a tree while he waited for the readings. Out of the corner of his eye Mergenschroer caught a glimpse of movement. Snake – or one of those huge dang spiders. Then a slot opened in a nearby door, and some food came tumbling out. Then the movement again, and a monkey ran right over and started eating that food. One of the guys quickly poked his head out the door, looked at the monkey, and said, "Thank God you're alive," and shut the door again. A few minutes later Mergenschroer gave the all clear. He and that monkey became good friends. At every SCUD strike he was shoved out the door, and the monkey learned to hop up on his shoulders and became his only company.

As the ground war into Iraq kicked off, the 786th jumped to its task, hauling fuel to the 24th Infantry Division as it and its armored vehicles tore first into Kuwait and then into Iraq; the 786th's unofficial motto was, "we pass gas." The plan called for the 5,000-gallon tanker trucks of the 786th to advance to logistic bases set up in Iraq and offload their fuel into massive fuel bladders. The Heavy Expanded Mobility Tactical Trucks (HEMTT) fuel haulers of the 24th, each capable of carrying 2,500 gallons of fuel, would then arrive and take on fuel from the bladders and distribute it as needed to the forward-moving vehicles of the division. One night, as the Mississippians rolled into Logbase Charlie to accomplish their mission, a helicopter arrived, circled, and then landed. It carried the commander of the 24th. His unit had moved forward so quickly that his tanks were running out of fuel. He just couldn't take the time for the 786th to offload fuel, transfer it to bladders, and then transfer that again to the HEMTTs. By then his tanks would be dead in their tracks. Instead, he ordered the 786th to continue rolling forward. It was going to be hairy, and everyone knew it. The Mississippians had no idea where they were going, and it was the middle of the night. As fuel haulers, the 786th did not have night-vision capability for a high-speed night drive through a war zone.

The 786th drove forward, and in a surreal series of events tanks would roll up out of the night and set a perimeter as other tanks loaded fuel directly from the Mississippians' tanker trucks. It seemed like an assembly line, with tanks in a semi-circle as individual tanks peeled away from the protective group and made their way down the line to fuel. Before all was said and done, the 786th had driven all the way to the Basra airbase in Iraq – the very limit of Allied advance into Iraq during the Persian Gulf War. As the night wore on, Jamie Davis was immersed in his duties, but he couldn't help but wonder about the smell. He had never smelled anything quite like it. Kind of mechanical, but with an undertone of something he couldn't quite place. When the sun came up, the source of the smell became obvious. There were knocked-out Iraqi tanks and vehicles littering the landscape all around. And dead Iraqis lay around the vehicles – some still hanging from the turrets of tanks and others sprawled out of the doors of the soft-skinned vehicles. Most of the bodies had been charred by fire. It was all like something out of a horrible nightmare. Davis was sure that he would never get that smell out of his nose or off his clothes, and he damn sure never wanted to smell it again.

REORGANIZATION

For the remainder of the 1990s, the US military struggled to come to grips with its relationship to and with the National Guard. It was clear that the Guard would be needed to augment the Regular Army in time of conflict, but it had become obvious that the existing plan to do that had fallen short in the Persian Gulf War. Training for the Guard was altered yet again, with many Guardsmen believing that such measures were just another way for the Army to discredit the Guard. The round-out idea was rather quietly dropped, in favor of the creation of enhanced brigades as the basic combat unit of the US military, with 15 of the enhanced brigades to be housed within the Guard. The plan was for the transformation to be complete by 1999, at which time the enhanced brigades of the Guard and the Army would have run through the National Training Center to demonstrate a readiness to be deployed overseas to battle within 90 days of mobilization.[*]

For the Guard units of Mississippi this transformation meant several things. Mississippi would house one of the Guard's enhanced brigades, the 155th Armored Brigade, which meant years of training and readiness across the board. Simultaneously the Guard, along with the military in general, suffered downsizing and cuts, making the transformation all the more difficult. The cuts and changes had a seismic impact on the local Guard. As an independent enhanced brigade, the 155th required more combat engineer capabilities than ever before. Under the old system, the Mississippi Guard had a single combat engineer company, the 134th based in Carthage. But now the 155th required an entire combat engineer battalion. As a result, what had been the 150th Quartermaster Battalion, based out of Meridian, was transformed into the 150th Combat Engineer Battalion. The 134th of Carthage became Alpha Company of the 150th. The 786th Transportation Company

[*]Doubler, *I Am the Guard*, 301.

of Lucedale became Bravo Company of the 150th. And the 785th Engineer Company of Houston/Okolona became Charlie Company of the 150th.

Implementing the change to combat engineers fell to the commander of the new 150th, Mike Gilpin, a Hattiesburg native and career Guardsman. The first matter at hand was getting those in the non-combat engineer units retrained, a truly massive undertaking. This meant dispersing Guard soldiers to military operation programs at several locations across the country. A second major issue was soldier retention. Some just didn't want to go through the rigamarole of all of the new training. Others were nearing the end of their careers and considered taking the opportunity to retire. Gilpin was somewhat daunted to learn that he had a maximum of three years to make the change complete.

The change had a profound impact across the state. The Lucedale and Houston units had proud histories, and their soldiers had valuable skills that had been honed through years of training. Now they would all have to be retrained to become combat engineers. The training cycle was slated to take two years, with each soldier having to start with individual training and progress through crew, squad, platoon, company, and battalion training, necessitating stints at training centers scattered across the country. As a long-standing combat engineer company, it fell to the Alpha Company troops from Carthage, under the command of Captain Trent Kelly, to train the Lucedale and Houston/Okolona units in their transition to combat engineer status. Certainly, the fact that Alpha was, well, the Alpha dog of this particular combat engineer world was validating. But there were some issues even on Alpha Company's side. Ken Cager, who at that time was an enlisted soldier in Alpha Company, spoke for many when he expressed doubts about the situation. The 134th had been something of a legendary company. Now it had to give all that up to be just another part of the 150th. The distinction of being *the* combat engineers in the state was gone. They were going to be just another company, and they were going to be saddled with the onerous task of training all these drivers and construction workers how to be combat engineers. Cager didn't look forward to the task at all.

The change to combat engineers was perhaps most difficult for the troops from Houston/Okolona. They had been engineers, but not *combat* engineers. Instead, they had been involved in construction – a very skilled task indeed. They had a proud history, having undertaken construction tasks across the state and internationally, especially in South America. Since their equipment had been based locally, almost all their drills had been local as well. As combat engineers, though, much of their equipment, including tracked vehicles, would necessitate drills at Camp Shelby, over a four-hour drive away. Paul Lyon, who held a training position with higher Guard command, saw the difficulty firsthand at an exercise at Camp Shelby. Trent Kelly's Alpha Company was tasked with running a training exhibition for Bravo and Charlie companies. The demonstration involved breaching a minefield with hand-emplaced explosives. Lyon was standing next to a construction guy from Houston watching as an M113 pulled up to the minefield and a soldier popped out, grabbed a detonation cord, then ran through the middle of the minefield and staked the cord to the other end. Then other soldiers got out and ran branches to each of the anti-tank mines in the field. Once done, the men returned to the M113 and there was a massive explosion as all of the mines went off at once. The soldier from Houston turned to Lyon and asked, "What if one of those men had stepped on a mine?" Lyon replied, "Well, that's why we have eight in a squad." The Houston Guardsman just shook his head, said "shit," and walked away. Before the transformation was complete, over 70 percent of the troops from Houston/Okolona had retired or transferred out of the unit. The losses from the Lucedale unit were not quite as dramatic but were still heavy. And, as a transport company, the Lucedale unit had been able to include women in many roles. However, most roles in the new 150th were reserved for men at this stage due to their combat status. So nearly all the women who had served in Lucedale retired or transferred.

Although the task had its share of immense challenges, the 150th Combat Engineers were validated in a ceremony on December 3, 1997. Gilpin was proud of his new command and wanted the 150th to have a real day in the sun. Senator Sonny Montgomery was the keynote speaker for the event. Veterans from the original 150th Engineer Battalion of World War II were on hand to welcome their new namesakes and brothers in arms. Just two years later, in 1999, the restructured 155th as a whole ran a successful rotation at the National Training Center. Both had been proven ready for war.

SEPTEMBER 11, 2001

The terror attacks of 2001 had a deep impact on the entire United States, but carried special importance for a National Guard that was undergoing a difficult transformation and for the men and women who served within it. Douglas Mansfield, who had joined the Guard in part because he had loved tanks, was in the middle of his basic training. September 11 was his birthday, but nobody knew; the first thing that he had figured out during training was never to stand out. Anything the instructors knew about you – whether it was your birthdate or whether you smoked – they would use mercilessly to belittle you. It was best to remain in the shadows. Mansfield and the other trainees were on a route march and had stopped for a short rest. At that point the drill sergeant disappeared. The trainees all murmured. That damn drill sergeant was off planning something and was going to come back and mess with the guys hard, and some unlucky trainee would pay the price. Maybe they would all pay the price. But when the sergeant came back, he was quiet and different. Almost human. His eyes were even glistening with what might be tears. He quietly asked if any of the trainees were from New York City or Washington DC, and a couple of trainees meekly raised their hands. Another trainer took those men away to call home. After those men left, the drill sergeant said, "Alright privates. The World Trade Center has just been hit by two aircraft. The Pentagon has also been struck with massive loss of life. And there is a fourth plane out there and its intentions are unknown. We have been attacked and we are at war. Welcome to the United States Army."

———

Larry Odom and Sean Cooley had grown up best friends in the Lucedale area and had become even better friends in the Guard. Larry deeply admired Sean's work as a trauma nurse, and Sean greatly respected Larry's serious nature when it came to his Guard work. And they shared a common love of pulling pranks on their Guard buddies. September 2001 found them on their way to taking an air assault course. Both men loved to push themselves physically, and air assault training also seemed like a good adventure. As they waited in the terminal for their flight to their training, the two men watched the planes impact the World

Trade Center on the news. Their training was delayed due to the closure of American airspace. The pair couldn't help but talk about what the strikes meant. The nation was at war, and they both knew that their time would come to be called to battle. It was a common refrain for Guardsmen and women across the country. Perhaps they had enlisted for college benefits. Perhaps they had enlisted for a better paying job. Perhaps they had enlisted for the valuable training the Guard provided or to get out of trouble with the law. Regardless of why they had joined, all now had to wrestle with the idea that they would soon be off to face combat in a distant land.

For Norris Galatas the news came as he was supervising the removal of some display vehicles at a Boy Scout camp. One of the park rangers ran up, nearly breathless, and shouted, "Hey guys! Y'all are fixing to go to war!" Galatas didn't believe him and asked why. The ranger responded, "They just flew a plane into the World Trade Center!" The Guardsmen went with the ranger to his cabin, arriving in time to see the second plane's impact. Together the men watched in horror as the succeeding events unfolded. Galatas couldn't believe his eyes as tiny figures leapt from the flames to their doom hundreds of stories below. He knew that his part in the war would come. America had been attacked, and he wanted to play what role he could in protecting the country and perhaps even seek a measure of revenge. For Brad Hollingsworth it all became crystal clear when he saw President George W. Bush visit Ground Zero. The President was speaking to first responders through a bullhorn when one yelled, "We can't hear you!" Bush responded, "I can hear you! I can hear you! And the people who knocked these buildings down will hear all of us soon!" Hollingsworth knew at that moment that America was at war, and he wanted to play his role in that conflict, to fight against those who had done this to his country. Ricky Tyler had dropped out of Petal High School at the age of 17 and had been engaged in hard, physical labor ever since. In 2001 he was already considering joining the Guard as a way forward when he saw the second aircraft impact the World Trade Center on television. That day and event made his decision simple, and straightaway he enlisted to better his own life and to defend his country.

Before September 11, 2001, the Guard, as was the case with the broader military in general, had been in something of a recruiting crisis. Competing with other jobs in the economic boom years of the 1990s had been difficult, especially when it seemed that the US military's forces would be called on for operations across the planet, from Somalia to Bosnia. But the terrorist strike on US soil changed all of that, as patriotic young Americans rushed to the colors as they so often have done in times of national crisis. Bradley Sharp was in high school in Wiggins, Mississippi, when his dad came roaring up in the family pickup to check him out of classes. America had been attacked, and it was time to prepare. With his father narrating the attacks and their likely aftermath, the duo wrestled two 55-gallon drums into the back of the pickup and went to load up on gasoline. His father was not a doomsday prepper, but wanted his family to be ready for whatever came as America embarked on a new war. Sharp went on to graduate high school and watched carefully as the events unfolded over the next months, especially the invasion of Afghanistan and the hunt for Osama Bin Laden. Inside him a feeling built up that he needed to be a part of these events, that he needed to be a part of something bigger than himself, and that he needed to help defend his nation. So, one year after the terrorist strikes Sharp joined the Guard. His father fairly beamed with pride, while his mother was more subdued, understanding the risks of his decision in an uncertain world. Others, like Joe Smith, had already done their service in the military. Smith had once played on the high school football team with the longest losing streak in the nation, so joining a winning team like the Navy had been an easy decision. By 2001, though, his naval career, and its attendant trips to far-off places like the French Riviera, had come to an end. However, in his words, "9/11 hurt me. It broke my heart; it really did. It made me so mad. I knew that something had to be done. And I knew that I couldn't do it, but I knew that I could help, so in 2002 I joined the Guard."

A RETURN TO SERVICE

Richard Rowland
Richard Rowland had already served with the 82nd Airborne and remembered thinking not too highly of the Guard when he and his fellow paratroopers had encountered a Guardsman perched atop a cooler of Cokes at Fort McClellan, Alabama. He had gone on to attend college at the University of Southern Mississippi and had married an exchange student named Keltoum. The pair had a daughter and

Richard had begun a career in finance. But then came the attacks on the World Trade Center. Richard couldn't help thinking that the wall of American security had been breached. Night after night he watched as events unfolded in Afghanistan and the Middle East. And he thought to himself, "That's where I'm supposed to be. That's exactly where I'm supposed to be. I'm not supposed to be sitting here on the couch, working for some damn finance company bored out of my skull. I'm supposed to be there in the fight."

Rowland figured that the quickest route to the fight was the Guard, and he fully understood how much the Guard had changed since that day at Fort McClellan. So, he got in touch with a Guardsman he knew, Jerry Bratu, a police officer from Meridian, and asked, "Jerry, what do I need to do to get back in the business?" Jerry responded that he was going to give Rowland's number to someone who would call him back. The recruiter who called him was Paul Lyon, who "promised everything in the world if I would just join." But Rowland didn't need much arm-twisting. He was ready to go. He realized that being a 35-year-old enlisted man would make him the grandpa of the 150th, but he could put up with that. But Bratu had other ideas and talked Rowland into going to accelerated Officer Candidate School. Bratu was a bit worried by Rowland's age, but he thought Rowland could handle it.

After 59 days of "pure hell," Rowland made it and was getting ready for graduation at Camp Shelby when an instructor pulled him aside:

He told me, "Rowland, you're going to stand there in formation. You're going to raise your right hand. You are not going to say the oath. We haven't finished your paperwork. Your security clearance hasn't come back yet." I fired back, "No shit? Why?" And he said, "Well, apparently there's some kind of problem." I was married to a foreign national, a French foreign national. And her father was Algerian. At that point in time, so soon after 9/11, everybody was suspect, especially if you were from certain parts of the world like Algeria. So, I got to go to a security clearance meeting; I basically sat in this hotel room with this dude for three hours, answering questions, "When was the last time you saw your father-in-law? When was the last time you saw your mother-in-law? When was the last time you were abroad? How many times have you been abroad? How many times have you talked to your mother-in-law?" And dude, most of the time it was, "Hold on a minute." I would grab the phone from the hotel room, dial my home phone. "Hey, Kel. When was the last time we talked to your mother? Two weeks ago? Did I talk to her? No? OK. Great. Thanks. Bye." After hours of this shit, I ask the dude, "Are we good?" He goes, "Yeah, yeah, yeah, yeah." I said, "Good. I got to run to the store and pick up something for this new exchange student we just got." And the guy looks at me, and he goes, "Exchange student? What exchange student? You never mentioned an exchange student." I thought, "oh, crap." So, I got to sit there and answer another two hours of questions with this dude in that little hotel room.

BONDS OF FRIENDSHIP

Jamie Davis and Robert McNail

Jamie Davis was from the small town of Stonewall in the rural fastness outside of Meridian with a family military tradition that ran back to the American Civil War. For him the military was a family rite of passage, and he had joined the Guard fresh out of high school, in 1988, when the unit from nearby Lucedale was the 786th Transportation Company. He had served in the Persian Gulf War, praying that the SCUDS wouldn't come through his barracks roof, before going on the mad fueling dash into Iraq. When the unit changed over to become combat engineers Davis wasn't particularly happy, but he had not reached enough years in service for a comfortable retirement, so he hung around. It wasn't until after the terrorist attacks of 2001 that he met his best friend in the unit, Robert McNail.

McNail, or Mac as everyone knew him, was from Meridian but had attended high school in Washington state because his father Marvin was stationed there in the Navy. There was a deep military tradition in the McNail family, with 16 members having served since World War II. So, it had seemed very normal when right after high school Mac joined the Army, where he had served his required years as a combat engineer, seeing his own service in the Persian Gulf War. Mac had gotten married and had a son, Edward, after leaving the military, but when Davis and Mac met, Mac's marriage was on the rocks, and he had moved back in with his parents. Like so many, Mac had rejoined after 9/11, choosing to serve in the local Guard unit, the 150th, where he and Davis met. They bonded over a mutual love of fishing, and Davis was anxious that

Mac would find love in his life again. And Davis could not help but admire Mac's ability with an armored combat earthmover, or ACE. Both men were in the Assault and Obstacle (A&O) Platoon of Bravo Company of the 150th. The task of the A&O Platoon was to set up or breach obstacles. Its heart was the ACE, which was essentially a big, armored bulldozer. It could build defenses in a jiffy or knock down enemy berms and earthen walls with great speed. But the vehicle was temperamental and would often fail or break down in the hands of an unskilled operator. And Mac was the best operator the unit had. He could make an ACE fairly dance, and under his watch they hardly ever broke down. He was the ACE man that everyone wanted for their job.

Fishing for catfish in local ponds is not particularly action packed, leaving plenty of time for conversation. It was on one of those fishing trips that the two men sat with their beer, waiting for some action, when Mac told Davis his news. Mac had long worked at the Naval Air Station in Meridian. Even with that job and the Guard, Mac held onto an idea that there was more out there for him. And he had found it. He was going to take nursing classes at a local junior college. He even pulled out his acceptance letter and showed it off. Davis was happy for his pal. Maybe this would give Mac the way forward after his failed marriage. Davis asked his friend if he knew that going to nursing school might well get him out of any upcoming deployment as America's war against terrorism deepened. Mac responded that he understood that possibility. But he would never take it. He had rejoined to serve his nation if it needed him. And he planned on answering that call if it came, no matter what.

FAMILY DECISIONS

Sean Cooley had secretly begun shopping for an engagement ring for Laura during an annual training cycle in 2002. He was also going to surprise her with a new car, but that car ruined the surprise altogether when the finance company phoned to ask her questions about her job and pay since her fiancé was trying to buy a car that was partly going to be in her name. Even with some of the surprise gone, the couple married in 2003 in Ocean Springs, which was followed by a honeymoon in the Smokey Mountains. Honeymoons are supposed to be all about romance, but Laura and Sean couldn't help but watch the news to follow the events of the US invasion of Iraq. Even though the Taliban regime in Afghanistan had crumbled, the Cooleys knew that the spread of the war in the Middle East made it increasingly likely that Sean would be called upon to fight.

Another main topic of honeymoon conversation was Sean's decision to become a nurse anesthetist. The career change would necessitate several rounds of schooling that the Guard would likely pay for. Both were sure that the call was coming, though, and Sean did not want the 150th to go to war without him. He couldn't let his buddies down. After 14 years of service, he knew and trusted those guys, and they knew and trusted him. Sean was sure that by being there he could help save lives. He couldn't miss that just to go to school. So, Sean and Laura decided to delay nurse anesthetist training until after any deployment of the 150th.

For Randall Jones there had been little choice about entering the Guard. His father had a main job at Ingalls in Pascagoula, but his passion had always been geared toward his service in the Guard. Randall's grandfather had been a drill sergeant at Fort Jackson. Military service was just what the Jones boys did, and Randall had enlisted in the Guard in high school. He also worked alongside his dad at Ingalls. Randall's little brother, Ben, also joined the Guard, and, while Randall was in the 890th on the coast, Ben was in the 150th in Lucedale. Randall's life changed one afternoon at the armory in Gulfport when he went to ask his platoon sergeant if he wanted lunch. The sergeant was seated at his desk with his back facing Randall. He looked busy, so Randall figured he would come back a bit later. After his own lunch Randall returned. His platoon sergeant was now lying on the floor, and by this time another Guardsman was tossing crumpled paper over the cubicle wall. Randall asked, "What are you doing?" and received the response, "Sarge is in there asleep and I'm messing with him." Randall decided to play a prank and to climb over the cubicle wall and startle the sergeant awake; and something of a crowd began to gather to watch the hijinks. Randall snuck over and in, and then jostled the sergeant. But there was no response. Jones noticed that the sergeant was stiff and cold; then he saw the pistol by his side. He had committed suicide.

Jones transferred out of the unit; he just couldn't work in that armory anymore. As he was sorting out his future, Jones knew that a callup for the Guard had to be coming soon. As it stood, he would be serving with guys he didn't know due to his transfer. Then came a bad break, and a good one. Working on a construction job, Jones was hit in the leg with a pipe, necessitating a visit to the hospital. His trauma nurse was Sean Cooley. Sean quickly identified that Jones' leg was broken, which had also caused life-threatening damage to one of his main arteries. It was Sean's way to keep up conversation to keep his patients' mind off their injuries. This time the conversation centered on military service and the possibility of pending deployment. Fresh from his honeymoon, Cooley had some advice: "Come join us in the 150th." With those words it all kind of clicked for Randall Jones. Randall's brother Ben was already in the 150th, so a transfer meant that if he indeed went to war it would be with his brother. While recuperating, Jones talked with his wife Amanda. She of course was worried about any deployment to a combat zone, especially since the couple had three children. But she also understood that Randall would sit at home every day worrying about Ben. She knew how much he would fret and how much he wanted to serve his country. She agreed that Randall should join the 150th and should answer the call that everyone knew was coming.

Robert Arnold was a solid student in high school, and had never really gravitated to working on cars like his father Larry and brother Larry Jr. Robert was a better trombone player than most, but he always had known what he wanted to be. His father was his role model. Hard working, kind, and smart, Larry worked so hard for his family that, as far as Robert knew, he had never once taken a vacation. Robert wanted to be like his dad, and to be like his dad Robert wanted to join the Guard and be a combat engineer. Robert's choice was made even easier during his sophomore year in high school when the terrorist strike hit the World Trade Center and Washington, DC. He was only 17, but he was in the Guard within a week. It was a split option, which meant summer training during high school, and Guard entry after graduation.

As Robert was going through training, his father Larry served with the Guard's 890th Engineer Battalion from the Mississippi Gulf Coast during the initial invasion of Iraq in 2003. Although there were occasions of fierce fighting, the opening phase of Operation *Iraqi Freedom* went remarkably smoothly, with the 3rd Infantry Division capturing Baghdad in under a month. Then began the slow march of events that would lead to a grueling insurgency, but for Larry Arnold the war ended quickly. He was evacuated from Iraq to

Germany with a medical condition and was not allowed to return to theater. Larry remained in the Guard and returned to home duty once his condition was rectified. He tried to get back to Iraq, but to no avail. As the situation in Iraq worsened, Larry couldn't help but be haunted by the idea that he had somehow failed. The job had not been completed. It didn't help that some in his unit whispered behind his back that he had tried to get sent home. That he was a coward. Those things ate at Larry's soul.

To almost any outside observer in 2004, it looked plain that the 150th would get called up to go to Iraq as part of the 155th. Larry knew that, and he wanted to go back to Iraq, finish the job, and let his demons rest. So, Larry put in for a transfer to the 150th, which was approved before the unit officially received its orders for the war zone.

Larry Arnold's phone rang in May 2004. His heart eased, knowing that he was going back. But there was the matter of his son, Robert, who was completing his training cycles. Robert would go to Iraq as well. Larry had already seen the worry in his wife Melinda's eyes when he had left for war in 2003. Now she would face the prospect of having both a husband and a son serving in Iraq. Larry did everything he could to get Robert transferred into the 150th so that he could watch over his son. He hoped that being there to protect Robert would lessen the burden on Melinda. It was October 2004 when Robert received the news. He was to transfer to the 150th immediately and would be serving alongside his father.

GETTING THE CALL

As Larry Arnold's phone rang in May 2004, calls were going out all across Mississippi to ready the 155th for war. Undaryl Allen was at work when one of his Guard buddies called and said, "Man. We're going overseas." Allen thought it was a joke and replied, "Man, whatever. Quit playing. We're not going nowhere." But his pal was adamant and continued, "Yeah, you have to bring all your stuff to Camp Shelby." Then it actually hit Allen, who thought, "Wow, we're fixing to go overseas for real. This is no joke." He let his family know the news, and they were all worried – especially his wife, who broke down into tears. The family went to church and prayed about the future, where Allen was overcome by a feeling that everything was going to be okay.

Bradley Sharp was in his first semester of community college when the call came, and it left him in shock. He knew that he was first going to have to undergo unit training and then the deployment to the war zone – a total of 18 months. He was proud to go and serve, but he did wonder what he was going to miss in those 18 months. He was 19 years old and ready to experience so much. But now a year and a half of that would be missing – if he survived. Living the busy life of a teenager was going to be replaced by the trials of war. As he sat there thinking about it in the break room at school, suddenly everything became more serious. This was going to be life-or-death stuff. He immediately thought of Larry Odom, a veteran who had already been to the Persian Gulf War. Sharp thought, "Heck. Ninety percent of us are so young we have never experienced anything." He did know one thing, though. As soon as the unit gathered, he was going to make a beeline to Odom and the other veteran soldiers to find out what they were all facing.

Ken Cager was one of those veterans. In command of Alpha Company, Cager felt chills run down his spine when he got the call. He knew that the upcoming training would have to be a new level of serious, because he was determined to bring all the men under his command back home safely. Cager and his wife Audrey had two children in diapers, and he knew that the deployment was likely going to be tougher on Audrey and the babies than it was on him. The young family prayed about it and came to terms with it, because, like it or not, Cager was off to war. Through it all, Cager couldn't shake the idea that he knew all his men so well. He had grown up in Carthage; he had known these guys and their families since grade school. He wasn't sure what he would do if he had to come back to Carthage after the war and explain to one of the wives or one of the children about how their son or father had been lost in combat. He would have to see those people every day for the rest of his life, carrying a burden that he would never be able to put down or even share. That phone call had changed everything.

For Chris Thomas, the timing of the call couldn't have been much worse. He was in law school and had just married his fiancée, Kristi. The ink on the marriage license was barely dry when the call came. The Guard did, though, allow him to report to Camp Shelby a bit later than the other soldiers to allow at least a bit of time for a truncated honeymoon. Thomas was only a month or so into the training regimen when he learned that Kristi was pregnant. He would be in Iraq when the baby was born. The circumstances amazed Roy Robinson, who would command the 150th in Iraq. There were so many soldiers like Thomas or Cooley who had legitimate reasons to avoid or postpone deployment. However, the numbers of the 150th didn't take a hit; instead, they went up. Retired Guardsmen from all over the state were calling daily trying to re-enlist in time to make the trip to Iraq. Soldiers in other units that were not scheduled to deploy were calling every day trying to transfer into the 150th to do their part in America's war. It hurt Robinson to have to turn some of them away, but the fact that so many were trying to join the 150th left him beaming with pride about the nature of the Guard and its soldiers.

Laura Cooley was snuggled up in bed, finally getting some sleep after a long night shift at the hospital. When the phone rang at 6:30 a.m., the frustration was plain in her voice as she gruffly answered. Larry Odom was on the other end of the call, and when he heard how unhappy Laura was, he said, "Hi Laura. This is Larry Mergenschroer calling. Good morning!" But the Guard is a tight family, and Laura instantly recognized Odom's voice. "Alright Odom. I know it's you. Why did you call us at 6:30? What is so important that it couldn't wait?" A few seconds later Laura was wide awake. The couple had already talked things out on their honeymoon and knew how to react when the call came. She hung up the phone, and Sean asked who it was. She replied, "It was Larry Odom, and there is nothing for it. You are going to Camp Shelby and then to Iraq."

2

Training

Lucedale plans a huge parade for the last day we're there, and it is a monster. They line the streets of the whole town with people with flags and signs, and they put all the unit on 18-wheelers with the flatbeds, with the families, and we go through town and never seen anything like it, really, probably four miles of people, and from a little, bitty town like Lucedale. So, we drove through town, and all that goes on, and we end up, and we stop, and I have buses set up at the end of town, so everybody gets off the flatbeds, say goodbye. Families figured out where that was, and they all scurry over there, and they give them the last kiss. And I'm in my car with my wife Jane and Victoria, my daughter, and other daughter, and we stop at a gas station right there in New Augusta, and then Tori tells me, "What time you going to be home tonight, Dad?" And I say, "I'm not coming home tonight. I'm leaving." And she breaks down, squalling; it just sticks in my mind, you know. They just weren't realizing what was fixing to happen.

PAUL LYON

A funny thing, I used to say it all the time: you don't have to wake anybody up in training sessions when we were in the mobilization training pipeline. Everybody was paying full attention because they knew where their ass was going within the next six months, and they didn't want to miss anything.

ROY ROBINSON

MATTERS OF COMMAND

As the 150th readied to head to Camp Shelby for initial training, the unit was commanded by Colonel Durr Boyles, who had been instrumental in maintaining unit strength, building up its training tempo and quality, and gathering a sterling battalion staff. Boyles, though, felt that the task of training the 150th and taking it first to the National Training Center and then to Iraq would be best suited to another commander. Officers rarely turn down the chance to lead men in battle. But Boyles' decision defined what was best about the National Guard. He wanted the best for his men and their families and he made a selfless decision to stand aside. The new commander was Lieutenant Colonel Roy Robinson, who married up with the 150th as it arrived at Camp Shelby. Boyles' stewardship of the 150th during his time in command had left Robinson with an embarrassment of riches. In Robinson's words:

> I walked into the absolute best situation you could ever walk into in terms of the battalion staff: the officers that I had on the staff. And they were uniquely qualified and very, very good. They just needed somebody to come in that had kind of a little more background on focusing, specifically, for mobilization and deployment because there's a lot more to it than just the maneuver stuff that goes on in support of the brigade. Getting a battalion out the door is a monumental effort of training, personnel issues, medical issues, logistical support issues, and for whatever reason, I had gone through a lot of different jobs that gave me a pretty good depth of knowledge for my age and my rank in a lot of those different areas. And having been kind of full-time, I think I had a pretty good grasp of what the mobilization process looked like.

The quality and experience of the battalion's operations section (S-3) stood as an example of the depth of leadership that the 150th possessed. At the helm of the S-3 office was Major Trent Kelly, who had long served as commander of Alpha Company, which had trained Bravo and Charlie on becoming combat engineers in the wake of the Persian Gulf War. Kelly hailed from the tiny town of Union outside of Philadelphia and had joined the Guard immediately after his high school graduation in 1984. He had been quite a sportsman in his small high school, even winning a golf state championship. Trent's father John had long served in the Guard, so joining the Guard seemed natural. So, when he and a few of his friends were standing in the parking lot of the Piggly-Wiggly one day, they decided to walk over to the recruiter's office. Kelly had always known that he wanted to be a lawyer in civilian life, so after years of service in the Guard it was off to Ole Miss to become a lawyer and then into private practice before becoming prosecutor in Tupelo, Mississippi. But for his position as S-3, it was being one of the most experienced combat engineers in the Mississippi National Guard that mattered. And, since the Mississippi Guard is a family after all, Trent's brother, Kevin Kelly, was serving with the 150th in Alpha Company.

Greg Wells was Trent Kelly's driver. The two had known each other all their lives. Wells was from Madden, a largely Black community very near to where Trent and his family had grown up. Wells grew up on a farm in a life full of physical labor, which led him to being an All-American high school sports star. He dreamed of playing pro ball, but was more practical than that and joined the National Guard while in junior college. He had reforged his links with Kelly shortly after joining and served as Kelly's driver for much of the remainder of his Guard career. Kelly knew that the Guard's community base and demographics had dealt the 150th a potentially troublesome card. Bravo Company from the Lucedale area was heavily white, while Alpha Company, hailing from Carthage, was predominantly Black. Race issues in Mississippi had softened a great deal since the fraught 1960s, but just to be sure Wells was given the task of ironing out any potential problems. And Wells knew just whom to reach out to in Bravo Company – Sean Cooley. Both men were greatly respected across the 150th and worked together to maintain racial harmony throughout the formation.

Kelly's senior assistant S-3 was Dexter Thornton, also a career combat engineer who had served two years as Charlie Company commander before a stint as assistant brigade engineer. Kelly's junior assistant was Allen McDaniel, who had grown up only a few miles away from Kelly's family outside of Philadelphia. McDaniel had also joined the Guard just after his high school graduation and was a successful lawyer. As the youngest in the group, McDaniel couldn't help but admire the wealth of experience that had been assembled in the S-3 office. Things weren't easy for McDaniel, getting called up to the assistant S-3 position and its attendant tour to the war zone in Iraq while leaving behind a four-month-old son.

But being around guys like Kelly and Thornton somehow made it all easier. These guys were good. Really good. He knew that he could learn a lot just by serving with them. And he quickly picked up on the rhythm of the office and its subtleties. Trent Kelly seemed almost addicted to Diet Mountain Dews. There was always one in his hand. And once that first one was finished it disappeared into his pocket, transforming into the receptacle for the spit from his snuff. The surest sign that you were in trouble or if things were going wrong was if Kelly took that bottle out of his pocket and spit into it while looking at you over its brim. If he spit twice and kept looking at you, it was going to be rough.

Robinson's company commanders were a group of long-service all-stars. Each of the company commanders had risen through the ranks, starting as enlisted men before attaining their command. Thus, all were familiar with the Guard at all levels, and all were trusted members of the Guard family. Commanding Alpha Company was Captain Ken Cager, who had begun his military life as an enlisted man in the 134th when it was in Carthage. He had then gone to Reserve Officers' Training Corps (ROTC) at the University of Southern Mississippi before taking another posting and then moving to become Alpha Company commander in 2002. In that position Cager found himself in command of men he had once served with in Carthage as an enlisted man himself. Cager had married in 1999, and he and his wife Audrey had two children, Richard and Phillip, who were born in 2000 and 2001.

Commanding Bravo Company out of Lucedale was Paul Lyon, who had also gone to the University of Southern Mississippi, but it turned out that he was not the best of college students. He left school to join the Army and did a stint in the infantry before joining the Guard as an enlisted man in 1985. After seven years he had risen to the rank of E-7 before he made the decision to go to Officer Candidate School (OCS). Paul got married, and his wife Jane became very involved in the family support unit for the local Guard community. The couple had four daughters – Tamara, Tabatha, Tori, and Kira – before Paul shifted back into the 150th after several stints in Guard units in the region. Just before the call to mobilize came, Paul took over command of Bravo Company in 2004.

In command of Charlie Company was Chris Thomas, who had joined the Guard as an enlisted man straight out of high school. Hailing from Purvis, Mississippi, Thomas realized that the successful folks in town were either doctors or attorneys. He decided on law school, but he realized he would need help to make that happen, so he gave the Guard a try. Fraternity life sidetracked him from his law school goals, and instead Thomas let some of his fraternity buddies talk him into going to OCS. After graduation Thomas opted for service with the combat engineers and took the Law School Admissions Test on a whim. After passing with flying colors, it was off to law school in Jackson with his wife Kristi. It was when he was studying for his second-year law school exams that the call came. It was time to go to Camp Shelby and take command of Charlie Company.

SEND-OFF

At armories in communities across the state, Guardsmen and women gathered to ready their equipment and supplies before shipping down to Camp Shelby for their pre-mobilization training. These small towns were sending their young men and women off to war, part of a Guard tradition that stretched back to colonial days. The next 18 months would be difficult, and everyone knew it. The departure would leave a gaping hole in each of these communities, with many of their best and brightest off to war. Each of the small towns turned out in force to send their young citizens off to an uncertain future.

Houston native Thomas Howell marveled at the support Charlie Company received in Houston and Okolona. The Veterans of Foreign Wars (VFW) post hosted all the soldiers and their families for a lavish meal, with speeches made by veterans and Guardsmen alike. The soldiers then boarded their buses for the journey to Camp Shelby, but the send-off wasn't over. The buses drove all over town as people lined the streets waving and shouting their well-wishes. Next the buses visited each of the local schools, where the parking lots were full of students carrying signs and waving. The schools had been let out that day for the goodbye. The same was true in Quitman, which hosted a platoon of Bravo Company.

Ken Cager, commander of Alpha Company, recalled the send-off in Carthage:

Carthage had a big patriotic send-off; the town gathered at the coliseum, and man, it was this big deal. I had no idea it was going to be this big. But they had all these people, and they brought them to the coliseum, and the unit had to be in uniform, and be standing out there. And then they made me, like, the keynote speaker. "OK. What am I going to tell these people?" Just tell them that we are looking forward to the training. I'm going to do my best to bring every one of them home. I mean, it's like – man, there's probably – oh, there's probably three or 400 people at this thing. I mean, we are talking about Carthage, Mississippi… they shut everything down for this thing. Probably one of the worst days of my life… there was crying out there, wives, crying. People taking pictures. They shut the schools down, and they had the kids lined on the road, the little flags… as long as we hung around with wives and mamas and daddies, man, it's just sad. And most people were thinking that some of these boys are never coming back.

The send-off in Lucedale was perhaps the largest of all. The entire town turned out, and Bravo Company climbed aboard flatbed trucks for a parade through the town before boarding the buses to Camp Shelby. Everything in town was closed that day, including the schools. It seemed like the entire population of the small town was there to wave goodbye. And, of course, the families of the men and women of Bravo Company were on hand to bid farewell to their loved ones. Laura Cooley, along with Sean's parents, beamed with pride. Sean was perched atop the first truck, chosen to lead the parade by his comrades in arms. Anice Lee was there to send her grandson Terrance off to war, and just seeing and meeting Sean for the first time filled her with confidence. She was most impressed, though, when she met Larry Arnold. It was plain that he and Terrance were close, as they chatted amiably and patted each other on the back. Anice was cheered by the idea that Terrance was going to war among friends; that he wouldn't be alone. Her eyes teared up, and she leaned in and gave Larry a hug. Larry put her head on his shoulder and said, "Don't worry about Terrance. I'm going to bring him back."

The younger Larry Arnold was also there with his mother Melinda. They were happy to see that father Larry was among friends and was plainly respected like a father in his unit. The younger Larry knew how good a father he had and was sure that he would serve that purpose well for the young men and women who were gathered around. Everywhere family members began to break out in tears as the gravity of the situation slowly dawned on them. But Melinda Arnold held it all in, standing there arm-in-arm with her son. She was not going to cry. Larry had enough to worry about without worrying about her. Just before he took his position aboard the flatbed truck, Larry told his son that he had just bought a 1949 Chrysler. That car was going to be their project when he got home, and that car would be his.

Topping off the ceremony in Lucedale was a short speech by the district congressman, Gene Taylor. He praised the Guardsmen and women, their families, and the community for its heartfelt support. He wished the soldiers well and concluded with a promise. "I'm going to bring y'all shrimp! I'll bring it to you where you are at: fresh shrimp from the Gulf!" And then it was off to Camp Shelby.

GETTING STARTED

Originally the Mississippi Guard was slated to train in Indiana, because Camp Shelby already had a brigade combat team from Tennessee training on-site. After some planning and calculations, though, it was decided that the 155th and its subordinate units, including the 150th, could just about be shoehorned into Camp Shelby alongside the Tennessee Guard. The staggered arrival of the 155th began in August, with the 150th being one of the final battalions to arrive on base. Being packed in cheek-by-jowl meant that there were bound to be some difficulties from the get-go. The Mississippi soldiers lived in long, concrete-walled barracks without any air conditioning amidst the heat of the late southern summer. Instead, doors and windows were left open and big fans stirred the humid air. Forty bunks were packed into each barracks, leaving precious little space. With men packed in so tightly everything became an issue, from lights out time to snoring. Eventually barracks sorted themselves out, with one barracks being known for lights out early, another for lights out late, and another for a perpetual game of cards. Not everyone, though, was eager to go and live under such luxurious circumstances. Gary Kinsey, the Bravo Company executive officer, even had to drag one unfortunate soldier out from his hiding hole under his parents' house to make him see the light of day. Going to Camp Shelby was surely better than living under your parents' house!

Everything was jumbled and hectic as the unit settled in. Mike Beal was from tiny New Hope, a village outside of Carthage that wasn't even big enough to have a stop sign. He had grown up "poor as dirt," working on a small farm with his grandparents. The farm barely produced enough for the family, but somehow his grandfather, Whitt Shepherd, always found some produce to give away to the even less fortunate members of the community. Strong and athletic, Beal had joined the Guard while still in high school and had then gone on to play football in college. It was after graduation from the University of Southern Mississippi that Beal decided to give Officer Candidate School a try. As the troops arrived at Camp Shelby, Beal was trying to get settled in as a newly promoted lieutenant and platoon leader in Bravo Company. He knew many of the men – the Mississippi Guard is a family after all. But he quickly had to figure out who was who. And it took all of about two seconds. Sean Cooley impressed Beal from the get-go. He knew that they were going to become close and that Cooley, as platoon sergeant, was going to be his rock.

As support platoon leader, it was up to Richard Rowland to make sure that the details of housing and transportation were locked up tight. For the freshly minted officer it was a never-ending task that had him dashing from one end of Camp Shelby to another. At this point he had heard of Lieutenant Colonel Robinson, the new battalion commander, but had never met him. Desperate to get everything done correctly, Rowland ran out of the battalion area one of their first nights on post. "I ran around the corner and ran smack dab into him. I went BAM! Damn near knocked him on his ass. Robinson jumped back and yelled, 'Whoa! Son, what in the hell is wrong with you?'" Rowland can't remember what he replied, having just about knocked over his commanding officer. But after a stammering explanation he ran off about his duties. In the end, he felt that maybe he had left a good impression on Robinson. After all, the other platoon leaders were all off in their bunks, but he was still out there "pulling the wagon and chopping the wood."

TRAINING, AUGUST—NOVEMBER 2004

The training for the Mississippians was handled by General Russell Honore and troops of the First Army, many of whom were veterans of the 3rd Infantry Division that had conquered Baghdad in 2003. The Guardsmen and women felt lucky to have such an experienced cadre in charge of their tutelage. The overall plan called for beginning with soldier readiness, to make sure that everyone had their records in order and was physically ready to deploy. Everyone then had to complete individual weapons qualification, common task training, land navigation training, improvised explosive device (IED) training, and cultural awareness training. Each company then worked on collective training before immersive training, in which soldiers dealt with realistic scenarios of cordoning villages and dealing with civilians in preparation for what they might see in Iraq.

What this meant for the soldiers was out of the rack at 0430 and then constant training, with a break for lunch, until 1900. Then lights out at 2030 and back at it again the next day. As expected, everyone in the 150th trained for the usually expected activity of combat engineers: building and breaching obstacles. But since the war in Iraq had devolved into an insurgent fight, everybody had to know everything. Combat engineers are infantrymen first, and much of the training was geared toward the realities faced by infantry fighting against an insurgent force that relied on IEDs as their weapon of choice. The training was intense and across the board, and the men and women of the 150th worked like their lives depended on it, because they did. Douglas Mansfield described the regimen as like "drinking from a fire hose. It was kind of like teaching a football player how to play baseball."

Captain Ken Cager explained:

It was so much stuff. We spent all those long hours, learning what a IED was, learning how to operate – how to be tactical convoys. Just to move from point A to point B, it was totally different than what we were used to. You don't drive with your lights on. You drive with your lights on in Iraq, it'll get you killed. Everything was – night-vision goggles, how to operate in the dark. And those 3rd Infantry Division guys, they knew how to keep us alive. They were like, "You don't do this. You don't do – I know you used to doing that, but you don't do that." Towbars, how to recover a vehicle quickly. I'm not talking about you taking two hours to recover a vehicle. I'm talking about drop a towbar, put a pin in it, you hook to that vehicle, and you dragging it off in, like, minutes, not hours. And our medical training. You have to be able to administer medical aid. How to stop bleeding. And everybody in that vehicle needed to shoot – learn how to fire every weapon you own because you may get somebody shot, that's a gunner, [so] that the driver may have to get up there and fire that weapon. Like, everybody in that vehicle needed to understand how to operate that weapon system in the dark. I mean, it was just that intense. We would practice different battles where we got hit by IEDs. The third vehicle gets hit. What will vehicle one and two do? If the last vehicle gets hit, what do we do? And we learned to raid buildings and villages. That was a big challenge, and how to clear buildings. We had never cleared buildings before. We're not infantry. We're combat engineers, but we had to learn how to do a four-man stack. How to approach a potentially hostile building. How to enter a neighborhood when you got snipers on top of the building. And this training saved lives. We practiced so much that it got mentally ingrained in everybody's head, and I'm convinced that saved lives because everybody knew the drill.

One important aspect of the training at Camp Shelby involved learning how to raid houses that might or might not contain insurgents. For Marty Davis of Lucedale, this was old hat. His civilian career was as an officer of the Mississippi Highway Patrol. As such he had extensive training and experience in breaching houses that might contain criminals, or perhaps they might just contain innocent bystanders. Marty got with Lieutenant Colonel Robinson and asked if he should get in touch with his Highway Patrol buddies to see if they would put on training demonstrations for the 150th. Utilizing civilian trainers is not a normal Army technique, but Robinson demonstrated that he was already willing to think outside of the box and gave Davis the go-ahead. And training with the Highway Patrol wound up being a huge success.

By the time the move to the National Training Center was imminent, the 150th had trained at all levels – from convoys, to setting and breaching minefields, to arms qualification, to Combat Lifesaver work, to hitting hostile villages and buildings, to cordoning peaceful villages and dealing with the local population, to locating and defusing IEDs. And in the training, one man stood out. Larry Mergenschroer recalled:

In training Terrance Lee showed himself to be a star soldier and armorer – at Shelby he was the best there was and will fix anything for you better than new. So, during qualification I had a guy that said his weapon kept hanging up. And so I give him my weapon and told him to go qualify. And I took his weapon and took it back in and give it to Terrance. I told him this thing wasn't working right. He took it immediately and tore it down, and I went up to battalion; wasn't up there ten minutes, and I'm back in the vehicle, going back out there. But he beat me back out to the range; it's thirty minutes out to the range. He beat me back out there with that weapon, and he was testing it on zero range, making sure it was ready before he gave it back. And he fixed that weapon and gave it to the guy, and he qualified with it. So, you have need for them kind of people. And so when he done that, it impressed the whole company.

LETTING OFF STEAM

Being rather local at Camp Shelby was both a good and bad thing. For the soldiers of Bravo Company, home was only about a 45-minute drive from the camp's front gate. Months and months of training with your wife and family so near, but you can't see them. And by this time cellphones were common, so men knew when their wives and children were having problems. The desire to go home and help out, or just to get to sleep in a real bed, was almost overwhelming. Official policy was that no soldier could go home at night. But as time wore on, Captain Paul Lyon* said "I ain't checking beds every night, but you're not allowed to leave. You get a ticket, you get put in jail, you don't show back up, or you show up late, I'm going to hammer you because you're not where you are supposed to be, but I'm not checking beds every night." So many of the Lucedale guys took to leaving Shelby at eight, spending the night at home with their family, and then getting on the road to return to Shelby at 4 a.m. There was never a single problem of someone getting arrested or showing back up late, because, as Lyon said, "They knew if they messed up, they wouldn't be leaving again." The men policed themselves, held themselves to the expected standard. It was Guard through and through.

For the Alpha and Charlie companies, the situation was different. Their homes were too far away to get there and back in the same night.

---

*Lyon was a first lieutenant serving in a captain's slot and was promoted to captain during the tour, so for simplicity's sake he will be referred to throughout as Captain Lyon.

And the men and women of those units couldn't help but notice the Bravo Company nighttime exodus. With family so nearby but still too far away, Cager and Thomas realized that they could not treat their soldiers like prisoners. The men had to be able to get some time to let their hair down and see their loved ones. So Cager and Thomas had to be a bit more inventive. Together they worked out a rotation where soldiers in their units got nights off and their families could come visit them, and they could all stay in hotels in nearby Hattiesburg. For soldiers without families to speak of, the bars and nightlife of Hattiesburg was their option. Of course, they had to operate under the same strictures as the soldiers of Bravo Company. Coming back late, or drunk, would cause privileges to be revoked – an issue that never arose.

Naturally, when you put a bunch of largely young men together in confined spaces for months on end someone is going to start pulling pranks. And everyone knew who that someone was. It was Sean Cooley. Somehow, he always magically had access to a nearly limitless supply of duct tape. A standard prank in his endless repertoire was to duct-tape the victim into his bunk as he slept. Come reveille in the morning, the victim would thrash about like a turtle on its back until someone broke from their gales of laughter and aided them in their predicament. Variations on the same theme involved stacking bunks up so when reveille sounded the victim rolled out of bed and crashed to the now distant ground. Everyone's favorite, though, involved plastic glowing chem lights. The kind when you snap them, they glow. Breaking the chem light open and pouring its contents on a sleeper would make the victim glow for hours.

One of Cooley's most memorable pranks, which elicited the greatest laughter, was a simple one. He put the sergeant's car up on blocks – just high enough where its wheels didn't touch the ground. Poor sarge just sat there and kept gunning his car, hoping to make use of his own night off. But nothing happened. He was sure his transmission was shot, but, of course, it was just Cooley. But even the great Sean Cooley was topped by an anonymous prankster in Alpha Company. As combat engineers, the soldiers of the 150th always had heavy machinery to hand. As the unlucky sergeant major of Alpha Company made ready to embark on his training regimen one day, he found his Humvee buried in the ground with only its roof showing. Sarge was all kinds of late for training that day, and his men heard about it. Cooley had to admit that he was impressed with that one. He just wished he had thought of it.

One of the unit's pranks was actually more of an experiment gone awry. Everyone had heard that if you took the heater out of a Meal, Ready to Eat (MRE) and poured the heater fluid into a Coke bottle, and then screwed the lid back down tightly, it would explode. Well, that was just too great a science experiment to pass up. The Bravo Company miscreants were in their barracks one afternoon and followed the instructions to a T before dashing out of the building. The resulting explosion was better than they could have hoped, surprising folks for blocks away, and blowing out three windows in the building. It was Captain Lyon who paid the price, getting chewed out by higher command and being told that those damn windows needed to be fixed by the next day. Lyon, as is customary in the military, passed the chewing-out down the line. The next morning Lyon had to admit that he was impressed. The windows were like new. That night at the battalion meeting, though, he got chewed out again. Turned out three identical windows in a nearby barracks had gone missing. Of course, the culprits claimed to know nothing about this.

Even though you might wind up duct-taped to your bunk, everyone loved Sean Cooley. He was the glue that held the unit together. Folks didn't just put up with his pranks; they loved them. And for his part Captain Lyon found himself getting closer and closer to Sean. The two would sit and talk for hours during downtime at training. With the men under his command facing a war zone, Lyon was only too happy to have Cooley and his medical experience in the company. Paul constantly mined Sean for information on how to handle life-or-death medical situations and told Sean that he would be one of the most important members of the unit when push came to shove and things got violent in Iraq.

Cooley had one final prank up his sleeve as training neared its end. Sean hadn't snuck out many nights to see his wife Laura, preferring instead to let others spend time with their families. But he sure as hell was going to sneak home on their first anniversary. The prank/surprise went a bit awry, however. Sean went to surprise Laura at home, but she had switched shifts at the hospital and was still at work when he arrived. Luckily, it was a slow day in the emergency room when Sean called. The conversation was more or less like when he called from Shelby; he didn't want to give up the surprise. But he did ask her when she was leaving.

He called twice more, and on the third call just told her to come home, because he was there waiting. Laura responded, "Well, shit! I could have left two hours ago!"

For his part, Robert McNail had kept up his reputation as the best ACE operator in the battalion during the training at Shelby, and he and Jamie Davis had kept their friendship alive. Meridian wasn't as close as Lucedale, but Mac had a special reason to sneak away from time to time. He had met Denise at church in April 2004, just before training began. They had been introduced by mutual friends and had begun dating by the middle of the month and were very quickly in love. But just like that, Mac was off to train at Camp Shelby. Denise visited any time she could, staying at a nearby hotel, and she became best friends with Jamie's wife Starla. Denise came to the relationship with two children, Daniel and Sheridan, which fitted Mac like an old brown shoe. He loved kids and got along with the duo famously. And Mac must have been open about the developing relationship with his family, because one Sunday at church Mac's father took Denise aside and told her that he knew that she and Mac were dating and that it was serious. Denise was a little taken aback, but Mac's father continued, "It's okay with me. You seem to make my son happy." He encouraged her to visit Mac any chance she got.

LATECOMERS

As the 150th was working to complete its training, it received transfers from other units across the state to make up losses due to physical issues. One of the new transfers was well known to many in the unit – Robert Arnold, Larry Arnold's son. Robert never knew exactly why he was transferred into his father's unit, but he had a strong suspicion that his dad had pulled all the strings he possibly could so that he could keep Robert safe in Iraq. When he arrived at Shelby, it was plain that his dad had been laying the groundwork for him by telling folks what a good soldier he was. At that point the two were in the same platoon but different squads, so they didn't see each other all that much. In fact, it was kind of like Larry was staying out of Robert's way so that he could be his own man. The two had to interact on occasion, though. Robert's squad was tasked one day with clearing a house of insurgents, and who was inside playing an insurgent? His dad.

Larry was bound and interrogated by the book, but broke free with a knife while the squad was interrogating another insurgent. There was heck to pay for that.

Ricky Tyler, who had joined the Guard in the wake of the 9/11 terrorist attacks, had wanted to serve his country in time of war, but had found himself in Kuwait as a chaplain's assistant. He was antsy, "bored to death," and wanted to do more. So he transferred to the 150th in an effort to see more action, showing up at Camp Shelby that October. Joe Smith had joined the Navy fresh out of high school so he could get away from Meridian, Mississippi and see the world. It sure worked; his first Christmas in the service was spent on the French Riviera. He had gotten out of the Navy after the minimum service total and had gotten married after a return to Meridian. Missing the structure of being in the military, he joined the Guard after the terrorist attacks of September 2001, and his wife supported his decision. His path was going to be different this time; he decided to be a medic, so it was off to Fort Sam Houston in Texas for medical training. Then it was on to join up with the 150th as it completed training at Camp Shelby. He knew that he was the odd man out, so worked to change that quickly. After all, these men would need to trust him soon with their lives when they went to war:

> Medics didn't have to go with the unit on training, but if they were out there, working, I wanted to be out there, working with them. And one day they asked me, said, "Medic Smith, why you out here, working with us?" And I'd tell them, "How am I supposed to know how hot you get, if I don't get as hot as you do?" Now, when they started calling me *Doc*, we were on our way, coming in from an exercise at Camp Shelby. In training we had a guy go down because of heat exhaustion, and I told them; I said, "We're going to pick him up; we're going to put him under a tree here. I don't want cold water; I want lukewarm water. We going to take his vest off; we going to take his top off." I said, "And I'm going to start an IV [intravenous fluid], and we're going to call in a nine line," which is basically a spot on the map where we were exactly, "and the helicopter's going to come in and land, and they going to take him, and they going to take him back to the hospital." And ever since that day, they started calling me *Doc Smith*.

NATIONAL TRAINING CENTER,
NOVEMBER–DECEMBER 2004

The next move for the Mississippians was to the National Training Center (NTC) at Fort Irwin, California. In the past for the 155th and the 150th that had meant mocking decisive battle, tank-on-tank scenarios. But the rotation in 2004 proved to be quite different. As the advance party touched down to prepare for the arrival of the troops, the weather was what you'd expect in California. Thomas Howell couldn't believe his luck, it was so pretty. In any free time he had he ran through the beautiful countryside and did so wearing shorts. But before the remainder of the unit arrived, the mercury dropped to record lows, meaning that the Mississippians would enjoy one of the coldest NTC rotations ever. And there remained some skepticism. The last such wartime rotation for the 155th had resulted in the unit not being cleared for deployment in time for the Persian Gulf War. Some wondered whether the Regular Army was going to play fair this time, or whether it was just another setup.

The unit's arrival was hectic. Since their own equipment was being shipped to Kuwait, they first had to marry up with equipment based at NTC. To put it bluntly, the Guardsmen and women didn't think that their new equipment matched up; it hadn't been maintained as well as their own. But once the grumbling settled and the details were sorted, and everyone had eaten a special Thanksgiving meal, the troops moved out to their forward bases. Upon arrival at the base, Allen McDaniel, one of the assistant S-3s, couldn't quite believe it. Everyone in the unit was going to be jammed into one big circus tent. A big empty tent with kangaroo mice jumping around in it. Once moved in, though, the National Guard showed that it was something different. Marty Davis, a platoon leader in Bravo Company, heard it from the NTC staff. There was no way that Davis should be letting his soldiers call him by his name. But Davis had grown up with these guys, and told the NTC cadre, "These men know me no matter what clothes I'm wearing and I guarantee that authority didn't come from just that rank. In the National Guard, especially in our hometown units where we grew up, if you had a weak spot, they know it. It's about being a respectable man. In the National Guard you are not going to get respect just because of what you sew on your collar. You have to earn it."

What ensued in training was something relatively new for the local opposition forces. The 11th Armored Cavalry Regiment (ACR) usually provided the opposing forces at NTC, which in the past had meant high-tempo battles – throwing everything they could at the trainees. But with the insurgencies in Iraq and Afghanistan, the regimen had altered. John Voccio, an Italian kid from the mean streets of Brooklyn, had learned from his old-school parents, "If you get into a fight, and you lose, you'd better fight them again." Taking his parents' advice, Voccio was known for fighting and for working hard to make money. It seemed like the Army was a good way to make that money, so Voccio joined fresh out of high school and went into the armored branch. He was coming out of basic training when the Persian Gulf War kicked off, and his drill sergeant told the recruits, "You're going to go over there. You're cannon fodder. You're going to be replacements. You're going over there to die." Voccio took him literally and decided to hurry up and get married. He survived that tour and loved it when he got assigned to NTC. He was there for the terrorist strike of 9/11, losing a brother-in-law when the World Trade Center collapsed. He still loved NTC and getting to beat up on all the trainee units, but he longed for a chance to be deployed to the war.

Instead of attacking the Mississippians with tanks, Voccio's 2nd Squadron, 11th ACR, had built forward operating bases (FOBs), roads, and villages. He and his squadron mates played the roles of civilians and terrorists. Their task was to simulate any possible scenario that the Mississippians might face. The buildings and villages were made from converted Conex shipping and storage containers. The simulations ranged from convoys, to both IED and ground attacks on convoys, to peaceful villages that needed to be searched, to searching for individual terrorists among the population, to all-out attacks on the FOBs. In something of an odd situation, Alpha Company of the 150th was placed with the 2/11th ACR. As it turned out, part of the 2/11th ACR was going to work with the Mississippians instead of against them. It wasn't a perfect situation. Thomas Howell, who served as executive officer of Alpha Company, spoke for many in believing that his unit felt like the odd man out during the NTC rotation.

For the remainder of the 150th, the training regimen was thorough and difficult, with Paul Lyon recalling:

They've built all these villages all over the desert floor, and now we have a FOB that we roll in on, and we take over this FOB. So we have to do takeover procedures for a FOB. I mean, you're loaded up. You got MILES [multiple integrated laser engagement system] gear on. You deploy like we're going into Iraq. You get all your vehicles loaded out. And they have people there that act like they're turning this FOB over to us, just like we would in-country. And then we do a left-seat, right-seat where you go out with the current unit to learn what they're doing before they leave. And then they leave, and we take over, and it's just like we're in-country. The enemy was as real as they get. And they all have MILES gear on, and everything is live. There's no, "OK. Stop. That was great." The whole fifteen days is live. You can get shot at any time, gassed at any time, everything. We do daily patrols, and you got the training that's going to go on that we do, too, where we do some live-fire demo and different things. But we did a full raid on a village looking for a particular terrorist. And my company is selected to do the raid of the actual village; Alpha Company's doing the outer cordon. Charlie Company's doing the inner, but Bravo is going to do the actual raid in the village, and we leave at like two o'clock in the morning and go conduct a big raid at NTC. We got blown up; they were dropping bombs off the top of the buildings on us. It was quite the mess, and they intended it to be. They want you to see what wrong, what bad looks like. So learning wise we learned a lot. It was a great exercise, and we learned what not to do in certain areas and different things, and then they took us back and redid it and showed us how it should've been done on different things, and it went well.

The training was taxing, and the conditions were horrible, but the Mississippians soaked it all in, making for one of the most successful NTC rotations in recent history. Douglas Mansfield recalled why he and his comrades were so motivated to do well:

You know people did not expect the 155th or the 150th to come out there and actually put that much blood, sweat, and tears and heart into those missions because it's training, right? Well, one of the things that does separate us apart is, "Man, I know you; I went to high school with you. You and I go way back, and if I have to go to this hometown and see your mom in Walmart or your cousin or your sister, I'm going to have to answer for that for the rest of my life." So, you know, a lot of people matured during training; a lot of people had the realization of we're no longer in a scrimmage; we're in the real game.

Of course, as with training at Camp Shelby, there were some notable moments and missteps. One night Richard Rowland had to make a quick run from one FOB to another. He dashed out of the tactical operations center (TOC) and told his driver to get a move on. The driver, a young private, responded, "Hey sir. We got a flat tire. I don't know what the hell to do about it." Rowland responded, "What do you mean you don't know what to do about it? Change the flat tire." But he was told that the Humvee didn't have a spare. Rowland was beside himself. These crappy local Humvees didn't even have spare tires? Rowland told the private that he didn't care what he had to do, but he needed to fix that tire. Twenty minutes later Rowland was back, and the tire had been changed. Great! And the duo was off to the next FOB. As his Humvee drove away Rowland noticed that the major's Humvee was up on a jack, and that his driver had reappropriated its right rear tire. He just hoped that the major never figured out who took it.

Most of the humorous moments revolved around the bitter cold. Again, Richard Rowland had trouble with the local equipment. This time his unit was on patrol and one of its M113 armored personnel carriers broke down. His unit didn't have any spare parts on hand, so it seemed like a disaster in the making. But then another unit drove by on the road, and he flagged them down. Sure enough, they had a maintenance guy. The mechanic looked in the engine compartment and magically squared everything away, and the patrol was ready to move out again. But Rowland's squad leader asked the mechanic, "Hey man, can you do anything about the heat?" As it turned out, none of the M113s had operational heaters, leaving the Mississippians in perpetual cold. The mechanic worked his magic once again, and the heater sprang to life. Everybody who possibly could jammed into the back of that M113 – the only vehicle around with a heater. Rowland recalled, "For three weeks I couldn't get them little bastards out of that 113. The only time anyone ever came out was to use the latrine."

One night Douglas Mansfield left his group of 113s that was formed up in a security formation for an overnight stop. After scouting the nearby territory, Mansfield returned to his unit and noticed that the troop hatch was open on one of the 113s, and light gleamed out along with a few trails of smoke. He wondered what the hell that could be, so he went over and poked his head in, saying, "What the fuck is going on here?" As he looked inside, his eyes had to take a moment to adjust due to the light. The guys had built a fire in an ammo storage can, and they had all huddled around. As he continued his inspection tour, Mansfield also took note that in another M113 two men had wriggled into the same sleeping bag in their vain attempt to stay warm.

It was even bad when the Mississippians were "safe" in their own FOBs. Paul Lyon recalled:

Between the rain, cold, and snow it was miserable. And the opposition forces were jacking with us. They would sneak onto the FOB by hiding "insurgents" in their observer vehicles, and they'd blow up the generator and cut off all the heaters, just to make it extra miserable. They would attack the FOB; so, they'd sneak into the FOB, and they'd run around, shooting everybody that were laying in their cots, freezing to death. And they kept doing that until the point that, I'll never forget; one of them came in, and it was two o'clock in the morning. And they'd cut the heaters off, and everybody's miserable after a long day of training. And they came in and attacked the place, and they're running around through there, shooting everybody. And everybody was like, "Just shoot me now, really. I'm dead." But I'll never forget; Major Trent Kelly was up there, and one of those "insurgents" came by and kicked his cot, and said, "Yeah. You're dead." And knocked the back end off the cot, and it folded up, and he fell off. And Trent got so mad; he got up and found that "insurgent" and made him go put his cot back together. They put his cot back together, and that night it was pretty much put out that, "If you come back in our area again, it won't be us shooting blanks at you. It won't be live ammo, but you won't like the reaction you get if you come back into our area again." We didn't get many attacks after that. It was well known: "Come on back in here; we got something for you, Mississippi style."

Terrance Lee, though, managed to beat the cold, at least for a few minutes. One morning Douglas Mansfield was all kinds of miserable walking through the cold slush to get some chow. Terrance was walking the opposite direction with a big smile on his face. Curious, Mansfield asked, "Hey T Lee. Why are you smiling so big? Why are you in a good mood in the middle of all this?" Lee responded, "Well sarge, I got me two cups of hot water. I'm going to get me a shower." Somehow Lee had talked the cooks out of two precious cups of hot water. It wasn't going to be much of a shower, but boy it was obvious that Terrance was going to enjoy it and had no intentions of sharing his newfound warm wealth with anyone.

The cold wore away at everyone, even Lieutenant Colonel Robinson. His stress level was crazy high; he wanted his men to be the best prepared for what awaited them when they reached the real war. There was so much to worry about, and so much to do. At NTC it never really stopped. Running low on fuel and stamina, Robinson could tell that he was getting sick. And he couldn't afford to be sick at NTC. One night he was in his bunk in the big circus tent that held most of the battalion, and his coughing wouldn't allow him any sleep. He knew that he also had a fever. Suddenly he felt someone sit beside him. He opened his eyes to find Sean Cooley. Sean felt his forehead and gave him some pills from a medical bag he carried, to help him sleep. And they did help. Robinson shook his head as Cooley walked away. That was the kind of guy that the unit relied on.

Sean Cooley, though, had a secret. In one of the 150th's mock raids, he had led the stack of men into a building. Protocol called for bashing the door in and then fanning out, looking for hostiles. It was Cooley's turn to bash in the door. He crashed into it with his shoulder, but the door had been wedged and didn't budge. And Sean's shoulder paid the price. As a nurse, he knew that he had torn it up pretty bad. But he sure as hell wasn't going to see any doctor. They might tell him to stay stateside to recuperate. And there was no way that Sean was going to let his buddies go to war without him. The only person he told about the injury was his wife Laura, and he swore her to secrecy. For her part,

Laura knew that there was nothing she could do. Sean was going to war with his unit, and that was that.

OFF TO WAR, DECEMBER 2004

At the close of NTC, the 155th returned to Camp Shelby before shipping out to Kuwait. The soldiers were ready. Everyone was tired of training and anxious to get into the fight. But there was a holdup. Everyone had to return all sensitive equipment, and one piece had gone missing. Somebody had absconded with, or lost, a pair of night-vision goggles. Most folks figured that it was a hunter who wanted them to get some deer at night. General Honore refused to give the troops their final home leave until the goggles were returned. Somehow, after a couple of days, they magically turned up. Everyone was sure that it wasn't the real goggles – that the replacement pair had been simply a reasonable facsimile. But it worked. The troops gathered for a graduation ceremony of sorts on the parade field at Camp Shelby, and Honore gave a speech. He praised the Mississippians for their very successful stint at NTC and assured them, "You will go over the berm into Iraq only with the best armor, vehicles, and gear."

After graduation the soldiers got to spend ten days home with their families over Christmas before shipping out. For many it was like a yo-yo. They had been through an emotional farewell before they departed for training, but now they were back. And this time, when they left, it would be for war. Randall Jones summed it up: "For the families it was an emotional roller coaster. 'Wait a minute dad. You're back. I thought you weren't coming back.' I don't feel it was fair to the families. It's like a Band-Aid. Rip it off. They were getting like, 'Well, dad's not really going. He'll be home in three or four days.'" His oldest son, though, was 12 and was able to work out what was really going on. The boy tried to be tough, saying he would do his best to be the man of the family. It was maybe even tougher on Jones' parents, sending both Randall and his brother Ben off to war with the 150th. Their mother took it hard, often weeping openly, while their father wore a quiet aura of pride. For his part Douglas Mansfield noticed an air of tension at home. He just wanted to do regular things like look at grass and trees, because the desert was going to be so different. His family members didn't really understand that need, and they also didn't know what to say to him. You couldn't really talk about the obvious, and nobody wanted to say goodbye, because that was bad luck. So big family meals were the order of the day. When talking is too difficult, eating together will suffice.

In small towns across Mississippi there were tears, awkward silences, talks with children to try to get them to understand, attempts to reassure worried parents, embraces with wives, and last feasts. And then it was back to Camp Shelby to ship out. The soldiers departed in waves, first boarding buses at Shelby to make their way to their overseas flights. Norris Galatas had an emotional departure from his wife Janis, who could only really tell him to stay safe. Then Galatas looked to his left and was surprised to see Winston Walker. The two had been fast friends for years, both in civilian life and in the Guard. Walker, though, had retired from the Guard to work as a nurse in a trauma unit nearer his parents. But when he had heard that the 150th was being mobilized, Walker pulled every string he could find to get back into the unit. Galatas looked at his old friend and grinned, and Walker replied, "Galatas, I'm right where I need to be." He then told Galatas that he planned to go on every mission that he could in Iraq to keep him and all his other friends safe. Nearby, Dexter Thornton held his crying three-year-old, who kept repeating, "Daddy, don't go. Daddy, don't go." It broke his heart and those of everyone around. Terrance Bloodsaw had never seen his mother and sisters cry so much, but he knew that he was doing the right thing. The buses were late, leaving many to sit with weeping family members for hours. Paul Lyon sat in his car with his wife and weeping daughters. He recalled, "That was the most difficult two hours of my life, saying goodbye to them."

The buses finally arrived and were loaded up. Chris Thomas handled getting Charlie Company all aboard and accounted for. One of the last soldiers to get onto the bus looked all of 12 years old. Thomas knew the lad well and had no doubt that he was a good soldier. As he motioned the soldier onto the bus, a hand grabbed his shoulder. It was the soldier's mother. She looked Thomas straight in the eyes and between tears choked out the words, "Please don't let anything happen to my baby." It hit Thomas like a punch to the gut. These men, these families, were depending on him. He had to get them back safely.

Robert McNail was at the very tail end of soldiers to hop aboard, and with good reason. While at NTC, he had sent Denise a letter asking her to marry him. He didn't want to go to Iraq without being engaged to her. The "real" proposal had come on Christmas Eve, when he got down on one knee in front of his family and the Christmas tree. The couple had thought about eloping, but Mac wanted a church wedding, so the date was set for March when he would get his short leave from Iraq. A nearby soldier could see that the couple was having trouble parting, so he came over and patted Mac on the back. It was Sean Cooley, and he looked at Denise and said, "Don't worry. I'll make sure that he gets back to you safely." Denise smiled and responded, "Thank you." And she watched the bus drive away.

Among the very last to ship out to Kuwait was assistant S-3 Allen McDaniel, who had to stay behind and make sure that everyone else got away safely. As he watched the other members of the 150th getting aboard buses and aircraft, McDaniel felt more and more alone. He wrote in his journal: "If we are going to have to go, I'm ready to get it over with. It's depressing watching everyone else leave. I miss Tara and Ford [his wife and young son]. I can't wait until I can look back on this from my home."

3

Welcome to the Sandbox

Saturday, Jan 08, 2005. Deployment day – Five months of training;
four at Camp Shelby and one at FT Irwin. It all comes down to this.
I'm on the second flight leaving from Keesler Air Force Base on a
C17. Everyone has their own expectations of what is about to happen.
Some are nervous, some you can't tell, some are sick to their stomachs.
Me… It's another chapter in my life. It hasn't hit me yet. Maybe
it won't. All I know is I miss my wife and kids. A year in theater?
Damn! I have no concept of that. I worry more for them than I do for
me and my men. The only thing that really scares me is that it hasn't
hit me yet. They say when it does, you'll get sick, your stomach will
knot up and the pucker factor reaches an all-time high. No one crosses
the berm leaving Kuwait without getting shot at. Maybe that's when
it'll sink in. I don't know. Everyone back home seems more worried
than I am. I'm just ready to get there and let the clock start ticking.

HAP PALMER, JOURNAL ENTRY

[The Mississippians] occupy FOBs held by the 24th Marine
Expeditionary Unit (MEU) up into their redeployment from theater
in February 2005… Contact there has revealed a marked demand
for CSC [Combat Stress Control] services due to the effects on service
members generated by contact with intense insurgent activity in this
area, in the form of frequent IEDs, patrol and convoy ambushes, and
mortar and rocket attacks on the FOBs, sometimes multiple times
a day. These attacks resulted all too often in the dismemberment or
death of service members in this area. Marines at these locations

presented clinically with visible manifestations of acute stress reactions
in response to the cumulative exposure to these traumatic events...
Given the fact that the 155th BCT has fewer people to perform their
mission in the most active and dangerous area of our AO, the op
tempo has remained consistently high since their arrival in theater.
The combination of personnel shortages, high op tempo, heavy
workload, and prolonged deployment cycle is a recipe designed to
generate a lot of business for CSC assets in this area... Based on our
observations, it is apparent that this area may represent a greater
demand for CSC support than any other site in the AO of the 1908th
Medical Detachment.

MEMORANDUM FOR COMMANDING OFFICER
1908TH MED DET (CSC) WRITTEN BY LTC
JOHN STASINOS, 1908TH SECTION CHIEF

The flights to Kuwait were staggered like the departure from Camp
Shelby. For most, this meant a bus ride to the Combat Readiness
Training Center in Gulfport to catch their flight. For Bradley Sharp,
what came next was hours in the small and uncomfortable holding area
while the aircraft was readied. Then the call came to board. But it was a
false alarm, and the men were all sent to a barracks to spend the night.
The flight was delayed for another entire day, with another anxious night
spent in the barracks. Finally, the boarding was for real, and the aircraft
took off for Frankfurt, Germany. Then there was another unwelcome
delay for hours as they awaited their flight to Kuwait. Marcus Wallace
couldn't believe how quiet that second flight was. Usually people talk
on airplanes. But the guys just sat there silently. The only noise was
snoring from the few who managed to sleep.

On his flight Richard Rowland also found silence; this allowed him
time to reflect, which turned into prayer. He told God, "Hey. Thanks
for my great life. If I don't make it back, it is what it is. But thank
you. Thanks for my wife Keltoum, my daughter Nadia, and my entire
family." Timothy Bolton was on another flight, and this one had some
talking. All his buddies knew that he was a long-service Guardsman. He
had joined in 1985 and had seen service in the Persian Gulf War. But
the guys he was sitting with were new to him. And when they figured
out that he had already been to war, they all began to ask him what to
expect. It all hit Bolton in kind of a funny way. He didn't want to be a

father figure to these guys and offer them advice. It wasn't because he wasn't fatherly – heck, he had four boys of his own. And it wasn't that he didn't want to share wisdom. But he knew that in war everything was random – sometimes good soldiers die while poor soldiers survive. You can do everything right and still not make it home. He knew that there was no trick to survival. IEDs and death could be anywhere at any time. What scared him most was, what if he gave these young men advice, and they died following that advice? Well, he was afraid he would never get over that. So instead he just tried his best to sleep.

FIRST THINGS FIRST

The first aircraft to touch down in Kuwait carried members of the advance party, who were tasked with sorting out accommodations for the 150th at Camp New York in Kuwait and with beginning the complex task of marrying up the unit with its equipment, which had been shipped in conexes to the nearby port. A tent city was set up for the soldiers, and convoy after convoy went back and forth to the port. Thomas Howell was feeling out of it. His flight from Gulfport had been delayed several times, he couldn't sleep on the airplane, and now in Kuwait sleep still wouldn't come. He looked like a wreck and felt like a wreck. He was on convoy duty to the port with Sean Cooley, who saw his distress. The two didn't know each other well, but Cooley looked at Howell and told him, "Look. It don't take both of us to do this. I'm going to take you back so you can sleep." Howell said that he was fine, but Cooley continued. "I'm good. I got some sleep. I got cleaned up. I'm going to take you back." Even though Howell was pretty sure that Cooley hadn't gotten any more sleep than he had, that is exactly what Sean did. Howell finally got some sleep, and he figured that he owed Cooley a big favor.

Then the main body of troops began to arrive. As Randall Jones looked around the camp, he got mad at his history instructor. He had always been taught that deserts were hot and dry. But Kuwait was cold and rainy. He thought, "Dude. This isn't the desert I pictured in my head. This sucks." Hap Palmer had grown up in Meridian and had long wanted to be a Marine until his cousin talked him out of the idea. So, after a stint in ROTC at Ole Miss, Palmer joined the Guard. In 2005 Palmer served as the Battalion Maintenance Officer of the 150th, meaning that he was in charge of the complicated and critical task of

WELCOME TO THE SANDBOX

keeping all of the battalion's vehicles in working order. He knew that the job would be never ending and would start the very moment that he touched down in Kuwait. Taking in his new surroundings, Palmer was amazed even by the trip to Camp New York, the major staging area that the 150th would occupy. The men were loaded on tall buses of Japanese make and shot like a rocket down the middle lane of a six-lane freeway with police escort. Even though the buses were nearly flying, luxury cars shot past them like they were standing still. The dead sheep and goats lining the road were testament to the difficulties of driving in the small country. He liked the camp though. Sure, the accommodations were big 70-men tents, but they had wooden floors and there was heat and air conditioning. The camp had hot showers, a great chow hall, a full PX, a Subway, a Burger King, and a nice internet center. It had everything. While getting their equipment ready to move out to Iraq, the Guardsmen and women also had classes on what to expect once there. Palmer wrote in his journal, "We had a mandatory class on the latest and most updated IED tactics in Iraq. Scared the living shit out of everyone. It was the first time I felt a trace of fear."

THE QUESTION OF ARMOR

One difference in capabilities between National Guard brigades and their regular Army counterparts was that... many National Guard units lacked the same modern equipment. While the Army had fielded the upgraded Family of Medium Tactical Vehicles in the 1990s, the workhorse vehicle of the National Guard wheeled fleet remained the antiquated "deuce and a half," or 2½-ton truck, a vehicle so old that the last one had rolled off the production line in 1977. An even more significant disparity was the National Guard units' shortage of armored vehicles, a problem that had bedeviled the coalition from the start of the war. By December 2004, the Army only had 69 percent of the armored or hardened vehicles that it needed in Iraq, and for National Guard units the shortfall was even more acute.
STRATEGIC STUDIES INSTITUTE[*]

[*]Colonel Joel Rayburn and Colonel Frank Sobchak, *The U.S. Army in the Iraq War: Volume 1; Invasion, Insurgency, Civil War, 2003–2006*, Strategic Studies Institute (Carlisle, PA: United States Army War College Press, 2019), 377.

As the 150th gathered its gear and made ready to move out to Iraq, Timothy Bolton looked around the vast complex. Regular Army units seemed to have the newest equipment – especially uparmored Humvees and M113s. He knew that small-arms fire would penetrate the Guard's unarmored Humvees, and .50-caliber fire would slice the sides of their M113s like cheese. He remembered General Honore's promise at the graduation speech at Camp Shelby that the Guard would go into Iraq with only the best equipment. He thought to himself, "Well. I guess he lied to me." Guardsmen all over Camp New York were coming to the same conclusion. And their fears were nothing new. In December 2004 Secretary of Defense Donald Rumsfeld had visited the base and had taken questions from a Tennessee Guard unit that was about to move into Iraq. Specialist Thomas Wilson complained that his unit had been left to scrounge through local landfills to find what armor they could to bolt onto their vehicles. Rumsfeld infamously responded, "You go to war with the army you have, not the army you might want or wish to have at a later time."[*]

The men and women of the 150th had heard of the issue before shipping out to Kuwait and had requested to uparmor their Humvees and M113s, but that request had been denied. They dared hope that the problem had been rectified and that there would be regulation uparmor kits awaiting them in Kuwait. Just in case, however, family readiness groups across the unit raised money to buy iron and steel and had that shipped with the unit in conexes. Aside from that, there were no cupolas for the M113s, and precious little iron and steel to go around. So the scroungers of the unit got to work. Randall Jones, Hap Palmer, Sherman Hillhouse, and many others headed to vehicle junkyards – where the shells of destroyed vehicles were stored – and looted the vehicles of whatever armor they could find. But the chief scrounger of all was Gary Kinsey, from the Mississippi Gulf Coast small town of Gautier. Frustrated by his slow progress in college, Kinsey had joined the Guard at the age of 22 to work on helicopters. Completion of Officer Candidate School necessitated a shift to the 150th in 2000. By the unit's arrival for training at Camp Shelby, Kinsey was serving as Paul Lyon's executive officer for Bravo Company. It was at Camp Shelby that Kinsey first became a

[*]Rayburn and Sobchak, *The U.S. Army in the Iraq War: Volume 1*, 377.

master scrounger. After all, it was his job to make sure that the men of his company were adequately supplied. It all started when he realized that there was a program to take old M113s out into the Gulf of Mexico and dump them to make artificial reefs. So, before those 113s were sent out to sea, Kinsey and a cohort of men had them looted of all potentially valuable equipment. That way, upon arrival in Kuwait, Kinsey already had a conex of 113 spare parts waiting for him.

Kinsey knew that he had to do something more, though. He had promised families at the going away ceremony in Lucedale that he was going to bring their sons home safely. And that couldn't happen if they didn't have uparmored vehicles. Not only did they not have the armor for the vehicles, but also there were no welding rods, no gas – nothing to fix anything. So, Kinsey went out to see what he could see. At one of the nearby camps there was a civilian contractor's welding shop. It had equipment everywhere. Literally everywhere. Hell, there was more spare armor in their dumpster than the 150th had in total. Kinsey played nice and asked if there was any way he could trade to get what he needed. His men were headed into the war zone after all. The answer was a cordial "no." Well, Kinsey wasn't going to take that. He went back to the 150th's area and recruited the fastest runners in the unit. Then he appropriated a Kuwaiti van that would attract zero attention. The group went back to the civilian shop, and Kinsey went to "negotiating" again with the foreman. Kinsey and the foreman talked about everything under the sun – both loved to hunt and fish and to tell tall tales about both. They got along famously, all while the fast runners were liberating everything they could find. Once back with the 150th, some folks asked Kinsey where he had found such a treasure trove of welding supplies and spare armor. He just told them that they didn't need to know.

Lieutenant Colonel Robinson was amazed, but he had expected no less. He knew that one of his unit's greatest strengths was that it was chock full of welders, construction workers, cops, road pavers, farmers – the list goes on. Each member of the Guard came to the table not only with their military specialty but also with their civilian career skills. Robinson had known that those skills would come in handy, but he hadn't guessed how soon. It seemed that all of a sudden, to Robinson's amazement, the 150th's scratch of desert in Kuwait had become a full-blown manufacturing line. Men were swarming over the vehicles like ants, with the noted gearhead Larry Arnold usually somehow in charge.

By the time the 150th rolled into Iraq, many of the vehicles had jury-rigged belly armor, door armor – you name it. Everyone just hoped that the armor would hold and prove effective under fire. Ricky Tyler couldn't believe that the vehicles could even move. They all seemed so weighed down with every chunk of metal under the sun, even including a jumble of old tire rims. Ken Cager thought that the "hillbilly armor," as it was known, made the vehicles look like something out of the television show *Sanford and Son*. And he couldn't help but complain inwardly, "Man. We are fixing to fight the same bad guys as the Army, yet we have substandard equipment."

Even though there was a good deal of worry over the issue of armor and equipment, the soldiers of the 150th took solace in the idea that their jobs as combat engineers would perhaps provide them with some protection. The general plan was that the 155th would take over several FOBs from Marine units that were rotating home or moving further west. Under the umbrella of Multi-National Force – West (MNF-W), the I Marine Expeditionary Force (MEF) held western Iraq, notably restive al-Anbar Province. The proposed plan called for the 155th to take over several FOBs from the Marines, including Kalsu, Duke, and Iskandariyah. The subsidiary task of the 150th was to break up into its component companies to provide combat engineer support to each of the maneuver battalions of the 155th on those FOBs. Support could mean many things, but generally would include building and maintaining the defenses of the home FOB. This remained the plan as the first Mississippians made their way into Iraq, with the 150th planning to operate as combat engineers as usual.

As the 150th made ready to move out, there was trepidation mixed with excitement. Jody Kyzar was from the tiny village of Sharon outside of Laurel. He had joined the Guard in college in part to help pay off his student loans. By 2005 he was an NCO working in the personnel division of the 150th, and he and his wife Angela had two young sons. As he readied to move into Iraq he wrote in his journal:

> Since being here [at Camp New York] I have talked to Angela on a few occasions. It is very hard to hang up the phone because I don't know if that will be the last time I'll get to talk to her. I miss and love her so much and especially the two boys. Death is something thought about [from] time to time. However, my strength and comfort in

the Lord helps me get through those troubling thoughts, although I have said that if it were my time to go, I would rather be in uniform fighting for my country. I truly believe in our cause over here and hope and pray that the Iraqi people get to enjoy the life of freedom that we Americans have. I would rather fight the terrorists over here than in the streets of America.

ADVANCE PARTIES

Chris Thomas led the advance party of Charlie Company to its new home of FOB Duke. At first Thomas could hardly believe his luck. Duke was way out in the middle of the desert, 20 kilometers outside the city of Najaf. It was a major ammunition storage site, so it needed to be well away from populated areas or threats. There was a main road joining it to the military supply network, and it was long and straight. Thomas remembered looking around and thinking, "Nobody is going to sneak up on us here. How did we get this lucky? How did we luck out and go to Duke?" He didn't want to jinx it, but he decided that if the commanders wanted to send his unit to the sleepiest FOB in Iraq for a year, then so be it.

But not all went well for the advance party of Charlie Company. Sherman Hillhouse and his group were slated to fly to al-Taqaddum Air Base (universally referred to as TQ), where they would catch choppers to Duke. What was supposed to be a 45-minute flight took nearly an hour and a half. He was a little worried that the aircraft let them off in the middle of nowhere, and there didn't seem to be anybody to greet them. They saw a red light in the distance and wandered over to begin asking questions. On the other end of that red light was a lieutenant who said, "Who the hell are you?" Hillhouse couldn't help but think, "Well, this isn't good." As it turned out, they had not landed in TQ but were instead in the city of Tikrit. It took them two days to find a flight out, and that flight was to an airbase outside of Balad. There the orphan group had to wait a full week before jumping aboard an ammunition supply flight to Duke.

Paul Lyon and the advance party of Bravo Company touched down without incident at FOB Iskandariyah. The FOB was located on the grounds of a massive powerplant hard on the Euphrates River just north of the town of Musayyib. The task of the advance party was to assess the situation and to report back to Robinson so that plans could be put in train for the future. Lyon figured that he and his men were largely going to be stuck on the base for much of the year managing all aspects of the base's engineering and defense. After getting sorted, the group grabbed a tent and settled in for the night. Larry Odom and Sean Cooley were in bunks near to Lyon, and they noticed that above Lyon's head was a hole in the tent; you could see straight out to the stars. Lyon asked a nearby soldier who had been there for a while how the hole had gotten there. He replied, "That's where a mortar shell went through a few nights back." Lyon's eyes widened as he thought, "Mortar shell. Hell. Maybe they are like lightning and don't strike twice in the same place," as both Odom and Cooley broke into laughter.

With mortars and rockets being a real concern at Iskandariyah, the advance party got down to the business of constructing bunkers that would provide adequate defense for the Mississippi troops when they arrived. The group was sitting the next day watching bunker demonstrations on Lyon's laptop. The demonstration film showed both mortars and rockets detonating on hardened bunkers. Odom recalled: "So, we were watching that, and all of a sudden we hear SSSSSSSSSSSSSSS! And Jimmy Mote was standing there. He says, 'Damn! That film has got good sound effects!' And I said, 'Sound effects, hell! That's the real thing!' And we all went out and jumped in the bunker. It was our first experience under fire in Iraq."

The group quickly decided that they were going to need better housing. Odom, Cooley, Mansfield, Mote, and Sharp had gotten close with some Special Forces guys nearby and were able to use their Humvee to scout out the base. Turned out that the Special Forces group had a wonderful compound and were about to move out. So, the Bravo Company guys just waited until the Special Forces group moved out, and took the building over. The new building was amazing. Marble floors, bathrooms, showers – and it overlooked the Euphrates. Heck, it was more like a vacation spot than a military building. And the Special Forces had left behind all kinds of food and other supplies. Iraq didn't look too bad after all. Typical platoon sergeant, Larry Odom tried to set everyone to work getting the place ship shape. But Sean Cooley had found a box of five Cuban cigars. Not many of the guys smoked, but this opportunity was just too good to pass up. Odom grumbled a bit, but Lyon told him, "How often do you get to smoke a cigar sitting on a balcony watching the sun set over the Euphrates River?" Even Odom couldn't deny that. And as the smoke wafted away on the breeze and the sun disappeared over the horizon, the men of Bravo Company felt at peace.

The advance party of Alpha Company made their way to FOB Kalsu, 30 kilometers south of Baghdad, where they ran into some old friends. Serving with the 155th in Iraq and based at Kalsu was the 2/11th ACR, who had been the opposing forces and had worked with the Mississippians when they had rotated through the National Training Center. While at NTC John Voccio and his men of the 2/11th did not have their own organic armor, meaning that in Iraq they would use Mississippi gear. After the NTC rotation, they had journeyed to Mississippi to familiarize themselves with their tanks and had married up with those tanks in Kuwait. Although Voccio didn't relish the idea of serving with the Guard, he had nothing but respect for the 155th after its rotation at NTC. If he was going to serve with the Guard, at least he was going to be serving with some of their best.

THE CHANGING SITUATION

Al-Anbar Province in 2005 formed the heart of the insurgency in Iraq. The Battle of Fallujah in late 2004 had dealt the insurgents in that city a severe blow, with an estimated 2,175 insurgents killed at the cost of 63 American lives, along with 600 wounded. Even so, most of the insurgents had fled Fallujah instead of fighting and dying. These insurgents fanned out into the smaller towns and villages of Anbar and Babil provinces, where they hoped to find fertile ground to continue their war. In addition to the insurgents that targeted US forces and interests, the Sunni militias of Abu Musab al-Zarqawi began to strike not only coalition forces but also Shia Muslims in Iraq. The combined effects of these developments posed a critical threat to American progress in their war in Iraq.[*]

The seismic shift in the insurgency away from Fallujah focused attention onto other sections of Anbar Province, including its eastern portion that ran along the Euphrates. Here the influx of insurgents

---

[*]Rayburn and Sobchak, *The U.S. Army in the Iraq War: Volume 1*, 394–396.

from the fall of Fallujah fatally met up with an ample supply of armaments and weaponry. At the time of the fall of Saddam Hussein's regime, endless tons of munitions had been smuggled out of Baghdad and the surrounding Iraqi military bases and had been buried in the desert of eastern Anbar. As 2005 dawned, that desert, pockmarked with caches of munitions dumps, became the supply center of the insurgency.* The area was home to the Albu Issa tribe, which was fractured in whether it supported the insurgency or the Americans. One of its powerful subtribes, the Owesats, tended toward siding with the insurgents, especially after being infiltrated by the insurgents after the fall of Fallujah. Matters were made much worse by money. The average monthly household income in Iraq was less than $80, while the terrorists paid young male Iraqis between $150 and $1,000 per attack and somewhat less for movement of bombmaking equipment.†

The deteriorating situation in eastern Anbar led to a spate of IED strikes that gave the area the grim nickname, "The Triangle of Death." But, even as eastern Anbar was becoming a thorn in the coalition's side, the Marines also faced a huge series of problems in western Anbar and along the Syrian frontier. As a result, the Marines decided that they had to shift more combat power to that area, which would result in the Mississippians having to take over more territory than had been planned as an economy of force mission. The solution was for the 150th to function as an infantry battalion that would take over its own area of operations (AO). This AO was slap bang in the middle of the Triangle of Death and squarely atop the insurgency's supply route at a forlorn forward operating base dubbed Dogwood.

A NEW PLAN

Lieutenant Colonel Robinson was already at FOB Kalsu overseeing the development of the engineer support plan for the base. In the

---

*Marine Corps Intelligence, *Study of the Insurgency in Anbar Province, Iraq* (Carlisle, PA: US Army War College, 2007), Chapter 6, 171.
†Lin Todd, *Iraq Tribal Study – Al-Anbar Governorate: The Albu Fahd Tribe, the Albu Mahal Tribe, and the Albu Issa Tribe* (Washington, DC: Department of Defense, 2006), 4-35-42, 6.47.

midst of the planning the phone rang. Robinson's aide motioned for him to come over. Robinson replied, "Hey. I'm busy. I got stuff going on. Who is it? What do they want?" His aide told him that it was Colonel Leon Collins, Commander of the 155th and Robinson's boss. "He wants to talk to you and talk to you now." Robinson got on the phone and was told, "Hey, you need to get on the next aircraft and come back to Kuwait. We have got to go through another brief, and you're fixing to get a change of mission." Robinson indeed hopped on the next flight and was told that the 150th was to go to and own some FOB called Dogwood. He didn't even know where it was or how to get there, much less the situation on the ground. The 150th was going to a place that it didn't know, to face an enemy of indeterminate strength, without properly armored vehicles, and to play a role that was not the chief focus of its training. It was time to learn, and to learn fast.

A tiny advance party, led by the battalion S-3, the operations officer Major Trent Kelly, rushed as quickly as it could to Dogwood as orders began to make their way down the pipeline. For the time being Charlie Company was to remain at FOB Duke. Bravo and Alpha, though, were both now headed to Dogwood, but with a twist. Ken Cager of Alpha Company had caught wind that someone was headed to Dogwood, but he didn't know who and kind of figured that it would be a traditional infantry unit. Cager looked up the area on the map and got a feel for what was going on there. He read about all the IED, mortar, small-arms, and rocket attacks going on in the region and thought, "Man. Whoever is going there is about to get into a fight." Then the phone call came in from Robinson informing Cager that it was him and his men who were headed to Dogwood. "Man, my heart sank. I thought, 'you have to be kidding me.' And I was like, 'Y'all need armor up there, but y'all sending engineers? Y'all want engineers to go up there in that cowboy country there?' And they responded, 'Yes. They need another maneuver element up there, and we are going to be it.'"

But there was more. Cager was to leave one of his platoons behind at Kalsu. Robinson, of course, knew the risks of having unarmored vehicles at Dogwood and had already done his best to mitigate them. He had arranged to swap an engineer platoon from Alpha Company for a platoon of armor from the 2/11th ACR. Voccio was more than surprised to learn that he and his platoon of tanks were headed with Cager and his men to FOB Dogwood. He recalled:

My commander apologized to me for sending us to support the Guard battalion at Dogwood. I asked, "What support will we have?" He answered, "None." I asked, "How long are we going to be there?" He answered, "I don't know." So I asked, "Where is it?" He was like, "I don't know." Then he said, "They're coming to pick you up in the morning." I said, "Come on sir. That's ridiculous, you know that? What are you doing, setting me up for failure?" So it was me, fourteen tankers, my lieutenant, one turret mechanic and four tanks that all went up to Dogwood. And I wasn't happy.

For Cager, it hurt leaving his 1st Platoon behind. He said, "It was almost like telling your kids that they have to go live with grandma." But there wasn't any choice. They were off to Dogwood. Hap Palmer recorded in his journal what most were thinking:

We had been planning for this [job as engineers at FOBs] since November back at Shelby. Now, we're going to be in this FOB with a couple of support elements and that's it. The cons: we are in a small FOB (troops and assets) and we won't get the same support the larger FOBs have. Our troops to task will largely be pre-occupied with Force Protection. The pros: We own this FOB and we can make it our own. We don't have to ask anyone for permission to do anything.

CONVOY

The members of the 150th had already carefully laid out their plans to convoy into Duke, Kalsu, and Iskandariyah, and the lead elements of the convoy had already moved out when their change of mission came in. Their new task was to replace the 2nd Battalion, 12th Cavalry Regiment (2/12th), which was presently holding FOB Dogwood on a temporary basis. The redirected convoy was to make two planned rest and resupply stops along the way. On their journey, the Mississippians were amazed to see Iraqis lining the road, some begging, others just gawking. Jay Standley had grown up in Oak Ridge, Louisiana and had joined the

Guard there in part for its educational benefits. College treated him well, and he soon found himself in graduate school at Mississippi State University, necessitating a transfer to the Mississippi National Guard. By 2005 he was a Platoon Leader in Alpha Company as the convoy rolled into Iraq. He recalled that seeing all those civilians meant that the "pucker factor" rose, not knowing if they were truly civilians or perhaps insurgents. But as the convoy reached its first overnight stop, it became clear that these Iraqis were friendly and wanted to make some money. Richard Rowland was amazed how many people swarmed up as the convoy slowed to a halt. The first one to reach his vehicle was a teenager, who slapped a CD that he had for sale onto the hood of Roland's Humvee – *The Greatest Hits of Reba McEntire*. Kevin Kelly made out like a bandit, scoring season five of the *Sopranos* for a mere $15. As he looked around, he realized that all the Iraqi vendors were making a killing that evening. The most successful entrepreneur, though, was an old man with a camel. For a dollar you could get on that camel and get your picture taken, and almost everybody wanted a picture.

On the second day's journey, the convoy got, in Lieutenant Colonel Robinson's words, "lost as hell." Somehow, in driving through the town of Hillah, the roads became too narrow for the convoy to continue. The massive convoy, even its 18-wheeler trucks, had to laboriously turn around on a two-lane road. Hap Palmer noticed that the people in this town weren't at all like the merchants they had met the night before. They were sullen, and "you could see the hatred in their eyes." Slowly the convoy extricated itself and resumed its journey. At Dogwood, Trent Kelly was already there as part of the advance party and joined a patrol from the 2/12th that was sent to show the convoy the final steps on their way to the FOB. The journey traversed Route Temple, which the 2/12th considered a "black route," one so dangerous that they would only travel it in M1 tanks. Kelly rode in the loader's position in one of the tanks to greet his comrades. He tried to exude confidence when the groups met up, but he couldn't help but worry for the guys in their hillbilly armor vehicles. Any IED would be devastating, As the convoy traversed the desert on the far side of the river, the soldiers of the 150th were transfixed. Jody Kyzar could hardly believe his eyes; there were IED holes everywhere – some as big as cars. Tension rose for everyone as they entered the unknown, with Randall Jones standing for all when he thought, "We ain't in Kansas anymore. This is fixing to get real."

ADVANCE PARTY

FOB Dogwood was located in the desert 25 miles southwest of Baghdad and 20 miles southeast of Fallujah on the west side of the Euphrates River. Dogwood had once been a sprawling base that had served as a divisional support command area in 2003 before being abandoned, and in 2004 had been occupied by a British task force of the Black Watch Regiment in a controversial move to aid in the impending battle in and around Fallujah, and to help stop Iraqi insurgents from fleeing the fighting there. The British press had labeled Dogwood, "bleak and miserable," with things getting worse quickly as the unit lost three men within days of arriving in the area.* The 800-plus British soldiers had pulled out in December and had been replaced by the 2/12th who were tasked with holding the area until their Mississippi replacements had arrived. The area of operations (AO) that the Mississippians inherited was larger than the size of New York City. The western side of the AO was mainly open desert, dotted with innumerable weapons caches left behind in the wake of Saddam's fall. The area along the Euphrates River to the east, though, was densely populated farmland sprinkled with villages large and small – villages often dominated by the insurgency. The Mississippians would arrive with only two line companies, instead of three, with Charlie Company remaining at FOB Duke. Alpha Company had a sapper platoon, an assault and obstacle (A&O) platoon, and a tank section. Bravo Company would arrive with two sapper platoons and a tank section. There was also a headquarters company. All told, the 150th would hold its AO with around 200 men, where the British and the 2/12th had deployed many more men and much more firepower and had still found the region to be deadly and incapable of control. From the little he knew at the time, Lieutenant Colonel Robinson was well aware that his undermanned and undergunned unit was being given a difficult task. But he had faith that his Guardsmen and women were up to the job.

Dexter Thornton and Trent Kelly were the first two from the advance party to reach Dogwood. Kelly had tried to arrange a flight to Dogwood through the Marines, but none was available, even though he pressed the urgency of the situation. A battalion was headed to Dogwood with

---

*"Bleak Mood at Black Watch Base in Wilderness of Mud," *The Guardian*, November 5, 2004.

no idea at all about the place. He needed to get there to get things rolling! Next Kelly tried to organize a convoy, but was told that nobody wanted to go that way. The roads were too damn dangerous. Things weren't off to a great start. Finally a patrol was spun up for the purpose of taking Kelly from FOB Iskandariyah to Dogwood, and it was clear that the drivers and soldiers on that convoy weren't too impressed with the whole idea. Dexter Thornton, though, was able to arrange a flight to Dogwood from FOB Kalsu. On arrival he couldn't help but believe that the base looked abandoned as his chopper touched down. He wasn't met by anyone, since the 2/12th didn't even know that he or the 150th were coming. He and Kelly soon found quarters and went about coming to grips with Dogwood and the new situation facing the 150th. And they sure got an earful. The 2/12th was getting hit by mortar and rocket attacks almost every day. Lieutenant Colonel Tim Ryan, the 2/12th task force commander, informed the duo that his men had detained 43 insurgents only the day before and had recently uncovered and destroyed several arms caches. One of those caches was so large that it had even contained an Iraqi jet – a find so big that television correspondent Geraldo Rivera was on his way in to do a show about it.

Kelly, Thornton, and the rest of the advance party got down to learning as quickly as they could, and for Kelly and his driver Greg Wells that meant going on as many ride-alongs with the 2/12th as he could. And it didn't take long at all to discern what a dangerous area the 150th was about to inhabit. The 2/12th had uparmored Humvees, and on one of their first patrols four Humvees traversed the dike road that hugged the banks of the Euphrates. Suddenly Kelly and Wells heard, WHOOM, WHOOM, WHOOM! The explosion of three massive IEDs. The convoy halted, and an accompanying Iraqi platoon caught the insurgent who had detonated the IEDs. For Kelly everything seemed to move in slow motion. He exited his Humvee and looked at the road. The three IEDs had been daisy-chained together, but had miraculously gone off between the Humvees, not under them. Then he noticed wire leading to a fourth IED, which had been directly under his Humvee, but had failed to go off. It wasn't until Kelly returned to Dogwood that he had time to process how close he had come to death on his very first day at Dogwood. He shivered at the thought, but it quickly passed. What concerned him most was the obvious danger of the area, and his troops were coming in without proper intelligence or uparmored vehicles.

Wells stood by Kelly's side and said aloud what Kelly was thinking: "Sir, if every day is going to be like this one, this will be a long year."

Soon the other elements of the advance party arrived, even as the convoy began its torturous journey from Kuwait. There would be three days for ride-alongs with the 2/12th to learn the area before they departed, leaving the Mississippians on their own. Advance party members went out on a variety of missions, each unsettling in its own way. For Paul Lyon of Bravo Company it was easy to work out one main problem. Since Dogwood was separated from the villages along the Euphrates River by kilometers of open desert, the insurgents in those villages could see the Americans coming, leaving ample time to escape. The chosen manner of escape was to jump into anything that could float and cross the Euphrates River out of the AO. When the 2/12th unit that Lyon was riding with reached the village, the only people left were women and children. The enemy had the advantage.

For Alpha Company in Ken Cager's ride-along, action was the rule of the day. The unit almost immediately received incoming fire and chased an insurgent to a nearby building. Already Cager thought to himself, "This ain't Camp Shelby. This is the wild west man!" The soldiers of the 2/12th fired rounds into the building hoping to chase the insurgent out. But he never appeared. Next followed an anti-tank round, razing the building. Cager reminded himself that the 2/12th had already fought in many areas of Iraq, when one of the men turned to him and said, "Well. That's one less place they can hide and shoot at us again." A search of the rubble turned up nothing – no body or trace of blood. Somehow the insurgent had escaped, perhaps through a tunnel. At that point the 2/12th captain turned to Cager with a map and pointed out the most likely places for hostile contact, especially the village of Owesat. The captain reminded him that he and his men really didn't know that much about the area. They had only been there for a month. He then pointed to the northern area of the map. "You don't want to go there. None of us has ever been out there."

The unit that Douglas Mansfield rode with went to a bridge that spanned the Euphrates. As the first of their vehicles crossed the bridge, the cavalry troops informed him that crossing the bridge meant death and was usually avoided at all costs. But on this day they were supposed to undertake some route clearance on the far side of the river for an incoming convoy. Just a few minutes later, a plume of smoke rose on the far side of the river, followed by the sound of an IED detonation. Soon thereafter the vehicles that had crossed the bridge came rushing back "Mad Max style," taking their wounded to Dogwood.

Sean Cooley was part of the advance party for Bravo Company. He and Douglas Mansfield accompanied a ride-along into one of the local villages in the middle of the night. As the members of the 2/12th fanned out to search for insurgents, they assigned Mansfield and Cooley an oddly shaped building for their search. Mansfield and Cooley approached with the utmost caution, relying on their night-vision goggles for guidance. On the count of three they threw the door open and burst inside, following all their Camp Shelby training. What hit them was not insurgent fire but instead the worst, most intense stink they had ever dreamed possible. There were eight holes in a porcelain floor. "Oh hell! It's the community shitter!" Mansfield turned to Cooley and said, "Man, those bastards got us good. They sent us over here to clear a shithouse, Sean." Covering their noses and trying not to lose their dinners, Mansfield and Cooley rushed back outside to find their 2/12th ride-along mates convulsing in gales of laughter. On the way back to Dogwood, the duo was alarmed to hear fire ringing out from the base. They were told not to worry by the men of the 2/12th. Wild dogs were a huge problem in the area, and the shots they had heard were merely one of the outposts shooting a K9 offender.

COOLEY BEING COOLEY

In their precious few moments off at Dogwood, Lyon and Cooley tried to figure out the best time to smoke their last two remaining Cuban cigars that they had liberated at Iskandariyah. They figured that it would be best to wait for the imminent arrival of the lost convoy and the rest of their buddies. Lyon's opinion of Cooley had risen even further after their arrival at Dogwood. Kevin Kelly, brother to Trent Kelly who was the battalion S-3, was serving with Alpha Company and had begun keeping a journal of his experiences, and that journal recorded the kind of man Sean Cooley was:

Our guys went out on a mission with the CAV to find a weapons cache. They found a 55-gallon drum with ammunition stored in it deep in the ground. They tried to reach down deep enough to get everything, but they couldn't. SFC Cooley got nominated by his peers (more like mandatory volunteering because of being the lightest one) to be lowered down into the barrel by his peers holding his ankles and dropping him down, picking stuff up and being brought back up. He was literally a human crane. Everyone laughed and joked about it. That is the type of guy he is. He will do anything anyone asks that will benefit anyone.

But, since Sean was Sean, that very same night he took toilet paper and rolled Larry Odom into his cot while he was sleeping like the Mummy.

Laura Cooley was happy back home in Mississippi. Her work at the hospital was keeping her busy, and since there were so few members of the 150th at Dogwood as yet, Sean had been able to call her most every night using a satellite phone. The night that the 2/12th made ready to depart as the Mississippi convoy rolled in, Sean called home. As luck would have it, Sean's parents, Jerry and Katherine, were also there with her to talk. Sean informed Laura that his calls might become a bit more infrequent as more men would be needing to use the phones. Dogwood wasn't much of a base yet and didn't have adequate phone or internet for the men. But it was something that they would endure. Sean told Laura about his recent missions into the nearby villages. The poverty and the need of the local population convinced him that he and his Mississippi buddies were badly needed there. He told her, "This is where we need to be. The people need us, and we are doing what is right." Laura agreed. He and the guys were there doing good things, bringing freedom and a new way of life to a people who needed it. She then turned the phone over to Sean's father Jerry. Sean reiterated for him his thoughts about the good that he and his fellow Mississippians could do for the Iraqi people. "Daddy, these people are pitiful, and they need our help." Jerry's response was blunt: "The hell with them people. You take care of yourself!"

EVERYTHING CHANGES

The main elements of the 2/12th began to depart Dogwood on February 2, leaving the Mississippians – under-resourced and deeply lacking in intelligence regarding their AO – to begin to develop their own operational tempo. Everything was new, from how and where to patrol, to the nature of the population in the villages, to how best to defend the sprawling base from attack; and all with so few men. Robinson and his team knew that to keep mortar and rocket attacks at bay, and to let the local populace know that they meant business, the 150th had to push out patrols. But they really didn't even know where to go. Sure, they had AO maps and initial intelligence, but where were the danger zones? Where was relatively safe? Where were IED attacks most likely to occur? All of that would have to be learned through on-the-job training. Initially the plan was for each company, Alpha and Bravo, to send out two patrols a day. HQ and A&O platoon members would be working to get the base into shape and to man defenses, along with Alpha and Bravo members who were not slated for patrol. Everyone who went on patrol that first day felt trepidation, heading into the unknown as they were, but the day went off without a hitch.

On the second day of patrolling, February 3, Bravo headed north, while Alpha headed south. Captain Paul Lyon rode in the same M113 as one of his platoon sergeants, Sean Cooley. Initially Cooley had lobbied for them to take a Humvee. It was more agile, and he could use that maneuverability to make it to any possible casualties quickly. But Lyon demurred, "You're not taking that Humvee. It has no protection. We're going in 113s." Lyon knew that even the 113s didn't provide much protection, but they were a damn sight better than a soft-skinned Humvee with a couple of sandbags on the floor. The patrol, consisting of three 113s, exited the gate and headed north. All eyes were peeled for the signs of IEDs that the men had been taught in training. A fresh hole in the ground. An oddly placed piece of trash by the roadside. Any kind of visible wires. And the group tried to stay off the road and opted to travel mainly through the desert, figuring it would be the least likely place for IEDs. The patrol went well; no contact of any sort, although Lyon got into trouble with Robinson for getting his guys out of radio range from Dogwood. But overall it was a success.

When it came time for the evening patrol, Sean Cooley was back again. He had already been on one patrol that day and did not have to go back out. But one of his buddies slated to go on the next patrol was having some issues. The threat of combat can get to anyone. And Sean felt that he needed to be there to help his buddy through that first patrol; to show him the ropes and give him confidence. He had dropped by to see his friend Gary Kinsey on the way out to ask him if he wanted to go on the patrol as well. But Kinsey couldn't – there was maintenance to be done on some vehicles that he had scrounged. He would have to go another time. So, as the evening patrol got ready to move out, Sean Cooley strode up alone to the vehicle. This time it was going to be a Humvee like he had wanted in the morning. Bradley Sharp was slated to drive, but Sean overruled him. The two were friends, so Sharp went along with Cooley's request. In the passenger seat was Stacey Ford.

Joining Cooley and Ford was Jack Walker, who manned the vehicle's main gun, and medic Joe Smith, who was to sit right behind the driver's seat. As conversation started among the four men, Smith tried to open the rear driver's side door. But it was jammed. All four men took turns trying to pull it open. Cooley even jumped inside and tried kicking it from the inside. But no luck. That damn door was as jammed as jammed could be. As Jack Walker made his way to his position on the gun, he kind of laughed. "Guess you weren't supposed to sit there today Doc." Nobody could understand what the hell was wrong, and some of the guys standing around the other vehicles were laughing at the sight. Eventually Smith just gave up. He would sit behind Stacey Ford and place his medical aid bag in the seat behind Sean.

The patrol then headed out on its mission, taking the same route through the massive berm that surrounded Dogwood as had the morning patrol. It consisted of three vehicles: an M113, followed by Cooley's Humvee, and a 113 bringing up the rear. In the lead 113 was platoon leader Lieutenant Mike Beal. He had only gotten to Dogwood the day before, and the thing that had surprised him most was the look in the eyes of the cavalry troopers who had been holding the base. They kind of stared right through you. He had noticed that on the wall of their building they had a mural of dog tags of the men that they had lost. These men had been hardened by death, and Beal knew it.

The idea for the patrol, once again, was to show the insurgents that the Mississippians were there, to get the lay of the land, and to keep any possible enemy mortar tubes out of range of the base. As usual, Cooley was full of humor, keeping the mood light. As the second vehicle in the patrol, the Humvee was relatively safe. As long as it stayed in the tracks of the lead 113 there would be little risk of hitting an IED – the better-armored 113 would hit it and set it off first. But the same was not true of direct fire. Cooley turned to Ford and said it was too dang bad that medic Smith was sitting in the back seat, and Ford chuckled.

"Yep," he replied, "Doc is in the hot seat." Smith wondered what was up and asked, "What do you mean hot seat?" With a grin on his face Cooley looked over his shoulder and said, "Well, normally the guy that's sitting in that back seat is the one that gets killed because that's where the RPG [rocket propelled grenade] hits." Cooley was looking back at Smith and laughing, and Ford was chuckling as he looked at Cooley. Smith replied, "Don't worry about it. I'm wearing my armored underwear."

At the same time Mike Beal's M113 cleared the break in the berm, leading the way for the patrol. Topping a hill, Beal could see Iraqi civilians in the area, and one dove for cover. Beal wondered what that meant. In the Humvee directly behind, Stacey Ford barely registered the massive explosion. Instead, it was more an onslaught of individual, seemingly unlinked assaults on his senses. A wave of heat, a massive flash that made his eyes burn like looking at an eclipse. The acrid burning of smoke. Smells. Gunpowder, burning rubber, boiling radiator fluid – blood. He was thrown violently upward and slammed into the side of the vehicle. And his ears were ringing. What the hell was that ringing? He could hardly hear. It was so loud that even thinking was difficult. In the back seat, Doc Smith had his head smashed into the machine-gun mount and could barely register anything at all. The first thing he saw was his door, and it was hanging there all funny. Something bad had happened; very bad. As he shook his head, trying to get the cobwebs to go away, he heard Stacey Ford yelling for him. "Doc – are you alive? Are you okay?" Gathering his wits, Smith replied that he was dazed but seemed unhurt. The two began to yell for Jack Walker. The blast had ejected him from his position, landing yards away, but he, too, seemed groggy but okay. Then they all suddenly remembered – Sean Cooley.

The soft-skinned Humvee had hit an IED that was buried in a depression in the road outside the berm. It had a pressure plate that would rock and make the connection to set off two 115mm artillery shells, each containing 22 pounds of explosives. Being in a slight depression meant that the tracks of the 113 failed to set off the explosives, where the driver's side wheel of the Humvee settled deeper into the depression, making the fatal connection. The blast was massive, ripping the unarmored Humvee to shreds. The driver's side front wheel, including the tire, rim, brake disc, brake assembly, hub, and a section of the front axle, was tossed more than 300 feet through the air due to the force of the explosion. The 113 following next in line was rocked back and forth so badly that its occupants thought that they had been hit by the explosion. There had been no warning of the IED; none of the signs that everyone had been trained to look for. Instead, this pressure-plate type IED buried in a depression in the road was something new, invisible, and deadly.

Immediately Ford and Smith began to search for their friend Sean Cooley. Ford got to him first and could barely fight back the tears as he looked at Sean's tortured form. Cooley lay more than 50 feet away along the side of the road in a fetal position in a ditch. The force of the explosion had amputated both of his legs below the knees and ejected him through the roof of the Humvee, with his head striking the rollbar on the way out. Ford could not comprehend how, seconds ago, the two had been chatting and joking, and now Cooley was almost unrecognizable. It seemed amazing to Ford how slowly time moved. The whole thing to this point had only taken a few scant seconds, but somehow it seemed like years. Smith, battling what he already knew in the back of his mind to be a severe concussion, or maybe something even worse, reached back into the flames of the Humvee for his medical aid bag. He could hardly believe it, but the thoughts ran through his mind like a medic. The patient didn't have much chance for survival – but any chance relied on getting him to a hospital quickly. So, the two, with the help of men who had rushed to the scene from the other 113s in the patrol, picked up Cooley and took him to the back ramp of one of the 113s to speed him back to Dogwood. Stacey Ford carefully grabbed Sean under his arms, cradling his wounded head on his own shoulder. As they neared the 113, Ford heard his friend's breathing become more labored. Shortly after they got back to Dogwood, as Mike Beal worked to give Cooley CPR, Sean's breathing ceased.

Medic Winston Walker was behind in the trailing 113 and recorded the scene:

> I exited the 113 to find a scene of chaos. Running to the vehicle I was first shocked to note the entire front of the Humvee gone including the 75% of the firewall. The focus of the blast was between the two front seats at the floorboard. Specialist Smith was sitting directly behind where the explosion occurred and is estimated to have been

unconscious for 2 minutes. After making quick assessments of the other soldiers and ensuring initial treatments by "combat live savers" was started I turned to see Smith crawling out of the smoking wreck looking as one would expect; covered in a mixture of dirt, sweat, blood and smut. He was upset he couldn't find his bag, many of his words were unintelligible, "No bag, no bag… wounded here… NO FUCKING MEDIC BAG!" One of the other soldiers started directing him I thought over to one of the wounded, so I resumed treating another. In a word or two the sight of Specialist Smith was both pitiful and humbling, still trying to do his duty but so disheveled and mentally scattered. It was then I realized how affected by the concussive and blunt forces Smith was. For approximately 40 mins he was uncoordinated, not always verbally coherent. Chaos all around and Specialist Smith on his knees wobbly, staring at me then a seemingly blank stare. Soon after he began to complain of nausea and headache.

The explosion had been audible from Dogwood, and Greg Wells joined a quick reaction force that sped out of the front gate to respond, but by that time the 113 carrying Sean Cooley was already quickly making its way back to the base. Wells began to police up any sensitive equipment at the site and picked up Cooley's flak vest to remove it from the scene, and blood came pouring out. Wells had not seen Cooley after the blast, but just by seeing that flak vest he knew that his friend was dead. Later he turned over Cooley's gear to Lieutenant Colonel Robinson, who accepted it with tears in his eyes. That moment hit Wells hard – Robinson wasn't just a commander. He was in mourning for the soldier who had been lost under his command.

Almost everyone at Dogwood had heard that there had been at least one KIA, and that it was Sean Cooley. Nobody could believe it, and a wave of emotion rolled across the base as a crowd gathered to watch for Sean's return. Hap Palmer recorded in his journal:

Two medics, SPC Joe Smith and SGT Winston Walker worked on him. When the vehicle stopped at the helipad the crew and medics brought Sean out onto a litter and continued to work. The first thing I saw as they brought him out was that his legs were blown off about 6–8 inches below his knees. His body was completely limp and his face bloodied. A medevac had been called and the bird was coming in as the medics picked up the litter and moved it to the other side of the 113 to shield it from the gathering crowd... But everyone still saw the black body bag. Captain Paul Lyon ... kicked the dirt when he saw the bag. I wanted to get close to Paul, but I couldn't. I didn't know what to say. There was nothing to say. [Later the destroyed vehicle was brought in by wrecker.] They led it to a secluded spot where it could be covered and hidden from the troops. It was demolished. How anyone survived is beyond me... I had to go look over the wreckage for any body parts or personal effects. We found one of his boots on the back seat. It was shredded... I remember seeing a destroyed Humvee back in Kuwait ... that had writing on it that read "Thanks General for the great armor."

Everyone was saddened; everyone was enraged. Why did it have to be Sean Cooley? He had been the very best of them all. It hit Mike Beal like a physical blow. Sean Cooley wasn't just a soldier, he was *the* soldier. How could the 150th lose its best on only its second true day in the war zone? And it was even more personal. Cooley was under Beal's command; and Beal's vehicle had rolled over the IED first and had not set it off. At once Beal felt both responsible and guilty for having survived. Why was he still here and Cooley was gone? Nothing made sense. Beal was a very religious man; faith and God were a mainstay of his life. But he found his faith wavering. There were so many questions, and so few answers.

Cooley's loss hit everyone, but Bravo Company suffered the most. Why had Sean gone out on a second patrol? Should one of them have stopped him? Well, it was Sean Cooley, probably nobody could have stopped him, but that didn't stop the second guessing. And he had so much to live for – a new wife. And they had been hoping for a child. And now it was over. It all seemed so senseless. And it had happened on only the second day of operations. They still had a whole year to go. How many more were they going to lose?

It hit the men who had been in the vehicle with Sean the hardest. Jack Walker, who had been blown out of the Humvee, had injured his back; he was sent for treatment in Baghdad and was eventually sent stateside. But Ford and Smith were still right there. Ford was enraged. He wanted to get back out there and hurt somebody. He knew that he should feel physical pain from the blast, but his adrenaline was too high. His buddy had died in his arms, and he was pissed. Doc Smith by now knew that he at the very least had a bad concussion. He was snapping in and out of reality but did, at least, have the time to give Sean his last rites. And he was covered in Sean's blood. A strange thought penetrated the fog. He needed to get his uniform cleaned; but it was too late. The laundry was closed. Maybe a shower in his uniform would get some of the blood and smell off; it was almost overwhelming. As he walked toward the showers he passed Hap Palmer, who figured that he had to be headed to the laundry and told him that the laundry was closed. Smith told him of his plan to shower and walked on. Palmer stood there lost in his own thoughts. Then another man walked past and told Palmer, "Hey Hap. You hear about Doc Smith? He got killed today." Palmer replied, "Well, that's kind of strange because I just saw him walking to the showers."

There was precious little time to mourn or to process the loss, which can be a good thing in wartime. Word came in almost the minute that the medevac had taken off with Sean's body that there was enemy activity outside the gate. Bravo Company, full of Sean's closest friends, had to rush to the gate defenses to deal with the threat. As they hurried to their positions, Kirk Dyer couldn't help but think that everyone in Bravo Company had grown up. There were no kids in the unit any longer. It was sad and sobering. But it was necessary. The war was now officially for keeps. Everyone was on edge. It was still only their second day there, and they had no idea what to expect. As it turned out the threat was a false alarm, but it did serve momentarily to keep the men's minds off how real the war had just become.

Cager's Alpha Company was still out at the incident site, searching for any vehicle or body parts. The final few men of the 2/12th on site were with them and told Cager that the local Iraqis liked to collect trophies after such strikes to parade them around and show off. Indeed, a group of Iraqi civilians began to gather. Perhaps it was just out of curiosity as to what had happened, but Cager and his men did have to wonder if there were bad guys in their midst. And after the loss of Cooley, many were beginning to wonder if perhaps all Iraqis were bad guys. Some of Cager's men asked, "They are getting close. Do we light them up?" Cager roughly told his men to hold fire. There was no way to tell if these were innocent civilians or combatants. No way at all.

But he sure as hell wasn't going to let anyone into the Alpha Company perimeter. There would be no souvenir hunting on this day.

By the next day both Ford and Smith were complaining of their wounds. The adrenaline had run out and their bodies were finally telling them the truth. Ford's leg was swelling badly, and there was a large knot on his head where his helmet had smashed into something. For his part Doc Smith knew that his concussion required rest, but rest was the last thing he wanted. He had to get back out there in the field to make sure that something like this never happened again. Mike Beal was right there with him; he too knew that he had to get back out there. Although his faith had taken a blow, he clung to what was left. The war had to continue. There was no choice. So, the duo went to Captain Lyon and volunteered to accompany him for the next mission outside the wire. And right by their side was Trent Kelly, the S-3. He needed to be there for his men; leaders sometimes have to lead from the front. And Kelly knew that how he was feeling – a mixture of enraged and scared shitless – was exactly what the men were feeling as well. Helping them conquer their fear and helping to make sure that their anger didn't boil over was something Kelly knew in his bones that he had to do.

Lieutenant Colonel Robinson knew what the Cooley incident meant, at so many levels:

Medic Walker tried to make me feel better, and he said, "Hey, sir. He never had a chance." I cannot describe to you what that does to you when you're sitting out there in the middle of the desert in a really, really nasty place, and you know that you are dramatically understaffed. I mean, it was truly a huge amount of territory, a bunch of really nasty enemy. There was a very active insurgency going on in that area. We didn't even – at that time we really didn't know the depth of the insurgency that we were on top of, and I have to say that was – everything that I've been through, life-experience wise, that was absolutely one of the most difficult times. I can tell you, losing that soldier that day, it really has a lasting effect that never goes away. I was screaming as loud as I could to brigade for additional assets that we desperately needed. But in my mind I was thinking, "You know what? If that happened to Sean Cooley, this thing is – we got to figure this out. We got to figure out how we're going to do this," because Sean was as good as any soldier we had.

Robinson knew that the 150th was in trouble. It was in tactical trouble, facing an unknown enemy with too few men and lacking the proper equipment. But the 150th was also in another kind of trouble. These men were brothers – they had grown up together and were the very best of friends. A tight-knit unit. Losing someone like Sean Cooley – the glue that holds the unit together – was going to hurt, and hurt bad. One of the first things that he had done once the accident had taken place was to shut down all communications on Dogwood. Internet, phones, satellite phones. It was all shut down so that news of the tragedy didn't leak out. Sean's family at the very least deserved to hear the sad news in the proper and most sensitive manner. Robinson also knew that the families of Guardsmen and women under his command were going to be shaken. And he needed to have a plan for that as well.

LOSS

Jerry and Katherine Cooley had just left Singing River Hospital where they had visited with Sean's wife Laura. They chatted a bit about how good it would be when Sean and the boys came home. The parade that they had for them would be even bigger than the send-off parade had been. Jerry and Katherine made their goodbyes; they wanted to get home in time to watch the evening news. As they sat there watching the television, while dinner was cooking in the next room, there was a report on the local news that a soldier from the area had been lost to an IED strike in Iraq. Jerry said aloud, "Goodness. You know that there is a family out there having a very bad day now." He and Katherine planned to do what they could to support that family; they were bound to be crushed by the news and in need of compassion. It was ten minutes later when a vehicle pulled up in their driveway, and two immaculately dressed military men stepped out. Jerry invited the soldiers in, as Katherine collapsed into the nearest chair in uncontrollable tears. Her son. Her Sean. He was gone.

Laura Cooley had stayed to complete her shift at the hospital after Jerry and Katherine had left:

So, I talked to him that night before I went to bed, and it was his morning. They knew they were going to go out on patrol; didn't know how the day was going to go. So, I get up that afternoon to get ready for my night shift, and I was just in a great mood. I got to talk to him before I went to sleep. Everything was sounding great. The next night, apparently the casualty team had just missed me at the hospital. They also missed me at my parents' house and had tried at my house a couple of times as well, but I had been out running errands. I had been at my parents' house, but we had left to go out to dinner. After dinner I went home. So I get home, and as I was closing the gate, a van pulls up into my driveway. And I'm like – and I don't know how I knew – because it's not a military vehicle; it's just a minivan – but I knew something was wrong. So, they're like, "Mrs. Cooley?" I'm like, "Yes." And they come inside and sat down on my couch and told me that Sean was gone. I actually knew the chaplain; I worked with him out at this hospital. They gave me their nice, predetermined speech that Sean was killed. They told me that they had already talked to Jerry and Kathy, but they had not been allowed to call me because they had to do it in person. Then my parents came over; my best friend that I went to college with came over and stayed with me. Jerry and Kathy came over, and we talked a little bit, and then we tried to figure out what we were going to do.

Laura wasn't entirely sure if she could go on. She had just met and married the true love of her life, and, just like that, he had been taken from her. It was like a thunderstorm had rolled in out of nowhere and upended her life.

But there was little time to worry; an immediate crush of events set in that kept everyone busy. Maybe it was a blessing; the work at least kept the grief somewhat at bay. There was funeral planning, life insurance details, and even dealing with the threat of members of the Westboro Baptist Church coming in to protest at the funeral. Sean's grandparents were devastated by the loss, and family came in to offer their support from all over the country, including Sean's brother Patrick who was working on the East Coast. Days later Sean's body arrived by airplane at the New Orleans airport. It was just a regular civilian flight, with nobody but the Cooley family really pausing to consider what the aircraft carried. Sean's casket, draped with an American flag, was loaded into a hearse for transport to Bradford O'Keefe Funeral Home in Biloxi. Laura rode in the car behind, and still couldn't believe that it was her Sean.

Laura's parents wouldn't take no for an answer. They didn't even really ask; they just moved in with her for a couple of weeks, believing that she did not need to be on her own while going through all of this. Sean was the first local soldier lost in the war in Iraq, so everyone called – from the governor, to all of the local media outlets, to people Laura was not even sure that she actually knew. On February 12, 2005, there was a funeral ceremony for Sean at the tiny Antioch Methodist Church nestled in the deep countryside outside of Lucedale, Mississippi. There was one wake in Ocean Springs, where the line to get in and pay respects was over three hours long. The outpouring of grief in the community was overwhelming. As the funeral procession left for Lucedale, the roads for miles around were lined by well-wishers. Tiny Antioch Church was full to overflowing, and folding chairs had been gathered from all around to line the lawn outside.

Sean was laid to rest with full military honors in a tiny cemetery just a short walk from his family home. It took a full thirty minutes for the throng of people to make their way the short distance from Antioch to the cemetery, in part because the tiny road was so overcrowded. For days everyone had wanted to shake hands with the Cooleys to tell them what Sean had meant to them. And everyone shared their favorite Sean Cooley story. "He took care of my mom; she wouldn't have made it without him." "He was such a joy; always smiling and bringing a smile to my face too." "He was the only thing that kept us going while Dad was in the hospital." Many people went with Jerry, Katherine, and Laura to the Cooleys' nearby home following the ceremony. Friends who had loved Sean donated an ocean of food, so there was plenty to eat for all. And all the wonderful stories about Sean made it seem like he was still alive. To Jerry Cooley, hearing from all these people who had loved his son made him feel there was sure some good left in the world. And that good is what Sean had died for.

REACTIONS

The 150th kept about its daily routine after the loss of Sean Cooley, which was a blessing that kept the men focused. And they needed it. Just four days after Cooley's loss, assistant S-3 Allen McDaniel was at a meeting in the tactical operations center to discuss Cooley's memorial ceremony. He left the meeting still mourning the loss of his friend.

As he stepped out of the TOC, "All of a sudden I heard a sound I will never forget. It was kind of a whistling sound like you hear in the movies. It was followed by a loud boom. We had gotten hit by a mortar round. Luckily it landed outside of the FOB and no one was hurt." The errant mortar round, though, shook McDaniel's confidence. The 150th had already lost one of its best, and the mortar surely indicated that the insurgents were in the fight for keeps. McDaniel couldn't help but wonder if he would make it for the entire deployment. It was a question that many in the unit were pondering.

On February 10, two days before Sean was laid to rest back home, the unit gathered for a memorial ceremony. Hap Palmer recorded the event in his journal:

> The memorial tribute to SFC Cooley was this morning at 1000 hrs. What a fitting way to honor this soldier. Bravo Company centered their formation on the stand adorned with the rifle, helmet, boots, and dog tags and photo of this incredible soldier. The other two companies horseshoed to the left and right. Colonel Collins spoke, 2LT Mike Beal of the 1st Platoon of Bravo Company spoke, SFC Larry Odom, 2LT Marty Davis, 1SG Larry Mergenschroer, 1LT Paul Lyon, and LTC Roy Robinson all spoke. All gave short summaries of what SFC Cooley meant to them. Every word spoken was true. Nothing glamorized; nothing made up. Nothing had to be. Cooley was just a good person, and everyone knew that. At the conclusion the roughly 200 people in attendance filed by the tribute stand and paid their respects by saluting this fallen soldier. Just prior to that 1SG Mergenschroer took to the stand to call roll: "SGT Arnold." "Here First Sergeant" was the reply. "SGT Brewer." "Here First Sergeant." Again we heard, "SSG Collins." "Here First Sergeant." "SFC Cooley." No reply. "SFC Sean Cooley." Again no reply. "SFC Sean Michael Cooley." After a long pause a reply came. "This soldier is not in this formation." I got chills. Attention was called, and Taps was played. Some cried and the rest acted like they didn't want to cry. Some of the prior service contractors cried like children. They'd seen this before.

It didn't take the emotion of the memorial ceremony for Robinson to know that the Guardsmen and women under his command had suffered a psychological and spiritual blow. And other losses would likely soon follow. Those kinds of emotions in a unit that was a family could make or break their year in Iraq, and he had a plan to help address the problem. The nearest combat stress control (CSC) officer was at FOB Kalsu, over three hours away, which was clearly unacceptable. Robinson wanted a CSC officer permanently stationed at Dogwood to help those who needed it. It took some pestering, but 1908th Medical Detachment eventually relented, and sent Lieutenant Colonel Rosalyn Morris to Dogwood.

Lieutenant Colonel Morris, Roz to her friends, had been raised in an orphanage in Chicago before moving with one of her friends to Kentucky where she went to college to study social work, in part to help vulnerable kids like she had once been. She also joined the Army. She figured that the government had raised her; why not try to give something back? She first enlisted in 1981 and then went through OCS in 1990. In an Army that was becoming increasingly aware of psychological injury, Morris' skills were in demand, serving tours in the Sinai, Egypt, Kosovo, Uzbekistan, and Afghanistan. Along the way she well learned to navigate the man's world that was the Army and had also learned to be self-sufficient (women's bathrooms weren't the norm in those days) and to NOT take no for an answer. In her position she had done everything, from ministering to psychological wounds, to working with prisoners, to helping in emergency rooms, to dealing with amputees. And in 2005 she was thinking about retirement. But Uncle Sam got the jump on her, and Lieutenant Colonel Morris found herself at FOB Kalsu when Robinson demanded a CSC officer. She heard that FOB Dogwood was isolated and that it was going to be a tough year there. But she thought to herself, "Well, I'm independent. I get shit done. I can do this. Let's go."

When Roz got to the base, Robinson let her know how glad he was that she was there. Roz already knew of the death of Sean Cooley, and Robinson informed her that his loss had hit the entire unit hard. Roz knew that she had her work cut out for her. And she knew that the soldiers would not want to talk to her. She had been around the military and war long enough to realize that men who had just been through trauma simply didn't want to talk about it outside of their closest circle of friends. And they sure didn't want to talk about it to a woman, a lieutenant colonel, a brain doctor. But she was determined to get the job done. The unit was in the process of setting up a tent for her, but she spent her first night in the TOC, where some netting was raised to give her a measure of privacy.

Her first priority the next day was to talk to the guys who had been in the Humvee with Sean Cooley – the ones for whom the trauma was the rawest. Medic Joe Smith recalled, "She made a beeline for me, and I really didn't want to talk to her. I really didn't, and I told her that too. I said, 'I really don't want to talk about it, not right now because I've got other things on my mind. I have to stay focused on what I am doing.'" Smith had already been out on another patrol, having to drive right past the spot where his Humvee had been hit. A shiver had run up and down his spine. A shiver that he felt would never go away. Larry Odom, who had been one of Sean Cooley's best friends, had a similar reaction. He didn't want to sit down with her; he knew that she couldn't change the way he was feeling. But he went through the motions when he had to.

Stacey Ford, who had been sitting next to Cooley in the Humvee, was one of the few who welcomed Roz's conversations. He recalled, "I need someone who is blunt and to the point. I don't want anyone who is going to be kind of whimsical and like that… I'm not here for the caring, touchy-feely at all. That's not me. And Roz was blunt. We talked quite a bit, and she helped me a lot… You know, I made my way through a lot of stuff, and she was the reason. And I am here today because of her."

Even though she broke the ice with Stacey Ford, Roz, who received the call sign and nickname "Psycho 6," knew that she had to reach more of the soldiers. One plan was to work on smoking cessation classes. Most vices were prohibited or simply unavailable in a remote place like Dogwood – but cigars, dip, and cigarettes were everywhere. Trent Kelly had figured that he might be in Iraq for a good long while before any shipments from home could come in, so he had come prepared with 234 cans of snuff. Some of the guys had laughed at him, but as time wore on at Dogwood everyone else began to run out, but not Kelly. Soon it seemed that everyone under the sun was asking him for a dip, but no way. That stuff was more precious than gold. Roz saw how prevalent tobacco use was, and she knew that in working on that problem she could reach a lot of men. Her other idea was a unit-wide meeting where everything was fair game for discussion. She presented the idea to Robinson, who gave her the go ahead. She told him that in such a meeting rank didn't matter – that the soldiers would be open to speaking on any grievance without fear of discipline. Even if that grievance was about him and his command. Again, Robinson agreed. The 150th had to move forward. It still had almost a year to go in the war zone. Taking the temperature of the unit with everyone able to speak freely would break the ice and allow the soldiers to feel a measure of relief that each of them mattered and that they were being listened to.

The men and women of the 150th certainly didn't want to go to that meeting. No way did they want to talk about their feelings in front of Psycho 6. But their company commanders rounded them up, and they all went. Roz began the session by asking everyone how they felt when they had received the news about Sean Cooley. Crickets. Nothing but silence. She asked again, and it became clear that she was going to keep asking until someone answered. One soldier raised his hand and asked Roz and Robinson whether it was okay to cuss in the meeting. They both said it would be fine. The soldier then responded. "Well, here is what I thought. FUCKEDY, FUCK, FUCK, FUCK!" There was some laughter, then more awkward silence. Roz thought to herself that she had lost the moment. But the ice had been broken, and everyone started talking. As Marty Davis, the highway patrolman of Bravo Company, sat and listened, something dawned on him. Here was Lieutenant Colonel Robinson – a true hard ass if there ever was one – sitting there and taking it. Nobody got ripped to pieces for what they were saying; it was all open and above board. To Davis, that moment is when Robinson went from being an officer to being the battalion commander.

As the conversation rolled forward, Roz realized something. The Guard was very different to the Regular Army, where all her previous experience had been. And the Guard processes trauma in a different way. Everybody knew everybody. They grew up together. They babysat each other's children. Their wives and families were dear friends. Sean Cooley wasn't another soldier. He was a family member. Losing him was like losing a sibling or a parent. It was deeper, more profound.

Albert Matlock was a good example. He was in Iraq with four cousins and more close family friends than he could count. As family, he knew that he could tell the other members of Alpha Company anything – even the officers and even if it was critical. He recalled, "I had more faith in Alpha Company than anyone else in the world, because I grew up with these guys. I know them and they know me, and we all got each other's back." However, he also knew the risk of potentially losing one of his Guard family and worked to set up emotional barriers between himself and trauma. "When it was time to go on a mission, I'd kind of back away. I backed away from my cousins; I backed away from my friends. Everybody knew what I was doing and respected me. Then after the mission everybody pulled together again, like a family."

Another thing that came out in the meeting was that the deep sorrow for Sean's loss was laced with a desire for revenge. Nobody wanted to stay on the FOB. They all wanted to get out and get the job done, and some hoped for more than that. Some were angry. Robinson and the other officers knew that they had to stop those ideas in their tracks. Ken Cager, commander of Alpha Company, recalled:

Many men were pissed and out for revenge. And I told them, "We're not going to go out and kill a bunch of civilians. We can't do that." Even thinking about that is wrong. So I told them, "We are here to defend. If we feel threatened, that's one thing. But we are professional soldiers. We are here to execute a specific mission, for a specific purpose. If we go and shoot wild, all the good work we've done is for nothing." So I had to try to communicate that to a bunch of 18- and 19-year-olds. I mean, think about it. Now, we were all deer-hunters; we were all country boys, and we were ready; they were ready to pull the trigger. But these are people we are trying to protect from the bad guys. I'm battling this thing going on in my brain. Even I think that I want to go after whoever did this. But I cannot allow my young soldiers free rein. That would make us as bad as them.

As Sean Cooley's closest friend, Larry Odom knew how badly everyone was hurting. But as a platoon sergeant he also knew that it was his job to control his men and point them toward the larger mission:

I had people tell me, "Hey. I just want to kill. I just want to kill one. Just let me kill one before I get out of here." And I said, "Wait. If you was having this conversation with me back in the United States, that would be premeditated murder. So what's different here?" Anything like that would be morally wrong and just create more enemies. So when you go on a raid, don't – if it's a bunch of women and children, don't destroy their houses, don't destroy their stuff just for the sake of just being mad at the culture or the people. Not only is it wrong, it just creates more terrorists is what that's doing. I told them, "think if this was your house, if this was your home, and these people were coming in there, doing that to you, what would you do?" Hey, I'd lash out probably in some form or fashion, if this is my home, and they're doing me that way. So you have to accomplish your mission but treating people humanely, too. You can't get caught up in the event.

Marty Davis of Bravo Company understood what a no-win scenario was from being a highway patrolman. He knew that, whenever a patrolman was called in, it was already a crappy situation. An accident, a home invasion, a domestic disturbance – nobody on either side ever wanted this event to happen. And it was the job of a patrolman to take the crappy, horrific event and make it make sense. They had to establish normalcy again. If they did their job well, the situation would improve. But they also held the possibility of making the situation infinitely worse if they lost control. To Davis, the situation in Iraq seemed eerily similar. Death and loss certainly made for a crappy situation, but he and his men had to take control in a correct and measured way. The other option was to make things spiral even further out of control. On a personal level, it helped Marty to know that he always had someone to turn to with his own problems; his brother Marshall was at Dogwood as well, serving as head of Robinson's Personal Security Detachment.

For Bradley Sharp it was simple. He was pissed at the Army for letting Sean go out on patrol in an unarmored Humvee. He was pissed at the local Iraqis for the IED. He was pissed, period. He wanted revenge and could see the desire for revenge in the eyes of others. But then he thought of Sean Cooley. He knew that if Cooley was there, he would have patted him on the back and told him to calm down and do his job. So that is what he did. For Robert Arnold, who was sitting there alongside his father Larry, it was all kind of simple. Cooley's death meant that they all could die; there is no certainty in war. So, he just figured that he was dead; his ticket was up. The two men didn't talk about it, but that realization made it easier for Robert just to go out there and get the job done instead of always wondering. For Mike Beal, there was no more wondering why they were in Iraq and what the mission was. His new mission was simple – to get through the deployment with the rest of his men alive. These men were his brothers, and he needed to bring them home to their families.

TANKS

John Voccio and his platoon of tanks from the 2/11th ACR pulled into Dogwood shortly after the arrival of Psycho 6. Much like Robinson had with the 150th, Voccio had something of a military come-to-Jesus meeting with his men before they left for Dogwood, telling them, "I'll do a lot of things for you, but I won't be an accomplice to murder. You will do everything in your power to do what's right. We're not going out there where you can shoot women and children just because you can. So, let's make that clear right now, if you do anything like that I'll be the first one to fucking bring you up on charges."

Voccio's arrival at Dogwood didn't inspire him with hope. It was just open desert with a few ramshackle buildings and tents dotted around. And nobody seemed to be expecting him. Finally, a soldier walked up and said, "Y'all the tankers?" Voccio replied that he and his group were indeed the tankers. The soldier, wearing a t-shirt and a boonie cap, motioned where they should go. Voccio had no idea whom he was talking to, and when he found out that the guy was Captain Paul Lyon of Bravo Company, he couldn't help but wonder what he and his men had gotten into. After getting settled, Voccio went to the TOC, where he was greeted with, "Hey. What you know good?" He responded, "What?" Only to hear once again, "What you know good?" Staring at the soldier, Voccio retorted, "Dude. What the hell are you saying?" Someone then translated, "He asked how are you doing." Voccio couldn't believe it. He and his guys were stuck in hillbilly hell with Billy Bob.

The next morning, though, Voccio's view of the 150th was abruptly changed. One of Voccio's tanks had already broken down. Bad starter. And, in the Army's infinite wisdom, he had been sent to Dogwood without any mechanics. As it turned out, though, the 150th was chock full of tank mechanics. The National Guard stores its tanks and larger vehicles at mobilization and training equipment sites (MATES). At those sites the tanks and vehicles are serviced and have their systems updated on a regular basis to be ready for exercises and training. The MATES technicians and mechanics who work on the tanks are largely Guardsmen who are also hired as civilian MATES employees. So, for these men their military job was to be a mechanic, as was their civilian job. It was tanks and 113s all day, every day. As a result, when Voccio strolled in to ask about his busted tank, he discovered that many of the Guardsmen at Dogwood were sure enough in a Guard combat engineer battalion, but they had also been working on tanks and 113s every day for decades. Tanks were their babies, and there were like 20 guys at Dogwood who knew tanks inside and out, and they repaired his broken tank in record time. It seemed like they knew his tanks better than Voccio's own mechanics did back at FOB Kalsu. Maybe working with the Mississippians wasn't going to be so bad after all.

4

Getting the Lay of the Land

*That was the first time I ever saw an IED go off with my own eyes.
Laying a buddy on the ground and trying to stop his bleeding is
something I would hope no one would have to do. It sucks… I can
close my eyes and clearly see the blast and the HEMTT slowly
rolling to a stop. The smell isn't like anything else in the world; oils,
blood, and gunpowder all mixed together. There's something distinct
about it. I showered when I got back. Washed my hair twice. I can
still smell it on me. It's a terrifying smell… I don't care if I ever
leave this FOB on another patrol again. But I know I'll have to.
It's part of my job. The way I figure it, we're 1/3 of the way through
this. We haven't seen all of the bad stuff we are bound to see. By the
nature of my job and all of the time I spend on the road, I could
very likely get hit myself. I realize that and all I pray for is to go
home alive and well enough to hold my children. I just want to
be able to hug my wife and children when they hug me. That's all
I ask. Anything above that is gravy.*
HAP PALMER, JOURNAL ENTRY

HOME SWEET HOME

Dogwood was a sprawling base in the middle of the desert, surrounded
by a concentric series of sand berms, and was of a size meant to house
4,000 men. But following the invasion of 2003, the base had fallen
into disrepair. The Black Watch and the 2/12th Cavalry had been mere

placeholders, so the FOB remained in bad shape when the Mississippians arrived. There were four hardened buildings that were worth that name, and a scattering of other buildings that were so badly off that nobody would have thought of moving into them. Even the four buildings that were habitable had been looted of everything of value, from their wiring to their flooring, and were mere shells. There were also a few large tents around to serve for housing, showers, and cooking facilities. Most had some form of air-conditioning, but broken doors, missing windows, and holes in the walls made temperature control challenging.

When the first Mississippians poked their heads into the hardened buildings, two of which they dubbed the White House and the Dungeon, they were greeted by an open bay setup, with cots lining the floors where the cavalry troopers were sleeping with only inches between themselves and the next man. The tents had a similar setup. But the soldiers of the 150th were having none of that. Once they took over, a transformation began. Lumber that had been meant mainly to construct defensive positions suddenly went missing. A unit that was heavy on construction workers and contractors meant that the ramshackle buildings suddenly had dividing walls, double and even triple decked rooms, and functional doors. Soldiers had to use ladders to reach the new second or third level where their cot now was, but in buildings that had ceilings that were 20 feet high there was ample room for everyone. Kirk Dyer was from Lucedale, the home of Bravo Company, but had joined the Air Force on something of a whim before moving to the Guard. Maybe it was his Air Force background, but Dyer didn't like the idea of living in those crowded buildings. So he and a couple of buddies chose to move into tents, also making them over with spare lumber into places worth living. For Ricky Tyler, having to wash his clothes in 5-gallon buckets was a bit of a pet peeve, but he was actually kind of happy to make his home within one of Dogwood's bunkers. Sure, it was impossible to keep the ubiquitous dust at bay. But at least when mortar rounds hit he didn't have to run anywhere to seek cover. He could just roll over on his cot and go back to sleep.

Food was an issue for all. Dogwood didn't have a nice chow hall run by contractors like many other bases. And certainly no McDonald's or Subway. At first there wasn't even a Mobile Kitchen Trailer (MKT); that was a couple of weeks down the road. So, it was Meals, Ready to Eat and Spunkmeyer muffins for all. And Kirk Dyer was amazed that even

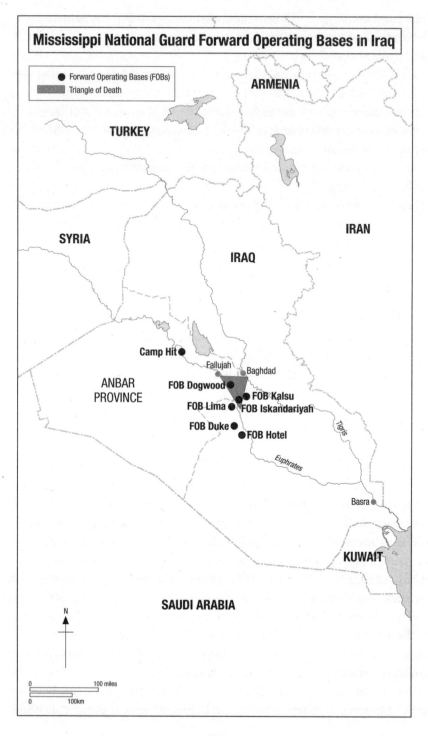

the MREs could go bad in the heat, with many getting sick as a result. The 150th had landed at the very end of the coalition's supply chain in Iraq. Robinson did what he could to alleviate the situation:

> We still had trouble getting supplies because they were coming from Duke and the 106th Support Battalion, and they would come, but it was not as routine as you would hope. It was very, very difficult to get resupplied. People were out scrounging all the time. I mean, we'd send elements up to Baghdad. We'd send elements to Fallujah. We'd send elements wherever they needed to go if they were trying to get things to scrounge that we needed to run the base, and we did a lot of that. I mean, I'll never forget; I got a congressional inquiry on why we didn't have any milk on the base, and the only option we had was strawberry milk because that's all we had. That's all we could get; we couldn't get anybody to bring anything up there, and I had to respond to a congressional inquiry on why we were not able to have things other than leftover strawberry milk on the base.

As it turned out, the soldiers just wanted good old milk for their cereal. So, Robinson made sure to send his Personal Security Detachment in the next convoy to FOB Kalsu with instructions to damn well come back with some milk. Jay Standley recalled that when those pallets of milk showed up, "you would have thought it was pallets of money everyone was so happy."

The 150th also didn't have much in the way of connectivity. The family support groups had sent the men with a supply of prepaid phone cards, but there was no phone center. At the outset, the unit had 16 computers and a very spotty internet connection, which allowed each soldier at most 30 minutes of internet connection a day. So, staying in touch with family and loved ones, something that was routine on bigger FOBs, was a glaring problem at Dogwood. But the major complaint of everyone was the toilet situation. Porta-johns set up in the desert heat. It was February, so it wasn't hot yet. But everyone knew that when it reached 120 degrees outside it was going to be 140 degrees in the porta-john. And, well, the smell was already unbearable. What would it be like in summer?

Waking up at Dogwood didn't present much of a problem, because one of the guys took to climbing the berm every morning at sunrise to do his best impression of a rooster. The "desert rooster" was there like clockwork every morning and became something of a tradition. But running the FOB was a constant headache given the tactical situation on the ground. Robinson knew that he had only two maneuver companies, Alpha and Bravo, to run operations throughout his massive AO. In general Alpha Company owned the southern part of the AO, especially the cluster of villages along that part of the Euphrates River, notably including Checkpoint 100 near the often-bombed bridge across the river, while Bravo Company owned the northern sector of the AO, including the troublesome village of Owesat. Making matters worse, the 150th didn't have nearly enough men to do the job. So, Alpha and Bravo companies had to pay a "FOB tax," which meant that some of their men had to be assigned to KP, or as tower guards, or gate guards, or detainee guards, or to man the internet café – or any number of things. All of this meant that Alpha and Bravo could, on a good day, send a total of 100 men each outside of the wire, which meant daily morning, afternoon, and night patrols. When not on patrols, the men would usually find themselves slated for some other duty, including being part of the quick reaction force. Days and nights were packed with activity for every soldier, and everyone knew that the patrols couldn't cover everything. The insurgents had the clear advantage.

MISSIONS

It fell to the 150th's battalion staff to make everything run smoothly, even with such a shortage of manpower. Trent Kelly's S-3 section was key to success, drafting the orders meant to set the area to right. As Kelly worked his way through his precious collection of Diet Mountain Dews, he and his assistants, Dexter Thornton and Allen McDaniel, worked their way through a mountain of details from managing the FOB tax to the rotation of missions. Through it all, McDaniel kept one saying in mind. Back at NTC, Robinson had told him, "An 80 percent plan that you can execute effectively is better than a 100 percent plan that you cannot adequately execute." It was about getting the job done with what you had; it was about action and results – not beauty. Another key member of the team was Jerry Bratu, who was in charge of the battalion staff at Dogwood. It seemed that everything, from planning, to supplies, to home leave, somehow made its way to Bratu's desk.

It was emblematic of the Guard that, even though Bratu didn't really have to go on missions given his staff planning position, he put together a squad from the 150th Headquarters that did indeed go out on many missions. Such is the Guard way. Finally, it was largely up to company executive officers, like Thomas Howell of Alpha Company, to make sure that their men had all the necessary support to undertake the missions designed by the S-3 office.

During all of the work, and only shortly after the loss of Sean Cooley, Trent and Kevin Kelly received the news that their father had died unexpectedly. That news hit the brothers like a hammer blow, but both men figured that their place was in Iraq helping the 150th. They could do nothing about their father's loss, but they could help their comrades in Iraq. Lieutenant Colonel Robinson, though, reminded the brothers how much their mother would be needing their support during such a difficult time. Both Trent and Kevin relented and went home on emergency leave. There were no convoys headed out at the time, so getting home proved an issue. At the last minute, though, the FOB laundry unit decided to make a run to Baghdad and allowed the brothers to tag along. This meant travelling on Route Temple, the most dangerous road in a dangerous area, in unarmored Humvees. But the brothers said a prayer and departed. As the convoy left the FOB the heavens unloaded a deluge of rain – and the local insurgents usually didn't attack while it was raining. Trent and Kevin were never happier to be soaking wet.

Patrolling from Dogwood was nearly constant, intended to keep the insurgents out of mortar range (there had already been three mortar attacks since the unit's arrival), to search for IEDs, and to search for weapons caches. Each mission began with the unit members gathering in a circle, locking arms, and saying a prayer. And, after the loss of Sean Cooley, the way the missions operated changed. Whenever possible one of the newly arrived tanks led the way, with the trailing vehicles trying to follow in its tracks. And no two missions ever exited or entered the base the same way or followed the same path. Never cross vehicle tracks that were already there. Many soldiers acquired civilian GPS systems which allowed them to plot a patrol's path so that they could never repeat it. And the very nature of Dogwood was a problem. As such a large base, it was surrounded by several concentric sand berms with exits cut into them. Those exits were a constraint, so the rule of thumb was for each new patrol to cut a new entrance into the more distant berms to avoid predictability.

The IED that had killed Sean Cooley was also a game changer. More uparmored vehicles were trickling in, but the vast majority of vehicles in the 150th only had their hillbilly armor. That armor had not withstood the blast that had killed Sean. Nobody stood a chance if they hit another IED like that. At Dogwood the soldiers of the 150th did what they could to compensate, especially in the M113s. They stripped the seats out of the back of the 113s and took up the flooring. In its place they welded 5/8-inch-thick steel plate. All hoped that, in the event of another IED strike, the welds would hold, giving any men riding in the back a measure of protection.

One of Bravo Company's first missions into an Iraqi village was in the northern sector of the AO, where they discovered three young men in a home where there were mortar primers. Since those could be used in the making of IEDs, they were a strict no-no. So, Bravo picked up its first three detainees. The next day an Iraqi turned up at Dogwood. He spoke perfect English, having gone to college in Texas, and said that the men they had detained were innocent. If the Mississippians gave one of them back, he would agree to provide what information he could on the insurgents. A deal was struck, and the 150th began receiving its first real intelligence on the area. Their informant was dubbed Barney, because Mike Beal thought that the informant looked just like one of their sergeants, Barney Houston. Iraqi Barney didn't seem to mind his new nickname, and neither did American Barney. So, all was well.

A&O PLATOON

But there was still so much to learn about operating in the area. One night elements of Bravo Company were making a run to Iskandariyah. Night-vision goggles don't tell you everything, so trailing vehicles in the convoy were alerted to any upcoming obstacles by the lead vehicle. But the convoy was moving too quickly, and when Marty Davis in the lead vehicle yelled, "IED hole," Larry Mergenschroer's vehicle was already in it, and got spun off the road, ending up in a field flooded with water. Even a Humvee couldn't make it out of there, so the guys knew that they were going to have to winch it out and tow it back to Dogwood. It was going to be a long night, and they were in the middle of nowhere, and who knew if there were insurgents around. The men set up a perimeter in case of attack and got down to work. Then the excited word came in, "There are guys walking towards us down the road! There is somebody coming; should we open fire?" Paul Lyon noticed that the men in the road had popped a chem light. He told his anxious men, "I don't think that the enemy would be walking down the road popping chem lights at night." It turned out that the men on the road had been on a foot patrol while manning an observation post outside of Iskandariyah and had fallen into a canal, shorting out their radio, and losing communications with their battalion headquarters. Once the Humvee was clear of the water, they begged a ride back to the base. Bravo called in the incident and the radio operator at Iskandariyah responded, "Well, thanks for finding our lost patrol."

The Assault and Obstacle (A&O) Platoon of Bravo Company had been left behind at Iskandariyah to be attached to the 1/155th Infantry Battalion at the base to serve both infantry and A&O tasks. In command of the A&O Platoon was Lieutenant Tucker McNeese, who had gone through ROTC during his time at the University of Southern Mississippi before joining the 150th during its training at Camp Shelby. The platoon's original assignment had been at FOB Kalsu, but it was in the process of transfer to Iskandariyah. Most in the unit had initially not been able to work out whether being at Iskandariyah was a positive or a negative. They were on a larger base with more amenities, and they had heard that Dogwood was a dump. But they were separated from many of their closest friends. The 1/155th treated them well, but there was a sense of loneliness. At least the A&O Platoon was all together, living in one big tent and keeping each other company. After their adventure with the lost platoon, and having gotten the supplies that they had come for, the men of Bravo Company looked in on their A&O Platoon pals. They all sat around and chatted. The Bravo Company contingent kidded their A&O guys about how good they had it. They even had a television in their tent! While talking the Dogwood guys downed as many Cokes and ate as many chips as they could. Who knew when they would see such luxury again? But the topic of conversation soon turned to Sean Cooley, with their A&O guys all expressing their sympathy and wishing they could have been there for his ceremony.

After their buddies from Bravo left, the men of the A&O Platoon got back to their own work. There was often incoming mortar fire, with shell fragments even landing in one soldier's cot while he was out on mission, but they felt kind of lucky that there hadn't been any for the last couple of days. For Robert McNail, getting back to work at that time meant studying. He had always been the best ACE operator in the unit, but since he had asked Denise to marry him back at Camp Shelby, he was working hard to make more out of himself for their future together. His fishing buddy, Jamie Davis, had encouraged Mac to take Combat Lifesaver classes, which would no doubt help with his return to nursing classes after they got home. Right before Mac went to the Combat Lifesaver class that evening, he shot off a quick email to his parents. He told his dad about the mortar attacks and how they were a real risk. He then listed the names of the 22 men in his platoon there at Iskandariyah in hopes that their local church would adopt the unit and pray for all the men. His own name was last on the list.

After Mac's departure for class, his best friend, Jamie Davis, was sitting in the communal A&O Platoon tent watching a movie when he heard a helicopter land nearby and then take off again. A few minutes later an officer made his way into their tent and told them that Mac was dead. He had been driving an unarmored Humvee to the Combat Lifesaver class when an armored, and much heavier, Humvee had slammed into Mac's vehicle. Medics had rushed to the scene to try to save Mac, but he had succumbed to blunt force trauma. He had already been picked up by the chopper, and his buddies would never see him again. The men of the A&O Platoon sat there in disbelief. Mac had just been there a few minutes before, and now he was dead, and his body was gone? None of it seemed right. Mac had been killed on February 11, one day before Sean Cooley was laid to rest back in Mississippi. Jamie Davis, who was also tasked with gathering Mac's personal effects, remembered, "I have tried lots of ways to get past losing Mac, but nothing works. It still comes back to bite me every now and then."

Even though Mac's death had taken place at Iskandariyah and not at Dogwood, news of his loss so soon after the death of Sean Cooley was another gut punch to the 150th family. Hap Palmer recorded his thoughts in his journal:

Two dead from the same company within the first 12 days in Iraq. Two totally unrelated incidents. To my knowledge we've done nothing but fire warning shots. Sure, we've blown up a few empty buildings with demo and our mortars and killed some of their wild dogs, but that's it. The mood was not the same for this one as it was with Cooley. We saw when Cooley was brought with medics scrambling to save him. We watched his troops cry, his commander and platoon leader wrench when the body bag was removed from the ambulance. This morning we just received word we had lost another troop. A good kid, always smiling, willing to help do anything. He never complained when given a mission or detail. He just went to work. Everybody liked him. It just wasn't quite as shocking and traumatic as what we witnessed with Cooley. Maybe we are all a little more desensitized to death now, or maybe it was just the sterile way we found out.

Allen McDaniel also recorded his reactions to the loss:

What's sad is that this is a death that could have so easily been avoided. It was inside the FOB with no enemy present. B Co seems to be in shock. I especially feel for their commander Captain Paul Lyon. Now he has lost two soldiers in less than a week. I'm still in shock. I hope that me being here means Ford [McDaniel's infant son] never has to go through something like this. I never want him to see what I've seen or miss what I've missed.

LOSS

Mac's fiancé, Denise, had just gotten off work and had gone to visit a friend who was in labor in the hospital. Communications had been shut off from the unit – no calls in or out and no email. And they had all learned from the case of Sean Cooley that communications shutdown meant that something bad had happened. Denise called her best friend Starla, wife of Mac's best friend Jamie Davis, asking if she had heard anything from Jamie. She hadn't. Both women understood that something bad had happened for someone, but it probably wasn't them. Their guys would call soon.

When Denise got home, she received a call from Robert's father, Marvin, who asked her to come to the house. The call wasn't unusual at all; Denise and Robert's parents had become quite close and often spent time together, especially in the evenings. As she pulled up, she noticed that there was a car in the driveway that she didn't recognize. As she entered the house, she noticed that Robert's mom, Linda, was sitting in a chair in tears, and also saw that the occupants of the vehicle were the preacher from their church and his wife. Linda looked up and between sobs said, "Robert's not coming home." Denise collapsed to the floor, barely able to breathe. Marvin and the preacher helped her up, and Denise told Linda, "No. This has to be wrong." But Linda wasn't wrong. The military had informed them of Robert's loss just before Denise arrived. Denise called Starla and then her own parents. She had two children from a previous marriage who knew Mac and loved him. She didn't want them watching television; they needed to hear the news from her, not from TV. Mac's young son from his own previous marriage, Edward, asked Denise, "You aren't going to leave me too are you?"

A few days later Denise was at the Barham Family Funeral Home in Meridian, Mississippi, where she got to see Robert again. He was in his dress uniform, even though the casket was closed for the wake. To Denise it seemed like the entire town of Meridian attended Mac's funeral. As in the case of Sean Cooley, Mac was the first soldier from the area lost in the war; the community – so closely tied to the National Guard – turned out to line the roads to the gravesite, and the waiting line for the visitation lasted for hours. Marvin and Linda could hardly believe how many phone calls and visitors they had over the next weeks. It was reassuring to know how much Mac had been loved and would be missed. But none of it replaced the hole in their lives left by the absence of their son.

INTO THE VILLAGES

As the 150th began to truly settle in, counter-mortar and presence patrols continued daily across the AO. These patrols were designed, largely, to keep the insurgents out of mortar range of Dogwood; also, keeping the insurgents guessing as to when and where US forces would turn up made it much more difficult for them to place IEDs or to dig up and transport munitions. Increasingly, though, moves were made into the local villages to gain information on insurgents, search for specific targets indicated by intelligence, and just to get to know the people. Some incursions into the villages involved the entire battalion, while most were much smaller affairs. It quickly became clear that the AO was a tale of two cities. Owesat in the north was an insurgent hotbed, while many of the villages in the south, including Baj al-Shamaly, were relatively cooperative.

The first real look at Owesat took place on February 12, and, as expected, all of the men were gone – presumably having swum or taken a boat to the other side of the Euphrates, out of harm's way. Only women and children remained. And Larry Odom was amazed. The women basically just ignored the Americans, going about their daily chores and duties like nothing out of the ordinary was happening. Universally, the Mississippians were surprised by what they found. Ramshackle, small cement buildings with dirt floors. Intermittent electricity at best, with maybe a beat-up old fan oscillating or the glow of a naked light bulb. Maybe a butane fire inside for cooking, maybe not. But most houses had a nice bed and a large collection of colorful blankets, all lovingly folded on shelves. Generally, the Mississippians took the women and children into another room while they searched for contraband or weapons, hoping to cause as little disruption as possible. Everyone was cognizant that any rude behavior would only make the situation in the area worse. But with all the men gone, there was little to be found or to be learned.

In Alpha Company's sector to the south, things got off to a more positive start. In the scattering of villages around Baj al-Shamaly more men remained around during the searches and, as Cager put it, the kids didn't throw rocks at you like they did in Owesat. While the mood was decidedly different, the conditions were still surprising to the Mississippians. Kevin Kelly recorded his impressions of his first visit to the villages in his journal:

> When you go into a house, you don't know how many people will be in there. There may be 3 or 15. They typically all sleep in the same room. In all the houses I went into (about 12) I think I only saw about 2 pieces of furniture and only 1 or 2 beds. The showers are something else. It's just a small closet with a piece of PVC pipe leading out into the yard. There is a tea pitcher or something of that nature with water in it. That makes up their shower. One of

the funniest things was when we were in one house and we were searching a room and we reached down to move something and there were 2 chickens there and they went crazy. Scared the mess out of us. It is amazing to see the houses, they are just like old rocks put together. Cracks in the wall and big holes, but yet they have bars up on all their windows. There are a lot of things you will remember, but this morning at around 6:30 a.m. and we are exhausted and sitting on our M113 with the ramp down and watching the sun rise up over the palm trees. Just a bunch of good friends watching it without saying much to each other. Then you look down on the ground and you see a donkey, skinny cows and dogs headed your way. Glad it lasted at least one moment.

THE WAR GRINDS ON

As the 150th struggled to comprehend its own losses and began to settle into a routine and to gather intelligence in its AO, tragedy continued to strike the wider Mississippi Guard. Hap Palmer recorded in his journal:

> We received word that the infantry lost two soldiers when a dike they were crossing collapsed and their Humvee flipped into the water. The bottoms of these rivers are thick with silt. It is presumed that the soldiers couldn't open the doors of their armored Humvee and drowned. Communications have been down since we heard the news. After communications were restored, I received an email from my wife and I realized that they have figured out that when an incident happens that we shut down commo. They talk to each other and figure out that no one has heard from their husbands in a while. They have broken the code… We're kicking out patrols as fast and frequently as we can. There are some real bad guys out there. We haven't done a whole hell of a lot to them other than run them off. We have lost two soldiers from this battalion. And we have yet to fire more than warning shots. The enemy is starting to get bolder every day.

The two 1/155th soldiers killed in the accident were Sergeants Joseph Rahaim and Timothy Osbey. Making the situation even more tragic, their comrades saw the vehicle plunge into the river and dove in to try to extricate them but failed. Rahaim, who had gone to Terry High School just north of Crystal Springs, where he was known for his sense of humor, went by Drew and had wanted to be a soldier since he was young; his favorite toy as a child was his G.I. Joe. Timothy Osbey was from the small town of Magnolia outside of McComb on the western side of the state. His preacher lauded the fact that, even though Osbey came from a difficult background, he had stayed on the straight and narrow and had made something of his life, joining the Guard right after high school. He had married only 11 days before shipping out to Iraq. Rahaim was 22 when he died, and Osbey was 29.

Back at Dogwood the boldness of the insurgents was becoming more and more apparent. Since the 150th was using less of the footprint of the base than had its previous occupants, its members decided to block some of the entrance and exits to the base through the surrounding berm. It fell to Jay Standley's squad to do the work. He recorded the incident in his journal:

We were ordered to go plug a hole in the berm. We did, and when Sgt McWillie backed his ACE off after finishing, we found two 155mm artillery rounds sticking out of the dirt. We called EOD [Explosive Ordnance Disposal], sent in an IED report, and backed off to pull security. After about 4 or 5 hours, EOD showed up, and investigated. The two rounds were daisy-chained together with red det cord. This IED had been planted in the berm, waiting for us to use this as a base exit again. Fortunately, our earth-moving had destroyed the setup, but we have no idea what the trigger device was. After we got back in, and were debriefed, it hit me as to how close that was. I'd parked the 113 near that cut in the berm, and stood atop the berm right there, as had a couple of others, pulling security during the digging. We were all very lucky to come home that day.

Tragedy struck again on March 2. The A&O Platoon at Iskandariyah undertook any number of tasks working with the 155th Infantry, everything from improvement of FOB defenses, to reconnaissance patrols, to security missions, to detainee duty. On this particular day,

Tucker McNeese was informed that his task was route assessment. The area had been hit by so many IEDs that the roads were becoming difficult to traverse. He and his men had to survey the roads to see how best to repair them. McNeese was given a platoon of infantry to accompany his men on the mission. At one point the patrol stopped to assess several craters in the road, with the infantry dismounting their vehicles to provide cover. Almost immediately there was thunderous IED detonation. McNeese rushed to the scene where two infantry soldiers were badly wounded. Seeing that the situation was dire, McNeese shouted for the medic. One of the badly wounded men, though, responded that he was the medic.

From Causeyville, Mississippi, Robert Pugh had shifted over to the unit when it became clear that it needed medics for its impending deployment to Iraq. Pugh suffered numerous shrapnel wounds to his chest and legs, but all his attention was directed toward saving the life of Sergeant Ellis Martin, who was also wounded in the blast. Martin was so badly wounded that he eventually needed 52 units of blood, and on the scene of the explosion Pugh directed McNeese and the other soldiers concerning how best to treat Martin's injuries until he passed out from his own wounds. Pugh, who went by Shane, died at the age of 25 and had been married for less than a year.

PSYCHO 6 AND THE ABSURDITY OF REALITY

While the 150th was not co-located with the 155th, the men in both formations had trained together for years and knew each other well. Any loss in the Mississippi Guard family deeply affected all. Roz Morris, Psycho 6, was being treated well by the men. In fact, they seemed to go out of their way to show her deference and respect. And she was making some headway in getting to know the guys through her smoking cessation campaign. But with all the loss and risk that was mounting up, she understood that she had to figure out a way to make a bigger impact more quickly before the stress these men were facing spiraled out of control. To her the answer seemed natural. She needed to go out on missions with the men. Having a lieutenant colonel female social worker out on active operations in Iraq was a distinct no-no. But Robinson knew a good idea when he heard it. He would take the heat from above if any came about allowing Roz into the field.

She wanted to go, and he knew that his men needed it. So, Roz Morris was headed to war.

———

War is so often a juxtaposition of the tragic and the absurd, as the 150th discovered. As trouble was brewing all over southern Anbar and Babil provinces, Bravo Company got word of an arms cache that needed to be checked out. When Paul Lyon's men got there, they discovered two massive 500-pound bombs, made for being dropped out of an aircraft. There was no way in hell that they wanted to get anywhere near those things. An EOD investigation, though, revealed that the bombs didn't contain any explosive, much to everyone's relief. But then word came down from Dogwood. The shell casings themselves could be put to use by the insurgents. So, Bravo Company wrestled the behemoths onto wreckers and brought them back to the base. It turned out that, with the help of some welders, 500-pound bomb casings made wonderful barbeques.

As the bombs were being hauled back to base, a story went around that quickly became legend. To deter the emplacing of IEDs, the 150th would send out sniper teams to overnight positions in the desert to keep watch for insurgent activity. One morning it fell to Jay Standley's squad to venture out and pick up the sniper team. Normally the snipers would take cover and remain hidden all night. But this morning when Standley arrived at the required grid coordinate, the entire sniper team was just standing around in plain sight. Some were almost weeping they were laughing so hard. Others just seemed perplexed. As the snipers had watched through their night-vision equipment in the dead of night, a sheepherder wandered into view with his flock. Well. Maybe sheepherders used their flocks for cover as they set IEDs. So, everyone trained their attention on the man, ready to fire if he started to set an explosive. Instead, all were transfixed as the shepherd took one sheep out of the flock, went out a ways from the remaining sheep, and had sex with the creature. There was no way this could be true. Nobody on the base believed the wild story, but different sniper teams saw the fellow and his amorous activities with his sheep four more times during the tour in Iraq.

A DIFFERENCE OF OPINION

It became more and more frustrating that all the intelligence that the 150th was gathering indicated that the village of Owesat was the heart of the insurgency in the area. However, even when night raids were conducted on the town in late February and early March, all the men had slipped away, leaving only women and children. And such night raids were fraught with danger. The narrow roads and rickety bridges over a spiderweb of canals near the Euphrates were difficult to maneuver on and through even during the daytime. After dark there was night-vision equipment, but it didn't allow for much depth perception – so if there was a hole or a ditch on the side of the road, you couldn't really see it. Thus, rollovers and accidents were a constant problem in Iraq. It was on such a night that Robert Arnold got his first experience driving an M113. He muscled the vehicle down the narrow, twisting pathways, arriving at the target village safely. But when the sun rose and he looked back at what he had driven through, he thought, "Oh holy crap! I'm lucky to still be here." On a mission two weeks later, Arnold wasn't so lucky. He was manning the turret gun in an M113 when it strayed from the road and hit a hole. The shock bounced Arnold around in the turret, slamming his face and the back of his head against the vehicle's armor. He put a battle dressing on himself and later the medics stapled his scalp back together without anesthesia. Fortunately, Robert's father Larry wasn't along for that ride. The two had been placed in different platoons so there was never the risk of losing them both at the same time.

One expedient that higher level command hoped would aid the Mississippians was to bring in an Iraqi National Guard (ING) component for them to train and work with. The training, overseen by Jody Kyzar, would help to transform the ING into more competent and capable soldiers, and, just perhaps, the ING would be able to unlock the cooperation of some of the local villagers for the Americans. The Iraqis were given their own little slice of Dogwood as their temporary home. Training went on for days, with smaller raids being undertaken as well. On March 14 it came time to put the new alliance to the test. Along with the ING the battalion conducted a raid of the villages in the al-Faddilyah area west of Checkpoint 100.

The raid proceeded like most of the Mississippi troops expected. There were few men around, leaving women and children in the village who mainly ignored the raid as best they could. Instead of following protocol in breaching houses, the Iraqis tended to pile in through one door all one at a time. Or they would mostly stand back and let one of their compatriots do all of the work. But one house was very different. There was a military age male detained from that home, and he was hopping mad, yelling at the top of his lungs and spitting on the Americans – it was pretty easy to see that this guy might be an insurgent. For Mike Beal it was a real wake-up call. He had never seen evil in the eyes of another person before, but he saw it in the eyes of this man. He knew for sure that this prisoner would happily kill him if he ever had a chance. The guy even had a mortar sight in his house. No doubt he was a bad guy. For the Mississippians, capturing this man, regardless of how he acted, meant taking him back to Dogwood where he would be evaluated and sent on for further questioning if the evidence worked against him. But for the Iraqis, he was guilty already. In conversation before the mission, Larry Odom remembered that one of the ING members, who seemed to all be Shia Muslims, had told him that everyone in the AO was bad since they were largely Sunni Muslims. And this ING unit hated Sunnis.

The Iraqis took the detainee away for questioning as the Americans moved on to the next house. Then there was some hollering. The Iraqis had used the sling of an AK-47 to wrap around the detainee's feet while two Iraqi soldiers held him in the air, and they were whipping the bare soles of his feet with a long chem light. Lieutenant Gary Kinsey couldn't believe what he was seeing, and told the ING soldier, "You can't do that!" The Iraqi replied, "Don't worry; when you whip them on the soles of their feet, nobody sees the bruises." Kinsey, Odom, and the others, though, took the chem light from the Iraqi soldier. Iraqis could treat each other however they liked on their own missions. But this was a 150th mission and would be run as such. The Iraqis weren't too happy to be called to book on the beating, but they did as they were told.

INTERPRETERS

As the Mississippians attempted to break the information barrier that existed especially in Owesat, it quickly became clear that working alongside the ING was not the answer. Instead, their interpreters became an ever more important link to the Iraqi people and to their trust. Each company in the 150th had two interpreters assigned to it, while the battalion had others that it could assign in need. Initially, some within the 150th, as with other units, were skeptical of Iraqis who wanted to serve with American forces. Perhaps these guys were spies? Even if they weren't spies, would they be reliable? Quickly, though, the Guardsmen came to understand that their interpreters were mostly just like them – people who worked hard and wanted the best for Iraq.

Born in Babylon, Joseph came from a Shia family, and his father had served in the Iraqi Army under Saddam Hussein in the Iran–Iraq War (1980–88).[*] From a large family, Joseph's parents always contended that he needed to go to college to make for a better life than the one they had known. Saddam's regime had always mistrusted its Shia population, a situation that worsened greatly with the outbreak of the Persian Gulf War. Joseph's memory of that time was of hardly any food, no electricity, and no schools. Practicing the Shia faith at all meant risking jail, with a visit to the Shia holy site of the Imam Husayn Shrine in Karbala punishable by three years in prison. In Saddam's Iraq, Shias were sometimes executed simply for who they were.

The situation only worsened after Saddam's defeat in the Gulf War. His regime survived, relying on deep brutality toward its citizenry, and the Iraqi economy collapsed. At that time Joseph was in high school and dreamed of maybe being a teacher himself. But schools were only open for Shia citizens on a sporadic basis, and the monthly salary for a teacher at the time was not even enough to cover feeding a family, much less housing and utilities. With his family always having to worry about where the next meal came from and with little future to hope for, Joseph was initially optimistic in the wake of Saddam's overthrow in 2003. Maybe the Americans would really bring democracy and opportunity to Iraq as they had promised. Instead, the nation had collapsed into civil and religious war wrapped inside an American conflict against

---

[*]American forces gave their Iraqi interpreters nicknames to help protect their identities. Joseph has chosen to go by one of the nicknames given to him by American soldiers rather than his real name, since there is still resentment in Iraq today against many who served with or alongside American forces.

foreign and home-grown insurgents. As Joseph put it, instead of one dictator – Saddam – there were now many dictators all over the country vying for control.

The new freedoms for Shia, though, did allow Joseph to go to college, where he decided to study English. He had a friend who was an interpreter with the Americans, and he said that the job paid well. Being an interpreter wasn't the only option for Joseph, but majoring in English certainly meant that there would be job opportunities when he graduated. It came time for a decision in early 2005. Joseph could get a job as a teacher of English at $350 per month, but being an interpreter for the Americans paid much more: $1,050 a month. That kind of pay would allow Joseph to save money – maybe even enough money to get married, buy a home, and start a family of his own. But Joseph also knew the risks. Serving with the Americans meant the possibility of being hit by IEDs, mortars, and ground attacks. But even worse, those who served with the Americans were often ostracized from Iraqi society, with many being murdered. It was such a risky job that Joseph only told his immediate family the truth. To everyone else he was moving to another town to teach.

In reality, Joseph was off to the main interpreter center at Diwaniyah, Iraq, for a proficiency test. He passed with the highest possible marks, which meant that he and four of his friends from his English course were sent to FOB Kalsu to await their assignment to American units. When it became clear that he and his friends were headed to FOB Dogwood, a veteran interpreter who was familiar with the area told them that serving there was pretty much a death sentence. In fact, he said, "An interpreter was killed on the main road past Dogwood just a few days ago; hit by an IED." The veteran sighed deeply and told Joseph that just getting to Dogwood alive was going to be difficult. "If you drive your car there you will be killed. It is the most dangerous road in the country. And if the Iraqis know that you are going to help the Americans then your life is over." Two of Joseph's friends quit on the spot. No way were they heading to Dogwood. But Joseph needed the money for his future, and he truly hoped that the Americans would bring positive change to his country in the long run. So, he hopped on a military convoy and headed north.

Once at Dogwood, Joseph was assigned to Bravo Company. His task was to accompany Bravo on its missions, especially those likely to involve dealing with Iraqi civilians. And for every 44 days of service, he would get five days of vacation to visit his family. Joseph had heard stories about how badly interpreters were treated, but most of the Mississippians welcomed him and treated him with respect. He even came to view some of the American commanders as father figures.

Events rushed forward at a blinding speed. The very next morning Joseph was out on his first patrol. The Americans seemed so calm, but Joseph was certain he was going to die. He spent the whole patrol waiting for the IED to go off, but it never did. Once back at Dogwood, Joseph began to get to know the other interpreters, who all shared two tents and had their own toilet facilities. Joseph liked the setup – it allowed him and his fellow Iraqis, the vast majority of whom were Shia – to practice their religion and observe the mores of their own culture freely. He quickly made friends with Assim, who went by the name of Ron and who also worked with Bravo Company. Assim had been there longer and helped Joseph find his way in navigating a military-style life – something foreign to the recent college graduate. Assim was from nearby Babil Province and was hyper-enthusiastic about the Americans, their culture, and the future of Iraq. Even though he had been there longer than Joseph, he was younger – only 17. He had lied about his age to become an interpreter; something that Joseph agreed to keep secret. Assim, too, understood the risks. His parents had been dead set against him working with the Americans, but he had been adamant. Assim believed that the Americans were the future: Iraq's best chance. And he might even go to school in America one day!

Assim, though, was keenly aware of the risks. He had been there for the loss of Sean Cooley. He knew the troubles in Owesat, and he knew the risks of being mortared. As he and Joseph became closer, the two made a deal. Whenever possible they would not go on patrols together. And when one went out on a mission, he would give all his money to the other to make sure that it got to his family if he was killed.

A TALE OF TWO CITIES

While Owesat remained a dangerous hotbed of insurgency, the villages around Sharmia to the south became ever more cooperative, allowing the Mississippians to work to gain the population's trust. The poverty of the area had been shocking to the soldiers of the 150th. Most children didn't have any shoes and were dressed in rags; many were filthy and covered in sores due to the general lack of medical treatment. Their teeth were often ragged and chipped, having lacked dental care for their entire lives. Conditions everywhere were unsanitary. It was like someone's nightmare of a Dickensian slum run wild. Seeing the dire need and understanding that basic medical care was perhaps the most pressing issue, the 150th launched Operation *Flintstone*. Soldiers wrote to their families and churches back home in their Guard communities to ask for donations of vitamins and medications, especially for children and pregnant women. Any assistance was welcome, from shoes, to clothes, to toys – but medical supplies for children was the focus. Lieutenant Colonel Robinson introduced the need by writing a letter to the Guard communities:

Dear Friends,

My name is Lieutenant Colonel Roy Robinson, a member of the Mississippi Army National Guard and commander of the 150th Combat Engineer Battalion headquartered in Meridian, Mississippi with units in Carthage, Quitman, Lucedale, Okolona, and Houston… I write you today not as a soldier but as a husband and father. Iraq, while modern in urban locations, still has rural regions that are very austere… Preventive medicine is not routine, and children are sometimes malnourished. The men and women serving in the 150th Combat Engineer Battalion want to have a positive impact on the lives of these children… Through "Operation Flintstone" our loved ones and friends in our local communities can help us to make a difference by donating children's vitamins and medicine. As we receive these items we will distribute them to the parents of children throughout the villages in our area. Growing up many of us remember taking Flintstone Chewable Vitamins with our breakfast. The name "Operation Flintstone" was picked to help everyone understand our intent to help children in Iraq grow up living healthier, happier lives… We greatly appreciate any assistance. It is our privilege to represent our nation and state not only as soldiers but also as humanitarians. Thank you for your help in protecting our country and building the future of Iraq.

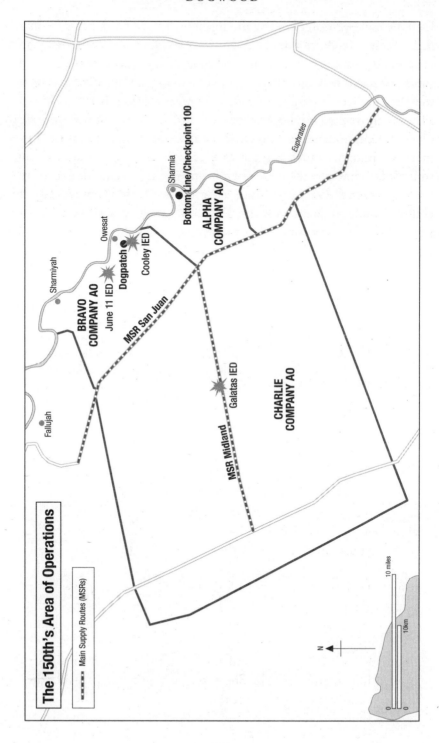

The 150th's Area of Operations

▪▪▪ Main Supply Routes (MSRs)

Fallujah

Sharmiyah

BRAVO
COMPANY AO

June 11 IED

Dogpatch

Owesat

Cooley IED

MSR San Juan

MSR Midland

Galatas IED

CHARLIE
COMPANY AO

Sharmia

Bottom Line/Checkpoint 100

ALPHA
COMPANY AO

Euphrates

N

10 miles

10km

Donations were soon flooding in, and in early March the 150th ran its first Medical Civic Action Program (MEDCAP) mission in the area, bringing doctors, medicine, shoes, and other items to the villages in the southern portion of the AO. As the cordon was set up and the vehicles were put in place, Kevin Kelly recorded in his journal that, at first, only a few Iraqis worked up the courage to walk up to see what was going on. Once it became clear that there were doctors offering medical care, and that the children would also get toys and shoes, "pretty soon we were swarmed." Some parents wept openly, being able to bring their children to a doctor for the very first time. Many of the children were frightened at the outset, especially when the doctor first pulled out a needle to give a shot, but toys and candy made it all better. And soon the stocks of vitamins, medicine, and toys were running low.

Much of the battalion was there that day running the mission, and seeing what was going on was a tonic. After the loss and the hurt, maybe they were doing something good in Iraq. Maybe this corner of their violent world would be made better by their presence. During the day, some got to know locals and their customs a bit better. Gary Kinsey and Kevin Kelly went over to a nearby house, where the women were working with some bread dough:

> They were making what looked like biscuits. I was dreaming of great big biscuits with some grape jelly. Lieutenant Kinsey and I were outside and were in the middle of this farm in the backyard with cows, goats, sheep and turkeys. Well the woman who was rolling most of the dough came out and started building this fire in a pot made of clay. She first put some straw in the bottom and then put some little limbs in it. Now comes the interesting part, if you remember, I said there were goats in the yard. Well, I guess that goat droppings are a highly flammable material. She took what looked like a 5-gallon bucket of goat droppings and poured them on top of the straw. She then put more sticks and palm tree leaves and started the fire. It didn't burn long, but the goat droppings turned into coals and heated the clay of the pot. She then took the biscuits and started slapping them until they looked like a pizza dough. She took that and put it inside the clay pot and slapped it against the wall and it stuck. They would leave it there for about 1 minute and then bring it out and it was

ready. Lieutenant Kinsey and I were so amazed and sick at the same time thinking that they would eat this pita bread cooked by goat droppings. Captain Lyon came by us and told us to get back to work because Epcot center at Disney World was closing. We started laughing and walked off.

In Owesat and its surrounding hamlets in the north, though, the situation remained volatile. Shortly after the loss of Sean Cooley, the Mississippians had detained three Iraqis and met an informant whom they had dubbed Barney who had offered them intelligence on Owesat. But it had been difficult for the soldiers of the 150th to get information from Barney without blowing his cover. Barney lived outside of Owesat proper, making contact a bit easier. Meetings, though, had been relatively few and had often taken place during raids in the area. Barney's house, like all the rest, would be searched and the family questioned. It was on one of those occasions that they hit the jackpot. Barney told them of a large cache of weapons buried near a local soccer field. The soldiers thanked Barney for his help but didn't treat him in any obvious way differently than any other civilian in the area, in an attempt to keep his cooperation a secret.

Bravo Company waited a couple of days, again hoping to keep Barney's role in the matter confidential, before running a seemingly routine operation that took it near to the soccer field. As the patrol approached the soccer field, Randall Jones noticed something quite odd. He turned to his seatmate in the Humvee, Bradley Sharp, and pointed to the field: "What's that? Something ain't right." Sharp asked him what he meant, and Jones replied, "How many guys have you ever seen working over here?" In every village they had been in to this point it had always been the women out in the fields working. The men were either gone or lounging around their home. Women did the work. But there were a bunch of guys digging near the soccer field. Guys that scattered like the wind when they saw the convoy approaching in the distance. That was a good enough reason to stop there. And the Mississippians made it look like a normal operation. They often pulled their convoy off the road and disembarked with minesweepers to search for caches, and today's mission looked no different.

It didn't take long for the minesweepers to get a hit. A massive hit. So, the men began to dig and quickly struck paydirt. Ammunition, rockets, rocket launchers, surface to air missiles. The find was unbelievably large. At first the men were excited, but as the digging continued and the pile of weaponry and ammunition seemed to have no end, fatigue set in. Voccio was there with his tanks to set up a perimeter as the men dug. After eight solid hours of digging, lugging ammo, and digging more, he heard a whistle. Incoming mortar fire. Time to hop back in the tank. Someone was damn unhappy about losing this stockpile of weapons to the 150th. Convoys came from Dogwood to pick up the ordnance to carry it back for destruction. But it never seemed to stop. Eventually, soldiers from both companies and the headquarters company took turns digging – for three days. Camp had to be set up in the desert at night to keep watch over the dig, and the work just kept on coming. Robinson would radio Captain Lyon from time to time asking when it would end, and nobody knew for sure. Robinson wondered if it would ever end. On the third day, as the radio conversations became more exasperated, Lyon finally told Robinson that they had found it all. Robinson asked how Lyon knew that for sure, and Lyon responded, "Well, that last shell had a note on it. The note said – that's it. You have found it all."

The find was indeed massive and included:

- (3) 30mm rifle grenades
- (3) 40mm rifle grenades
- (2) 60mm rifle grenades
- (138) 60mm mortar rounds
- (67) 73mm RPG rounds
- (93) 80mm mortar rounds
- (11) 85mm RPG rounds
- (13) 100mm mortar rounds
- (4) 107mm rockets
- 120mm mortar tube
- (143) 120mm mortar rounds
- (82) 122mm artillery rounds
- (128) 125mm artillery rounds
- (33) 130mm artillery rounds
- (5) 155mm artillery rounds
- (159) 122mm missiles

- (7) surface to air missiles
- (10) rockets
- (35) hand grenades
- (5) rocket motors
- rocket propelled grenade launcher
- (8) AK-47 assault rifles
- (8) heavy machine guns
- (40,000) rounds of assorted small-arms ammunition
- (5,000) feet of detonation cord
- bags of high explosive
- (3,000) time fuses

The men had felt good about helping the children in the southern villages through Operation *Flintstone*, but the cache find in the north was maybe an even better feeling, if different. Kirk Dyer and Jody Kyzar both recorded that they thought that this find was going to hit the insurgency hard. And it felt so good that each of the weapons found was one less IED, one less incoming mortar, one less sniper round.

Reality soon settled back in, though. A few days later Barney's body was found in the desert. He had been executed by the insurgents for having helped the Americans. In a later raid, Bravo Company went to Barney's house again. His family was inconsolable. They told Paul Lyon that insurgents had broken in during the night and had cut Barney's throat and dragged him out into the desert. It all infuriated Lyon. Barney had tried his best to help the Americans, but they had had too few troops to keep him safe. And now they even couldn't help his family, who made it clear that giving them gifts or support could get them all killed. The insurgency was brutal, and working with the Americans in and around Owesat was plainly a death sentence.

IED ALLEY

All the patrolling, working with the population, and cache finds, though, seemed to have little impact on the frequency of IED strikes, which were increasing by the day. During the last week of March and the first week of April, there were five major IED incidents in the

150th's AO. Two of the incidents involved hiding IEDs in the carcasses of dead animals, which was quickly becoming an insurgent staple. On one of its patrols, Alpha Company noticed a dead dog on the side of the road – not all that unusual a sight in Iraq. But this dead dog had visible wires coming out of it. EOD was called in, and a robot made its way to the dog's carcass and disabled the device. Kevin Kelly recorded another Alpha Company find in his journal:

> Today during a patrol outside the wire, we noticed that there were two dead cows laying on the side of the road. Since insurgents typically use dead animals to hide IEDs, well, we fired on them with a .50 cal. machine gun, but really didn't do much to them. We then fired at it with a M-1 tank. Needless to say, I don't even think there was more than a grease spot left. It might seem crude to some people, but it could have saved a soldier's life today.

Other incidents saw IEDs explode, causing only limited damage. Even so, these were moments of terror that continued the slow buildup of trauma and fear that accumulated day by day. Hap Palmer recorded in his journal:

> I go to Karbala every Wednesday for the brigade maintenance meeting. We take a route that leads us down ASR [Army Service Road] Midland across the desert for about 1 hour and 30 minutes. The security escort takes me there once every week. Same bat-time, same bat-channel. Last Tuesday one of the water trucks hit a pressure detonated IED while crossing the one hill on Midland. Two more were found that didn't detonate. Everyone around here thinks it was intended for my trip the following day. I don't know. I don't care. It still pisses me off. No one was hurt, but the truck was destroyed. We changed our usual route and went down ASR San Juan. San Juan is a nasty little road. One little spot is nick-named Swiss Cheese Alley because of the craters that line both sides of the road left by IEDs. We picked the right time to move through. The streets were lined with kids. Assholes don't care if the kids get hurt, but it's not good PR for them. Kids present is usually a good sign. When we made it back the following day we found out that Abraham (one of the local informants) was decapitated along with his son in Baghdad.

The local assholes didn't want a direct link to the murder, so they had their boys in Baghdad do it. Abraham was a pretty well-respected fellow in his village. He just didn't want the terrorist assholes setting up shop there. Yesterday morning A Company took some equipment to Iskandariyah. They were hit by an IED right along Swiss Cheese Alley. No injuries, no significant damage to the M916 [an equipment transport vehicle]. Just some busted glass in the windows/windshields.

Other such strikes did lead to catastrophic casualties for the units involved. Hap Palmer was on the recovery team sent out to clear the site where a Military Police (MP) unit had been hit while crossing through the 150th's AO. He recorded:

When we arrived, parts and pieces of the vehicle were scattered all about. The door of the level 1 armored Humvee was thrown about 50 meters from the wreckage. The fender was 20 meters on the other side of that. One of the tires was probably 100 meters from the wreckage. That door takes 4 men to lift. One of the guys injured had to have his mangled legs amputated. They all had been medevaced when we arrived. As soon as we arrived we started to get garbage bags and clear up the small pieces. You don't want... [an insurgent] to know how much damage his work did. It took three hours to recover the vehicle. It was a pressure detonated device. Ironic that the Humvee that was hit was the last in order of march. This was a pressure device on a road that women and children civilians use. There is not a room in hell hot enough for the asshole that did that.

Robinson had his men step up patrols and raids, even launching a heliborne raid onto an island in the middle of the Euphrates that was a presumed insurgent hideout. But nothing seemed to make a difference. The insurgents' early warning system at Owesat always meant that the bad guys slipped away before the Americans arrived. And, of course, in an insurgent war firing on presumed civilians swimming or paddling across a river trying to evade a raid was not an option. So, the drumbeat of war continued.

HOME SWEET HOME

In April Congressman Gene Taylor kept his promise that he had made back in the going away parade in Lucedale and visited the Mississippi troops on their FOBs in Iraq. He even brought with him the supreme delicacy that he had told the men to expect – fresh Gulf shrimp! Bravo Company of the 150th was running a resupply convoy to Kalsu when the men there told them that they had just eaten fresh shrimp provided by the congressman. "Son of a bitch! He didn't bring us no shrimp at Dogwood!" The soldiers of the 150th felt let down – especially those from Lucedale who had been there for the promise. But they also kind of understood. Even military helicopters avoided Dogwood, only ever touching down there in times of great need – the area was just too hot for a congressman. With the constant threat of IEDs and mortar or rocket attack, it would be a long time before the 150th got any shrimp.

Dogwood was in such a dangerous area that civilian contractors would often just ditch their trucks and loads instead of driving out in such conditions. This tendency left Dogwood chronically undersupplied, so the master scrounger Gary Kinsey stepped in on behalf of Bravo Company, and Thomas Howell did the same for Alpha. The scroungers headed to bases all over Iraq in search of whatever their men needed. They, along with Marshall Davis, took Robinson's personal security detail and headed out to the various FOBs where supplies for Dogwood were getting hung up. Often this meant trips into Camp Victory in Baghdad. On some occasions Kinsey and Davis "lied their asses off" and told the contractors how safe it was, which led to the contractors relenting and following them back to Dogwood. On other occasions they had to offload the supplies onto their own vehicles. Kinsey would often alternate between running active missions into the villages and then finding himself getting a shopping list for his next convoy run.

Among the things that Kinsey really wanted to procure were cupola shields for the gunners of the M113s, along with more steel for additional hillbilly armor. In his many visits with Marshall Davis to the nearby FOBs, Kinsey made sure to befriend their local scroungers. This effort paid off with huge dividends at Camp Victory. The chief wheeler-dealer there was a Cajun from Louisiana, so he and Kinsey got off on the right foot immediately. Bravo Company had a wealth of window-unit air conditioners that had been sent with them through a local donation. But they were the wrong voltage and were therefore still sitting there at Dogwood all boxed up. Well, Camp Victory had a large surplus of steel, but needed air conditioners badly. Voila! A deal was struck. The 150th had its steel and armor, and the soldiers at Camp Victory were able to stay cool. In his continuing travels to other FOBs, Kinsey became an invaluable middleman, linking people to their needs across the area simply by talking and befriending folks. At Camp Anaconda, he worked a deal for the cupola shields the 150th needed. You name it, Kinsey seemed to be able to find it. His only requirement was that you never asked him *how* he got it. And Thomas Howell asked the same of his company commander Ken Cager. Just no questions please.

Kinsey had two especially great moments as a scrounger. Another unit stationed in Baghdad at Camp Victory had its updated equipment arrive late, while it was already leaving to return home. That equipment included four brand-new uparmored Humvees. There was some sweet talking to a master sergeant at Camp Victory. A name was signed on an invoice, and suddenly the 150th had four brand-new uparmored Humvees. Evidently you could do a lot with a new coat of paint and some changed bumper numbers. His other crowning achievement involved a tank that was down with a bum engine. The few tanks at Dogwood were lifesavers, and having one non-operational was critical. It was on another visit to Baghdad that Kinsey gave the sad but true story of the tank being down and how badly it was needed. But, he told them, we were only "shade tree mechanics without the tree." So, good as they were in the 150th, they couldn't get the tank up and running again. The local master sergeant looked around surreptitiously and said, "wait here." Then, from around the corner came a forklift with a brand new tank engine. These things cost hundreds of thousands of dollars, and you were only supposed to be able to get a new one in a one-for-one trade with an old one. But here Kinsey was getting one scot-free. From this point on, Kinsey always had an extra tank engine to trade to keep his tanks running. Folks were sure enough happy to have that new engine, but this one brought Kinsey a fair number of uncomfortable questions. Still, for all the uncomfortable questions, Kinsey and the other scroungers like him could take real solace in that they were keeping members of the 150th alive. Uparmored vehicles; operational tanks; cupolas on the 113s. It all made the 150th safer.

With scroungers like Kinsey on the job, though it was not safe enough yet for congressmen and their cases of Gulf shrimp, the Mississippians were able to take several steps to make Dogwood a more comfortable home. Besides working on the amenities of their own personal spaces, the 150th had gotten its own Morale, Welfare, and Recreation (MWR) tent set up and running, which now had a big screen television (especially for local college sporting events), two smaller TVs for Xbox video games, a ping-pong table, and a pool table. But somehow the ping-pong table lacked paddles and balls, while the pool table didn't have any legs. There was always room for improvement. So, it was Gary Kinsey to the rescue again. On one of his many trips to other FOBs, Kinsey got to talking to a government contractor who had been there for a couple of years about how he had hundreds of guys who were slap bang in the middle of the desert on an FOB with very few recreation options. They were working or they were bored. Pushups, sit-ups, and running only went so far after all. What they needed was a gym. Well, the friendly contractor had just what he needed: two conexes of nautilus weight equipment. The good stuff. Another unit had ordered them but had departed before they arrived. A few days later the 150th now had a massive new gym. Outdoors there was volleyball (of the full-contact variety), and the desert served as a golf driving range. And there was Wiffle ball, for those who were not faint of heart. One problem was that many of the fielders sometimes couldn't see through the smoke of their cigars and cigarettes well enough to catch the ball. There wasn't yet a PX, but the soldiers themselves ran something of a small store selling items that they had bought or traded for while visiting the bigger FOBs. With the shortage of stock for sale, care packages from home were always a huge hit. And some of the stealthier families and friends learned to send liquor that had been placed into empty bottles of mouthwash to the guys.

While Kinsey and others were scrounging where they could, the higher level of contracting FOB improvements had become the bailiwick of Allen McDaniel. With a legal background and some proficiency in Arabic, McDaniel had seemed a perfect fit. So, ever so slowly, his job shifted from being assistant S-3 to working with contracts to keep the FOB afloat and supplied. His first great success had come in February, with getting approval from upper commands to gravel a particularly soggy part of the base. Even as a lawyer he found the process to be byzantine and inordinately difficult, but he learned the ropes and soon became a master of his craft. One of his first priorities was phones to keep the men in touch with their families. He knew that an adequate phone network was critical to maintaining morale. He decided to work the issue through both Army and Marine channels.

The Marine contracting team that McDaniel worked with was located in Fallujah, meaning that he was a frequent flyer on the trip northward. He soon befriended the Marine captain on site, and thought he had a deal worked out for several satellite phones. At the same time, though, he received word through Army channels that Dogwood had been approved for a trailer that contained 16 individual phone booths. What to do? Should he let the Marines know that he had gotten the Army phones? Or should he keep them in the dark and take their kind offer of satellite phones as well? When he walked back into the meeting with the Marine contracting officer, McDaniel came clean. The Army was giving Dogwood phones, so they could keep their own. The Marine broke out into laughter. He had long known that the Army was sending phones to Dogwood. He just wanted to see if McDaniel was going to be honest or not. From that point on, McDaniel and the Marine contracting officer were fast friends, with the Marine promising that he was going to look after Dogwood.

The Marines were true to their word. Soon the food situation at Dogwood improved with the arrival of a Mobile Kitchen Trailer (MKT), but Dogwood still lagged far behind the culinary amenities of the more developed FOBs. And the quality and quantity of food remained an issue. McDaniel also convinced an Iraqi market vendor in Fallujah to relocate to Dogwood to ply his wares. The market proprietor, known as Ferris, brought a small sea of pirated DVDs to the base, and sold televisions and all manner of electronics. He was always ready to make a deal, but also seemed to be a constant source of headaches for McDaniel.

One of the most important new buildings on the FOB was the chapel. Church services were always well attended, with worship remaining a high priority for the Mississippians, most of whom had been raised in very observant households. The chapel was named for Sean Cooley, and there were hymnals everywhere for singing – hymnals that Thomas Howell had "liberated" from the Marines. There was also an internet café so that soldiers were able to keep up with the home front better than ever before, which was something of a double-edged sword. Sometimes having such instant access reminded the soldiers too much of what they had left behind. Connectivity impacted all the soldiers at Dogwood, and all in different ways. Ken Cager knew that if he talked with his wife Audrey and his children Richard and Phillip too much, he would only become depressed by the thought of the important things that he was missing. And his men depended on him for their lives; he couldn't be effective if he was depressed.

Everyone used the phones, but one of the true regulars at the phone bank was Terrance Lee. He had a lot of people to keep up with. The person he called the most was his new wife Stephanie, checking up on her pregnancy. She was due in August, and Terrance just couldn't wait to be a father again. He would also call his older children, Terrance Jr. and Raemone. Terrance Jr. had started playing baseball, with Terrance Sr. serving as his coach before the unit had shipped out to Iraq. So, Terrance had to call to catch up on his son's latest sporting triumphs; and the kid was *good* at baseball. He also had standing calls to his grandmother Anice and mother Dinah every Thursday and Sunday, to let them know how he was doing and what the situation in Iraq was like. On the phone his grandmother and mom always sounded worried, but he would reassure them, saying, "I'm straight. Don't be worrying about me. I'm straight. Everything here is good." Like so many of the others at Dogwood, Terrance did not bother his family with tales of IEDs and loss. It was bad enough that they had to see those things on television. He and the rest of his Guard family did their best to keep their loved ones back home from needless worry. There was nothing that they could do to help, so why frighten them needlessly? But Terrance did ask for their help in one very specific way. Even with the MKT, Terrance detested the food at Dogwood. And what he wanted was quite funny. His brother Darius had been shocked when Terrance had come back from basic training with a taste for tuna straight out of the can. Terrance could never get enough of that stuff. And it grossed Darius out to no end. But the family kept sending him endless cans of tuna, with Stephanie especially sending Terrance case after case of his favorite meal.

MAINTAINING

Keeping the 150th's vehicles ready for their constant patrolling and missions was a deadly serious undertaking, with much of the work passing through the very capable hands of Jerry Bratu. Any shortfall in fueling or maintenance could be the difference between life and death for the combat companies. Below Bratu's level it was the duty of Norris Galatas as the platoon sergeant of the support platoon and his men to keep Dogwood stocked with precious fuel and to keep the vehicles topped up and ready. Fuel came in via convoys of massive tanker trucks, with Galatas and his section having to pump that fuel into their HEMTTs, which took hours. He saw to it that a 350-gallon-per-minute pump was magically scrounged up to do the job in minutes, not hours. He and his men ran the Dogwood fuel point, keeping the steady stream of vehicles ready for action. When not manning the fuel point, they, like everyone else at Dogwood, had other duties of manning the defensive outposts, or serving on quick reaction forces, or taking their HEMTTs to retrieve damaged vehicles.

The mechanics at Dogwood worked seemingly endless hours, tasked with guard duty and all the other base requirements, as well as maintaining the constant supply of broken-down equipment. The job was relentless. To John Voccio, who was in command of the tanks on loan from the 2/11th ACR, watching the Guard mechanics at work was watching true artistry in action. He had once wondered how bad it was going to be to serve with a Guard unit, but he was well past that by now. Voccio had been very unhappy to learn that one of his tanks had thrown a sprocket when it had been hit by an IED. Replacing a sprocket like that could take a whole day, perhaps more, depending on the situation. The Mississippians, though, knew a better way to get the job done – replacing it in record time using a method that Voccio himself had never before seen. The Mississippians really knew what they were doing.

At the center of it all was Larry Arnold. He wasn't a mechanic per se in the unit, but he was the resident gearhead whom everybody trusted. As Bravo Company went about its business, there was Larry, working alongside the mechanics and double checking everything on his beloved vehicles. When the vehicles rolled back in from patrol, there was Larry, whether he had been on the patrol or not, checking weapons, checking engines. And when the next patrol made ready to roll out, there was Larry, running all the pre-mission checks. Larry Mergenschroer recalled: "He was just out there like an old bulldog. And he made dang sure that every time we went out, we didn't have no problem with the vehicles or a weapon." As the oldest guy in the unit, Arnold had taken on the role of a father figure for many. It seemed that he could fix people's problems as well as he could fix an engine. He never yelled, like an officer might, but was always there to talk and lend a hand. It got to the point where the younger guys in the unit simply called Arnold "Pops," and had made him the dad in their expansive family of soldiers.

Even though conditions at Dogwood had improved, the overall situation in the AO continued to cause deep concern. On April 16 there was another IED strike, with only good luck keeping anyone from being badly injured or killed. Ken Cager recalled:

[With our more uparmored vehicles] we thought we were prepared; we thought we had the proper equipment, and again, I always told my guys, "Man, let's not get complacent. Let's not get lazy. Be vigilant." And what happened is when there was an intersection that we always used to either go left to go to the village or go right to go down towards Route San Juan. Right there you had this paved surface, and then it turned; it was like a T. And what happened: the tank decided he just wasn't going to go out to the – he wasn't going to stay on paved surface; he [was] just going to cut across, like, be lazy and just make that turn and just instead of going and pivot-steering and getting on the hardball, he just cut across, like, the soft shoulder of the road. So what happened: they had a daisy chain IED right there that we didn't know about, and there's no telling how many times we drove by it. And they had it buried; I mean, you couldn't even see it. Well, man, it took six road wheels off of that tank.

It was good fortune that it had been the tank that had hit the IED. Had it been a Humvee or an M113, the results could have been disastrous. But, with all the IEDs that had impacted the unit and the AO in previous weeks, everyone knew that it was only a matter of time before the 150th's luck ran out. And everyone couldn't help but wonder if they were going to be the next one blown up. Was it going to be this patrol, or perhaps the patrol tomorrow? Nobody knew when or to whom, but the next big one was coming.

TRAGEDY STRIKES ON MIDLAND

Captain David Martian had no reason in the world to ever think that he would serve with the Mississippi National Guard. He had grown up alternating between living in North Dakota and Alaska – pretty much as far from Mississippi as a person could get. He had joined the Army for a stint, but really wanted to be a teacher in the public school system in North Dakota. And for that he needed college. And for college, he needed money. There he was, standing in Dickenson State College looking to enroll, when he saw a poster proclaiming that service in the North Dakota Guard would provide free college tuition. Well, that was a no brainer, and he joined up. Martian hit a comfortable stride teaching and working with the Guard. Along the way he married Daniela and the couple had two children, Ashley and Trevor. Daniela was in the Air Force and got an assignment for pilot training, something everyone in the Air Force wants. So, it was off to Columbus, Mississippi, for that training, with Martian transferring to the 2nd Battalion, 114th Field Artillery out of Starkville so he could be near his wife as she trained.

It was just over a year later, on Mother's Day weekend 2004, when Martian got the word that his unit had been called up and would be going to Iraq. Within the 2/114th Martian served as the commander of Alpha Battery, which meant being stationed at FOB Lima outside the city of Karbala. The soldiers of Alpha Battery were the only Mississippians at Lima, serving alongside Marines and Iraqi forces. It was something of a lonely existence, but FOB Lima was largely quiet, which was a very good thing in Martian's view. There was real drama in early April, though, when a platoon of Alpha was directed to provide security for a convoy bound for Baghdad. That convoy wound up smack dab in the middle of the infamous terrorist attack on Abu Ghraib Prison, with five of Martian's men being wounded.

Other than the Abu Ghraib incident, life at Lima mainly meant working with the resident Iraqi battalion or running security for other convoys. On April 19, that meant running a convoy up to FOB Dogwood. As it turned out, FOB Lima was to be closed, and Martian's men were tasked with picking up two Marine officers from Dogwood who would oversee Lima's closure. Martian knew the route to Dogwood well and knew how dangerous it was. Army Service Road San Juan was the most utilized route into Dogwood, but it was a noted IED hotspot. And Martian knew full well that it was best to keep the insurgents guessing by taking different routes. So, for this mission he chose for the platoon-sized convoy to utilize Route Exxon and then Main Supply Route (MSR) Midland to make their way to Dogwood. Martian was in the second vehicle in the convoy, and it was just a normal day. The weather was actually kind of nice, and there was no traffic at all.

The sound of the massive IED strike really didn't register with Martian. It was much more what he saw. A blinding flash, followed by the uparmored Humvee in front of his vehicle being tossed into the air. The damn thing weighed over 10,000 pounds and had been tossed over 20 feet into the sky before flipping and landing with a crash upside down. Fire spewed forth from the stricken vehicle and its ammunition began to cook off, sending rounds in all directions. The spectacle took only seconds, but its awful majesty remains seared into Martian's mind.

The trailing vehicles in the convoy quickly stopped, and Martian and his men rushed to the flipped Humvee. Everyone quickly thought of Stephen Brooks. As gunner on the Humvee, Brooks had been atop the vehicle and had no doubt been crushed. Gunners hardly ever survived violent rollovers. Fire raged in the Humvee, and rounds were still cooking off. Only one door to the vehicle remained operational, so everyone inside had to be manhandled out of that single door – and it was agony for the wounded. But there was no way around it. One by one, the men were wrenched free of the wreck, with the last being Brooks. Somehow the force of the blast, or perhaps the airborne flip of the Humvee, had pulled him back into the vehicle before it had crashed to the earth.

The scene was one of horror. All the occupants of the vehicle – Terrance Elizenberry of Clinton, and Melvin Gatewood, Wyman Jones, and Stephen Brooks, all of Columbus – were badly burned. All had to be medevaced, and their injuries would take months of excruciating treatment for proper healing even to begin. Tommy Little, though, suffered the most grievous wounds: a broken arm, broken leg, broken ankle, puncture wounds to the shoulder and stomach – and he was paralyzed from the waist down. Little was first treated in Iraq, but then sent to Landstuhl Medical Center in Germany and then to Brooke Army Medical Center at Fort Sam Houston, Texas, where he died on May 2, 2005. A native of Aliceville, Alabama, Little was the youngest of 11 children and had joined the Guard after working at the cotton mill in Aliceville at the age of 24. Little's sister Idella said, "He loved that National Guard. We tried to talk him into resigning, but he never did. He'd get angry when we talked to him. And he didn't mind going overseas." Idella spoke to her brother only two days before he was hit by the IED, and she recalled, "He said, 'Bay, pray for me.' I said 'Tommy, is it that bad?' He said 'Bay, it's rough.' And that was the last time I talked to him." The family was able to see Little in the hospital before his death. And, while he could not respond to them, they all felt that he knew that they were there.

For David Martian and the survivors of his platoon, the war just chugged right along. Once the incident was complete, the convoy continued its mission to Dogwood, picked up the two Marines, and then returned to FOB Lima. The men of Alpha Battery united in prayer for Little and the others who had been wounded that day and kept up with reports on their conditions. It was weeks later when they learned that Little had succumbed to his wounds while in the hospital in Texas. The entire incident was a true wake-up call for Alpha Battery. And, with FOB Lima about to close, they could only hope that their next destination would be a safe one.

NORRIS GALATAS

Norris Galatas was proud of his service in Iraq – he and his men had done their main jobs of keeping the complex fuel situation in the unit under control. But they had also gone out on patrols and had manned many positions at FOB Dogwood. And he was the perfect person to keep the fuel flowing efficiently. He had a dogged determination and a very detail-oriented personality. Sometimes that combination came off

Bravo Company soldiers holding a banner signed by children from the Lucedale school district at their send-off ceremony. (Paul Lyon collection)

Larry Arnold (right), alongside his wife Melinda, his son Larry Arnold Jr. (left), his grandson Anthony and his daughter-in-law Tanya at the Bravo Company send-off parade in Lucedale. Arnold was killed in an IED strike on June 11, 2005. (Paul Lyon collection)

150th soldiers undergoing riot training at Camp Shelby before their deployment to Iraq. (Paul Lyon collection)

150th company commanders at the National Training Center. Left to right:
CPT Chris Thomas (Charlie Company), 1LT Paul Lyon (Bravo Company),
CPT Hap Palmer (Battalion Maintenance), CPT Ken Cager (Alpha Company).
(Paul Lyon collection)

MAJ Trent Kelly, 150th S-3, on a mission with Alpha Company.
(Paul Lyon collection)

Troops of the 150th Combat Engineer Battalion stand in prayer before crossing into Iraq in their convoy to FOB Dogwood. (Stanley Walker collection)

Hap Palmer, 150th Battalion Maintenance Officer, on a mission in a Humvee with hillbilly armor. (Paul Lyon collection)

SFC Sean Cooley petting a horse of the opposing forces at the National Training Center. Cooley was killed in action in an IED strike on February 3, 2005. (Paul Lyon collection)

Advance party of Bravo Company at FOB Iskandariyah. This is one of the last pictures ever taken of Sean Cooley (seated on right). (Paul Lyon collection)

The Humvee that was carrying Sean Cooley, seen after the IED strike of February 3, 2005. (Paul Lyon collection)

150th Battalion memorial service at FOB Dogwood for Sean Cooley. (Paul Lyon collection)

FOB Dogwood, seen from atop the battalion headquarters building.
(Paul Lyon collection)

1LT Mike Beal, platoon leader in Bravo
Company. (Paul Lyon collection)

An M1 Abrams tank of the 2/11th ACR
departing FOB Dogwood for a patrol.
(Paul Lyon collection)

SFC John Voccio, platoon sergeant of the 2/11th ACR tank platoon that was assigned to the 150th at FOB Dogwood, on a mission near the village of Owesat. (Paul Lyon collection)

LTC Roy Robinson, commander of the 150th, being awarded a Bronze Star by COL Leon Collins, commander of the 155th Brigade Combat Team. (Paul Lyon collection)

Members of the A&O Platoon at the National Training Center, with Robert (Mac) McNail standing in the center of the group. McNail was killed in a vehicular accident at FOB Iskandariyah on February 11, 2005. (Paul Lyon collection)

CPT Gary Kinsey and SFC Kevin Kelly training Iraqi soldiers for a mission at FOB Dogwood. (Paul Lyon collection)

SFC Norris Galatas of Headquarters Company. Galatas was wounded in an IED strike on April 19, 2005. (Janis Galatas collection)

1LT Thomas Howell (left) and 1LT Eric Kimbrough in the center, along with Alpha Company soldiers, standing with the contents of an arms cache that they had discovered. (Thomas Howell collection)

LTC Roz Morris (center) along with 2/11 ACR soldiers atop an M1 Abrams tank at FOB Dogwood. (Paul Lyon collection)

SPC Terrance Lee at the send-off
ceremony in Lucedale. Lee was killed
in action on June 11, 2005.
(Paul Lyon collection)

Stephanie Lee, wife of Terrance Lee,
at a postwar awards event that
highlighted her involvement in cancer
research and charity. (Photo by Gary
Miller/FilmMagic/Getty Images)

Iraqi interpreter Assim (left) working with Bravo Company commander CPT Paul
Lyon in the village of Owesat. Assim was killed in an IED strike on June 11, 2005.
(Paul Lyon collection)

Iraqi interpreter Joseph (right) working a mission with 150th troops in the village of Owesat. (Paul Lyon collection)

Bravo Company soldiers searching a vehicle at a roadblock outside of Owesat, just after the vehicle had backed up to the roadblock before the detonation of an IED. (Paul Lyon collection)

Charlie Company soldiers on operations after digging out a munitions cache. (Chris Thomas collection)

LTC Roy Robinson, commander of the 150th, at a combined planning session with the Iraqi Army in battalion headquarters at FOB Dogwood. Seated to the left are company commanders CPT Paul Lyon and CPT Ken Cager. (Paul Lyon collection)

Platoon leader Richard Rowland scanning for threats outside of FOB Dogwood. (Paul Lyon collection)

Alpha Company and the construction of Bottom Line near Checkpoint 100 using local contractors. (Thomas Howell collection)

Alpha Company soldiers on the banks of the Euphrates after a raid on Owesat. They are standing with one of the boats the insurgents used to cross the river to escape. (Thomas Howell collection)

SGT Chad Dauzat of Charlie Company of the 150th. Dauzat was wounded on August 19, 2005. (Greg Fernandez collection)

Greg Fernandez (right, kneeling) on operations with Charlie Company. Fernandez was wounded on August 21, 2005. (Chris Thomas collection)

The three sheiks of the Owesat tribe who came to meet with the leadership of the 150th on September 24, 2005. (Paul Lyon collection)

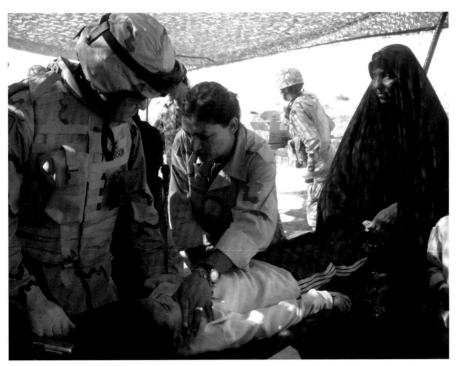

An Iraqi mother looks on as her daughter is treated by a US military physician during a MEDCAP mission in Owesat. (Paul Lyon collection)

Medic Joe Smith handing out toys to children on a MEDCAP mission in the Alpha Company area of operations. (Paul Lyon collection)

1LT Jay Standley (center), who took his platoon of Charlie Company of the 150th to Hit. (Paul Lyon collection)

2/11th ACR SPC Chang Wong, who was wounded by an IED on May 24, 2005, adjusting to his new prosthetic legs. (Photo by Myung J. Chun/Los Angeles Times via Getty Images)

Alicia McElroy (now Alicia Thornton) and Dane McElroy standing with a photo of James McElroy at a remembrance graveside ceremony. (Alicia Thornton collection)

as gruff to others, but the men he had known for a long time loved him for it. He didn't even seem to mind the nicknames – Eeyore or Uncle Fester were the two most popular. But whatever you did, everyone knew not to call him Galatas. He would bristle and huff, "My name is Norris. NOT Galatas."

Norris Galatas didn't have any reason to expect a day that was anything but ordinary. After being roused by his alarm, he ate a Danish and drank a Coke that he had secretly squirreled away for months out of sight of the others. It just seemed like a good time to drink it, even though it was kind of stale and very warm. As he finished the final fizzy drops, word came in that he and his men were needed. Bravo Company had responded to an IED strike on the 2/114th Field Artillery, set a perimeter, and called in the medevac chopper. It was the task of Galatas and his men to venture out in heavy trucks to retrieve the Humvee that had been destroyed. Galatas knew just what to do – jump in the Palletized Load System (PLS) vehicle. It was huge, armored, and fully capable of the job. But the PLS was still loaded with supplies that had been brought in the night before and had not yet been offloaded. It might have taken only 15 minutes to unload the PLS, but that was 15 minutes that Galatas didn't have. Instead, the team jumped into an unarmored HEMTT, and the convoy rolled out of Dogwood. An A-1 Abrams tank was in the lead, followed by a Humvee, then Galatas' HEMTT, followed by a second HEMTT in the rear.

Suddenly there was a shocking jolt, followed by a sound so loud that it seemed to be alive. The whole 10-ton truck seemed to jump into the air. Galatas immediately knew that it was an IED, yelling, "Fuck me! Fuck me!" As the truck settled back into place and rolled to a stop, Galatas wondered why he was covered in sand. Then he remembered; he had placed two sandbags in the floor of the HEMTT – his only protection against an IED. The sandbags had been blasted apart, throwing gritty sand into his eyes and hair. And he began to feel wet, which meant he was bleeding. Calmly, Galatas reached over and engaged the parking brake – years of habit had ingrained the motion into him fully. His door already seemed to be open, so Galatas began to make his way out of his stricken vehicle.

Many rushed to Galatas' side, including Hap Palmer and medics Winston Walker and Joe Smith. Palmer, assisted by Jeremy Utsey who had been sitting in the HEMTT alongside Galatas, helped Norris to the ground. Palmer later wrote in his journal:

> When Galatas hit the IED, it wasn't loud; it wasn't big. The whole thing was just sort of surreal. It all happened in slow motion. Robert stopped our wrecker. We were directly behind Galatas so we couldn't immediately see what damage had been done. I jumped out of the gunner's hatch and eased off the road to the left. I walked far enough out and could see the front axle was gone. That's when I ran to Galatas. One of the guys was pulling Norris out of the HEMTT. When I first got there, I helped them lay Norris down. As we laid him down, I saw blood spilling out of his back and onto my boot. Once we saw his back it didn't take long to see the gaping hole in his right buttocks. Blood was pouring out. I put pressure on his wound. I had to squeeze together the 3-inch hole with my hands and push down.

Galatas seemed stunned and was bleeding badly, but the two men could already hear Walker and Smith rushing to their side. Walker got there first and was worried when Galatas was unable to respond to his first questions. But then Galatas' eyes opened and he half-moaned, "My butt hurts." By that time the assembled medics had begun cutting Galatas' clothes off to get access to his wounds. Norris couldn't help but notice that one of the new medics was female. He looked at her and asked, "Aww, man. Do you have to cut them off?" When she replied that they indeed had to, Galatas turned a bit red in the face and told the female medic that he hadn't worn underwear that day. She laughed, and said, "Oh, that's all right. They are all small and scared."

Walker and Smith first tried to apply pressure to the gaping wound in Galatas' buttock, shoving an entire roll of gauze into his butt cheek to staunch the bleeding. Next it was on to wounds in his back and his legs. Walker also started a large-bore IV before a physician's assistant arrived at the scene. Palmer remembered:

> I lifted Galatas' shirt and found another big hole in his back. It looked like it was right over his spine in the middle of his back. Winston cut away the clothing around it too. Before we turned him and put him on the litter, Winston took an entire role of gauze (about the

diameter of a coke can) and placed it in the hole in his ass cheek. Norris was out of it, kind of incoherent. By the time the MEDEVAC bird arrived he was making sense again and being his usual cynical self. We were all scared to death that the shot to the back might've hit his spinal cord. We were relieved when he was able to cross his legs. I asked him what he wanted me to tell his wife Janis. He said very clearly, "that I'm alright." I was covered in blood and hydraulic fluid that had spilled on the ground while we knelt over Norris... [on the trip back to Dogwood after retrieving the vehicle] I was still terrified. I haven't ever been scared like this.

Everyone was relieved when Galatas moved his legs, but he had lost so much blood that they were in danger of losing him. Frantically, the physician's assistant looked at the assembled medics and asked if any of them had any Hextend, an experimental compound starch injection that was capable of arresting hemorrhagic shock for a limited time before lost blood could be replaced. Well, medics sure as hell weren't supposed to have Hextend. That type of thing had been restricted to use by doctors. But Joe Smith just happened to have Hextend. He had "liberated" some from the physician's stores after the loss of Sean Cooley. He was damn sure that he was going to have every tool at his disposal if they were needed on the battlefield to save a life. He figured that he could spend time answering questions after the life was saved. Smith reached into his medical bag and handed the Hextend to the physician's assistant. The assistant raised his eyebrows, hooked the Hextend up to Galatas' IV bag, and then told Smith that the two were going to have to talk about how he had gotten that Hextend later.

Back at Dogwood, Trent Kelly was working the radios and handling the reaction to the IED strike on Galatas. Once it became clear that there was a need for a medevac, and quickly, it was Kelly who put in the call. But the reply was that it was going to take over half an hour before a chopper could arrive on scene – half an hour that Norris Galatas did not have. Kelly was livid, but there was nothing that he could do. But there was a chopper en route to another incident outside of the 150th's area of operations. And the soldier it was rushing in to save had died of his wounds while the chopper was inbound. So that helicopter diverted instead to the site of the IED strike on Galatas, and arrived in under five minutes. That chopper carried a flight surgeon and blood for a transfusion. All of those events intersected to save Galatas' life. Galatas got a look at his HEMTT when he was loaded onto the medevac. He was damn lucky to be alive. The hood had been wrenched from the vehicle and the whole front wheel had been blown away – the entire wheel assembly was just gone. As the chopper made ready to take off, Galatas' friend Winston Walker patted him on the shoulder and told him that this was his ticket home. The nurse on the chopper was nice, assuring him that he would be at the hospital in less than 20 minutes. Once there, Galatas remembers being asked only a few questions about allergies before he passed out. His next memory didn't come until days later in Walter Reed Hospital in Washington, DC.

FURTHER LOSS

Even as the soldiers of the 150th labored to come to terms with the tragedy on ASR Midland, news filtered in of losses in the wider Mississippi Guard family in Iraq. On April 6 a guard tower caught fire in Mahmudiyah, badly burning several. On watch that night were troopers from the Headquarters Troop of the 2/11th ACR, who served alongside the Mississippians. Two of the most badly burned, Specialist Tyler Dickens and Private Casey LaWare, eventually succumbed to their wounds in Brooke Army Medical Center and Landstuhl Regional Medical Center respectively. Dickens was 20 at the time of his passing and was survived by his wife Elisha and the couple's infant son Austin. LaWare was a 19-year-old Californian who had joined the Army while still in high school. His family had been quite surprised that he had chosen to enlist due to his gentle nature. When all of his buddies had gone deer hunting he had always demurred; he just could not conceptualize shooting a living creature.

A few days later into April, the brigade phones and internet connection slammed shut yet again. To all, both in Iraq and back home in Mississippi, it seemed that the brigade's net was down almost more than it was up, causing constant worry and wonder regarding who would be receiving the surely devastating news. On April 22, an IED strike hit a patrol outside Iskandariyah, killing Specialist Kevin Prince of the 2/11th ACR. Prince was from Plain City, Ohio, and his grandfather was a World War II veteran who had talked him out of joining the Marines, but couldn't talk him out of joining the Army. Prince joined straight out of high school, where he had been a soccer star, and hoped to use his accruing benefits to attend college one day. He was 22 when he was killed, and his mother and father, Susan and Ron Prince, made it their duty to tell their son's story so that he would "not be just a number."

Only six days later a vehicle-borne IED detonated at a traffic control point in Diyarah, killing two more members of the 2/11th ACR, Captain Stephen Frank and Captain Ralph Hartling. Both soldiers were from Michigan, Hartling from Union Lake and Frank from Lansing. Both attended and graduated from West Point, Hartling in mechanical engineering and Frank in geography. Frank was survived by his widow, Laurel, and a two-year-old son. Hartling was survived by his widow, Jennifer, a two-year-old daughter, and a one-year-old son. Jennifer was pregnant at the time of his death and had her doctors induce labor so that the couple's new son would be there to welcome his father's body back home.

PROGRESS IN THE SOUTH

While so many losses rained down on the brigade, progress in the southern villages around Sharmia provided a needed tonic. On top of Operation *Flintstone*, which was going very well and resulted in the distribution of a wealth of vitamins and childcare products, the 150th had begun to collect candy and clothing, hoping to further improve the lives of the children of the region. However, the soldiers quickly learned to be careful with their candy requests. The village children tended to pop the entire piece of candy into their mouths, which was a problem when they first tried "fireballs." The hot candies were like nothing the kids had ever had before, often resulting in them crying and running away. But the lure of new candy always brought them back.

The next goal in the area was to adopt the local school, which was jam-packed with 100 children. The guys wrote home and requested school supplies of all types – notebooks, pens, pencils. And by April they were ready. Kevin Kelly recorded the first visit to the school in his journal:

We went into the school and talked to the teachers and handed the kids candy and stuff. They were very receptive. A very run down school that is packed with kids in very small classrooms with the desks you used to see on *Little House On the Prairie*, plus no air conditioning. After we finished with the teachers and kids in school, we went back to the streets and talked to a lot of kids and adults there. All they wanted was our watches, pens or sunglasses. I had a big green laundry bag over my shoulder full of candy and toys and everyone made fun of me saying that I looked like Santa Claus. But I've never seen Santa Claus delivering candy and toys in 110 degree Christmas Eve with sweat rolling out of every pore.

JOSEPH

As the war ground on, Joseph, the Bravo Company interpreter, made the decision to go home for one of his short leaves to get engaged. He had long debated the idea. He knew that his life was in danger every day on patrols outside of Dogwood. And he knew that his life would be in danger back home if anyone found out that he was working with the Americans. But he was in love and wanted to be married, so he decided to take the risk. Joseph took a military convoy to Kalsu, where he was met by his cousin driving a civilian vehicle, but with an AK-47 on hand for protection. But back in his hometown there was trouble afoot. His girlfriend's father had learned the truth of Joseph's employment. He was furious, and told Joseph, "I will not let this marriage happen, because your life is in danger working with the American troops. I'm not ready to give my daughter to a dead man." After rounds and rounds of arguing, it was decided. The couple could get engaged, but there would be no wedding until Joseph had survived his tour with the Americans at Dogwood.

When he returned to Dogwood, everyone was happy to hear Joseph's news, especially his best friend Assim, who also was an interpreter for Bravo Company. The duo was excited about the future and talked endlessly into the evenings. Assim wanted to know everything about Joseph's fiancée. How pretty she was, what her hopes and dreams were. And for his part, Assim was more than ready to talk with Joseph about his own hopes for the future. He had been talking to every American who would listen about his desire to go to the United States for college. Many of the Guard soldiers were very supportive of Assim's goals, even offering to put him in touch with people they knew at universities in their home state of Mississippi. Things were looking up for Joseph and Assim. While they were talking, there was a knock at their tent's door. It was Captain Lyon of Bravo Company. He had heard Joseph's good news and brought him a red blanket as an engagement present. Lyon had come to realize the special place that blankets held in Iraqi society, and Joseph loved his gift. He treasures it to this day.

RECOVERY

As the wheel of war slowly turned in Iraq, the life of Janis Galatas had been turned upside down. She had received a call at 10:15 in the morning on April 20 informing her that her husband had been badly injured by an IED attack. All she could initially learn from the phone call was that Norris was alive but had suffered severe injuries to his buttocks, midsection, and lower back. Twenty minutes later she learned more when Rickey Posey, a retired Guardsman and one of Norris' friends, called. He was heading the Family Assistance Center at the armory and gave her a complete rundown on her husband's condition and his impending move to Walter Reed Hospital in Washington, DC.

As usual after a major incident, all communications from Dogwood had been shut down. By now families had long since learned to worry when their communications with their loved one ceased. It was like a macabre lottery. Someone had lost a loved one killed or badly injured in Iraq. Where would the wheel stop? Who would get the call? This time it had been Janis Galatas. When communications came back up, Janis heard from many of those at Dogwood who had been closest to her husband, singing his praises and offering their well-wishes. She also heard from Lieutenant Colonel Robinson, in command at Dogwood. He told her in what high regard he held her husband and those who had saved him: "I truly believe that the overwhelming and immediate response saved his life. It is difficult to describe to someone; the reality here on the ground can be overwhelming when someone we care about so much gets into trouble, but these guys block all of that out and focus on the job they are trained to do. I just want you to know how proud I am of the soldiers who assisted, and how proud you would have been."

On April 25 Janis arrived in Washington, DC and saw Norris for the first time since he had left for Iraq. She recalled, "He looked dead. He was swollen like a toad and yellow. His eyes were closed, and the respirator was still breathing for him. I took his swollen, puffy hand and it felt like it could burst at any moment, so I just talked to him for a few minutes." It wasn't until April 27 that Norris woke up again:

Janis was the first thing I saw when I opened my eyes. She was holding my hand and looked troubled. She looked like she had been either crying or up all night. She asked me if I knew who she was, and I nodded … something was in my throat [his respirator] and I couldn't breathe. The next time I woke up my throat was sore and dry, and Janis was there. She asked me if I knew her, and I nodded again. She asked me this time if I knew where I was and I looked around me but didn't recognize anything. I knew it must be a hospital, but I didn't know where. I wondered if I was still in Iraq. I raised my hand to reach out for her, and she looked like I had just said "I love you" or something. I was still in a drugged fog and although she told me several times where I was, I was still in that world that was uniquely mine. She told me I was in bad shape and that I was at Walter Reed Army Medical Center in Washington DC. I had no clue and went back into my drug world. I just couldn't get it through my medicated brain where I was, but I wanted that damn thing out of my throat.

Norris had open wounds on his buttock and in his stomach, which had been left open with a drain and wound vacuum. He also had a colostomy bag. Norris was heavily sedated and drifted in and out of consciousness for several days. On April 30 he complained that he was itching and wanted to get the heck out of there. He told Janis that he was fine and was ready to get up and go. She told him that he had to stay in bed, that he wasn't fine. Well, that made Norris mad, so Janis went to dinner and warned the staff that they had better keep an eye on her ornery husband. The doctor just smiled and said, "Don't worry. He can't get up." When Janis returned an hour later, all the wires and tubes that were poking out of Norris had been switched around. She asked the nurse, "He got up, didn't he?" The nurse gave Janis a bit of a frightened look and said that he had gotten up and had tried to leave. So, they had put him back into bed and given him some extra medicine.

It wasn't until May 12 that there was much for the Galatas family to celebrate. Norris had moved to being fed through his IV, had expelled his first waste into the colostomy bag, and had stood on his own for the first permitted time. By May 17, there was more good news. They removed the packing and wound vacuum in his stomach. Janis got to watch the procedure and was amazed: "His abdomen was completely open, and his organs were tucked neatly into a mesh bag that make him look like a turkey about to be put into the oven on Thanksgiving!" Worse news came on May 19. Norris had awoken during his eighth major surgery and had vomited, resulting in stomach acid burning his lungs. For Norris Galatas it was back to an induced coma and back into intensive care. Back to square one.

By May 30 things were beginning to look up again, until a visit from Secretary of Defense Donald Rumsfeld, who was there to give Norris his Purple Heart. Janis knew that this was supposed to be a stirring and patriotic moment. But she didn't particularly feel that way. Rumsfeld had told her husband and all the other Guard soldiers back at the beginning of their tour that they weren't going to get uparmored vehicles. That they had to fight with the army they had. Well, she wished that it had been Rumsfeld and not her husband who had been driving around Iraq in an unarmored vehicle. A day later she brightened when she got a note from Lieutenant Colonel Robinson. The troops had just observed Memorial Day, which had focused Robinson's mind on the losses that the 150th had suffered. He wrote:

It is difficult to explain how a bunch of soldiers in a combat zone can be so emotional [after remembering their fallen in a ceremony at Dogwood], then after the ceremony they just wipe the tears away and return to their duties. I think it is safe to say that we are all forever changed by the experience, neither positive nor negative, just changed. I pray for Galatas every day and I feel a personal responsibility for everything that has happened while we have been here. That is just part of the deal. The guys are continuing to perform miracles, doing a lot with a little.

Janis returned to their home after 57 days with Norris in Walter Reed. Norris, though, was not cleared to go home until July 23, over 90 days since his wounding. And even then, he was just headed home for a visit. There were many more surgeries to come, so he would have to head back to Walter Reed after two weeks of convalescent leave. Norris was in his uniform and hobbling on a cane as he entered the aircraft for home. One of the passengers wouldn't take no for an answer and gave Norris his first-class seat. And he knew just what he was going to do next. Order a gin and tonic. And then keep ordering. When Norris got off the aircraft in Meridian, there were hundreds of people there cheering his return home. They treated him like a hero, but he thought otherwise:

But there were, you know, just tons of people there to greet me, and you know, they treated me like a hero. I wasn't no hero; I just happened to live through an ordeal that would have killed most people, but like I tell everybody that asks about the story, I said, "I'm stubborn and hardheaded." I said, "That's what kept me going was I wasn't going to die. I wasn't going to lay down and die."

5

No More Doors Left on the Hinges

SGT Wong with the 2/11th was injured when the tank
he was in hit an IED. Fragments shredded his feet...
I saw Wong just about every day with the rest of his
crew in the motor pool. He was a good kid. I'm tired of
all of this. I'm tired of watching kids get hurt! They say
you can get desensitized to it. I haven't. Every day you
either see it or hear about someone in the brigade that
either died or got hurt. I don't even like asking who it is.
I'm scared I may know them. Whether I know them or
not, it's exhausting hearing about it all the time. A guy
died last night over at KALSU from an IED with the
2/11th. Four guys were killed the same day SGT Wong
was hurt. They were with the infantry at Iskandariyah.
I'm tired of this shit! I want it to end!

HAP PALMER, JOURNAL ENTRY

SUPPLY AND DEMAND

At what seemed to be the very last link of the supply chain in Iraq, FOB Dogwood had improved, but was still in need of almost everything to make it a true military base. On top of the normal daily activities of counter-mortar patrols, presence patrols, raids on villages, and cache searches, there were also innumerable scrounging runs to bases all over the region. One of the favorite places to go scrounging was at the vehicle graveyard at FOB Duke. Many of the vehicles, though hit by IEDs or riddled with gunfire, still had parts that you might need. But after a visit there, Hap Palmer couldn't quite get the place out of his head. It had the same smell of oil, blood, and fire that he remembered from the day that Norris Galatas had been hit by the IED. He also was shocked that some of the vehicles were still covered in blood or contained body parts. He silently determined that none of the vehicles of the 150th would ever wind up that way.

On the return trip from Duke, Palmer's scrounging convoy was joined by some maintenance guys who were coming to Dogwood to work on some of the air-conditioning issues. The maintenance men were just kids in his view, and they were shit scared. So, they put them in the ninth vehicle in the convoy. No trouble back there. The convoy had just entered the 150th's AO, at the road junction known as Swiss Cheese Alley because of all of the IED craters, when an IED went off. And, of course, it went off on the maintenance men's vehicle. Happily, though, the IED had been set in a crater left by a previous IED. It was command detonated – set off by a person (often using a cell phone) instead of being set off by the pressure of a vehicle. Since the IED had been so deep in a crater its blast went straight up, and it was off the road next to the maintenance guys, not under them. So, while some of the guys were shaken, there were no injuries.

The difficulties of supplying Dogwood were made the clearest on May 12, when an IED hit a supply convoy, killing a Kellogg Brown and Root (KBR) driver who was hauling a generator to FOB Dogwood. Reuben Ray Miller was proud to be supporting the war effort in Iraq by driving for KBR. It felt like a calling to him. Known as "Scooter" to his friends, and a lover of Harley-Davidson motorcycles, Miller was known for keeping the rest of his KBR buddies entertained with tall tales. He paid the ultimate price to help keep FOB Dogwood operational.

On the same day the brigade internet and phone connections again went silent. An IED strike on a convoy outside of Iskandariyah killed Sergeant John Smith, who was serving with the 2/11th ACR alongside the Mississippians there. The Wilmington, North Carolina native had been in Junior ROTC at New Hanover High School before joining the Army. He had been in the 82nd Airborne before his transfer to the 2/11th ACR, and a number of his paratrooper buddies attended his funeral. Sergeant Sean Lee was asked what trait best defined John Smith.

Lee replied, in reference to a battle earlier in the conflict, "Courage. There were rounds firing all over the place; it was chaotic. I remember looking up to see where Smitty was, and he just had this grin on his face, so I started grinning too. You could draw your courage off him."

As the grim toll of war continued to mount, the efforts to supply Dogwood were indeed transforming the FOB. Soon Allen McDaniel had engineered through his Marine contacts in Fallujah the arrival of a KBR dining hall, complete with steaks and lobster from time to time. There was a well that produced non-potable water for washing clothes and vehicles. Its non-potable status didn't stop men from swimming in it, though. There was a complete weight room, softball games, and volleyball for recreation when there was downtime. There were even forms of risky recreation off-base. The Charlie Company executive officer had once heard that General Dwight Eisenhower had told his men during World War II to seize the day, because many of them would not survive to make it home. Seize the day. Lives were being cut short. Make the most of every minute. Around Dogwood that mantra meant that some of the guys would swim when they could in the deep Iraqi wells cut into the desert. For others, it meant fishing in the Euphrates with hand grenades. By now the seasons had changed and it was well over 100 degrees during the day, with sandstorms a real threat. If you left a tool out in the open sun and then grabbed it, you risked getting burned. Leaning on the hood of a vehicle risked the same.

Living conditions were still hit or miss – some lived in the converted old buildings and others in tents. The latrines still were old, steaming hot porta-johns. But everyone had access to cheap bootleg DVDs of the latest movies. Usually they had been filmed by someone sitting in a movie theater – so you just had to kind of ignore it when someone got up and walked in front of their camera. There was even a massive tent that could hold battalion formations. At this rate, helicopters would soon start landing at FOB Dogwood.

TURNING THE TABLES ON OWESAT

In the Bravo Company sector, the village of Owesat remained the largest sore spot of the entire battalion. Everyone knew that the village was shot through with insurgents – the same insurgents who had killed and wounded so many across the AO. But there was no way to get the drop on them. There were far too few Mississippians to take and hold the village. And raids on the village netted nothing, since the insurgents saw them coming, crossed the river, and could not be fired upon. But Robinson, in conjunction with Jerry Bratu and Bravo Company, had come up with an idea. In the planning, Bratu's experience as a police officer was of great importance. He and Bravo Company commander Paul Lyon would often sit into the night conversing about how to crack the insurgent nut that was Owesat. And there seemed to be a weakness. Owesat and its fertile surroundings were nestled into a curve in the Euphrates River. The village had but one main road, one that sat on a raised dike and hugged the riverbank. All traffic into and out of the village used that single road. And, since it was on the far side of the village, away from FOB Dogwood, its traffic was largely unmonitored. The idea was to use bulldozers to cut that dike road to both the north and south of Owesat, making it impassable. Then traffic into and out of the village would have to divert through the Army service roads that ran through the desert between Dogwood and Owesat.

On May 14 the bulldozers rolled in, cutting 30-foot-wide gaps into the dike road at points where the road traversed marshes. Nobody was going to use that road again until it was laboriously rebuilt. The Mississippians were also sure that the dike road was a major artery for the transfer of weapons to the insurgents, so cutting it would be a significant blow to their supply lines. Traffic the next day began to divert into the desert, where the soldiers could keep a better eye on it. And everyone got the feeling that the insurgents were going to react violently to the changed state of affairs. As things were beginning to change at Owesat, the 150th went through a significant change as well, as S-3 Trent Kelly was transferred to work at FOB Kalsu to train Iraqi forces. As a professional soldier, Kelly understood and did what the Guard needed, but he was going to miss his brothers in the 150th greatly.

HELP FOR MOHAMMED

In the southern part of the AO, Alpha Company was still working to expand its humanitarian operations. On May 14 a patrol cordoned off a tiny village of just seven houses and began handing out candy and searching for any contraband. The Americans were in for quite a show.

One of the local cows took their visit as a time to run in circles mooing excitedly, with the local Iraqis cheering her on and throwing dirt clods at her to make her run faster and moo even more. The cow was joined by a featherless, extremely ugly chicken and her many chicks, which added their noise and frenzied antics to the mix. Like magic, a three-legged dog then turned up, and a sheep stampede followed.

After the farmyard displays were complete, the group moved off to a new house where they saw a small boy, perhaps seven years old, with his parents. The parents started talking in animated tones before lifting their son's robe. The guys were horrified to see that the lad had no penis, and that his bladder was hanging outside of his body and had flies buzzing around it. The parents were plainly at their wits' end as to how to best help their child. Captain Cager and his men promised to report on the situation to their doctors and see what could be done.

Three days later the soldiers of Alpha Company returned to the home, with a doctor and an interpreter. It turned out that the child was named Mohammed and that he had been this way since birth. The doctor examined the child carefully and took pictures, informing his mother that he was going to try to get him treatment at an American military hospital in Baghdad. Mohammed's mother collapsed to the ground in tears. Plainly this was the first time that she had dared to hope for a normal life for her son. A week later, on May 21, the big day arrived for Mohammed. Kevin Kelly recorded the scene in his journal:

Today started out with an early wake-up to go pick up Mohammed at his house. When we got there this morning early, he was up, dressed and ready to go with his little backpack over his shoulder. His dad was outside and came up to us and you could just see the joy in both of their faces. We took them to the HUMVEE to put them inside and we told the father that we hated to do this, but we would have to blindfold him until we got to our FOB. He said he understood. We headed back and got back to the FOB and we took them to the aid station to wait for the helicopter. People were coming in and out to greet them and to see the boy everyone had been talking about. They brought him a coloring book, SFC Arthur had brought him some matchbox cars, others brought toys, food, Gatorade, and even money. It was like Christmas for the little boy. When I got back, he was watching the *Polar Express* on someone's laptop and eating a sucker. The father pulled the interpreter and I to the side and told me that he never thought that there could be so much generosity, thoughtfulness, and humanity shown to someone from another country and especially since there was a war. He then told me that Mohammed couldn't go to school because little kids made fun of him, and also no one would really play with him either. He just kept saying *Shukran* (Thank You) over and over. I just told him that if I was in the same situation that I would want him to do the same for my son. We finally got up to the top of the hill when the helicopter was due. LTC Robinson came out to meet both of them. Before he came out there, Clay had asked the little boy if he was ready to go on the helicopter and he said very quickly, NO. Everyone laughed and he just smiled. The helicopter flew in and I carried his bag to the bird and helped him in. I then handed him his backpack that was full of little green apples to eat and all the stuff everyone had given him. He just kind of threw up a hand and waved and that was all the thanks we needed. The bird took off and our little boy was headed to Baghdad. I remember Clay coming up to me and saying, "If that doesn't get to your heart, something is wrong with you."

INTO OWESAT

Three days later, the battalion ran a dual-purpose mission into the insurgent hotbed of Owesat. A double-strength cordon would seal off the village, followed by a house-to-house search for terrorists, while on the outskirts of the village soldiers distributed blankets, school supplies, and care packages, and a medical team handed out medicine, wheelchairs, and walkers. If the insurgents couldn't be caught, perhaps a softer hand was needed to win over the local populace. Plainly the Americans were still regarded with distrust, with only 25 villagers showing up to take part in the bonanza.

The search of homes in Owesat followed the same frustrating pattern as every day previous. The men were gone, presumably having taken boats or swum across the Euphrates upon word of the soldiers' approach. As interpreter for Bravo Company, Joseph could tell that the pressure was building. There had been so many losses, and yet no insurgents had paid the price. In searching one home, he became suspicious.

There were only a mother and young child present, but the home seemed like it had recently housed more people. Joseph asked the woman where her husband was, and she replied that he had been killed by insurgents because of his service in the Iraqi Army. Joseph told her that he believed her, but later gave her son a piece of gum and asked him where his father was. The boy replied that he had left ten minutes ago and crossed the river.

The house was indeed the home of an insurgent, but the only people left were an innocent wife and child. There was nothing to be done. In another home a woman spoke up. Her family did have a weapon (each home was allowed one weapon), but, she said, the terrorists had more. She waved her arms, indicating the other homes in Owesat, and said, "Most of the people here are working with the terrorists. They help them. The terrorists stay in their houses." With Larry Odom and others of Bravo Company listening, Joseph asked the woman why everyone cooperated with the insurgents. She raised her voice and almost screamed, "Because they are dangerous, and they kill us. If we cooperate with you or the Iraqi forces, they will kill us. So, we have to work with them or die. There is no other way." Odom wiped the sweat away from his brow as the temperature rose past 110 degrees. Some of his men had clumped into what shade was available from the buildings. But all were at a loss. The insurgents seemed to be hitting them harder every day, but even cutting the road into and out of Owesat had made no difference. The elusive terrorists always escaped, leaving behind only their human hostages. Suddenly the ground shook, and there was a roar like thunder. Another IED.

CHANG WONG

Chang Wong had moved to the United States with his parents from Malaysia at the age of two. It was not until he was a senior in high school that Wong had received his coveted Green Card. With his new status he hoped to attend Pasadena City College in his now hometown. Sadly, though, the tuition was too high, so Wong decided to take a year off to save money before trying again. Some of his high school buddies were in the same financial boat and had joined the Army for its educational benefits. In 2001, those buddies convinced the newly graduated senior to join them in the military. It seemed a great idea to

Wong – adventure, college money. Heck. It was all good. His mother cried when she heard the news, but Wong had made up his mind.

Wong wound up in Voccio's platoon of the 2/11th ACR and was the gunner of one of Voccio's tanks on the raid of Owesat that day. Wong's tank hit an IED. Wong was hit by a rush of heat, but he didn't feel any other impact, so he decided to stand up and get out of the tank. But he couldn't. Then he looked down. The lower part of one leg was crushed and dangling at an odd angle; the other was simply gone.

Joseph Hammonds, a Guardsman from Sand Hill, Mississippi, was riding in the convoy behind Wong's tank when the IED hit. He couldn't believe his eyes. Two massive road wheels came flying off the tank, and shrapnel of all kinds arced through the air and began to pummel Hammonds' Humvee. Medics rushed to the scene and pulled Wong's mangled body from the tank. The loader and tank commander had also suffered shrapnel wounds, while the driver had torn a ligament in his shoulder. The medics first worked on Wong, who was deep in shock, and tied tourniquets to both of his legs. Wong and two other wounded crewmen were evacuated to Baghdad by a medevac chopper.

Once in Baghdad, Wong's condition worsened dramatically. Although he had taken no shrapnel to the torso, the immense concussion of the IED blast caused his lungs to begin failing due to acute respiratory distress syndrome. Wong was dying. Desperate for a life-saving solution, the doctors hooked Wong up to an interventional lung assist device known as a Novalung – a machine that allowed gas exchange in the lungs via simple diffusion. The device was entirely experimental, only having been used on a total of 100 patients worldwide. Even though the device had not received US approval for use, Wong was the third soldier sent home from Iraq with the device.

Next it was off to Germany for more treatment; the doctors were hoping to stabilize Wong's lungs and legs enough to allow him to be transferred to a hospital in the United States. While in Germany, Wong was visited by his parents and, even though he remained in a coma, he was awarded his American citizenship. After three weeks in Germany, Wong's ventilation tube was removed so that he could finally speak to his parents again. Then he was off to Texas for further treatment. Now, with his mind free of the fogging effect of the worst of the pain medication, Wong was left to confront the rest of his life as a double amputee. He was in his mid-20s and both of his legs were gone below the knees. Fearing what the remainder of his life could become, Wong slipped into a depression – nothing that his parents and friends could lift him out of. Wong remembered, "I had a hard time sleeping. I didn't want to go to sleep because I was afraid that I wouldn't wake up."

TRAGEDY IN THE SOUTH

Even before the 150th had really begun to deal with the IED strike on the tank, news filtered in that a patrol of the 155th outside Haswa had been hit by yet another massive IED, killing four. Haswa was just south of the 150th's AO and was another noted IED hotbed. The news hit the soldiers of the 150th hard – many had served on several occasions with the men who had been killed. And some were close friends.

Sergeant Saburant "Sabo" Parker had worked at a lumber yard in Angie, Louisiana, and had spent time on the Southern Championship Wrestling circuit. Parker was a 16-year Guard veteran. He had met his wife, Kitza, in Columbia, Mississippi, and had transferred over to the Mississippi Guard. The couple had two children together, Merissa and Sheliah, and the group loved fishing together. One source of friction in their marriage, though, was Sabo's choice of music – Bluegrass. Kitza recalled, "He loved bluegrass music and tortured me with it."

Bryan Barron was from Biloxi, where he and his wife Amanda lived with her daughter Haley. The couple had a child of their own during basic training at Camp Shelby before the trip to Iraq. Like Sean Cooley, Barron was a practical joker. He had joined the Guard just in time to make it to training for the Iraq mission. His sister, Jodi, remembered how gung-ho he was about his service and how he had planned on making the National Guard his career.

Audrey Daron Lunsford, whom everyone just called Daron, was from Sardis in northern Mississippi. After high school, Lunsford had been a police officer and had served a stint in the Army before joining the Guard in 2004, just as the call for mobilization came in. He had met his wife Vangi while on the police force, and the couple had been married two years before he shipped out. The pair had their first child, Paris-Audrey, during training at Shelby, and, even though she wasn't talking yet, Daron called her every day from Iraq, often talking her to sleep at night. He even sent Paris-Audrey emails that she wouldn't be able to read for years. One of his final emails read,

"I'm counting the days until I can be with mommy and you, but until then, keep mommy busy and stay that beautiful little angel that I love and cherish."

Daniel Ryan Varnado was from Saucier in the southern part of Mississippi. He was known through high school and college as one of the bright young baseball stars of the state. Former teammate Dale Young remembered that "Watching Danny play was watching magic." He had hopes of going pro after college but had joined the Guard to serve and protect his country in the aftermath of the terrorist attacks of 9/11. He was survived by his wife, Sharon, and his two-year-old son Cannon.

Brigade communications had just come back up, when a mere three days later they were shut down again when an IED went off, hitting a Humvee outside of Diyarah, killing Sergeant Mark Maida of the 2/11th ACR. The Madison, Wisconsin, native had already completed his military service, but had been called back to action as part of the stop-loss program, which extended terms of service in time of military need. Maida was a consummate outdoorsman, and loved to hunt, fish, skydive, and listen to Lynyrd Skynyrd. After service in Iraq he planned to marry his sweetheart and enroll in a local college. Plans that were never to be realized.

STILL A TALE OF TWO CITIES

Even as the situation around Owesat became ever more deadly and frustrating, just a few miles to the south the population by and large continued to be supportive of the American presence. The 150th formally adopted Albaroodi and Albrodey schools and adopted a small clinic near Checkpoint 100 – the main road intersection in the area. Kevin Kelly recorded in his journal:

> We went on a mission into the village today to deliver school and medical supplies. Our first stop was the medical clinic. We gave them so many medical supplies to stock up their pharmacy and medicine cabinets. I've never seen so much stuff getting unloaded off the truck to give to them. The doctor was very appreciative. We then moved to the school and had a lot of stuff we gave them. We put everything in the middle of the school yard. There was no

control of the situation and before you know it, there was stuff thrown everywhere and kids running around crazy. It looked like a tornado had come through and stuff was everywhere. I pulled out my Santa Claus bag and was handing out candy. I had my own little following. I bet there was 20 kids following me around saying, Mister, Mister. We then went to the next school. When we got there, we did the same thing with all the school supplies, but this was much better organized. At one point, though, the line started pushing and started grabbing things, but the teacher went into the office and brought out a limb that was about 3 foot long. The kids ran like crazy. One kid wouldn't leave, so the teacher made him hold out his palms and he hit him with the switch. Once we left the school, we visited a few more places in the village. We actually had one guy that ran from us, so we tried to catch him. He ran toward the Euphrates River between some houses and I guess he swam to get away. I walked all the way to the edge and like to have slipped in, but no way was I swimming after him.

Everyone was also cheered by news about the child Mohammed. Doctors in Baghdad had examined him and confirmed that they would be able to undertake surgery to place his bladder safely inside his body. However, the doctors also had identified Mohammed as a hermaphrodite – he had organs of both sexes, but neither were fully developed. Surgery to correct the situation was possible but would have to take place in a much more advanced hospital, preferably in the United States. Although the news was mixed, Mohammed's progression was a tonic. Maybe the soldiers were doing something good and lasting in Iraq despite all the loss. Mohammed's first surgery was scheduled, and the unit got down to the business of raising money to send him to the States for the more complex procedure.

A GIFT FOR ASSIM

By this time Joseph's best friend among the Iraqi interpreters, Assim – whom the Americans called Ron – had become great friends with the Mississippi soldiers. They had all found out that he was only 17 by this point, and many had taken him under their wings as father figures. Assim was so enthusiastic and dedicated to the cause of a free Iraq.

He hung around the Americans more and more, constantly asking questions about their homeland and expressing his desire to enroll at an American university. Of course, the various supporters of Southern Mississippi, Mississippi State, and Ole Miss all tried to win him over to their chosen school. And it didn't hurt that Assim was great at his job. He was skilled at interacting with the local Iraqi citizens, and the Americans always knew that he had their backs if anything ever started going sideways.

Assim so admired the Americans that he did his best to replicate their attire. Somehow, he purchased his own body armor and uniform, in part so the insurgents couldn't pick him out of the crowd. He had even acquired a holster for a pistol, and he told everyone that all he needed to complete the ensemble was the pistol itself. The Mississippi soldiers were impressed with Assim's ingenuity – he looked great. But they informed him that policy restricted interpreters from carrying arms. There would be no pistol. Assim looked crestfallen, but he understood. For the next few days of missions he just carried that empty holster. But a few days later a pistol magically appeared in the holster. The guys took Assim aside and told him again that a pistol, though it looked wonderful on him, was not allowed. Assim then took the pistol from its holster and pulled the trigger. It was a cigarette lighter. Looked a hell of a lot like a pistol, but it was just a lighter. And Assim could get much more than a lighter that looked like a pistol. If the Americans wanted anything – DVDs, electronics, souvenirs – he was the man who could get it for them.

Assim's birthday was in late May, and the guys had a great gift for him. His own car. There was an entire small junkyard of cars at Dogwood that had been confiscated by units that were there before the 150th arrived. Nobody used them; heck, nobody even owned them. So, a couple of the guys got out their tools and whipped one of the vehicles into shape, and Assim got the best birthday gift ever. The following weekend Assim used one of his break periods to drive the car home to show his family. But then he returned by convoy and without the car. The guys all poked fun at him: "We gave you that car and you went home and sold it!" Assim told them that he had left the car with his brother to use, and that his brother would keep it safe. But the whole time there was a gleam in his eyes, so many still suspected that the car was long gone.

LARRY ARNOLD

The rising level of insurgent activity in the northern sector of the AO, especially around Owesat, concerned Larry Arnold. He had a sneaking suspicion that things were going to get worse before they got better. But in his communications home to his wife Melinda and his sons Larry Jr. and James, Larry remained breezy and conversational. He often talked about how great it was to be there in Iraq with his other son Robert. The two were a big help to each other. He also often mentioned his position as father figure to the guys, given that he was 46 and many of the soldiers were 19 or 20. He felt a deep need to protect these guys – to keep them safe. That was part of his near obsession in making sure that each of their vehicles was in the best shape possible. When speaking to his family about missions, Larry didn't focus on the potential danger involved. Instead, he focused on the good that they were doing for the Iraqi people. The children especially were so poverty-stricken and needy. And, from handing out vitamins to providing school supplies, Larry and his comrades were making the kids' lives better a little bit every day.

As June began, the Arnolds had something extremely exciting to talk about. Robert was coming home on leave. He had thought about postponing his leave to take some extra training with the Marines. However, the luck of the draw had him slated to go home in June, so he decided to stick with it. Melinda was so happy to hear that Robert was coming home. She rarely showed it, but the strain of having a husband and a son in a war zone was debilitating. So many had already been lost to either death or horrible wounds. But at least Robert would be safe for a short while. When Robert got on the chopper for the flight to FOB Anaconda, his dad Larry was there. They hugged, and the chopper took to the skies. Larry and others had told Robert to only pack a single uniform. It was a quick trip, there was limited space for luggage, and he would be wearing civilian clothes at home anyhow. One uniform was plenty. But one of the guys on the chopper didn't seem to like the flight all that much and puked his guts up. With the door open and the wind from the rotor blades whooshing all around – well, that puke went everywhere. Robert couldn't believe it. One damn uniform, and now it was covered in puke. Fortunately, at Anaconda he scrounged up a PT uniform and had time to get his one uniform cleaned. But the trip home was not off to a good start.

TERRANCE LEE

Nobody had been more excited to see that Dogwood had received a "liberated" set of Nautilus weight equipment than Terrance Lee. He and his platoon leader, Mike Beal, became workout buddies, constantly pushing each other to lift more and get in better shape. There was good-hearted ribbing about who was getting stronger faster, each determined to outdo the other. Ricky Tyler, Lee's team leader, was impressed with the result, thinking, "That dude is a stud. I'm glad he is on my team." Lee was already known across the unit as the guy who would just not stop smiling no matter the situation. He was also the weapons guru – the dude could fix anything that ailed pretty much any weapon. But he became best known as the guy you could always find in the weight room. He and a couple of his buddies, often Voccio's tankers, lifted religiously and often had competitions with each other. Something had drawn Lee to the tankers; they had bonded, and they often hung out outside of the weight room, usually playing video games or minor level gambling on cards.

On the evening of June 10, Lee and the tankers were playing cards and telling tall tales. And, even with Roz Morris' best efforts, there were cigars being smoked in that room, so the air hung thickly. As the game neared its end, someone brought up the now legendary story of Christopher Dueitt. A month back Dueitt had gotten hold of a green smoke grenade and had bombed one of their card games, leaving everyone to run out of that particular card game coughing up lungfuls of green smoke. On this night there was no prank smoke attack, and Lee excused himself early to go and call first his grandmother Anice and then his wife Stephanie. He chatted with Stephanie awhile as married couples do, asking after each other and talking about the children. Terrance always liked to check in regarding his oldest son's baseball games. Terrance Jr. was going to be a star, it seemed. As the call neared its end, Terrance got around to some important details. He had finally finished the paperwork to make Stephanie the beneficiary of his life insurance. He also told her that he had set up a special savings fund for her, "in case something happens to me." It was the first time that Terrance, always so happy-go-lucky, had expressed anything like fatalism or fear for his future. Stephanie jokingly reprimanded him. She was glad for his work on the insurance policy, and any savings account made her happy. He was a good steward of his and the family's money. But he was going to be fine, and they would spend that money together once he returned. Terrance agreed and then let her know that he had to hang up and turn in. He was headed out on a patrol the next morning and needed to get some sleep.

TRAGEDY

On June 11, Bravo Company's task was to head to a village in the northern part of the AO that was not often visited given the constant need to keep a wary eye on the insurgent-dominated village of Owesat. Since his unit didn't often go to this location, Captain Paul Lyon reasoned that there might be the discovery of a cache. So, on that day the Public Affairs Officer (PAO), Danny Blanton, and a cameraman accompanied Bravo Company, hoping to take some pictures and develop a writeup on what was found. Normally Assim rode with Lyon on such missions as his interpreter. But, because the PAO and cameraman were in the vehicle, Assim was going to have to ride with some of the guys in an M113. For Assim that wasn't a problem at all; he made a beeline for the 113 that was going to carry his friends Larry Arnold and Terrance Lee. He loved talking to those guys, so it was going to be a great day. For his part, Larry Arnold wasn't even supposed to be going on the mission. His platoon leader, Lieutenant Mike Beal, had taken Arnold's name off the list that day. At 46, Arnold was older than most of the company, and Beal figured that he could use some rest after having run a long mission the day before. But Arnold told Beal that he was good to go; he wanted to do his duty just like everyone else.

Voccio led the way in his tank, followed by Lyon's Humvee and three M113s. Lyon got on the radio to Voccio to remind him that the route north would be through the desert and to take care not to cross tracks in the sand left by any previous patrol. That was where insurgents just loved to bury IEDs. Voccio responded in the affirmative, and the convoy headed out. Hap Palmer was standing there as the vehicles made their way out of Dogwood. As they filed past, he couldn't help but think how brave these kids were. Most of the guys in the vehicles were young guys. After missions and on downtime they liked nothing more than to do what other folks their age did – play video games. In a more peaceful world that is exactly what the guys would be doing, playing video games, going to school, and going out at night to meet girls. But in Iraq they faced death each day and did so without flinching.

As the patrol made its way north, Voccio couldn't help but feel sorry for the guys driving behind his tank. The treads and the huge turbine engines of the tank churned up quite a dust storm in its wake. And on a hot, windy day like today, those guys were going to be covered in sand. In the northern villages there was really nothing of interest – they searched a few houses, and talked to some women and children about why their husbands and fathers weren't there. The usual. And no caches were found. Just a boring day. On the way back to Dogwood, the patrol went a different route, being assigned a new counter-mortar mission. In Lieutenant Beal's M113 Beal stood in the gunner's position, with Michael Martin driving and David Landrum sitting to his side. Arnold and Lee were seated at the far back, staying as far away from the incoming dust as possible. Assim was seated just a bit further forward. Their day was coming to an end, and dinner and a rest were on their minds. When Beal looked back, he saw Lee and Arnold both fast asleep. It had been another long, hot day with little to show for it.

Driving through the desert meant dealing with hills. And Voccio's tank, with its greater power, was pulling a bit further ahead of what the other vehicles were able to manage. Then Voccio started up a particularly large hill, and Lyon made ready to call him to slow him down somewhat. That tank could plow straight forward and was doing exactly what it was supposed to do in avoiding whenever possible the tracks of previous patrols. But this hill was so steep that Lyon's driver had to veer outside of the tank's tracks to make it up the hill, and the rest of the patrol followed. In so doing, the Humvee crossed the tracks of a previous patrol. Lyon couldn't help but shudder, but nothing happened. Maybe they had gotten lucky. Lyon passed the spot; the next Humvee passed the spot. Luck did seem to be with them. But when the M113 carrying Arnold, Lee, and Assim reached the spot, there was a huge explosion. Mike Beal didn't even have time to register a blast, or heat, or anything. He was just flying through the air, having been blown out of the gunner's turret of the M113. He landed with a thud atop the stricken vehicle, knocked out.

The patrol came to a quick halt, with everyone taking care. Where the insurgents placed one IED they often placed others. Lyon, along with Marty Davis, turned to look from their Humvee and saw sand and smoke rising from the M113, but it had not been torn to shreds like in previous IEDs. Maybe everyone was okay. Quickly a defensive perimeter was formed, and rescuers rushed back to the stricken vehicle. Among the first to the scene were Lyon, Davis, Voccio, and medic Joe Smith. Davis had been part of many deadly scenes as a member of the Mississippi Highway Patrol, and he knew that in such scenarios the most valuable thing he could do was to remain calm amidst crisis and provide leadership. And they could hardly believe the scene that awaited them. Atop the vehicle lay Beal, shaking uncontrollably. He seemed almost in a fog but quickly recognized Lyon and the others running up, even though to him they seemed to be moving in slow motion. He shook his head to clear the massive cobwebs further and joined in the search of the vehicle. The explosion, caused by a 155mm artillery shell hooked up to a pressure plate, had gone off directly under the rear quarter of the M113 and would have thrown shrapnel all through the vehicle, killing everyone. But weeks before at Dogwood the M113 had been augmented by hillbilly armor, a 5/8-inch-thick steel plate welded beneath the rear of the vehicle where troops rode. That plate had held the shrapnel at bay, but its welds had given way, bending the steel plate upward with a massive crushing force.

First the group found David Landrum, whose left leg was crushed below the knee and was dangling at an odd angle. He was in horrific pain, but he would survive. Next, they got Michael Martin out of his driver's seat. He was dazed, but miraculously otherwise unharmed. Smith and Voccio then attempted to open the back door of the 113, but the crumpling armor had jammed it. Next, they scrambled to the top hatch where they were able to reach Arnold and Lee. Mike Beal joined in but felt all the strength leave his body as he saw the scene. The massive force of the blast had crushed much of Lee's skull and had blown off one of his legs. Smith took some grim solace that Terrance Lee, that constantly smiling presence, had died instantly, never knowing a moment of fear or pain. Larry Arnold almost certainly had a broken neck, had all his teeth blown out, and had a host of other broken bones, but he was still breathing. The men, though, could not reach Assim. The mangled armor didn't allow them access to him through the top hatch, but they knew that he was in there. So, Voccio crawled over to the emergency hatch and opened it. There was Assim. The crumpled armor had pinned the lower part of his body. He didn't have a pulse that Voccio could feel, and, although he figured it was useless given the state of the armor, he gave Assim's body a tug to see if it could be pulled free. Voccio was surprised when the body moved easily, and when he got Assim through the escape hatch he discovered why. One of his legs had been shorn off above the knee by the force of the armor's crumpling. After placing Assim on the ground, Voccio went back inside the tortured 113 and retrieved his leg.

Two were KIA, and Larry Arnold was in deeply critical condition. With the perimeter up, Lyon put out the call for a medevac chopper. Hopefully Arnold could be saved. But it was plain that he had massive internal injuries and was having great difficulty breathing. Hoping against hope to buy Arnold time, Smith performed an emergency tracheotomy, allowing Arnold to breathe more freely. He turned to Lyon and yelled that the chopper had better get there soon; he didn't know how much more time Arnold had. But Lyon could hardly believe it. The damn choppers from Baghdad hemmed and hawed about coming. There was a sandstorm brewing and a landing zone in the area might be hot and under fire. Lyon was nearly frantic. Time was the most precious commodity, and the choppers were wasting it. Should Arnold be placed in another vehicle and be taken to Dogwood? Just then the news arrived: the choppers were inbound. But 20 minutes had been lost. The men had set up a landing zone for the chopper, but it landed instead atop a nearby hill 500 feet from where the casualties were.

The chopper carried a doctor from Baghdad who got out to assess the situation. Assim and Lee had passed, so they were not his issue. He went straight to Larry Arnold, who still had Joe Smith kneeling at his side. The doctor took Arnold's pulse on his fingertip and, finding none, pronounced him dead. Medevac choppers were for the living, not the dead, so Arnold would have to be loaded up along with Assim and Lee and taken by vehicle back to Dogwood. Smith looked up and told the doctor that Arnold did have a pulse, but it needed to be checked at his neck. It might be faint, but it was still there. Smith and Lyon both pled with the doctor, and Lyon was pretty sure that some of the guys in his unit were ready to beat that doctor's ass if he didn't comply. Checking Arnold's neck did indicate a faint pulse, so the doctor got to work at a frenetic pace, and Arnold was soon placed aboard the chopper and was off to Baghdad. Not too long after, though, Lyon received the call over his radio. Arnold had died on the flight to the hospital.

The bodies of Lee and Assim were loaded aboard another M113 to be taken back to Dogwood before they were returned to their families. After Voccio had carried Assim to the vehicle, one of the guys was asked where his other leg was. Voccio had forgotten and went back to fetch it from the side of the destroyed vehicle. As Assim and Lee returned to base, and the 150th made ready to deal with another great loss, it was time to strip and retrieve the stricken M113. The quick reaction force was on site, including Hap Palmer. Both he and Voccio were determined that the M113 would not become a spectacle in the vehicle graveyard at FOB Duke. And they greatly wished to honor the memories of their fallen comrades. So, while others stripped the vehicle of its sensitive items, Palmer and Voccio crawled into the crumpled crew compartment and cleaned away any human memories of that horrible moment.

JOSEPH'S DILEMMA

Joseph was with the other interpreters when word came in that his friend Assim had been in an IED incident. At first, they didn't get much news at all; then came the rumor that he had been taken to a hospital and was going to be okay. It wasn't until the following morning that they all learned that Assim had been killed. Joseph was devastated. As was usual with the two friends, he had Assim's money. They each entrusted their money with the other when going on missions, with instructions about how to get that money to their families. And Joseph had a job to do. He had been instructed to reach out to Assim's family to collect his body for burial. It was about the last thing on earth that he wanted to do, but Joseph called Assim's family to give them the news. He certainly owed his dear friend that much. Assim's brother answered the phone. He paused for a few seconds of silence after hearing Joseph's dreadful news. But then he told Joseph never to call again. Assim was already dead; he had died to the family when he had chosen to serve with the Americans. Assim's brother begged Joseph never to visit and never to tell anyone that Assim had been killed by an IED serving with

American forces. Such a revelation could only cause his surviving family members great trouble.

Joseph and the other interpreters were devastated by the decision. Assim would be buried in a pauper's grave with no proper recognition. They owed him more than that. He was their friend, and he had given his life for a better future for Iraq that he had truly believed in. While they could not provide Assim with a burial, the interpreters arranged a traditional Islamic memorial service to honor his life and times.

Joseph took a short leave to visit his family after the loss of his friend: a leave that he spent wondering if what he was doing was worth it. His psyche was in deep turmoil. Were the Americans really making Iraq better? Was serving with them worth losing his own life over? Making matters worse, in his hometown there was more suspicion than ever of Iraqis who chose to serve alongside Americans. They were thought to be the worst kind of spies. Joseph's cover story of working as a teacher in another town seemed to be holding for the moment, but he started sleeping with a pistol under his pillow just in case. Any knock at the door might be someone who wanted him dead. Turmoil and death were rampant in Iraq; terrorists were endemic; religious militias were everywhere, spreading death and terror. The Americans might not be there for the long haul, but they did seem to be bringing peace to part of the country. And the motivations of the men he served with in the 150th seemed to be pure. Continuing to work with them appeared to be the best choice among a host of bad choices. And the money he was able to set aside would mean the world to the future of his own family. So, instead of resigning, he returned to Dogwood.

LARRY ARNOLD

It was a joyous occasion in the Arnold household. Robert was back! He arrived in the morning and moved his stuff into a little man-cave apartment separate from the main house. Then he and his mom Melinda went shopping. Her boy was home, and she was going to treat him right, and a great dinner was the next step. After shopping, Robert went to his apartment to get some shut-eye as Melinda began work on dinner. Larry Jr. came home with his family as well. It was going to be a night of happiness. Then there was a knock at the door. Somehow

Melinda knew what that knock meant. She looked out the window, and sure enough there were two military men out there in dress uniforms. She screamed and fell to her knees. Picking herself up a few seconds later, Melinda went to the door. The men asked to come inside to talk. She said, "No. You can leave," and closed the door in their faces. The men retreated to their car to sit. They weren't leaving without passing on the information that they had come to give.

Robert had heard his mother's scream and had come from his apartment to see what was the matter. The car was parked there with the two military men inside. Larry Jr. was standing there staring into space, deeply wrapped in thought. Robert quickly discerned the nature of the situation and went inside to be with his mom. Those men sat in that car for more than an hour before Melinda was ready to receive them. They carried the news that the family had feared. Larry Arnold Senior had been killed by an IED in Iraq. Melinda sat inconsolable with the chaplain for over an hour, and then she suddenly snapped back into place. It was like the flipping of a switch. Larry still needed her, and her family needed her. As her son Larry Jr. recalled, she never cried again until the funeral, and then only for a short period.

Larry Arnold Senior arrived in New Orleans on Father's Day in 2005. It was like the whole airport shut down when his casket was removed from the aircraft with a flag draped over it. Crowds stood saluting or with their hands over their hearts in silence as Melinda accompanied her husband on his journey to McDonald Funeral Home in Picayune, Mississippi. Robert had been left to wonder why he was home when his father had been killed in Iraq. Could he have done something to save him? He should have been there. But as Melinda began to navigate her new world in the wake of her husband's death, Robert realized that he was right where he was supposed to be. A part of himself would always live with a sense of guilt for not being there for his dad, but he was a rock for his mother in her time of greatest need.

Westboro Baptist phoned Melinda threatening to picket Larry's funeral, and boy did she give them a piece of her mind. It seemed that all Picayune turned out for Larry's funeral. Roads were lined for miles around with mourners. The police and fire departments lined the way, saluting and carrying American flags. The Patriot Guard riders were there on their motorcycles just in case Westboro Baptist did happen to show up, but they didn't. There was a 21-gun salute, the folded flag, and a bagpiper. Jerry Cooley attended the funeral. If anyone knew what Melinda was going through, it was him. She rested her head on his shoulder and the combined loss was almost too much to bear for both, but sharing it somehow seemed to help.

In the wake of the loss, Robert was in a hurry for his home leave to be over and to get back to Iraq. He was determined to do his part in honor of his father. But that was not to be. The command of the 150th believed that the Arnold family had suffered enough. Melinda could not be allowed to lose both a husband and a son. Robert would be transferred to a position at Camp Shelby instead and, no matter how many times he asked, he would not be returning to FOB Dogwood. At first the decision hurt Robert. He wanted to be there with his buddies doing his service. He wanted to complete his father's mission. But after a while he decided not to fight the decision. His mother was going through the greatest crisis of her life. He knew that he couldn't make that crisis worse by returning to the war zone. He knew that she needed him there. As much as he wanted to return to Iraq, his place was at home helping her.

TERRANCE LEE

Anice Lee, Terrance's grandmother, was tired from mopping the house and was just sitting down to watch a movie on *Lifetime*, and her husband Robert Earl was napping in the back room. She noticed a big white van pulling up in front of her house, followed by a throng of people, hundreds of them. Her local community was very tightly knit, and the strange vehicle winding its way through the neighborhood boded ill, so it had attracted a crowd. She then saw immaculately dressed military men step out of the van and knew what it had to be. After they knocked, she opened the door and said, "What are y'all coming here for? I know there ain't nothing wrong with Terrance. I just talked to him yesterday." Weeping, she rushed at the men and started hitting them. Robert Earl appeared at her side and calmed her before asking the men in. It couldn't hurt to hear what they had to say. The news was as she had feared; her little Terrance was dead.

Terrance's mother, Dinah, had been reading the newspaper in the break room at work two days before, and the story was about the loss of two soldiers in Iraq. She turned to her coworkers and said, "I'll be glad when my son comes back out from over there. Glad when he is home safe." On this particular evening, she had just sat down to dinner at Olive Garden with friends after a long day at work when her phone rang. It was a neighbor telling her to get to Anice's house quickly. Some military men were there. She turned to her friends and said, "We got to go; Bertha says that military men are at the house!" But they hadn't even gotten their food, much less paid for it. A woman at a nearby table who had overheard the conversation said, "The military is at the house, and you got somebody in the military – just go! I'll pay for it." Dinah called the police to see what was going on, and they promised to meet her at the entrance to the neighborhood. The road was packed with so many people that they would never be able to make it there. She was informed of Terrance's death as she made her way through the crowd in Anice's front yard.

Terrance's wife, Stephanie, was out that evening when the news came in. Although the military tried to reach her, she first learned of her husband's death by hearing people in town talking about it. It took all the wind out of her; Terrance couldn't be dead. He just couldn't be. She was due to have the couple's child in two months' time. She made her way to Anice's and found herself surrounded by those who loved Terrance, which is something that she desperately needed at the time. But she still didn't believe it. She just couldn't. Not until, on Father's Day, the family went to New Orleans to meet his body. Due to her advanced pregnancy Stephanie couldn't make that trip, but she did see Terrance in Marshall Funeral Home in Biloxi. And it really was him. It was him – he had too much makeup on, but it was him. She then ran her hands through his hair, something she had loved to do, and found herself touching wax on top of his head, masking the wound where part of his skull had been crushed. At first Stephanie thought about suicide. Terrance was gone and nobody would miss her. But then she realized that she had to live for her daughter Kamri and for Terrance's child, which was due soon. Stephanie gritted her teeth. She was going to live the life that Terrance had wanted them both to live.

Terrance's funeral was so packed with well-wishers and mourners that it had to be moved from the family church to the much larger First Baptist Church. The entire community turned out, and the funeral was a perfect example of an immaculate military ceremony. The guns fired over his grave site, and the folded flag was handed to Stephanie and Terrance's children. For weeks after, people streamed by the family's homes. Nobody had to cook for themselves for nearly a month, the outpouring of community support was so great. But as the crowds began to dwindle, the family had to figure out how to try to move on in Terrance's absence. And Stephanie was about to give birth to Terrance's child.

REACTION

Back at FOB Dogwood, reaction to the deaths of Assim, Terrance Lee, and Larry Arnold varied from stunned disbelief to deep anger. For Mike Beal it was like a malevolent kind of déjà vu. Sean Cooley, the rock of the unit, had been lost under his command in a vehicle that had somehow hit the IED that Beal's own vehicle had missed. Now he had lost three more men under his command. He couldn't help but think that he was responsible. In moments of quiet, the incidents ran on a constant loop in his mind. What else could he have done? What had he missed? It ate away at him and at his bruised faith. And he had a depressing feeling that the guilt would never go away. Beal kept his life of faith alive – it helped to go to chapel, to pray, and to sing. Beal went on missions – as many as he could. Out there on missions he had to focus and didn't have as much time to dwell on events. But one thing was for sure, Mike Beal knew that he was a dead man. He wasn't going to survive; Iraq was too deadly and unpredictable. His turn would come.

Across the 150th nagging doubts set in. What were they doing here? They kept losing good men, and for what? Maybe they should stop patrols altogether and sit on the FOB and just survive for the remainder of the tour? Others, of course, blamed the Iraqis more than ever. Surely they couldn't all be terrorists, but there sure as hell weren't many Iraqis turning on the terrorists. Maybe Owesat just needed to go away? Jody Kyzar spoke for many when he noted in his journal, "No words can explain how we all feel. It is so hard to fight an enemy you don't see and don't know where they are or what they are doing." Ricky Tyler, who had been Terrance Lee's team leader, had to fight off bouts of anger toward the local population. At the beginning of the tour, he had understood that the Mississippians were there to drive away the bad guys so that the population could live without fear. But he now began to wonder if everyone was a bad guy in this area. Even with those thoughts, he knew deep down that the local people were caught on the horns of a real dilemma. Recent history suggested that the Americans might not be there for the long haul. If that was the case, supporting the Americans might be a death sentence for the people of Owesat. The cognitive dissonance was nearly deafening.

Even though she had been going out on a few missions and had customers in her tobacco cessation classes, Roz Morris was still let down by the low numbers of men she had been seeing. On her walk-arounds on the base, she could tell that there were hurt soldiers out there that needed her. But how could she serve them better? She couldn't make them come in, after all. She had only seen 20 men so far, and most of those conversations dealt mainly with tobacco. After June 11, though, the numbers skyrocketed. She saw more than 80 soldiers in the days after the loss of Assim, Lee, and Arnold. It saddened Roz deeply that the soldiers needed her – that their trauma was so deep and so raw. But she was glad that she was there for them. Voccio even ordered his entire tank platoon to make a standing schedule of visits to Roz's office.

Others got down to work with typical National Guard ingenuity. The armor on the bottom of the 113s had to be modified to withstand an IED blast. The welders got together and tried to jury-rig V-shaped armor beneath the vehicles to better direct the force of any blast outward and away from the crew compartment. Another idea was to rig giant rollers for the tanks to push across the desert, detonating any IEDs in their path. The simplest idea, though, was for many of the men to ride atop the 113s when at all possible. They might go flying in an IED blast, but they would survive. None of the solutions was ever truly finalized before the 150th returned home, but that did not stop anyone from trying. Impossible was not a part of their vocabulary.

BREAKTHROUGH IN THE SOUTH

The very day after the loss of Assim, Lee, and Arnold, the S-5 (civilian affairs) section of the 150th along with the leadership of Alpha Company got a surprise. The village leaders of Baj al-Shamaly wanted a meeting. The village was ready to cooperate, and the elders looked forward to working with the Mississippians in any way they could to keep the insurgents at bay. On the same day, the S-5 and Alpha Company leadership met with the farmers of Faddilyah village to begin work constructing an agricultural cooperative – Operation *Amber Waves* – which was designed to increase local crop yield. Kevin Kelly was there for the meeting, and, even though he didn't particularly trust the village elders, especially after the IED incident just the day before, he did enjoy hanging out with the local children:

> As I was walking to my vehicle, one of the kids I know walked up and gave me a whopping 50 Dinar, which is worth about 3 cents. He gave it to me because I'm his friend he said. He didn't want anything in return. I gave him about 5 Ozark suckers, and he was off on the run. I was looking down at this one little boy who was about 6 years old and all of a sudden he let out one of the longest and loudest burps I've ever heard. I busted out laughing. This started a chain reaction and the next thing you know, I had about 10 of them burping what sounded like a song.

Deliveries of medical supplies and farm goods soon followed, and the relationship quickly bore more fruit than the leaders of the 150th could have hoped for. The leaders of Baj al-Shamaly reported that they were forming a local security force that would aid the Americans in policing the area. As a gesture of good faith, they also provided intelligence as to the locations of four insurgent leaders in the area, most of whom frequented the northern village of Sharmiyah. They were living in plain sight. It was a bonanza of information that was a real game changer, and Lieutenant Colonel Robinson knew it.

ORPHANS

Chris Thomas' Charlie Company had felt itself somewhat lucky to be located at FOB Duke apart from the rest of the 150th. Duke was well into the desert outside Najaf, far from any potential threat of insurgent attack. Like everywhere else in Iraq, IEDs were a concern, but Thomas and his men had not been impacted and thanked their lucky stars that they weren't in the more active area around Dogwood. Charlie Company's main job was to secure the FOB, which seemed a pretty cushy detail. Company executive officer Brad Hollingsworth knew how good they all had it. You could order specialized omelets in the morning, there was a seafood feast every Friday, and the latrines were air conditioned. This sure was better than what he was hearing from FOB Dogwood. Then came a shift when Charlie Company was moved to FOB Hotel, which was in the outskirts of Najaf itself. In 2004 the Marines and Iraqi forces had fought a bitter battle in Najaf against the militia of Muqtada al-Sadr. The city had been subdued, but there remained a great hatred of the Americans among its people. When the resident Marines briefed Charlie Company on what to expect, they told Thomas and his men to make sure to bring enough ammo on patrols. If they received any incoming fire, they were to attack with everything they had. Thomas sat there listening and thought, "OK. This is life and death now."

There were telephone services at Hotel, and Chris Thomas talked with his wife Kristi as often as he could. While on the phone, he could often hear his infant son crying in the background, and he could tell from the tone of her voice that she hadn't slept in days. They had named the infant, born while Chris was in Iraq, Christopher Thomas Jr.; they figured that if Chris Sr. was killed in action then there would still be someone to carry on the name. Of course, Kristi told him that everything was okay, but Chris knew better. He could use force to drive away the insurgents who were shooting mortars and keeping him awake at night, but there was no way to silence a baby who had colic when you were a single mother. He needed to be there helping her. But he couldn't be.

Charlie Company ran patrols all through Najaf, sometimes on foot. And every time the locals gave them a wide berth along with hostile stares. It was obvious that the people neither liked nor trusted the Americans, but they had learned not to be violent in the massive battle of 2004. One task that the Marines gave Charlie Company was to bolster the defenses of one of their outposts in the center of town. It was a seven-story building that provided overlook of much of Najaf – a perfect spot. But it was a shambles, and Charlie Company had to fix that. Richard Rowland was in the group that reconnoitered the building, and he was shocked. There was nothing with which to build defenses. No concrete, no concertina wire, no nothing. And what awaited him on the second floor was even worse:

> All the Marines were sleeping on the second floor. It was one huge room of cots, man, just pushed up next to each other, nothing but cots everywhere. And on the very edge of the cots was where they stacked all their piss pots. Man, there must have been 200 goddang full piss pots in that damn room. They're like, "Oh, yeah. Y'all can have this room while you are here." And we were like, "Naw. That's okay."

Operations for Charlie Company at Hotel settled down into a routine, with Thomas even being able to stop at a local merchant's for souvenirs. The overall situation was so good that one of the officers at Hotel took to riding a four-wheeler off base with buckets full of candy, tossing the coveted sweets to throngs of children. But back at Dogwood, Lieutenant Colonel Robinson was livid. He had to deal with the threat of Owesat. With the loss of Assim, Arnold, and Lee, it was beyond time to end the insurgency there. He needed Charlie Company on hand so that he could have enough combat power to take the war to the enemy. So, the word came in to Charlie Company in mid-June. It was off to FOB Dogwood.

Thomas' Charlie Company, though, was not the only 150th orphan. Alpha Company had left its 1st Platoon behind at FOB Kalsu in return for Voccio's tanks. At Kalsu the 1st Platoon operated much as the bulk of the 150th at Dogwood. There was a continuous stream of counter-mortar and presence patrols designed to keep the very active insurgency in the area at arm's length. The area was one of extreme danger, having cost the 2/11th ACR so many casualties, especially during April. IEDs remained a constant threat. Terrance Bloodsaw of the 1st Platoon hit his first IED on February 21, but he and his buddies were lucky; their M113 was jolted but not penetrated. The force of the IED had struck next to them rather than under them. His driver, who was also one of his high school pals, wrenched his hip, but otherwise they were lucky. His second IED hit was in September. He was driving that day, and when he heard the BOOM! he didn't have any time to react before the M113 lurched uncontrollably to the right. He tried to regain control, but the vehicle flipped, ejecting him.

He was flung more than 20 feet clear of the wreck, landing on his head, and was knocked unconscious. He woke up that evening in the hospital staring at a nurse, wondering where he was. 1st Platoon remained at Kalsu for the duration of the deployment, often engaging in humanitarian missions with the local population while dodging the ever-present IEDs.

CHARLIE COMPANY ARRIVES

The stories about Dogwood, the danger, and the lack of amenities on the FOB meant that nobody in Charlie Company looked forward to their change of scenery. When Thomas and his men rolled in in mid-June, they noticed that the soldiers at Dogwood didn't look the same as the last time he had seen them. They had a coldness and serious nature that marked them as different; they had been through it. Richard Rowland made his way to the TOC, where he was going to set up shop. He couldn't help but notice that the door was a "flimsy as shit" piece of plywood. This didn't bode well. When he opened the door, there was the whole staff to greet him with a sign, "Welcome to Dogwood Lieutenant Rowland. Did you bring us a tee-shirt from Disneyland?" He thought to himself, "Well, if FOB Hotel was Disneyland, what was FOB Dogwood?" For Thomas, the difference between Dogwood and Hotel was made apparent that night on his first patrol. He was standing up looking out of the vehicle using his night-vision goggles. As the vehicle made a turn, he half-noticed that everyone else was getting down. Then someone said, "Hey, sir. You better get down. We have a lot of IEDs here, unless you want to get your fucking head blown off."

For Brad Hollingsworth, Charlie Company executive officer, the situation was similar. On his first day at the FOB, Hollingsworth was excited to bump into his friend and Mississippi State fraternity brother Eric Kimbrough, who was serving with Alpha Company. When Kimbrough asked if Hollingsworth wanted to accompany his unit on their patrol that night, Hollingsworth jumped at the chance. The patrol took Hollingsworth down to near the disused bridge across the Euphrates near Checkpoint 100. Kimbrough informed his friend that, while their side of the river was relatively quiet, the far bank was a no-go zone. And right on cue green tracer rounds cut through the night sky from across the river. It took Hollingsworth a few moments to realize that someone was trying to kill them. Lights were on in that village like there was some sort of celebration underway. Women and children were thronging the streets. And the fire kept coming. Kimbrough and the soldiers of Alpha Company didn't seem too surprised or worried. They took cover behind a nearby tank, but with no great sense of urgency. The casual nature of the violence took Hollingsworth by surprise. The Dogwood area certainly was the real deal, much different than FOBs Duke or Hotel. He hadn't even been there an entire day and had already earned a Combat Action Badge.

Raymond Vreeland was free and open about what he thought of Dogwood. It sucked. On his very first day his cigarette lighter blew up from the heat. On his second night there he pulled guard duty in one of the towers. He and his buddy had a couple of muffins and a cup of coffee apiece to stay awake during the night:

And I was sitting there looking out the window, and all of a sudden, I heard something on the little shelf in front of me. It was pitch black. So I got my NVGs, night-vision goggles, out, and I looked on the little table, and it was a mouse, stooped over in my coffee cup. And I told the other guy; I was like, "Hey, man, there's a mouse in my cup, drinking my coffee." He said, "Oh, yeah. Let's catch it." And we were going to kill him because he had been eating our food. I said, "All right. If he comes back up, on the count of three, I'm going to put my hand here on the left, you put yours on the right, and we're going to trap him." Well, the mouse came up, and we seen him. I said, "On the count of three, you just throw your hand up there, and I'm going to shine the light on him." Well, we did that, and we had the light on him, and the mouse ran to my hand, and then he ran back to my buddy's hand. And then he ran back to mine, again. Well, I seen the mouse look at my arm, and then I looked at my arm, too, and my sleeve was wide open. And that mouse ran up my shirt and ran all around. I was hopping around. I had body armor on; I was hopping around, screaming, and the other guy was on the ground laughing at me. And he crawled all up in my shirt. I slung my body armor off, and I was hollering and screaming. I stopped. I thought I had done slung him out my shirt. I said, "Well, I think he's out." And all of a sudden he went to crawling on my back and everything. And I went to slapping myself, and I was screaming and everything. I took my shirt off and everything. He crawled up my neck, and jumped out my collar, and I was just, it freaked me out. Of course, he went back and told everybody, but I was mad. I called up on the radio, "We need mousetraps."

The next few days involved some transition at Dogwood. Charlie Company transferred its 2nd Platoon to Alpha Company to make up for Alpha having to leave a platoon behind at Kalsu that it had exchanged for the tanks. In exchange Charlie Company was assigned a platoon from the Vermont National Guard. Also, Richard Rowland moved from the TOC to being the 2nd Platoon Leader in Bravo Company. He was excited by the change – he wanted to get out there into the war, not be at the TOC. On his second mission with the platoon, he was tasked with providing security for an overflight by a Raven drone. The Ravens were eyes in the sky that always kept the insurgents guessing. Rowland watched as the squad assigned to the Raven went through preflight checks and peered into the flight viewer to make sure that all was good to go. After the Raven took off, its operator came to Rowland a bit sheepishly. They had forgotten to turn the recorder on, which meant the Raven was flying freely and could not be controlled or brought back. It was gone. Rowland just knew that he was going to get fired on his second mission outside the wire. Desperate, he climbed on top of his M113. He knew that it made him a wonderful sniper target, but he just had to see if he could catch a glimpse of the Raven. What he saw was two Iraqi farmers jumping up and down and waving. He walked over to check, and there was the Raven, nestled among some very startled sheep in their pen. He wasn't going to get fired that day after all.

CHANGE OF MISSION

With Charlie Company on hand the 150th was nearly up to full strength. And Lieutenant Colonel Robinson was ready to change the mission. With the help of Roz Morris he called a meeting – a second meeting where everyone could say whatever they wanted. Grievances could be aired without the threat of repercussion. The Guard was a family, and this was a family conference. These kids were under his command, and Robinson wanted them to feel like everything possible was being done to ensure their protection. Questions came in from all around, and Roz Morris was everywhere orchestrating the proceedings. Robinson again reiterated that, while the insurgent threat was all too real, most of the people – even those in Owesat – were civilians who were helplessly caught in the middle. They shouldn't be mistreated in any way. Instead, they should be treated with respect and liberated from the grips of the insurgency. But he also let the men know that it was time for a change. Owesat was going to be locked down. He wanted to send a signal to the insurgent leadership there. Entries into Owesat should be hard entries – and it was time for the kid gloves to come off. Searches were to be more aggressive. Everyone needed to watch the outcome of their actions, but, he said, "I don't want any goddamn doors left on the goddamn hinges."

6

On the Offensive

*Last night, we had another big raid. We hit the village around
22:30 or so. There was no way we could find each other in the dust
and confusion, but we had the grids to our houses in our GPSs so
it was easier to just hit the target houses, as planned. Then, as we
headed north, my crew, Sgt Sherman Hillhouse, Norwood, Clowers,
Bell, and Reeves, couldn't find our way to the houses. The map and
graphics we had didn't show the series of berms and ditches between
us and the houses. I decided to just park the track behind another
target house, so Reeves, on the gun, could watch it, while we trekked
up to the school and other house. I will say, that the doors up in
this village are made a lot better than the ones we've encountered
previously. The school was empty, and the house had no one except a
very, very old man there. We then headed back to the other cluster of
target houses. We herded one group to the central holding area, and
then hit the last four houses. We then herded those 8 or 9 individuals
to the holding area. It was a sight to see. Several LMTVs, HMMVs,
and 5-ton trucks were arranged in a semi-circle, with their headlights
illuminating a circular concertina wire holding area, or "corral,"
containing around 200 detainees. Not long after we'd gotten our guys
"checked in" and numbered, the source [an Iraqi informant] arrived
to point out the bad guys. With him were a couple of spec-ops guys.
We would escort a detainee up to the HMMV where the source was,
and he'd say "good" or "bad." In the case of "bad," then the name,
status, and crimes of the individual would be read aloud. All in all,*

*we brought back 39 "keepers," some of which were apparently pretty
big fish. We got back in around 5:45 am, or so, just as the sun was
coming up. The next day, the commander of 2nd MEF (Marine
Expeditionary Force), the group we fall under over here, called to
congratulate our BN. Apparently, he'd seen a list of the names we'd
brought in, and he'd recognized several of them as being insurgent
leaders in the area.*

JAY STANDLEY, JOURNAL ENTRY

BOTTOM LINE

Lieutenant Colonel Robinson and the soldiers of the 150th already had
ideas of how to proceed against the insurgency once they had enough
men for the job. As a National Guard unit, having soldiers that were
also welders, construction workers, architects, and the like had meant
that FOB Dogwood itself had been transformed by those skills. But
the Guard was also full of police, state troopers, farmers, and nurses.
Many of these skills helped in community outreach to the portion of
the population willing to accept it. Other skill sets were more useful in
developing a plan to shut down what was, in some ways, a vast criminal
organization in Owesat. Using the expertise of law enforcement officers
in the 150th, especially Jerry Bratu and Marty Davis, Robinson and
his Guard soldiers worked out a plan that was well outside the normal
military box for the time. The first order of business in taking the war
to the insurgents was to strangle their access to the villages of the AO.
Cutting the dike road in Owesat had been a first step, but it had not
had the desired result. There needed to be an American presence much
nearer to the villages to staunch the flow of insurgents and arms. The
first step in the plan was to seal off the AO from the south. Checkpoint
100, which sat near an unused bridge over the Euphrates and the
junction of two major roads through the area, seemed a natural spot. It
was the junction of the two roads that was known as Swiss Cheese Alley.
It was also near to the friendly villages of Baj al-Shamaly and Sharmia
that the 150th knew well.

Stage one of the plan involved concreting a wide swathe around
the road junction, making planting IEDs there almost impossible.
Allen McDaniel worked to hire local Iraqi contractors and workers to
undertake the job, being careful to take Imodium before his meetings

with them since those meetings always involved eating and drinking the local tea, which it would be impolite to refuse. Everyone seemed to think that the contractor was an uncle to one of the interpreters, but if it was more than rumor nobody ever seemed to know. The work was "crappy and slow," and had to be protected by units from Alpha Company, but it came along nicely, and IED attacks in that area dropped off to nothing. Before the arrival of Charlie Company, Robinson had never had enough troops to hand to allow for such operations. Everyone had been needed for patrols. But now his hands were no longer tied.

Next, right next to the brand-spanking-new intersection, Alpha Company began to erect a fortress. Hesco barriers were unfolded and jammed with sand and gravel to create a small enclosure easily capable of holding and providing defense for a platoon. As combat engineers, such construction was second nature to Alpha Company, and the small fortress went up in record time. It wasn't long before Alpha Company platoons began to rotate through the fortress, manning it permanently. Any good fortress needs a name, and this one became known as "Bottom Line," named after a seedy nightclub back home that many in Alpha Company had frequented. It wasn't easy duty at Bottom Line. All food and water had to be trucked in, there were no amenities at all, and units had to be on 100 percent alert because they were marooned 8 miles from any help at Dogwood. So, the risk of a ground attack by insurgents was real.

Usually augmented by Iraqi Army troops, the Americans at Bottom Line set a roadblock consisting of a concertina wire barrier across the road. By this time, all vehicles in Iraq knew full well to stop at such a roadblock. The vehicles were searched. If they contained nothing of interest, which was the case the vast majority of the time, the driver was sent on their way. If there was contraband or weapons, the driver was detained. If a driver refused to stop, the order was to open fire, because any vehicle could be a vehicle-borne IED meant to destroy Bottom Line. Voccio was there with Alpha Company when it faced its first such incident. The subject car just kept on coming, so shots were fired into its engine block, putting it out of commission. Turned out the driver was just having an argument with his passenger and had not seen the roadblock. But everyone was okay. Although there was little drama as yet at Bottom Line, the 150th had effectively cut a major artery of arms delivery in the area, putting a real pinch on the insurgency.

RAID IN THE NORTH

As elements of Alpha Company worked on Bottom Line, in the far north of the AO, the 150th undertook a battalion-sized raid on the village of Sharmiyah. The raid was part of a wider series of raids undertaken by the 155th across the region, known as Operation *Azil*. In the raid, Alpha, Bravo, and Charlie companies, augmented by Voccio's tanks, cordoned off Sharmiyah in the dead of night. Next came a house-by-house search. The 150th had never had enough troops to raid distant Sharmiyah, so the nighttime operation came as a surprise to the locals, with many insurgents failing to flee. Most homes were occupied by innocent civilians, with many still asleep on their rooftops, as was often the Iraqi custom in the heat of the summer. In all 20 insurgents were identified and captured. The soldiers of the 150th carried with them pictures and identity information on many insurgents, and being captured with weapons or IED-making materials was a sure ticket to detention. Kevin Kelly recorded aspects of the raid:

> While I was getting one suspect ready to be searched, we found several weapons and a big bag of loaded AK-47 magazines that were being stored in a hiding place. We had asked him if he had any weapons and he said no. When I showed him what we had found he said it wasn't his and that someone must have done it to get him in trouble. By the time we got him to a collection point, the man was crying. We had one man that said he didn't have any ID because he didn't live here and was just visiting. He also said that someone had taken off with it in a car. When I told him where he could possibly go if he didn't have an ID, he said he thought of where he might have one. When we got back to the house, he produced 3 of them. Pretty significant find when just a few minutes earlier he didn't live here, but he went directly to a drawer and pulled it straight out and handed it to me... [Later] 1SG Stiles said we had a runner. We had noticed this guy run into this house and we had surrounded it. When we went in, we started searching again and of course none of the women had seen him run in. I found that so amazing that they were all gathered up in the room where the front door opened up to. I took a couple of guys on the rooftop and there were about 15 young kids lying on blankets. I saw one blanket that was over someone's head and he looked a

lot bigger than the typical 5–10-year-olds that were up there. I kept yelling for him to get up, but he just lay there. When I yanked off the cover, he started rubbing his eyes like we had just woken him up. I guess he thought we wouldn't recognize the glasses he was wearing, his size, clothes and what his face looked like.

With the 150th at its full complement of manpower, life at Dogwood had moved from survival to attack, and real pressure was being placed on the insurgency. Just two days later, though, a signal came that the fight was far from over. A patrol reported a dead body on the side of the road north toward Sharmiyah. Explosive Ordnance Disposal was immediately called in. It was well known that insurgents often hid IEDs inside bodies. The EOD robot went out and poked around the body. No IED. Charlie Company was tasked with its identification and retrieval. It was an Iraqi policeman, killed in reprisal for the raid on Sharmiyah. The insurgents were making it quite clear that any suspected involvement with the Americans meant death for Iraqis in the area.

SHUT OWESAT DOWN

After the IED strike of June 11, Robinson ordered a halt to all missions into Owesat and instead ordered Bravo Company to place a moving blockade onto the western approaches into the village. In essence, Bravo Company set up positions on the outskirts of Owesat and stopped all vehicle traffic into and out of the village utilizing roving patrols in the desert. Owesat was under siege. A week of the blockade pushed the insurgents to the edge, with Bravo Company patrols often taking direct and indirect fire from the village. Plainly Bravo Company was getting under the insurgents' skin.

The insurgents were determined to make the Guard pay for the blockade. Late one afternoon, Captain Lyon and his soldiers were on patrol, stopping and searching vehicles that came through. Roz Morris was there on the mission. Taking part in the dangers of missions such as these was the only way she could really get close to and understand the guys. The unit had stopped and cleared a host of passing vehicles, and it was almost evening. A sedan pulled up and was searched as normal. The occupants didn't match any descriptions of known terrorists, and the vehicle didn't contain any contraband or weaponry, so it and they were waved through. The car rolled down the road a ways and then came to a stop. Then it started backing up. Standing nearby, Richard Rowland spoke aloud, "Well, this shit ain't right." Cars NEVER came back to an American roadblock. Something was seriously wrong.

With all the Americans' weapons now trained on them, the occupants of the car stopped the vehicle and got out. The men seemed very unhappy and told the interpreter that the Americans had stolen thousands of dollars from their car. Lyon never believed that for a minute. But the Iraqis were adamant. Lyon, Morris, Rowland, and a few others carefully approached the vehicle to search it again alongside the Iraqis. Together they looked in the trunk and opened the door to look in the back seat. WHOOOOOMP! An IED went off. Roz was knocked over by the force of the blast; Rowland was tossed onto the hood of the car, along with Lyon. Their ears were ringing terribly. A command-detonated IED had been set off no more than 10 meters from where the car had stopped. Someone in Owesat had been watching and waiting patiently for the Mississippians to be in the right place. As good fortune had it, though, the IED was just far enough away, was buried too deep, and was in front of the car while Lyon and his men were to the car's rear – horribly frightening, but not deadly.

Lyon and his men quickly regained their wits. The driver of the vehicle was running away. The passenger was just standing there screaming. They must have known that the IED was there and had backed up to lure the Americans to the spot. One of the men of Bravo Company stopped the fleeing driver dead in his tracks and then kicked him hard in the chest. The driver crumpled to the ground, and the soldier jumped on him, ready to make him pay for what he had done. Lyon ran over and got that soldier off the Iraqi civilian, telling him that he would personally kick his ass if he kept it up. Maybe these guys were insurgents and had lured them to the spot, if a bit poorly. But maybe they were innocent civilians who were in the wrong place at the wrong time. That was not for them to judge; the men would be taken back to Dogwood and would go through the legal process of military adjudication.

Roz Morris had gotten to her feet and watched the scene unfold. She could understand the soldier's anger. He and they had very nearly died; a few feet further would have been all it took. And they were all shaken. Everyone had been steps from death. For his part, Lyon couldn't help but wonder why he was still alive at all. On June 11 his vehicle had run over the IED that had killed Assim, Arnold, and Lee, but had not set it off. Here, only two weeks later, he had missed being killed by a hair's breadth again. All these guys had been through something like that; they had all been near death. And even with all that, Roz was amazed that the Mississippians continued to exercise the proper restraint. Yes, Rosalyn Morris was proud of her men. And she was equally *sure* that at least one of the Iraqis was innocent. The passenger in the car had not tried to run away; instead, he had shit himself thoroughly and still stood there sobbing. And now the guys were arguing about who had to have him in their vehicle to take him back to Dogwood. But a compromise was reached; Shitty Pants, as he quickly became known, rode to Dogwood on the hood of the vehicle and got a good shower and a change of clothes before anyone would talk to him.

A few days later Roz Morris was surprised to see everyone waiting for her in formation at the FOB. It was a ceremony to award her a Combat Action Badge, a distinct rarity for women in the military at the time – and an even greater rarity for a lieutenant colonel combat stress control specialist. The men loved her for taking risks with them. Numbers of men seeking her care skyrocketed. Some went under the cover of requesting help with smoking cessation, but everyone knew why they were going. It was easy to tell, because the guys walked around with a nicotine patch on their arm and a cigarette in their mouth after their visits. Roz's boss, the commander of the medical detachment back at Kalsu, was livid when he heard that she had been going on missions and had come so close to getting blown up that she had received a Combat Action Badge. But he knew that there was no stopping Roz Morris.

ACTION IN THE SOUTH

On July 2 the command team of the 150th met with the leaders of both Baj al-Shamaly and Faddilyah villages. The elders asked for more medical aid, specifically dentistry, and continued help for their farms. In return, they provided more intelligence regarding insurgents in their area. At the same time, the routine at the nearby Bottom Line checkpoint had paid off in many ways. Having a mix of American and Iraqi troops there did make for some interesting tensions, though.

The Guard troops always had food brought to them from Dogwood for the night, and Alpha Company executive officer Thomas Howell for one was amazed to watch the Iraqis capture, skin, and cook sheep for their repast. But the great ongoing issue was sanitation. The Iraqis were notorious for not knowing how to properly use a porta-john. Instead of sitting, they would stand on the seat and – well their aim was notoriously bad. So, the porta-johns at Bottom Line were always a mess, leading many just to utilize the great outdoors. But even then there was a problem. The Iraqis refused to go far from the safety of the Hesco barrier to relieve themselves, so one of the outer portions of the barrier was essentially an open Iraqi sewer.

Even with the sanitation and culinary issues, Bottom Line was proving to be a rousing success. Cager and his men wouldn't stop every car. Predictability was asking to get hit by a vehicle-borne IED. But the cars they stopped paid great dividends. One was almost a dead giveaway from the get-go. Most traffic was either beat-up old vehicles, even donkey carts. But here came this luxury car, complete with a driver in front and a well-dressed passenger in back. As the guys began to look through their photograph intelligence collection of black-listers, the Iraqi interpreter started jumping up and down. The guy was the equivalent of a brigade-level commander for the insurgency. He was quickly whisked away to FOB Kalsu, and that was that. Just two days later, a taxi came through and was pulled over. Both driver and passenger exited the vehicle. The cabbie came over to the interpreter and told him that the Americans might like to check the trunk. They did, and sure enough, there was a mortar tube in there. One more terrorist arrested.

Medic Joe Smith was at Bottom Line a few days later and was part of a group that stopped a rather nice car. They didn't expect much, since there were both a man and a woman in the vehicle. The presence of women or children usually kept the insurgents at bay. But they stopped the vehicle anyway. The woman was heavily pregnant and obviously deep into labor. She and her husband were on their way to Baghdad for the delivery. A quick look, though, revealed to Smith that her water had already broken and that there was no way that the couple was going to reach Baghdad. They were having their baby at Bottom Line instead. The husband was livid. It was a distinct cultural no-no for an American man to be involved in such an intimate situation with his wife.

Smith told him through the interpreter that he was just going to have to get over it. The baby was being born here, whether the husband liked it or not. A few hours, and lots of screaming later, Smith delivered the couple a healthy baby boy. At that point the husband perked up again, and he even worked up a smile for Smith. The medic cut the cord, and now the trio was off once again to Baghdad.

The dangers of working roadblocks were made crystal clear on July 16 with the death of Sergeant Travis Cooper. Cooper was working with the 2/114th Field Artillery based out of Starkville, Mississippi. He was engaged in searching a vehicle in his unit's AO when an IED exploded, leading to injuries that caused his death. Cooper was from Macon, Mississippi and had attempted to join the Guard while in high school but had been rejected because of a tattoo he had on his neck. He was so anxious to serve his country, though, that he got a job at a local grocery store until he saved the $2,500 to get the tattoo removed. Then it was right back to the Guard for Cooper. His family took solace that he died doing something to which he was so dedicated.

THE SCREAMING CHICKEN

Now the time came finally to deal with Owesat. Pressure had been put on the insurgents for weeks with Bravo Company's rolling blockades. And now Robinson had the troop strength to make a difference. The moment came when naval intelligence informed Lieutenant Colonel Robinson that it had made reliable contact with an insurgent leader from Owesat who was ready to turn and give up his fellow terrorists. There had been nights when Navy SEALs had swooped into the AO for a snatch-and-grab of a particular insurgent. But this operation was to be massive and was designed to clear out the bulk of the Owesat insurgency; an operation that required the entire strength of the 150th. Robinson and his staff got down to planning the details of the mission, which led to several sleepless nights. And then, on July 20, the insurgent defector was brought into the FOB. He wore a mask to cover his face and had naval handlers with him. But he came with a list of a host of target houses and promised to point out who was a member of the insurgency and who was not. Robinson got a bit of a chuckle out of the informant's code name – Screaming Chicken.

For the raid itself, the plan was for mechanized patrols to swoop in from north and south, cutting the insurgents off from their presumed escape across the river. In addition, helicopters would be circling overhead, helping to coordinate movements. And, with the information that they had to hand this time, if anyone fled across the river it was presumed that they were a combatant. The choppers would finally be allowed to fire.

To ease the insertion of the mechanized elements into Owesat, the 150th was assigned a Husky, a vehicle with a V-shaped hull and an onboard mine detector. It was presumed that the roads into and out of the village were strewn with IEDs. The specialized Husky was designed to detect mines, and its V-shaped hull could set off IEDs without being badly damaged or its crew incapacitated. ACE bulldozers followed to fill in any IED craters left behind or any obstacles that the insurgents had cut into the roads.

The operation got underway at 3 a.m., and many soldiers followed Thomas Howell's example of gulping down some Red Bulls to try to shake the cobwebs out of their minds. From the south the Husky led the way, with Charlie Company following behind, hoping to cut off Owesat from the river and any possible escape quickly. Disaster nearly struck, though, when a 5-ton truck of Charlie Company's patrol hit an IED that the Husky had somehow missed. Nobody was injured, but the truck was disabled and held up progress. The incident threw off the careful timing of the operation, leaving Charlie Company's advance nearly stalled. Richard Rowland and elements of Bravo Company were following behind and heard yelling and hollering coming in over the radio. Where was the element that was supposed to be cutting off the river? Rowland grabbed his driver over the shoulder and told him to hit the gas. Even though they had lost contact with the Husky in an area that was thick with IEDs, they were going to rush forward and cut that damn river escape the hell off. Luck was with Rowland and his men; they didn't hit any further IEDs. Rowland's quick thinking allowed the mission to achieve success.

Although much of the village had been occupied quickly, the insurgents were good at this kind of warfare, and many of them had made their way to the river in time to escape – no matter the speed and success of the mission. And Robinson heard it all narrated from the chopper pilots. "Men approaching the river. More gathering at the river.

They have gotten on boats and are crossing the river." Then Robinson gave them permission to fire. The Apache pilots almost didn't believe it. On other operations in and around Owesat they had flown over and helplessly watched as the insurgents had fled to safety. But this time they finally got the go-ahead. Those tiny boats and their inhabitants were blown to bits.

From deep in the night and well into the morning, the 150th searched every house in Owesat – well over 175 homes. Captain Ken Cager of Alpha Company was amazed to find a guy who only really had half a head; he had suffered a traumatic injury long before, perhaps in the Battle of Fallujah. But the guy was adamant. Even with half a head he was yelling shit about the Americans and proclaiming his allegiance to the insurgency, making him an obvious target for arrest. Kevin Kelly recalled that, after daybreak, a civil affairs team truck rolled in with a loudspeaker calling on any remining males to come out of their homes. After that, the loudspeaker took to playing Jimi Hendrix's "Purple Haze" as motivation. Alpha, Bravo, and Charlie companies were each searching their assigned areas and returning with suspected insurgents. It was hot and dirty work as the sun rose into the sky. Sherman Hillhouse of Charlie Company remembered his favorite part of the day. He and his buddies were parched as they marched 30 detainees to the gathering area. Then he saw a couple of children standing along the side of the road holding watermelons. He called them over and offered them a dollar for each watermelon they could come back with. Those were the best watermelons that Hillhouse ever had, and those boys loved making some American folding money.

From darkness into the dawning day, each of the men detained in the raid was brought in front of a Humvee that was parked in the center of town. In that Humvee sat the Screaming Chicken, with his own personal security detail standing menacingly around the vehicle. Behind his sunglasses and mask, he would look at each individual brought before him. He would then speak to the driver of the vehicle, who would give the suspect a thumbs up or a thumbs down. Thumbs up meant release; thumbs down meant a trip first to Dogwood and then to Abu Ghraib Prison. It was as simple as that. After the mission was over, the Screaming Chicken and his security detail was whisked away. But over 100 insurgents had been detained. And the Screaming Chicken was entirely accurate, with all the detainees later proving to be members of the Talwid al-Jihad, Ansar al-Sunna, or 1920th Revolutionary Group terrorist organizations. Joseph was elated. In speaking to the prisoners before they were hauled away, he was certain that they had captured the IED maker who had killed Assim, Terrance Lee, and Larry Arnold. The capture would not bring those men back, but it meant a bit of closure amidst the great sense of loss that he still felt for his friends' deaths. In addition to the captures, the raid discovered and destroyed a significant amount of weaponry, including:

- (173) 60mm mortar rounds
- (13) 120mm mortar rounds
- (3) 122mm artillery rounds
- (13) rocket propelled grenades
- (2) rocket propelled grenade launchers
- (65) hand grenades
- (8) cans of small-arms ammunition
- (500) pounds of explosives
- (4) mortar sights
- (2) sniper rifle scopes

AFTERMATH

The insurgency in Owesat had been dealt a fearsome blow. But it wasn't giving up without a fight. There were so many insurgent detainees at Dogwood that everyone was at a loss as to how to hold them. The quick solution was to get the dozers to dig a 30-foot-deep hole in the ground and ring it with concertina wire. It wasn't pretty at all, but it would do for the moment. The next day the prisoners were given food and boxes of water and were escorted to restrooms. There wasn't too much reason to worry, because most would be out-processed in a matter of a day or two. But that night, it was Alpha Company's duty to keep an eye on the prisoners. Exhausted from days of labor, though, the men on watch went to sleep. Somehow, eight of the prisoners clambered up the side of the sand wall and used the boxes that the water had come in as cover to cross over the concertina wire. In the morning there was chaos. Were they still on the base? Were they a threat? A quick reaction force set off following the prisoners' trail, but they were nowhere to be found. It was presumed that they had returned to Owesat, perhaps to fight another day.

Even worse, in the desert northwest of Owesat, over a week later, 15 Iraqi bodies were discovered. They had been zip tied and executed, presumably in retribution for the losses suffered by the insurgency on the Screaming Chicken raid. The bodies had been in the desert for a few days and were in bad shape. An Iraqi Army unit was called in to police up the area. It was the worst thing that the 150th soldiers who made the discovery and set the perimeter would ever see.

For Lieutenant Colonel Robinson, the Screaming Chicken raid resulted in some deep soul-searching. It was he who had ordered the choppers to open fire on the insurgents in the river. He did truly believe – and all intelligence pointed to the fact – that those in the boats were insurgents, enemy combatants. But Robinson couldn't help but wonder if there had also been civilians in those boats. The thought continued to nag at him. He felt the loss of every soldier under his command deeply, but this was a different kind of hurt. A Catholic priest made rounds to Dogwood once a month, and on his next visit Robinson went to confessional in the FOB chapel, which was named after Sean Cooley. He told the priest his fears, and the priest responded in a kindly and reassuring manner. It was a war zone. People sadly get caught in the middle in a war zone. It was not Robinson's responsibility to sort all of that out. The reassurance allayed the worst of Robinson's fears, but the cost of that decision would remain with him always.

DOGPATCH

In the wake of the major success of the Screaming Chicken raid, Bravo Company put into place the next idea – one to deal directly with the threat posed by the village. Cutting the dike road had been a start, forcing traffic onto the desert side west of the village. But FOB Dogwood was so distant that it did not allow for effective traffic control or overlook of the village. Also, for raids the 150th wanted instant access to Owesat instead of driving in from the desert, which always gave the insurgents time to escape across the river. Captain Lyon and his men thought that they had the perfect answer. There was a lone, abandoned house on the western outskirts of Owesat. Lyon proposed taking that house over and making it a forward observation post. Robinson gave the go-ahead, and soon there were Hesco barriers surrounding the house and crew-served weapons on the roof. Like Bottom Line at Checkpoint 100 to the south, the new position outside of Owesat, which became known as Dogpatch, was occupied by a platoon of soldiers on a rotating basis. Unlike Bottom Line, though, Dogpatch was within observation and support distance from the other outposts at Dogwood, especially OP3, allowing the footprint of the base to be extended ever outward. It had long been Robinson's goal to push observation posts further out into the desert to help hinder any possible mortar attacks on the base, which had worked wonders. Now the outpost system there was a permanent American position that kept constant watch on Owesat and oversight of almost the entire Dogwood AO. In addition, the location of Dogpatch allowed for raids on foot into Owesat that were designed to keep the insurgents off balance. Such raids took place nearly every week over the next months – small raids with small targets based on intelligence. The raids kept the insurgents guessing and made Owesat an increasingly difficult place for their operations.

One of the first such surprise raids into Owesat, aimed at the homes of two suspected insurgents, was not without its difficulties. It was after midnight that elements of Bravo Company formed up and set out toward its carefully chosen target houses. Intelligence had again indicated the presence of a major player in the insurgency, and his house was the key. The area in and around Owesat was crisscrossed by small canals, used both for irrigation and as the local septic system. And within 20 yards of leaving Dogpatch, the first of the troopers had tumbled in. He came up sputtering and remarking that the water that had gotten all in his mouth and nose tasted like shit. That's because it was full of shit, his buddies told him. The dude started retching on the spot, with everyone trying to stifle their laughter lest the sleeping inhabitants of Owesat hear them. But by the time the mission was over, nearly everyone had taken a shit tumble. It was so bad that, on the next day, the laundry unit refused to wash their nasty clothes.

It quickly became clear that the insurgents didn't like the new American presence at Dogpatch. Chris Thomas and his men were at Dogpatch one day pulling duty when one heard "pop, pop, pop" followed by colors in the sky. Thomas remarked, "Oh, look at that. Those are tracer rounds. Somebody's shooting at us." Then it registered more completely. "Oh shit, someone is shooting at us!" He and his men all hit the dirt. Several of the first platoons stationed at Dogpatch had a similar experience. Sometimes it was just boring duty, with Kirk Dyer remembering that some soldiers entertained themselves by waiting until one of their buddies had to use the porta-john. Then they would shoot a dummy round from a grenade launcher into the side of the porta-john and let the hilarity begin.

WHO LIKES A VISIT TO THE DENTIST?

Life for the 150th in its AO continued to ping-pong between the hard hand of war on one side and humanitarian outreach to the civilian population on the other. In some ways, the back and forth was confusing; having to turn on and off war and compassion. But it was the reality of the 150th's conflict. Only ten days after the massively successful Screaming Chicken raid on Owesat, Alpha Company led one of its largest humanitarian missions in the southern village of Sharmia. Kevin Kelly recorded the results in his journal:

When we finally got everything set-up, we had our first customer. Most of the people they saw were kids. They didn't know what they were getting into. I believe they thought we were going to give away stuff if they let the dentist look in their mouth. Wrong answer, there were teeth that had to be pulled first. The first little boy was about 10 years old and scared to death. Once I told him I had a bag of toys and candy for everyone, he sat there like a champ and didn't move. While he was sitting there, the dentist applied a local by needle and then pulled the tooth right there. I don't think any of them had ever been to a dentist or had a tooth pulled before. They didn't know what to do when their mouth went numb. They were drooling everywhere and not sure if to spit, swallow or just hold everything in their mouth. It took a little coaching.

We did have a 90-year-old man that showed up for them to look at his teeth. When I say teeth, I mean TWO of them. That was all he had left in his mouth. One of them was infected. When he sat down in the chair, he told the dentist that his wife had told him that if he came home with both teeth pulled, she would leave him, and he could find another wife. The dentist then had a little boy around 7 years old that sat there ready for a tooth to be pulled. The doc actually pulled out two. When he was done, the doc pulled out a dollar bill and explained to the boy that in America when you have a tooth pulled, you put it under your pillow and a tooth fairy comes and gives you money. He told the boy since he was a U.S. Govt. representative of the tooth fairy, he was granted special permission to give him the money now. When he told the little boy that, the little boy opened his mouth and pointed in his mouth and said he had another one that was hurting and it needed to be pulled. He was proud of his dollar, but no other tooth had to be pulled.

Our last patient was a little boy that we knew had already been through and didn't have any problems. He wanted another toy out of my Santa bag. I told him to let me look. He opened his mouth and I told him he was fine and he could leave. The dentist had another treat for him. The dentist had him sit down and when he looked in his mouth this time, he said that he was going to have to pull 5 of them. The little boy jumped up and started saying that nothing was wrong with his teeth, and that they all felt wonderful. Everyone started laughing and he ended up getting another toy. We all thought he deserved it.

I think we ended up seeing about 60 patients in a 4-hour timeframe. Not bad.

OPERATION *MUDJAHARIN AL-ANSAR MOSQUE*

The humanitarian missions in the south and raids to obtain information in the north had paid off. Combined intelligence indicated that insurgent leaders were set for a secret meeting in the mosque in Sharmiyah in the far north of the AO. It was discovered that the meeting was preparatory to an attack on Abu Ghraib Prison, and included several leading insurgents, including Jamal Ahmad Dahal, a former Iraqi Army chemical weapons officer, and other key members of the Talwid al-Jihad and Ansar al-Sunna terror groups. The sensitivity of the intelligence necessitated very quick planning, which would involve most of the battalion. Accompanying the 150th would be the Hillah Swat, a hundred-man team of specially trained Iraqi police.

The raid got underway at 10 p.m. on August 4, with US forces navigating their way to Sharmiyah using night-vision devices. The troops swung well to the west in the desert, using a new route far from the prying eyes of any villagers to the east who might tip off the insurgents. Even so, with night vision unable to discern depth, a few vehicles ran afoul of a depression in the desert. It was worst for the Iraqis, though. Many of the Hillah Swat members rode in the back of armed pickup trucks. Larry Odom was in a vehicle riding behind the Swat members when they hit the hole in the desert. Hillah Swat members came flying out of the pickup like kernels from a popcorn machine. But they scrambled back to their vehicle and rejoined the formation.

Until this point, the village had been relatively peaceful. It was far to the northern edge of the AO, and the 150th had been undermanned and focused on Owesat, so missions into the village had been few and far between. It had been the arrival of Charlie Company that had made possible the first major raid on Sharmiyah back in June. But still the insurgents felt the village to be safe enough to have a planning meeting there. Expecting nothing, the insurgents were caught totally by surprise. US Special Forces preceded the 150th into Sharmiyah to hit the mosque itself, capturing eight specially targeted individuals. The battalion then roared in and set an outer cordon around the village and got down to the urgent business of rousing out additional insurgents. Breaking the village up into sectors, the 150th began to round up detainees. Every home in the village was raided, with some of the guys noting that the doors here were tougher to kick open than those in Owesat. In total more than 100 detainees were rounded up. Then they had to be taken to a vehicle in the center of town where the Screaming Chicken once again sat masked and gave the thumbs up or thumbs down to each detainee.

Part of Bravo Company was to link up with the Special Forces troops at the mosque so that they could depart with their bounty of specially targeted insurgent leaders. Once Bravo Company arrived, the Special Forces operatives loaded their top targets onto a chopper and departed, leaving numerous other detainees for Bravo Company to deal with. As Bravo worked to catalogue the captives, a drone reported that a vehicle had fled Sharmiyah and was headed to another nearby village. Robinson reported that the house the insurgents had fled to had been identified and marked. Captain Lyon was tasked with going to hit the new target house. Leaving most of Bravo Company behind to manage their haul of detainees, Lyon departed with a patrol numbering just a single squad, led by a tank, to the new site. It was four vehicles rolling into a new village, facing an unknown threat. Kirk Dyer could hardly believe their bad luck. The dangerous mission was almost over, and now he was part of a tiny group rolling into the unknown in enemy territory.

Lyon's makeshift squad reached the target house without incident and set up a quick cordon. Dyer led the stack of men and burst through the front door, but there was nobody inside. Methodically, the group made its way to the roof, where Dyer surprised two military age males. Both were detained and made ready for transport back to link up with the rest of the battalion. But all the vehicles were full; there was no place for the detainees to sit. So, it was a ride back on the hoods of the vehicles for them. Once back in Sharmiyah, the two were hauled before the Screaming Chicken. Both got the thumbs down. Later it was discovered that one of the two men was the regional commander of the insurgent group Ansar al-Sunna and was one of the most wanted insurgents in the entirety of Iraq.

In all the 150th captured 39 identified insurgents that night. In addition to the Ansar al-Sunna leader netted by Lyon and his men, two of the other insurgents identified were among the top leadership of the Talwid al-Jihad terror group. Both insurgent organizations were crippled by the raid. The planned attack on Abu Ghraib fizzled, and the Talwid al-Jihad and Ansar al-Sunna terror groups were so unhappy with events that they blamed each other for the word slipping out on their meeting. As a result, the two groups began to feud, greatly limiting their ability to conduct operations in the area. It was a signal success for Lieutenant Colonel Robinson and his men. The positive relationship with the citizens of the area had led to gaining critical intelligence that had crippled the local insurgency. Coupled with the tremendous success of the Screaming Chicken raid on Owesat, the insurgents in the 150th AO had taken two tremendous blows.

THE CHANGING SITUATION

As Commander of Multi-National Force – Iraq, General George Casey faced a difficult situation as 2005 dragged on. There was still major fighting, with a focus along the Iraq–Syria border, but the war had obviously, in his view, become more suited to counterinsurgency than main force operations. As the Mississippians were raiding Sharmiyah, Casey sent out a team of advisors led by Colonels William Hix and Kalev Sepp to survey the actions of US units in-country. What they found was an Army all too likely devoted to the main force operations that had been their doctrinal bread and butter for decades. In their view, Hix reported, 20 percent of US units "got" counterinsurgency, 60 percent were in the middle, and 20 percent clearly did not get it. Their recommendations included raising the number of American troops in Iraq to make counterinsurgency more feasible. Getting off bases and working with and among the people was key to hamstringing the insurgency, in their view. Eliminating insurgents remained important in their thinking, but stopping them from returning was perhaps even more important.* What Casey and his team were calling for, and what would become the hallmark of General David Petraeus during the subsequent "surge" of 2007, was second nature to the troops of the Mississippi National Guard in eastern Anbar Province. Thinking outside of the military box is how the Guard operates, and it was paying dividends in the 150th's AO – dividends that would help chart a more successful course for the entire war going forward.

THE DRUMBEAT OF WAR

Regardless of the 150th's effective tactics, or perhaps even because of them, the insurgents weren't going down without a fight. On the evening of August 19, it fell to Charlie Company to kick out the counter-mortar patrol for the day. The basic idea was to flush any potential insurgent mortars out of range of Dogwood by the sheer presence of the US patrol. As usual, a tank led the way and took care to not cross any previously left tracks. Unpredictability was Charlie Company's ally. Manning the .50-caliber in the lead M113 was Chad Dauzat, who had been born in Thibodaux, Louisiana. When Chad was nine, his parents divorced, which brought him to Amory, Mississippi. He played football and did well in school. He got married in high school before his graduation in 2001 and was greatly impacted by the terrorist attacks of 9/11. He went straight into the Guard, and in 2004 had volunteered to transfer to the 150th so that he could go and fight for his country. Chad was known for many things in Charlie Company, chiefly his dedication to his country and his never-failing good humor. Dauzat was an experienced gunner,

---

*Rayburn and Sobchak, *The U.S. Army in the Iraq War*, 445–446.

one of the most talented in the 150th, and August 19 was just another patrol. So, he was taking it easy, allowing his arm to rest atop the armor of the .50-caliber's cupola.

A command-detonated IED went off beside Dauzat's 113, and shrapnel tore through his arm, shattering his wrist. Captain Chris Thomas immediately brought the patrol to a halt and rushed to the M113. The IED had detonated next to the vehicle rather than beneath it, so the 113 itself was unscathed. Dauzat was a different story. Thomas reached him, not really taking time to worry about any secondary IEDs in the area, and found Dauzat covered in blood with his hand dangling at a bizarre angle. The guys told Dauzat that he had a "million dollar wound" and would be headed back to the States. Dauzat seemed partly in shock but remained cheerful as the medevac chopper came in and took him to the hospital in Baghdad. Sure enough, Dauzat's buddies were right. The wound was bad enough to see him shipped first to Germany, then to Walter Reed in Washington, DC, and next to Fort Gordon in Texas for treatment, before he was finally sent home. He never returned to the unit.

Dauzat's best buddy in the unit was Greg Fernandez, who didn't happen to be on the patrol that evening. Fernandez hailed from Grenada in the northern part of the state and had joined the Guard in 2003. He had been working with heavy equipment for his uncle's trucking company since he was 15 years old, so working with similar equipment as a combat engineer seemed to be a natural fit. Originally, he was with the 223rd Engineers, but had finished his basic training too late to allow him to go on their 2003 deployment to Iraq. Instead, he was transferred to the 150th in 2004, showing up at Camp Shelby in October after most of the unit's training was already complete. He made fast friends with Dauzat; the two loved to head to Hattiesburg and hit the bars on their nights off. Trying to catch up with the others, though, caused problems. Fernandez took all his overseas shots on the same day – all nine. He got "sick as a dog" and had to be isolated to his barracks for nearly a week. The doc asked him what the hell he had been thinking, and Fernandez could only tell him that he wanted to get ready for Iraq as quickly as possible.

Like the rest of Charlie Company, Fernandez had not headed to Dogwood to start; instead, he made the rounds of FOB Duke, Hotel, and Kalsu. While at Kalsu he was assigned to widen the entrance to the base, so he got his dozer and a dump truck and headed out, getting the job done in an afternoon. The base commander was amazed. It had taken the Navy Seabees over a week to complete a similar mission in the past. When asked how he could have done it in an afternoon, Fernandez simply responded, "Well, sir. I'm a combat engineer. That's what we do."

Fernandez had arrived at Dogwood with the remainder of Charlie Company in mid-June, and he had been singularly unimpressed with the FOB, considering where he had been before. It was only a week later that his M113 had been hit by its first IED. It was a small one, and it had been buried poorly, which focused the blast upward rather than out. And it had been command-detonated, exploding beside rather than under the vehicle. No damage or injuries, but it sure meant that operations at Dogwood were the real deal. Fernandez had actually enjoyed the major raids on Owesat and Sharmiyah. It meant that they were making headway.

Like almost everyone else in the 150th, Fernandez got assigned to resupply convoys, and on August 21 he headed out on such a mission. He was driving the 916 tractor-trailer truck, and this one was a bit worse for wear. Its headlights were stuck on high beam and its brakes were wonky. But he was an experienced driver and felt very comfortable behind the wheel with Virgil Scott riding by his side. The first stop was FOB Kalsu, where the 150th's vehicles met up with a convoy of the 2/11th ACR headed to Baghdad. The convoy departed in the dead of night for safety reasons, and Fernandez was given a handheld radio for communications with the other vehicles. The makeup of the convoy baffled him. There was a lead truck, followed by two 916s, then a gun truck, then a 916, then his vehicle. Behind him was another gun truck, another 916, another gun truck, and then two HEMTTs, with a gun truck in the rear. The odd issue was that the HEMTTs were the slowest vehicles in the convoy. The slowest should be in the front, he thought, so they wouldn't fall behind. No matter. It was time to move out. Radio check. The damn batteries were out on his radio. He got out to tell the convoy leader to wait while he got new batteries. But he was told that there was no time, and the convoy took off, leaving him to scramble back to his truck to try to catch up.

He had that 916 floored; it was still falling further and further behind. But he was going fast enough to outpace the vehicles behind him. In 30 minutes the taillights of the vehicle in front of him were lost, and now Fernandez was flying blind alone, in the middle of Iraq. He was pissed, scared, and had no radio contact. He was sure as hell going to yell at someone when they got to Baghdad. Then he saw it. Lights in the middle of the road. It was another American convoy coming toward him, and it was coming to a halt. Fernandez knew procedure. A lone vehicle on the roads approaching a convoy would be fired upon – presumably an insurgent vehicle-borne IED. But his lights were on bright, blinding the oncoming convoy, and his brakes were so crappy that they wouldn't stop him in time. Virgil tried the radio, but the damn thing was still dead. All Fernandez could think of was to reach up and pull the air horn. Surely the oncoming convoy would recognize its sound as American.

Fernandez had to sit up and look up to reach the horn. Then the windshield exploded, peppering his eyes with more than 100 small shards of glass, and he lurched backwards as the bullet struck home, straight into his neck. He could hardly see anything, and yelled, "Virgil, I'm hit! I'm hit! I'm hit!" Virgil couldn't believe that Fernandez had been shot and said, "What?" Fernandez yelled, "Dude, I'm fucking hit!" Safety of the vehicle no longer a concern, Fernandez reached down and popped the main brake, and the truck screeched to a halt. He jumped from the vehicle and tossed his helmet aside and pulled off his body armor. That is when he felt the blood. He was soaked in blood from the neck to the waist, and it was flowing like a river. He thought, "Shit. This ain't good." He didn't hurt much – his body was in shock and didn't allow much pain. He reached into his neck to the middle knuckles on his hand. "That ain't good either," he thought. He could still feel the bullet in there.

Seconds later the oncoming convoy realized what had happened and a soldier rushed to his side, Aric Seiber. The bullet had severed both the jugular vein and carotid artery, leaving Fernandez only minutes to live. Seiber was not a medic but had Combat Lifesaver training and even had a medical bag. He put pressure onto the wounds and bandaged the jugular and carotid as best he could to stop the geyser of blood. By this time, Fernandez had worked out the seriousness of his condition. He was dying. And he had one thought. Get his weapon and shoot the dumb motherfucker who shot him. Fernandez yelled, "I know that dumb fuck shot me," and reached toward his weapon.

Seiber stopped him and asked him how the hell was he still so alert given what was going on with his body. Fernandez responded, "I'm a damn country boy from Mississippi, that's how!" Seiber shot back, "Well, I'm a damn country boy from Tennessee, and I ain't gonna let you do that."

Once he settled down a bit, Fernandez realized that he didn't blame the guy who shot him. That was convoy security protocol after all. And, as it turned out, the other convoy was made up of soldiers who had just arrived in Iraq. This was their very first convoy. Their very first night off their FOB. Seiber started looking at Fernandez funny, which meant that he was dying. Someone had started three IVs, slamming him with fluids to try to stave off the inevitable. All of this took barely a couple of minutes. Then the medevac thundered in. They were in such a hurry that they tossed him onto the damn thing, and just a couple of minutes later it landed at the hospital so quickly that it bounced three times. It was at that time that Fernandez finally passed out; he didn't think that he was going to sleep. He knew he was dying.

Three days later Fernandez woke up at the US military hospital in Landstuhl, Germany. The nurse on duty told him that someone had been waiting to see him. Turned out that it was Chad Dauzat, who was still recovering from his own wounds. Part from surprise, part from being so sick, Fernandez promptly barfed everywhere. And Chad Dauzat didn't like it when folks barfed, so he politely excused himself and told Fernandez he would catch up with him later. Fernandez figured that he looked like a pin cushion. He had a chest tube, a drain hanging out of his neck. And his eyes were swollen and not crossed exactly but looking outward. His right pupil had been destroyed, his lenses knocked out, one of his optic nerves had taken heavy damage, and the muscles had been shorn (which explained the eyes-looking-out part). He had 25 staples holding part of his neck together, and over 52 on his leg from where they had taken a vein to replace the carotid artery. His jugular had just been sealed off. The docs told him that whoever had bandaged him in the field had saved his life.

Fernandez's mother, Betty, was in the hospital herself, having just had gallbladder surgery, when she heard that her son had been wounded. She had tried to call but had never been able to make it through to his room in Landstuhl. Well, that wasn't going to work. So, she called Senator Trent Lott about the whole mess. A little later, Fernandez was surprised when a full-bird colonel walked into his room and handed him a cell phone. "Son. You had better speak to your mama." After the talk Fernandez went to give the phone back to the colonel, but the officer said, "No. You hang on to it for a while and call whoever you want." On the phone with his mom, Fernandez had talked about next steps. He was going to be sent to Walter Reed in Washington, DC, in a couple of days. His mom said that she would meet him there. No amount of protests from Fernandez about his mom's fragile health dissuaded her. Then she hung up. She had to make her flight arrangement soon, because there was a storm in the Gulf of Mexico bearing down on Mississippi, and she was going to be lucky to get a flight at all before it made landfall. Fernandez asked her the name of the storm. Katrina.

THE GATHERING STORM

Even with all the recent events, the mood at Dogwood was bright. Sometimes it is the simple things that mean the most, and the FOB had just seen the opening of real, honest-to-God, functional toilets. No more stinking, boiling hot porta-johns. There were even workable showers now too! Even the upgraded chow hall seemed about ready to open. It was about that time that reports had begun to trickle in about the massive storm in the Gulf of Mexico. Now these were Mississippi Guard soldiers. They had all been through hurricanes before and had often been tasked with disaster relief following such storms. Everyone in Mississippi had been there and done that. But this storm seemed unlike anything ever seen before, at least since Hurricane Camille had destroyed the Mississippi coast in 1969.

Missions still had to be run, and posts occupied, but the most popular place at Dogwood quickly became the Morale, Welfare, and Recreation tent, where a packed crowd watched Katrina roll ashore on a 52-inch television. The storm first wobbled toward New Orleans, but then took a dead aim on the Mississippi coast and many of the 150th's families. The mood quickly darkened and everyone who lived south of Jackson tried to call home. The phones were jammed, but everyone had to get through. For Kirk Dyer it was a hugely cathartic moment, the most difficult of his entire deployment. He had always been the one at risk, telling his family that he would be safe and not to worry.

He had always known that he just had to put his head down, do his job, and survive. He never had to worry about himself, and it was so comforting to know that his family was safe and sound. But suddenly everything was topsy-turvy. His family was in the crosshairs of the most massive and destructive storm that anyone could remember. And no amount of reassurance from his wife could assuage his fear – a fear so palpable that it seemed like a presence in the room. Suddenly he realized what the families at home had been going through since February. The shoe was on the other foot, and it hurt badly.

Richard Rowland was finally able to get through just as the leading winds of the storm began to lash his home. The wind was so damn loud that he could hear it on the phone over his wife Keltoum's voice – and she was inside. He heard the cracks and booms as the tall pines of the area were shattered and came crashing down. Keltoum was cheerful, kind of narrating events. "The wind is really picking up. Listen, those are trees coming down." Then there was a massive WHUMP! And Keltoum said, "Wow! One just came down on the house..." Then the phone line went dead. Stacey Ford, who had been injured in the blast that had killed Sean Cooley, was on the phone with his son-in-law at the same time. His son-in-law kept having to talk louder to be heard over the din as the first of 16 trees came down nearby. Amidst the crashing, Ford heard his son-in-law yell, "There goes another..." and then the line cut out and buzzed with static. The same story was repeated over and over, especially for those of Bravo Company from the southern part of the state. Power went out everywhere, communications went down – like the reverse of the situation when the communications were cut after a death or injury in Iraq. And the news stations were fixated on the disaster that befell New Orleans. There was no way to get information on the southern part of the state of Mississippi. Everyone stared at everyone else in the MWR tent. Were their homes still intact? Had their families survived? Nobody knew, a situation that persisted for days. And the men still had to go out on missions and to fight their war, even while they feared for the lives of their loved ones.

AT HOME

Laura Cooley couldn't follow the orders to evacuate the Mississippi coast. As a nurse, her presence was deemed essential. Then she started to think. She had never been able to make herself go through Sean's belongings after his death in February. Now the predicted storm surge meant that all her memories of Sean were at risk. She packed everything she could of Sean's and put it as high as possible in her home. It was like going through his life in double-time speed. In some ways Katrina was good for Laura, forcing her to confront his loss and to see all those pictures of them so happy – moments that would never be repeated. She took Sean's truck over to her parents, who lived on higher ground, hoping that it wouldn't flood there. But the move didn't pay off. Her parents wound up with 6 feet of water in their home; Laura wound up with 3. Furniture, walls – all destroyed. Sean's truck was totaled. But at least the boxes and pictures were safe.

Laura's parents had a generator, so the first couple of nights after Katrina were spent in their sodden house. Next, she stayed with an uncle for a couple of nights, but that wasn't a long-term solution. Finally, she moved in with a friend and her child. She stayed in the ruins of their home, which was torn down to the studs (at least their water was working), for two weeks before a FEMA trailer turned up for her. She had been living in homes with no electricity, barely any food, and only a trickle of running water for six weeks. Through it all, she had to work and could only wear the few clothes of hers that had survived the flood. All while still wrestling with the previously unconfronted death of her husband. On one steaming evening while getting ready for work, Laura sat there in the Mississippi humidity and darkness as the obligatory cloud of mosquitoes moved in and thought, "I will never survive another year like this one. I'll just throw in the towel if anything like this ever happens again."

The Lee family was still trying to come to grips with the loss of Terrance. His grandmother Anice and his mother Dinah sat and talked about him every day, trying so hard to keep his memory alive. But it was Terrance's two sons, Terrance Jr. and Raemone, who had the most difficult time adjusting. They kept asking where their daddy was and could not come to grips with the idea that his life had ended and that he would never come back to them. For Terrance's wife Stephanie, her advancing pregnancy with the couple's child was an ever-present reminder of the void his absence left in her life. It was so bittersweet. She looked forward to welcoming Terrance's child into the world but was also distraught that he would never meet that child.

As Stephanie neared her due date, the weather reports began to become more alarming as Katrina bore down on the Gulf Coast. And damned if it didn't look like the storm was going to hit just as her baby was due. The Lees, who lived much closer to the coast, evacuated barely in front of the storm, but Stephanie was determined to stay put. Her home was in Lucedale, about 50 miles from the coast and from what was expected to be the worst of the weather. But Lucedale was far from spared by the storm. Trees were down everywhere, many smashing homes; roofs were gone, roads were next to unpassable, and power was off for weeks. And, since Lucedale wasn't in the path of Katrina's eye, rescue and cleanup efforts came there only in fits and starts, with crews focused more on New Orleans and the devastated Mississippi Gulf Coast.

With power out everywhere across the southern part of Mississippi, and with nobody knowing when it might come back on, family and friends urged Stephanie to evacuate. So, Stephanie got Terrance's pistol, hopped into the family pickup, and left for Shreveport, Louisiana. But she wasn't going to evacuate. No sir. She was headed to Louisiana to buy a generator and then return home. Others could run away or flee. But not Stephanie. She was determined to bring her baby to *her* home – the home she had planned to share with Terrance – and that *her* home was going to have electricity when her new child entered this world. It took two days of fighting through roadways jammed with evacuees, but Stephanie completed her journey and returned to Lucedale, then went straight into the hospital and gave birth to the couple's daughter, Marchelle. And then she went straight home to be alone with the children. She wanted nothing more than them and the memory of Terrance.

Melinda, Larry, and Robert Arnold had also spent the last two months attempting to navigate the emptiness left in their lives by the loss of Larry Arnold Senior. The increasingly frightening reports on Katrina, and the mandatory evacuation order, jolted the family into the present. Melinda and Larry evacuated north to Arkansas, but Robert decided to stay behind. Their home was projected to be directly in the path of the massive storm's eye, but Robert wasn't leaving. Robert was in a particularly dark place, having lost his father and then not being allowed back to Iraq to serve out his tour. His head was spinning with loss, grief, guilt, and a deep anger. He figured that he didn't have anything to lose in the storm, so he stayed. And he was going to make for damn sure that nobody looted their home in the wake of the storm. Nobody was going to touch his father's cars and belongings – the tangible testament of his life. Those things were staying put.

The area around the Arnolds' home was devastated. Power and water were out, in places for months; everywhere seemed a tangled mess of fallen trees. Homes were shattered. Nobody was spared. Looters did try to come by the Arnolds' on one occasion, but that once was enough. There was no more trouble after that. It was during that lonely time – with the desolation and isolation reminding Robert of the desert – that Robert got to think. He wrestled with the demons of loss, anger, and guilt. Nobody was going to save him. He was alone. But in that struggle came redemption. Amidst the solitude, Robert came to the decision that his mother and family needed him more than ever. He had to crawl out of his own well of despair for them. The past would never be put behind him, but Katrina helped him look to the future.

ESQUIRE

Tom Junod knew how to write a story. An award-winning writer, he had worked for nearly every big magazine including *GQ*, *Life*, and *Sports Illustrated*. In 2005 he was working for *Esquire* and had become interested in the war unfolding in Iraq. Mark Warren, his editor at *Esquire*, had heard of the loss of Larry Arnold in his dealings with the Iraq War and had noticed in August that Katrina was bearing down on his hometown. He thought to himself, "Jesus Christ. How much can one family take?" Warren decided to chronicle the story, and met up with Junod in Atlanta to discuss "the doubly devastated: those who'd lost a father, son, brother to the war that year and then had lost everything again." First, they made their way to Picayune and to Robert Arnold's trailer.* Melinda and Larry had only been able to evacuate to Arkansas in the first place by using some of Larry Senior's death benefit. But they had lost touch with

---

*Much of the information in this section comes from a blend of interviews with Larry and Robert Arnold and the Lee family, combined with Tom Junod's article "Mississippi Goddamn," which appeared in *Esquire* in November 2005, and the podcast "Mark Warren on the Odyssey of Stephanie Lee, 'Patient Zero,'" *Esquire Classic*, 2016.

Robert since the phones were out and had taken to reading casualty lists from the area, hoping not to see his name. Seventeen were confirmed killed in Pearl River County, Mississippi, but Robert's name was not on the list. So, Melinda and Larry bundled into the car to return to see if Robert was indeed safe. They found Robert amidst devastation that they couldn't believe. But the family's trailers were intact, and Robert had protected their precious belongings. For the Arnolds it was all so surreal. The hubbub of reporters and attention that had come with Larry Senior's loss had returned. Larry appreciated that Junod and others cared about his father, and approved of the article that he eventually wrote. But in some ways it also seemed so wrong. It seemed like his father wasn't important until he got killed. He thought to himself, "Where were these people when dad was alive? He was a great man when he was alive. They are here only now to find out who dad was, instead of finding out who he was while he was alive."

Junod and Warren were touched by the story of the Arnolds and of their perseverance through loss. But they were floored by Stephanie Lee. Interviews with Anice and Terrance's family were revealing and difficult. But getting to know Stephanie was like getting to know a force of nature. There she was, hunkered down in her home with her newly procured generator keeping the lights going. Stephanie informed them that she had named her daughter Marchelle Elyses, the name that she and Terrance had chosen together before his departure. And Junod witnessed a reunion. It took two days before Anice was able to make the journey to Lucedale to see her great-grandchild. She just wasn't sure if she could take meeting Terrance's new daughter without having Terrance there. So, she asked her husband Robert Earl to pull over to give her time to collect her thoughts as they neared Stephanie's. Stephanie just happened to be returning home to meet them at the same time and saw them pulled over, so she pulled over as well. She was in Terrance's truck, riding with Terrance's baby. Anice trembled now that the moment was here. She forced her legs to allow her to stand and go over to the truck. Then she locked eyes on Marchelle and it was like looking into Terrance's eyes. That was all that it took. Anice turned to her husband and said, "Robert Earl, you go on. I'm getting in the truck with that baby."

Warren and Junod were greatly impressed by the fortitude and perseverance of both the Arnolds and the Lees in the face of unimaginable loss and hardship. They published their article in *Esquire* and then moved on to other stories. But somehow they couldn't shake the idea that the tale of these Mississippi families was far from over.

BACK TO THE WAR

At Dogwood days went by as men began to piece together what had happened to their families and homes. Some heard quickly; for others it took up to an agonizing week to learn their loved ones' fate. Some, especially those who lived from Jackson northward, were relieved to hear that all was well. But the southern part of the state was devastated, especially impacting those of Bravo Company. Douglas Mansfield stood for many when he was finally able to get through to his father via an old-fashioned land line. Power was out and trees were down, leaving Mansfield's elderly father to sleep outside on a cot at night. Mansfield's father was prepared with a generator, so not all the food in the fridge was destroyed, but that generator made noise. People had already come once to try to steal Mansfield's generator, forcing him to chase them off with a gun. Gary Kinsey was from Gautier, well within the flood zone for the massive tidal surge caused by the storm. His car and back deck were just gone – carried away by the flood waters. There had been 4 feet of water in his home, destroying everything.

Everyone from the southern part of the state was hearing similar tidings. Damage, no power, no chance of getting power or water anytime soon, looting, danger. Some in the unit were impacted so deeply that they required emergency leave to go home and lend a hand. But that list potentially included nearly everyone in Bravo Company. So, dealing with the leave situation became a massive problem. Surely not everyone could go home at once. Instead, leave was parceled out in dribs and drabs to allow the 150th to continue to function. Gary Kinsey, who had lost everything, was one of those allowed to return to set his family's life to right. It was a hard-working home leave to say the least, spent ripping out sheet rock and insulation, and working to get electricity running again. Everything had to be bleached as well. With the help of family and church friends, Kinsey was putting sheet rock back up when it was time to return to Iraq. Those at Dogwood who found out good news that their property had avoided significant damage and those who were able to go home to help greatly admired those who suffered but were unable to return. Here they were – helpless, unable to aid their families in their time of greatest need, but still they went out on missions every day. Still, they soldiered on. To Greg Wells, who had long served as Trent Kelly's driver, the moment was inspiring and touching. As the units gathered for their patrols, they paused for their traditional prayers, and as Wells looked on he noticed that many of the soldiers had tears running down their cheeks for what they had lost, for the uncertainty. Yet they went out the gate and returned to war.

Through it all, loss continued. At home, Joshua Russell of the 890th Engineer Battalion, who had already served in Iraq as part of the original invasion, was helping with hurricane rescue efforts when his Humvee struck storm debris, killing him. He was on his way to rescue his own grandparents at the time and became the first Mississippi Guardsman killed conducting relief operations on state active duty. Carl Carroll was a Williamstown, Pennsylvania native who was working as a contractor at FOB Kalsu. He had retired from a long career in the Army flying helicopters. He felt that he still had more to give to his country, though, so he had signed on with the Titan Corporation for work in Iraq. He died from wounds from an IED attack, as Katrina slammed into the coast back home.

At FOB Iskandariyah, word came to Tucker McNeese and his A&O Platoon that it had been assigned a mission to travel to a nearby village to assess the schools in the area. It was hoped that working with families and perhaps even adopting local schools could help stem the tide of the insurgency around the FOB. Major Gregory Fester and a contingent of the 322nd Civil Affairs Brigade accompanied McNeese and his men on their mission. Fester had completed his military service but had been called back as part of the stop-loss program and found himself part of the unit supporting the Mississippians at FOB Iskandariyah. After assessing the schools, the convoy was hit with an IED on its return trip, killing Major Fester. His friends were left to open his last care package that day sent by his wife Julie, which included a picture of her.

Finally, Major Lowell Miller of Flint, Michigan, who was assigned to the 1/155th at Iskandariyah, was killed by insurgent fire near the FOB while working alongside an Iraqi Army unit on a training mission. Miller was a graduate of the Virginia Military Institute, where he had fallen in love and gotten married. He and his wife

Jennifer had two daughters. These losses represented the continuing rising pressure of the steam boiler of the Guard's war, each impacting the 150th more and more, even as their families dug out from the wreckage of Hurricane Katrina. The war didn't seem to care about what was happening back home.

A SPECIAL BULLDOZER OPERATION

On September 6, Captain Chris Thomas of Charlie Company got a special mission. He was tasked with bringing dozers and earthmoving equipment to FOB Kalsu. Main Supply Route (MSR) Tampa, near to the entrance of the FOB, was one of the most IED-heavy areas in the 155th's AO; indeed, it was very near to where Carter Carroll had been killed only two weeks prior. Thomas and his crew were to bulldoze and clear an area a football field wide along a stretch of the MSR, to make placing IEDs much more difficult. Thomas realized that this operation would require one of his very best dozer operators. And Thomas knew just the guy. Albert Matlock of Alpha Company had joined the Guard while he was still in high school in 1983. As a long-service Guard soldier, Matlock had been working with and on heavy equipment for more than two decades. He could fix anything, and he could drive anything. Perfect for the job.

After the small convoy arrived outside of Kalsu, Matlock got that dozer to work, flattening down the earth next to MSR Tampa. As Matlock set to his job, Thomas and the others in the group stood in a semi-circle some 30 yards away and chatted as they watched his progress. About ten minutes later there was a massive explosion that lifted part of the dozer off the ground. Matlock had hit an IED. After being knocked to the ground, Thomas first directed his attention to Matlock and the dozer. He couldn't help but think that the scene looked like something out of a Yosemite Sam cartoon, with smoke and dust swirling madly around the dozer. Thomas jumped up thinking, "Oh my God! Matlock's dead!" But then, through the cloud, Matlock came staggering. Looked like he had been hit by a bull, but there he was, walking.

Matlock hollered that his ears were ringing something fierce, but otherwise he felt okay. Then Thomas heard Lieutenant Kevin Brown yelling, "I'm hit! I'm hit!" Looking over, Thomas saw Brown face down in the dirt, with his pants ripped to shreds. Through the shorn trousers

Thomas saw the gleaming white of exposed bone. Thomas ran to his side, and Brown's legs were covered in dirt and blood. He couldn't wait on a medic, so Thomas stooped to get a look at Brown's wound. Then he stopped and stared. That wasn't exposed bone. That was Brown's ID card. A piece of shrapnel had tumbled between Thomas and the man he had been standing next to, with no more than 2 feet between them, and had hit Brown a glancing blow to the ass. But it hadn't hit him directly in the ass; instead, it had sliced his wallet in half as it whizzed by, leaving the ID card exposed. To Thomas the bizarre incident laid bare the randomness of war. Matlock had hit the IED but was more or less okay. A piece of shrapnel that should have killed him had missed by inches, and instead of "de-assing" Lieutenant Brown, it had only left a couple of painful cuts and half a wallet in its wake.

Thomas and the rest of the squad were left to contemplate their good fortune. But for Matlock it was back to work. He had a job to do, and ringing ears weren't going to stop him. So, as Thomas and the others gathered their wits and a medic attended to Brown, they all looked in amazement as Matlock got back aboard the dozer and started his job anew, with a fresh hole in the ground that needed fixing. Thomas just shook his head. That is who Matlock was, he thought: the old salt soldier was like a dog that lived next to a two-lane country highway and had been hit six times by cars, but just wouldn't die. Matlock was the definition of toughness. Later, when Matlock returned to Dogwood, everyone was relieved to see him. The rumor mill had gone wild: Matlock had his legs blown off; he only had half a head. But there he was, okay. He did report to the medic the next day about the ringing in his ears. His hearing even shut off from time to time. After he left the medic, Matlock called home, but not before he told everyone in the unit to not tell his wife a damn thing about his accident. He certainly wasn't going to tell her. He knew that there would be hell to pay.

OPERATION *OWESAT CHECKUP*

Although there remained violent incidents in the AO, especially IEDs, the recent run of successful raids on Owesat and Sharmiyah led the 150th to believe that it had the insurgents on the run. So, it was time to turn up the pressure once again and try to finish the job. Since the Screaming Chicken raid in late July, which had crippled the insurgency in Owesat, there had been three major raids into the village. Using troops that had been pre-positioned at Dogpatch, the raids had been able to enter the village before the insurgents could flee across the river. As a result, in late August the 150th received intelligence that the insurgent presence was abandoning Owesat for more friendly areas outside of the AO. With that good news, Robinson reasoned that it was time to play the Dogpatch card again. On September 16, troops were shuttled to Dogpatch in secrecy and gathered for a surprise nighttime raid on foot. No vehicles; no noise; no warning. Soldiers of Bravo Company moved out on foot to ensure surprise, and were joined later by Alpha and Charlie Company troopers driving in from Dogwood. But first there was a sartorial issue that needed fixing. One of the guys in the company didn't like his false teeth. Said that they hurt when he wore them, so he usually went just plain-old toothless. However, the way that he looked without his teeth tended to scare the Iraqis, so the deal was he had to put his teeth in for missions. So, first thing was a tooth check. He had them in that night, but he didn't like it. Magically, just a couple of weeks later those teeth came up missing. He just couldn't find them anywhere.

The soldiers of Bravo infiltrated Owesat and then took up ambush positions along the dike road next to the river – which was the escape route of choice for insurgents. Once the Bravo Company ambushes were in place, Alpha and Charlie companies rolled in simultaneously from the north and the south. The plan worked like magic. Reacting to the approach of the vehicles of Alpha and Charlie companies, insurgents from across the village raced for the dike road. And they ran straight into the waiting arms of the Bravo Company ambushes. The ambushes used infrared spotlights to mark the insurgents as they ran up – lighting them up like Christmas trees for any US troops wearing night-vision goggles, but leaving the insurgents themselves unaware. They only knew that Americans were around when one popped up from the blackness, tossed the insurgent into a ditch, zip tied them, and then hid to wait for the next insurgent to be hit with an infrared spotlight. By the end of the raid there were almost 20 insurgents piled up in that ditch.

Larry Mergenschroer was in the stack that hit a target house that supposedly housed an insurgent bigwig. Choppers had shown up on scene and let everyone know that nobody had fled the building or had boarded boats to cross the river. The terrorist had to be in there.

With practiced precision, the guys checked the house from top to bottom, but he wasn't there. The house did back up to the Euphrates River, but the chopper pilots swore up and down that the target had not fled that way. They were using heat sensing technology and were certain they would have seen him leave. Mergenschroer and the other soldiers went to the bank of the river nonetheless. Nothing but a bed of reeds in the shallow water.

Then Mergenschroer noticed a black snake poking its head up between the reeds. "Odd damn place to see a snake," he thought. He looked closer. It was a black hose. One of the other soldiers waded in and yanked the hose away. A few seconds later an Iraqi sat up out of the water. He had been lying there submerged, with his sodden shirt wrapped around his head to fool the heat sensors on the choppers, and he had been breathing through the hose. Well, he wasn't breathing through it no more. They had their insurgent leader.

Nearby, Alpha Company rounded up more suspects and disabled any boats capable of crossing the river. In some ways "boat" was a kind name. Many of the craft were just sheets of tin with the edges folded up – barely able to float. As the sun began to rise and the mission wound down, more Iraqi civilians came out into the streets. At the head of the group were the children, asking for any candy or toys the soldiers might have. But one of the Iraqi mothers figured that it still wasn't safe, as this was obviously a military mission, not a humanitarian one. The woman tried to shoo the children away, and when that didn't work, she took to hitting them with a switch and throwing rocks at them. The kids got the message and started to run back inside their homes. One of the children got caught up in a fence, and it was his unlucky day. That Iraqi mama started whooping that kid something fierce. Many of the Guard soldiers broke out into peals of laughter, having been the subject of such rough summary judgement when they were children. In all, the raid was a success. More than 30 insurgents were apprehended, and the villagers seemed more accepting than usual, with the possible exception of the switch-wielding Iraqi mother. Perhaps even Owesat was turning around, and that would be the best news possible.

7

Everything Changes

Today is Thanksgiving day. Last night, SGT Villaneuva, one of the 2/11 medics, was killed by an IED in the cemetery… This morning, one of my soldiers engaged and killed the driver of a truck that came down Rte. Cherry. The boundaries of, "you will be shot if you come any further" are clearly marked. Why the man continued down the street after warning shots is anyone's guess, but the Sergeant on the guard tower followed the rules of engagement exactly. He did his job well this morning.

JAY STANDLEY, JOURNAL ENTRY

When those sheiks came in to talk, it all changed. I remember meeting with them. The commanders were talking with them, and my platoon had security duty. So I was sitting up in the turret. I'll never forget. So they are sitting there talking and this one little girl comes out with a little silver platter holding it up to me. I see a teacup there. And I think, "I don't know man." But I don't want to be rude in the meeting. So I drank it. Barely warm and tasted nasty. Gave me the shits for three days. It hit me so hard that I had to get an IV from the medic. God that was miserable.

RICHARD ROWLAND

LIFE AT DOGWOOD

Due in large part to noted scroungers like Gary Kinsey and Thomas Howell, FOB Dogwood now had everything an FOB could hope for: a full chow hall, a PX, a well. The soldiers had even moved out of their communal tents and run-down buildings and into personal, air-conditioned conexes. You always knew that you had made it as an FOB when chopper pilots shut down their machines and hung around awhile for food and recreation. And now the chopper pilots all seemed to be stopping there. A rumor was even floating around that Mississippi's governor, Haley Barbour, might even come by to visit. Maybe he would finally bring the guys their fresh Gulf shrimp. Another new arrival was a National Guard unit from Puerto Rico.

A platoon of the Puerto Rican contingent joined Chris Thomas and Charlie Company, replacing the platoon from Vermont that had served under him for a few months. Thomas knew all of about 12 words of Spanish and tried to use them all in welcoming the new soldiers. He led off with the obligatory "Buenos días" before introducing himself and giving the new men their duties in the upcoming mission. The soldiers looked on attentively. At the end of his monologue, Thomas turned to the unit's platoon leader, Lieutenant Morales, and asked if he or the men had any questions. Morales translated this phrase for the men, and nearly all their hands shot into the air. Thomas thought to himself, "Hell, they didn't understand a damn word I said." Although there was a bit of a communication barrier, the Puerto Ricans proved to be brave and competent soldiers. And the Iraqis couldn't make heads or tails out of them – because to them the Puerto Ricans looked Iraqi.

Another Puerto Rican unit ran the FOB Dogwood laundry. And, lo and behold, one of the laundry soldiers was the prettiest woman that many of the men had ever seen. This development meant that the soldiers of Dogwood had some of the cleanest uniforms in Iraq. Some of the company commanders noticed that their men were washing their clothing twice a day. "Didn't you wash that earlier today?" "Well, sir, I got it dirty again."

THE THREE SHEIKS

For Randall Jones, September 24 started as just another boring day. It was the turn of his platoon to man Dogpatch on the outskirts of Owesat. Not much had been happening lately, so he thought that he might even get some rest. Little did he know that it was the most important day of the 150th's tenure at Dogwood. In the late morning Jones had to blink his eyes to make sure that he was seeing things right. There were three older men, dressed in traditional Arab cloaks and wearing nice turbans, making their way toward Dogpatch from Owesat. And these guys were carrying a white flag. The observer on duty called the scene into the TOC and asked if they wanted him to open fire on the men. "NO!" was the loud and quick response. Once they got within earshot, Jones told them that they had gone far enough, and then he said, mostly jokingly, "Are y'all here to surrender?" Well, as it happened, that is exactly what the men were there to do.

The three men, Sheik Abu Mohanad, Sheik Abdul Hameed Abbas, and Sheik Najim Abdallah Sarhan, were leaders of the Owesat subtribe that dominated the immediate area and were elders of the village of Owesat. And they had come to parlay with the leaders of the 150th. With his interest now thoroughly piqued, Jones radioed into the TOC with the news. Since Owesat was within the Bravo Company AO, Robinson sent Captain Paul Lyon to the scene to figure out what was up. Lyon arrived to hear once again that the trio wanted to parlay with the American command. Robinson gave his approval to bring the men onto the base for a meeting but asked that they be blindfolded first in case they were there merely to get the lay of the land for the insurgents.

Once the sheiks were seated in a makeshift meeting room and offered some water, Robinson and Lyon got down to a good cop/bad cop negotiation. The sheiks opened with how offended they were to have been blindfolded. Robinson countered with how offended he was that people from their village were killing his men with IEDs and mortars. The sheiks understandably responded that they had not done any such thing. Robinson shot back, "You are letting those things happen from your village. That is the same as you doing it!" The sheiks began to argue and protest their innocence, but Robinson was having none of it. He said, "No. There's no arguing here. I'll tell you what is going to happen.

The next time y'all shoot mortars out of your village at my FOB or we are hit by IEDs, I'm going to take those bulldozers and tanks you see sitting right over there, and I'm going to push all your houses into the water!" Lyon couldn't help but think that the negotiations weren't going quite as he had hoped or expected.

Lyon then interceded as the good cop, asking Robinson if it was okay if he took over the negotiations. Robinson put on a show of making a very difficult decision, but eventually left the room growling and telling Lyon very loudly that he had better come away with some wonderful intelligence. With the bad cop gone, Lyon played his role in calming the sheiks and asking them what they really wanted. The trio reported that insurgents had been holding the village hostage since the fall of Fallujah, but they had been forced to leave by the recent string of raids in the area. Owesat was free from threat, and the villagers were ready to work with the Americans now that there were no insurgents to threaten them with death for doing so.

The sheiks also informed Lyon that the cutting of the dike road, along with the checkpoints at Bottom Line and Dogpatch, had effectively strangled all trade into and out of the village, leaving the people there in desperate shape. They very much wanted the roads to be opened again. And they were tired of the constant raids, getting their doors kicked in, and their homes searched. Lyon responded that those certainly seemed like reasonable requests. However, he couldn't agree to reopening the dike road – it would attract the insurgents back like bees to honey as a way to move munitions around Iraq. But the desert road near to Dogpatch could be improved and allowed to flow more freely. And raids on the village could certainly slow and even allow for more humanitarian aid in their stead. But Lyon demanded one thing. There could be no more mortar attacks or IED attacks from Owesat, or there would be renewed hell to pay.

The sheiks carried the offer of a cessation of raids and an opening of traffic in return for peace to their people, and Lyon went to Robinson to flesh out the details of a plan. A few days later the sheiks returned, white flag and all, and reported that the people of Owesat had enthusiastically endorsed the Mississippians' offer. Then Robinson and Lyon sweetened the pot. The sheiks didn't like the road that ran near Dogpatch – it was a dirt road that was often difficult to traverse. Well, Robinson and Lyon offered to improve that road, perhaps even pave it. But then they got to the good part. The Mississippians would supply the machinery and materials but would pay civilians from Owesat to do the work. It was a stroke of genius. The needed road would get built, placating the leadership and people of Owesat. The workers on the road would get paid more by the Americans to build the road than the insurgents had once paid them to plant IEDs and to fire rockets. And those workers, the same military age males who had been swimming the river, would now be working daily under the supervision of the Americans. They would be a happier people: a people who no longer had an economic reason to work for the insurgents; and a people under watchful American eyes. Although the counterinsurgency manual that would change the nature of the war in Iraq was still in the works, the 150th's solution to Owesat was counterinsurgency at its best. The sheiks went back to Owesat with the good news, and the Mississippians prepared for a new type of war.

A NEW OWESAT

For the remainder of their deployment, the Mississippians met with the sheiks of Owesat once a week to go over any concerns either side had, with Allen McDaniel working the contracting side of the operation and always careful to take his Imodium. In what once had been a relationship of bitter animosity, the Mississippians and the people of Owesat became close, getting to know each other well and developing a mutual respect in the process. What had once been a feared, no-go area of the Triangle of Death had been transformed into a model oasis of calm amidst a spiraling war. One constant source of disagreement, though, was the obligatory tea that popped up at every meeting. While Lyon and Robinson never developed the violent intestinal reaction to the concoction that soon came to plague Richard Rowland, nobody – and I mean nobody – could come to like the Iraqi tea. It was a lukewarm slurry that everyone hoped had at one time been heated to a high enough temperature to kill whatever worms lived in the Euphrates water. But Lyon had an idea. On the fifth meeting with the sheiks, he brought tea himself. Good old Mississippi iced sweet tea. At first the sheiks were quite taken with the idea of drinking American tea. But their faces wrinkled up in disgust, followed by a quick smile. They dare not offend their American partners in the tea ceremony. They gave a few half-hearted compliments to Lyon's tea, but they made damn sure to bring their own local tea to every meeting following, while Lyon brought his own sweet tea. Problem solved.

One of the first true signs of the lowering of tensions with Owesat was that the 150th began to run Medical Civic Action Program (MEDCAP) missions there. Kirk Dyer recalled that these initial humanitarian efforts were a bit tense; after all, the soldiers of the 150th were headed into a village that had so often been the source of danger, loss, and heartache. The first such mission was set up at the main new entrance to Owesat, and the troops set a perimeter to ensure safety. Most of the battalion's interpreters were there that day to facilitate communication with the locals. At first only a few trickled into the American lines, and then it became a flood. Troublesome Owesat was only a few miles distant from the more cooperative villages to the south, meaning that the residents of Owesat had often heard of the benefits of seeing American doctors and dentists. Sure, there were some horror stories of teeth being pulled, but the Owesats had not had access to modern medicine for several years by this point. So, on they came to get the medical benefits that their neighbors to the south had been enjoying for months. Having so many civilians around in Owesat kind of spooked Dyer and many of the men – was there any real way to guarantee that these folks were "friendlies"?

The doctors and dentists did a thriving trade that day, with children being the main customers. Many were malnourished, several had worms, many needed teeth pulled, and others simply had the bumps and bruises associated with childhood. Roz Morris was there taking part in the sea change event. As the Iraqis became more comfortable with the American presence, they got down to normal life amid the hubbub of the MEDCAP. And normal life meant dinner. Roz looked on with mixed amazement and horror as the locals bled, slaughtered, and then dressed a sheep for their meal. For Roz, and for many within the 150th, that act of preparing dinner, even if a bit bloody, helped to normalize the people of Owesat. These were people going about their lives just like the Mississippians. Sure, there were different levels of technology and wealth, but the Iraqis were caring for their families and trying to make their way in the world the best that they knew how. They weren't that different to the people back home.

As the MEDCAP continued at Owesat, troops of Alpha Company also got great news from the southern part of the AO. Mohammed's parents had been working constantly with doctors in Baghdad concerning the boy's care. His bladder surgery was scheduled in just two days' time, which would address his most immediate problems. The second round of surgery had also been addressed, with local American doctors contacting colleagues in Pennsylvania to enquire regarding the possibility of undertaking the procedure there. The soldiers of the 150th continued to raise money in hopes of making that surgery a reality.*

HEADED WEST

Along with success in the 150th's AO came the first real sign that the unit's time in Iraq was nearing its end. On September 26, the official lists came in of what the soldiers would need to keep with them and what they should start packing so that it could all be sent home. At the same time, though, the situation in western Anbar Province heralded another change. The area near the Syrian border had been particularly restive during 2005, and by September higher command in Iraq made securing that border one of its chief missions. As part of the push to lock down the border and put pressure on the insurgency in the area, Regimental Combat Team 2 undertook Operation *Hunter*, aimed at the cities of Hit, Haditha, and Husaybah. But to free up forces for the mission, the Marines also undertook Operation *Green Light*, designed to bring the 2/114th Artillery of the Mississippi National Guard in as reinforcements for the coming struggle in the city of Hit.†

David Martian and Alpha Battery of the 2/114th had hoped for a quiet assignment after the closure of FOB Lima and the massive IED strike on MSR Midland that had killed Tommy Little, with the follow-on strike wounding Norris Galatas. For a few months the unit had been shuffled from pillar to post, including a short stay at Dogwood. Then the news came in that Alpha Battery was headed to Hit to take part in the Marines' combat surge in the area. Martian was

---

*The unit lost touch with Mohammed's family after its withdrawal in two months. Nobody in the unit nor the author has been able to ascertain whether the second surgery ever became a reality.

†Kenneth Estes, *U.S. Marines in Iraq, 2004–2005: Into the Fray* (Washington, DC: History Division, United States Marine Corps, 2011).

part of the advance party to Camp Hit, and quickly discovered that the new assignment was not what he'd had in mind at all. The Marines gave Martian the grand tour. There was Camp Hit proper, which seemed relatively safe to Martian, but there were also outposts beyond the main camp, called firm bases, which were isolated in the city. Firm Base 1, which was to be Alpha Battery's home, was an old dormitory right next to the Euphrates on the edge of Hit. The Marines warned him that Hit was chock full of people who didn't want the Americans there and were violent in the disapproval of their presence. Offhandedly, they mentioned that Firm Base 1 was usually hit by RPGs or small-arms fire pretty much every day. But that wasn't the worst of it. Alpha Battery would also be responsible for an isolated combat outpost in the city of Hit known as the Pink Palace. Only large enough for a platoon, the Pink Palace was even more dangerous. No; being stationed in Hit was not what Martian had in mind at all. But at least his guys weren't at Firm Base 2, which was located deep into the city and was, thus, the most vulnerable. Martian couldn't help but feel pity for whoever wound up there.

The situation was far from ideal. Alpha Battery was due to go home in a couple of months and found itself mired in one of the most violent corners of the war in Iraq. That their return home was so near made the stint in Hit even more difficult for the Mississippians, but there was nothing for it. They had to get to work. Patrols had to go out every day, working in tandem with Iraqi Army forces. And, sure enough, there was an IED strike on day two, and incoming RPG and small-arms fire right on cue. Casualties weren't heavy, in large part since Alpha was equipped with uparmored vehicles. But stress levels were off the charts. And there simply weren't enough men to do the job. It didn't seem that the Marines or the 2/114th were putting a dent into the insurgency in Hit. They needed more men and resources.

In October the call went out for a platoon of combat engineers to join the 2/114th in Hit, and the luck of the draw fell to a single platoon of Charlie Company to pick up stakes from Dogwood and relocate to Hit. Lieutenant Jay Standley had been shifted to Charlie Company as a platoon leader and got his men ready to go. He and his men choppered into Camp Hit, to be met with a conex of their supplies and gear later. Camp Hit wasn't too unlike FOB Dogwood at this point, but Standley and his men could see right off the bat that the Marines in the area had been through the wringer. Just something about their demeanor and the way they held themselves was different. These guys had seen a lot, and it was alarming for the Mississippians. There were a couple of days of ride-alongs with the Marines to get the lay of the land. Hit was a good-sized town on the banks of the Euphrates – it had real hardened structures and LOTS of them, unlike Owesat. And everyone was warned that the enemy was all around. Hit was an insurgent hotbed, and they sure as hell weren't giving up without a fight. Firm Base 2, the destination of Standley and his men, was slap bang in the middle of Hit. And there was no way to get to Firm Base 2 other than driving right through town. But, the Marines told them, Firm Base 2 was more secure than it had been, because an Iraqi vehicle-borne IED had blown up the bridge just a couple of weeks before, which made it harder for the insurgents to move around.

What Standley and his men found at Firm Base 2 was not reassuring. It was a single-story building that had once been a sports center and was surrounded by three-story buildings. That worried Standley greatly – any insurgents would have an overwatch position on him and his men. There were fences and wire surrounding the building, warning any vehicular traffic to stay away. There were also guard towers made out of Hesco barriers dotted around the structure and guard towers atop the roof. The towers were manned 24/7 and each boasted a machine-gun position. Sherman Hillhouse took some comfort in knowing that at least the defenses around the building were solid. Hillhouse was less impressed, though, with the interior of the building. There were rooms off the main corridors for everyone to sleep in, but there were also Iraqi troops, so it was sure going to be cozy. There was a courtyard in the center that was open, which would be kind of nice in peacetime. But what caught Hillhouse's eye the most was the abundance of full piss jars. The damn things were everywhere, left behind by the departing Marines. Hillhouse couldn't help but wonder why there were so dang many piss bottles. The first time that he went outside to relieve himself and got shot at answered that question thoroughly.

Standley and his men soon settled into a routine at Firm Base 2 – four days of patrolling followed by four days of guard duty and quick reaction force duty. Patrols in Hit were different than anything Standley and his men had ever seen. For one, there were Iraqis everywhere and instead of wide-open spaces there were the narrow and congested roads of a city. And IEDs were everywhere as well. In Hit, the IEDs were very unlikely to be buried in the ground with a pressure plate. Paved roads and narrow corners didn't allow for that. Instead, the IEDs were implanted in anything imaginable alongside the roads – from animal carcasses, to old boxes, to random bits of trash. You had to keep your eyes peeled. But Standley had his secret weapon, Mike Reeves. A Mississippi country boy, Reeves had a sixth sense about IEDs. He could just spot anything that was out of the ordinary and could certainly tell if anything was there today that had not been there the night before. On Standley's first two patrols, Reeves had spotted IEDs. But then came day three.

Standley recorded in his journal:

In our first two days of patrolling, we found 2 IEDs which we called EOD [Explosive Ordnance Disposal] to blow, and we found one more the hard way. We hit an IED in our M113 on the way home from a supply run to Camp Hit. I was in the lead track with SSG. Hillhouse's crew. With me were Hillhouse, Sutton, Reeves, Clowers, Rogers, and Burrell. We were rolling along, and BAM! I got a face full of soot, water, and cordite. Bell kept driving, to get out of the kill zone. I think he drove about 800 meters, or maybe a click before we got him stopped. Everyone was checking on each other, and thinking the worst. We'd had a couple of boxes of MRE's [Meals, Ready to Eat] and a couple of cases of water on the rail on the side of the track that got hit. When the round exploded, water and MRE went everywhere, bathing all of us. We'd assumed it was someone's blood. We were, needless to say, very relieved, but very angry. My goggles had been blown off of my head, and my eyes were full of soot and cordite. They were burning, and I was blind for a few moments, but was very relieved to still have my eyes, and be otherwise ok. I also think I lost some hearing, actually, all of us did. We had hearing protection, but a 155mm artillery round went off right beside us, so it's not surprising. I guess I should consider myself lucky to have only lost some hearing from the incident. Also, we've been mortared here in the Firm Base (FB2), three days in a row. Today, they got one right outside the back door, and one by the Iraqi Army washpoint. Several Iraqi Army soldiers were injured, along with two US personnel receiving minor shrapnel injuries to the face.

As soon as it was safe, Hillhouse inspected the damage to the 113. One road wheel was almost out of action and the armor had taken several hits. He couldn't help but think that the dents in the 113's armor looked like Play-Doh that a child had forced their thumb into. And he also couldn't help but think that if the 113 had not been uparmored, they would have all been dead.

THE NEW NORMAL IN HIT

The very next day Standley and his men were on a return run to Camp Hit, and, before they cleared the densely packed center of town, Reeves shouted "IED!" The M113 came to a halt right at a major intersection. It was there that Reeves had seen the IED, and civilian vehicles were whizzing all around. It infuriated the Mississippians that the insurgents had no respect at all for innocent lives. It was much more likely that a civilian vehicle was going to set off the IED than an American military vehicle. But the insurgents didn't care in the least. Standley had his vehicles fan out to try to stop civilian traffic into the intersection, and, once that was under control, the EOD came in with its IED robot.

The robot slowly rolled off but didn't go to where Reeves had seen the IED. It missed its mark by 20 meters. Standley was on the radio trying to get the robot back on track when, BOOM! A second IED rocked the intersection; one that nobody had seen. The flash was followed by a cloud of dust and debris, and Standley looked up just in time to see a chunk of brick that had blown away come tumbling through the air and punch Captain Kloppenberg right in the head. Kloppenberg wasn't wounded, so it was kind of funny. The robot then went and disarmed the IED that had been identified. At the same time, the troops looked up to see a black station wagon pulling into a nearby driveway. Just such a station wagon was on the intelligence list, so the Mississippians went to check it out, and bagged their first major insurgent target in Hit, sending the unlucky occupant of the vehicle off to questioning with the Marines.

On October 13, Standley, Hillhouse, and their squad were part of the quick reaction force that in the early evening replied to the sound of gunfire a few blocks from Firm Base 2. A sniper team had engaged with a trio of insurgents who were caught red-handed placing an IED inside the body of a dead dog. Once given permission to fire, the snipers had opened up on the trio, producing the gunfire that had drawn Standley and his men to the scene. It fell to them to police up the area. The snipers reported that all the subjects were down, but they were only certain that they had hit one. The others could just be pretending to be wounded or dead. So, Standley and his men advanced with great care and with weapons at the ready. As they cautiously approached the scene, two of the insurgents raised their hands to surrender, and the third convulsed mildly as he bled out his last moments of life. The Mississippians breathed a sigh of relief; at least it was safe. Then they got down to the work of dealing with the insurgents.

Standley could hardly believe his eyes. The two who had surrendered were just Iraqi kids – maybe 14 years old, if that. And the one who had died was at most 17. These were kids who should be in school, playing video games, chasing girls. But now one was dead on the side of the road and the others were so badly frightened that they were weeping uncontrollably. All of that just for the bit of money that the insurgents paid them to emplace IEDs. The two young lads were zip tied and sent for questioning – there was nothing that could be done about that. Standley and his men placed the older child into a body bag and made ready to deliver him to the local morgue. But they had to wait for the EOD guys to get there and blow the IED that had been placed in the dead dog.

The guys took up formation in and around the vehicles and made ready to wait. Then a civilian Iraqi vehicle came driving toward them at high speed. Goddamned if that wasn't all they needed right now – an incoming vehicle-borne IED. A trooper named Hayden took aim and shot a warning round past the car. As the tracer cut through the early evening sky the car screeched to a halt. The driver got out in a state of near panic and started talking animatedly. The interpreter listened carefully and then reported that the man's wife was pregnant and in labor, and they were just trying to reach the hospital that was about a block away. Sure enough, the woman was very pregnant and screaming in pain, so they were allowed to pass. After all that excitement, the EOD did its job and removed the IED, allowing Standley and his men to take the dead child to the Iraqi morgue. Once there, Standley and his men carried the body inside. The doctor on duty there unzipped the bag. Plainly this was nothing new to him. He looked inside and gave just a bit of a jolt before looking at the Americans, saying, "I knew this child. He was a good boy, such a good boy. And smart. How did it all have to come to this?"

BACK AT DOGWOOD

As the trouble picked up ever further at Hit, at Dogwood preparations for the unit to return home were underway in earnest, while relationships with the villagers, especially those in Owesat, continued to improve. And, although a couple of IEDs exploded just south of the 150th's AO, the peace with the local villagers held. One topic that kept coming up in the weekly meetings with the sheiks was how much the town could use a tractor. That way they could maintain their own roads and use the tractor for more efficient farming. So, an old orange tractor was procured and, given its bright color, it became a welcome sight of change, constantly in motion in the town and in the fields.

Next came another major MEDCAP. This time the unit staged near the gate in the wall of the local school. Locating there made the crowd more manageable, since people had to approach the medical setup by passing through the narrow gate in the school's wall. Next came visits to the doctors and dentists. Only then did the locals get to their main goal, a truck full of blankets, heaters, walkers, wheelchairs, candy, toys – you name it – to give away. As the troops milled around giving stuff away, they couldn't help but notice that the school had no running water. Upon asking the sheiks, they learned that water was hauled into the school from the Euphrates. Everyone knew right off the bat that that water was the chief culprit in many of the illnesses they were seeing. So, over the next two days, the 150th hauled in giant water tanks for the school. And every week the men returned to refill those tanks with fresh drinking water.

One of the biggest opportunities for violence at Dogwood took place in the Morale, Welfare, and Recreation tent on October 16, when Ole Miss played mighty sixth-ranked Alabama in football. Many of the guys from the northern part of the state were Ole Miss fans, but all the Mississippi State and Southern Miss fans sorely wanted Ole Miss to get thrashed by the Crimson Tide. So, the MWR tent was standing room only for the tilt, and you had better not get up to use the latrine, or your seat was flat gone. Everyone was talking trash, and the game was a nail biter. It all nearly came to blows when Voccio got up and changed the channels. The brash New Yorker made it clear that he didn't see what all the damn fuss was about these cheesy southern teams. Order was quickly restored, and the game ended with a 13–10 Alabama triumph. The Ole Miss fans could take heart in a pyrrhic victory, while the Mississippi State and Southern Miss fans could let them have it hard. And Voccio and his tankers could just stand there and wonder at the scene.

MORE TROUBLE IN HIT

Back in Hit, David Martian and his troops of Alpha Battery at Firm Base 1 were well and truly ready for their stint in Hit to end. Daily IEDs and harassing fire had kept up a constant pressure on Alpha Battery, and there seemed to be little to show for the effort. But on October 15 everyone had reason to hope that all of that would change. The Iraqis had written a constitution, one lauded as being designed to unite the country and to pave the way for an American withdrawal. And on October 15 there would be a massive election in which Iraqis hopefully would unite behind that constitution and stake out their future. All of the US forces in Hit were utilized to prepare for the election and then guard the polling places. It was truly all hands on deck. But, after all that effort, the election fizzled. After all that fuss and buildup, at Alpha Battery's polling place only two Iraqis showed up to vote the entire day. Well, maybe this constitution wouldn't be the magic bullet after all. It was back to normal, which for Standley's platoon at Firm Base 2 meant a four-day stint of overwatching the critical junction of routes Bronze and Uranium outside the city. Given the junction's remoteness, this was a welcome, if rustic, respite from the constant danger of operations inside Hit. Indeed, while the Mississippians were on their mission at the road junction, a mortar shell had crashed into Firm Base 2, killing Sergeant Jacob Dones of Dimmitt, Texas, who was serving with the 2/11th ACR, which also had an element at the firm base. Dones had joined the Army fresh out of high school, and his sister, Priscilla, had joined the Marines. The two loved to argue about which service was the best. Next for Standley and his men were two relatively peaceful patrols, followed by a raid on the home of a suspected terrorist on October 26.

The raid involved a great deal of planning with an Iraqi Army contingent that was due to accompany the Mississippians. Standley, however, wasn't sure if the Iraqis were understanding his plans and orders, so he was up until well after 1 a.m. planning the 5 a.m. raid. He then got settled into his cot, wearing full gear, for a short nap before it was down to business. Next to him was Sherman Hillhouse, and the two chatted about the upcoming raid for a couple of minutes before dozing off. Just minutes after hitting their racks, all hell broke loose in Firm Base 2. A rocket burst through the western wall of the building, shattered through one room, and careened down the hall before detonating just outside the room where Standley and his men were trying to sleep. Amazingly, nobody was seriously injured. A soldier from the 2/11th ACR had been hit in the face by some of the exploding wall as the rocket buzzed a foot above his head, but that was it. Just a couple of feet further, though, and all the Mississippians could have been lost. Another rocket had tumbled between the two guard towers on the roof of Firm Base 2 before ricocheting off the roof and flying away. A search of the building across the way yielded two rocket launchers that had been wired to a car battery and a washing machine timer.

With everyone a bit shaken and happy to be alive, the raid set out at 5 a.m. on schedule. Intelligence had indicated an important terrorist in the neighborhood, necessitating searches of several homes. In one of the dwellings was a military age male, who was overtly belligerent, which was unusual. But there proved no reason to hold the suspect. The team from the Iraqi Army were happy to find and "liberate" a locked box full of DVDs. It was obvious to everyone that they figured the DVDs to be pornography and planned on screening them once back at the firm base. Standley and Hillhouse didn't much like it but couldn't stop it. After the raid, Standley was brewing some coffee and trying to process the night's events, when the Iraqis burst into his room shouting "Osama Bin Laden; Osama Bin Laden!" The videos that they had seen were not the hoped-for porn, but instead were al-Qaeda recruitment videos. As they made ready to return to the target's home, Hillhouse opined that there was no way that the dude was stupid enough to still be there. But, sure enough, when the team kicked his door in, there he sat. The guys figured that of all the terrorists that they had ever captured, this guy was the dumbest.

It was only four days later that Standley's little group of men ran into perhaps their worst trouble. The narrow road in front of Firm Base 2, known as Route Cherry, was lined with Iraqi shops, many of which had awnings that obscured sight lines down the road. Those awnings were a danger and had to go. The task was for the Mississippians to head out of the firm base and to destroy those awnings using explosive charges. Sergeant Clowers and two Iraqi Army soldiers took the lead, heading to the most distant awning, while other teams fanned out to the closer ones. Sherman Hillhouse and Sergeant Sutton were detailed to inspect other sites for potential demolition. Suddenly, a car screeched up just outside the Mississippians' perimeter, and out jumped two insurgents, one armed with an RPG launcher and another with a Russian-made machine gun.

Two RPG rounds shrieked overhead before detonating just meters away, followed by a spray of incoming automatic fire. Standley's platoon and its Iraqi Army allies hit the ground and returned fire as pandemonium reigned. Bullets were pinging off the Hesco barriers and off Firm Base 2 itself all around. Standley reported the contact and began to direct fire in on the insurgents, but with echoes of firing bouncing off buildings from all directions, it was difficult to discern their location. Standley next went about locating his most forward elements – Hillhouse, Sutton, and Clowers. Once it became apparent that they were safe, Standley had his men cover for each other as the forward elements drew back into the secure perimeter around Firm Base 2. Standley was impressed; his men reacted like true professionals under their first real baptism of fire, and the withdrawal went off without a hitch. Then, suddenly, the incoming fire just ceased. The insurgents had fled to fight again another day. It had been chaos for a few minutes, then it was all over. Nobody had been wounded, but it was a very closely run thing. The attack on Firm Base 2 was seen as such a big deal that the insurgents released their own news report on the event saying, "A group of your mujahidin heroic brothers in the city of Hit, in western Iraq, was able to mount a military attack on the youth center in the middle of the city, which is used as headquarters for the Crusader forces, using RPG mortar shells and automatic sub-machine guns. A fierce confrontation took place and the infidel forces sustained heavy losses. The operation took place last Sunday [31 October 2005]. Praise be to God!"

As the fighting in Hit continued, the Mississippi Guard family suffered another blow with the loss of Lieutenant Robert Oneto-Sikorski to an IED strike on October 31. He was serving in Iraq in the 155th, along with the mother of his children, Clare Rager. Oneto-Sikorski was from Bay St. Louis, which had been heavily damaged during Hurricane Katrina. Both Oneto-Sikorski's and his mother's homes had been inundated by the massive storm surge associated with Katrina, with his three children, Robert, PJ, and Hannah, having evacuated with family members to the Memphis area. Having suffered such a loss due to the storm, Oneto-Sikorski could have come home on leave to help out, but he had let his men take that opportunity first. In discussing his decision to stay in Iraq, his mother sympathized, but she also told him to be careful. He only had two more months left in-country. Just two more months before he was home with his loved ones.

BACK AT DOGWOOD

Back in the Dogwood AO, positive changes continued. Weekly meetings with the sheiks of Owesat, along with the leadership of many other of the local villages, progressed, as did humanitarian aid to and cooperation with the populations of those villages. People on both sides, though, remained wary. Just a few months back they had been bitter adversaries, and everyone understood that the situation could change in a heartbeat. Paul Lyon thought that the best summary of the situation that he had heard came from a local farmer. As a MEDCAP was underway in his village, Lyon asked the man through an interpreter whom he supported, the Americans or the insurgents. The man replied, "I support whoever is standing in front of me with a gun." American action had driven the insurgents away, so now the local population supported the Americans. Pragmatic and true.

In seeking to create a more durable solution, the Mississippians continued humanitarian operations across the AO. In Owesat, that included installing pumps along the Euphrates River, which allowed for much more efficient irrigation of crops. In addition, advanced seeds were supplied to local farmers. And, since there were many farmers among the Mississippians, there was a great deal of practical demonstration of more modern farming techniques. Everyone expected the following year to provide bumper crops for the local farmers, and the sheiks were very open in their profuse thanks. MEDCAPs continued, with local health benefitting greatly. And everyone at Dogwood had written home to families, schools, and churches for anything that children might enjoy. To Douglas Mansfield it all seemed kind of surreal. When they had first arrived at Dogwood, Owesat inspired fear and uncertainty. Then it was the hotbed of insurgency – Owesat was the enemy. Now, as November began and the 150th's tour entered its last month, Owesat "looked like Mardi Gras on Canal Street." Children were scampering in all directions, following the Americans in hopes of toys, soccer balls, beads, candy – you name it. Mansfield and Kirk Dyer spoke for entire 150th in saying that the change wrought in Owesat was immensely gratifying. There had been many days after the loss of Sean Cooley, Larry Arnold, Terrance Lee, and so many others that they had questioned why they were there. What good were they doing? Were the losses worth the results? But now they felt that there was a real reason for them being there. They felt like they were doing good.

Ken Cager remarked:

> We had moved into a vacuum, and the enemy knew it. I mean, it was just kind of a sucking chest wound right there in the central part of Iraq, and that's what the bad guys exploited. You take a bunch of engineers out of the state of Mississippi, and you give them a mission that we were not trained for; we just figured it out. We figured out what worked, and we did it on the fly, and we did a pretty damn good job of it, in my opinion. We were given a mission that we did not ask for, but we took the resources that we had; we employed those resources, and I really believe we affected the way that – I believe we shaped the whole landscape of what the whole war looked like in 2005 because we denied the enemy access to that critical location. And I'm convinced, had the 150th not been in that area at Dogwood; had we not have gone there and done the things we did and engaged with that population up there, and then engaged the bad guys directly, I'm convinced that things would have looked totally different in the central part of Iraq.

MORE IEDS

Regardless of the impact of the Mississippians with the population in the Dogwood AO, the war in Iraq rumbled onward. On November 8 at Hit, Standley, Hillhouse, and their men had a two-IED day. On a supply run to Camp Hit, Mike Reeves – who could still spot an IED from a mile away – noticed something funny at the junction of routes

Strawberry and Bronze. This was a place that yielded at least one IED a week, so Reeves' warning came as no shock. A cordon was set, and the EOD came in with its robot. The payoff was disabling an IED made up of three 120mm artillery shells augmented with four 2-liter bottles of gasoline. And this was an intersection within Hit very near a civilian bus stop. Again, it was clear the insurgents cared nothing about the possibility of innocent lives being lost.

When the IED was gone, the patrol proceeded to Camp Hit, loaded its cache of supplies, and headed back. Once again, as the patrol made it to the intersection of Strawberry and Bronze, Reeves shouted, "IED!" This time it was a 55-gallon drum placed next to the intersection. Everyone knew the drill by now. Set up a perimeter and await the EOD. As usual, the little robot went out to inspect the IED. But this time, BOOOOM! The 55-gallon drum vaporized into a ball of fire that incinerated the EOD robot. Once back at Firm Base 2, the guys printed out a picture of Johnny 5 from the movie *Short Circuit* and had a bona fide robot funeral.

There were even parting shots to the Mississippians in the Dogwood AO. The area's insurgents weren't entirely calling it quits. The area around Dogwood was the insurgents' armory, and they wanted it back. It was only the effort of the Mississippians that was holding them at bay. For Bravo Company that meant finding the body of a sheik from one of the southern villages in his car. He had been assassinated for cooperating with the Americans, and his wife was left behind to tell the cautionary tale to the other villagers. Also, as November was drawing to a close, Chris Thomas and Charlie Company were on patrol in the southern sector of the AO, away from Owesat. As they rolled near to the bridge that crossed the Euphrates, near a host of villages, a small IED went off just behind the lead tank of the patrol. With no damage to report, the patrol went on. After 100 yards, there was another boom. This time shrapnel from the IED slightly wounded one man. After caring for the wounded man, Charlie Company got underway again, only to be hit by a third IED. At this point Thomas had seen enough. Time for the patrol to return to Dogwood. He yelled to the tanker, "If one more fucking IED goes off, I want you to fire!" Sure enough, just a couple of minutes later there was another boom. Again, no injuries, but this particular boom was followed by the report of the tank's main gun. The shell whistled into the bank on the far side of the river and exploded harmlessly. But that show of force seemed to be enough. There had been a long lull in IED activity in the area, and the four that hit Charlie Company would be the last in the Dogwood AO.

LOSSES IN HIT

On the night before Thanksgiving, a foot patrol went out to reconnoiter a nearby cemetery that was often used as a site to launch mortar fire at Firm Base 2. Patrols often targeted the cemetery, making it a preferred site for IEDs. On that night, Specialist Javier Villanueva, a medic serving with the 2/11th ACR, was hit by an IED and killed. Villanueva hailed from Waco, Texas, and got married to Felicia Owens just before he enlisted in the Army in 2003. The couple had an infant child, Taliyah, at the time of Villanueva's death. The patrol evacuated Villanueva's body before completing its mission.

In all the chaos and confusion of the cemetery encounter, though, one of the patrol's radios was left behind. As a sensitive piece of equipment, it had to be retrieved, so another patrol set out from Firm Base 2 for the cemetery. Sergeant Meadows asked for a few volunteers for the scratch mission, with both Standley and Reeves joining the crew. The search for the radio was fruitless, but Standley was taken aback to find a US soldier's boot in the middle of Route Star. The boot had been blown off by the IED, and flew over the wall of the cemetery and into the road. Standley was even more surprised when he picked up the boot to find that the soldier's foot was still inside. He stood there in shock for a few seconds, staring at the foot. He knew that he couldn't just leave it there. It had to be taken back to Firm Base 2 where it could be shown proper respect. The boot was placed in a backpack and returned, where it was sent to be buried with Villanueva. It had been one of the most surreal experiences of Standley's life.

After returning to Firm Base 2, as the sun rose in the morning sky, a truck came barreling down Route Cherry toward the front entrance of Firm Base 2. There were signs all over in several languages that warned drivers that they would be shot if they advanced any further. Such signs were a normal part of Iraqi life at this point. Everyone knew NOT to drive up to an American base without slowing and stopping – the risks posed by vehicle-borne IEDs were simply too high. But this truck just kept coming. Warning shots were fired from the guard towers atop Firm

Base 2, but still the truck kept coming. Shots were fired into the engine. It just kept coming. It had to be a vehicle-borne IED, and the base made ready for impact. Then came the kill shot from atop the Firm Base. The vehicle careened to a halt amidst the Hesco barriers in front of the building. There was no blast, and soldiers made their way cautiously to the vehicle. It was just an empty panel truck. The driver must have been greatly distracted, having broken every major rule of the Iraqi wartime road and paying the lethal price. And the guard was left to wrestle with the fact that he had killed an innocent man. Standley assured the soldier that he had done the right thing. He had followed the rules to the letter. It was the driver's fault, not his. But Standley could see in the young man's eyes that he would carry a sense of guilt with him always.

PARTING SHOTS

There was great news the next day, November 25. Lieutenant Colonel Gary Huffman, battalion commander of the 2/114th Artillery, was inbound to both Firm Base 1 and Firm Base 2. Since the Mississippians were soon to be on their way home, Huffman was showing the incoming Marine commander whose troops would be replacing the Mississippi Guard where all the trouble spots in the area were. At Firm Base 2, Standley couldn't keep a smile off his face while showing Huffman and his Marine counterpart the lay of the land. The Marines were going to have to stay on their toes. Hit was a difficult assignment, with threats coming from any direction day or night. The Marine lieutenant colonel listened attentively, taking it all in. Then the patrol pulled away, off to visit David Martian and Alpha Battery at Firm Base 1. For Martian and his men, it was something of a reunion. Huffman had needed a gunner for his Humvee, and the task had fallen to Greg Tull of Alpha Battery. Tull was from the 1st Battalion, 194th Field Artillery of the Iowa National Guard, but he had been on assignment with Alpha Battery for most of the tour and had become one of the guys. Martian felt bad for Tull, being taken away from his buddies for the last part of the tour, but such is the way of the military. As the officers got down to their business, Tull went around and reconnected with all his pals quickly before driving off again. Then there were handshakes all around before Huffman and the Marines headed out for Camp Hit.

Before the patrol went very far, though, it was hit with an IED. Both Huffman and his incoming Marine counterpart were wounded. Exposed in his position as gunner, Tull took the brunt of the blast and was killed. David Martian and Tull's friends of Alpha Battery were the quick reaction force but could do nothing for their fallen friend. The force of the IED blast had killed him instantly. Tull had had less than a month remaining in Iraq. As the Mississippians looked on while Tull was placed in a body bag, many wept openly. Only two people had shown up for that damn election. Hit wasn't getting any better. The enemy was not on the run. And here was Tull, paying the ultimate price when he had almost made it home. And for what? Greg Tull was from Pocahontas, Iowa where he had been an all-conference basketball player and leading scorer for his high school team. He had enlisted in the Guard while still in high school and looked forward to the idea of defending his country in the wake of the terrorist attacks of 9/11. The entire town of Pocahontas shut down for his funeral to bid goodbye to its favorite son.

GOODBYES

At the beginning of December, it was all over. The final patrols had been pulled out of Bottom Line and Dogpatch on November 27, and the main body of the 150th made ready to depart by December 5. For Standley and his men at Hit, departure could not come quickly enough. The strike on Huffman's patrol showed them all that death could come even while leaving Hit. And, as was fitting, the convoy that took Standley and his men to Camp Hit for the first leg of their journey found an IED at the roadside and had to wait for an EOD robot to investigate. Although they had been through this dozens of times by this point, waiting out that last IED seemed like it took an eternity. For David Martian and Alpha Battery, it was even worse. On his next to last patrol in Hit, Martian's Humvee hit an IED. The explosive device had been poorly placed and had not even badly damaged the vehicle, but it sure as hell shook up Martian and his men. Iraq seemed out to get them. And then the news got even worse. When they left the next day, they were not choppered out like the rest of the guys. Instead, they had to drive in a convoy all the way from Hit, through Baghdad, down to FOB Kalsu, traversing some of the most dangerous terrain that the war-torn country had to offer. It seemed like a great way to die, and the pucker factor was at an all-time high. Somehow, they made it safely. But the war had one final dark card to play before the Mississippians departed for home. On December 8, Milton Rivera-Vargas, who was at FOB Kalsu as part of a Puerto Rican National Guard unit attached to the 155th, died of a heart attack in what would have been one of his last nights on guard duty before he was to return home. He left behind seven children ranging in age from seven to 34.

Back at Dogwood, there had been a slow-moving frenzy of activity for well over a month to prepare for the complex task of withdrawal and redeployment home of the 150th. By December everything was in an organized shambles as the unit made ready to ship out in earnest. Everyone was happy to get home – to see their families, to have survived, to see what Katrina had left them. But then came the punch. The Marines, who controlled Anbar Province, had decided that they were going to close FOB Dogwood. The base would be destroyed and the American military presence permanently removed from the area. As word of the decision reverberated around the unit, the questioning began. Why the hell had they been sent there in the first place? What of the sacrifice of Cooley, Arnold, Lee, and so many others? What would come of all the progress that they had made in the area? What had it all been for?

Ken Cager of Alpha Company spoke for everyone when he recalled:

When we got word that they were going to close Dogwood it was like a kick in the nuts. We lost lives up there. And now you had to ask the question, "Why did y'all send us up there in the first place?" I couldn't figure it out for the life of me why the Marines decided to do that. I mean, this was a hot area: a critical area. This was the Triangle of Death. If anything, you should have wanted to expand that footprint inside the heart of Iraq. We were thirty miles from Baghdad, and you wanted to lose this ground? And they had spent a lot of money building it up; like, we eventually got a top notch dining facility up there. Dogwood was like a thriving FOB now. I mean, we had a stress doctor; we had a nice gym, and it is all going to be gone. It was a disheartening decision. Nobody was going to remember that the old 150th Engineer Battalion had gone to Dogwood and succeeded.

It's unfortunate, man. And we lost good people in the process, but then they gave it all up. They gave it all away.

Paul Lyon of Bravo Company took the Marines out on their ride-along to meet the three sheiks of Owesat at Outpost 3. He had to fight back anger in the meeting. He knew that the Marines were quickly going to pull up stakes and leave, but he couldn't tell the sheiks that. Trying to put on a brave face, Lyon started the final encounter with some humor. He asked the sheiks if they had started to spend some of the money that they had received for their part in some of the road-building contracts in the area. He figured that maybe they had bought something nice. One of the sheiks replied in the affirmative. He had bought something nice. A new wife. He called her his coalition wife. Lyon smiled and congratulated the sheik. And he introduced the men to the Marines by his side. He told them that the Marines would now take care of them like the Mississippians had. He couldn't say what he really wanted to say, "Hey. These assholes are going to leave you and the insurgents will be coming back, so be careful." All he could do was shake hands with the sheiks and give them hope for the future. Hope that he knew to be unwarranted.

As the meeting went on, Larry Mergenschroer watched a scene that had become comforting to him over the past months. Nearby, that orange tractor that the 150th had provided to Owesat slowly went back and forth, working to smooth a road. Seeing that tractor on its daily missions had become a talisman for Mergenschroer. It meant peace. It meant progress. There weren't IEDs in Owesat anymore. There weren't mortars being fired from Owesat anymore. There wasn't gunfire from Owesat anymore. It was a village at peace. It was the village of the orange tractor with its waving driver. And it hit Mergenschroer harder than he expected that, with the Marines and Dogwood gone, that tractor would soon be destroyed. That the IEDs, mortars, and gunfire would return. That the good work of the 150th would be undone.

By the time the 150th pulled out, it had brought peace to its corner of the Triangle of Death against all odds. It had conducted over 1,500 combat patrols, over 150 combat logistical patrols, and over 150 company-sized operations. It had captured over 377 insurgent detainees, including some of the most wanted men in Iraq, crippling the insurgency in the area. It had also wrecked the insurgent supply lines through the destruction of an enormous amount of ordnance, including 2,007 mortar rounds; 386 artillery shells; 2,214 miscellaneous shells; 210 cases, 519 cans and 67,142 loose rounds of small-arms ammunition; 633 rocket-propelled grenades and 47 launchers; 303 rockets; and a host of other items, notably including four Milan guided missiles, 24 Sagger missiles, 4,410 pounds of high-explosive compound, and nine antiaircraft guns.

As the Mississippians made their way first to Kuwait and then home, Roz Morris returned to FOB Iskandariyah to see out the remainder of her tour in combat stress control. She had come to love and respect the Guard soldiers with whom she had worked so closely at Dogwood, and she had developed an affinity with the Iraqi people in the area. That affinity had grown in the latter part of the tour as violence had given way to MEDCAPs and humanitarian aid. She made it a point to keep up with developments in the area. Conexes and other portable items were moved to other bases, but most of Dogwood was just burned to the ground. So much of what was burned could have greatly assisted the local population, but that was not in the Marine playbook. She knew the mentality. The incoming unit had to make its own name; it had to do things its own way. Within weeks word came to her that the insurgency was on its way back to Owesat; that the work of the 150th was already being undone. She couldn't help but shake her head and wonder, "Didn't you learn anything from the Mississippi National Guard?" But the question was rhetorical. She already knew the answer, and it left her cold inside.

8

Aftermaths

I was just telling my wife the other day that I actually miss it a lot. Imagine 365 days of a roller coaster ride; the adrenalin you get from roller coasters but like times ten. And I'm actually having problems because I'm so used to that adrenalin waking up every morning. You know there's mortars landing in the base or we're going on a raid or we're doing this, we're doing that and it's always go, go, go, go, go and there's was always something exciting happening; now, you know, I don't have that. So I've got to try to fill in with the adrenalin and it's just not working out.

GEORGE TRIERWEILER

The 150th shipped back home in stages starting in mid-December, with many members of the unit home in time for a family Christmas. But for some it took a good bit longer. Two of the last to leave Iraq were company commanders Ken Cager and Chris Thomas. Both had to undertake a standard full accounting of their unit's equipment before they could return home, but there were complications. In Thomas' case it was because his company was short by one truck – reappropriated by another unit in Kuwait no doubt scrounging for vehicles as the 150th had done a year prior. As Thomas worked out all the details and headaches about that damn truck, he couldn't help but notice how great the troops in Kuwait had it. They even had a Coke machine, something he hadn't seen in a year. He remarked to a passing officer, "That Coke machine must be hard to handle." Not catching his sarcasm, she responded, "Sure is hard to handle. It hasn't had Cokes in it for three weeks." Thomas just shook his head. Here he had been bombed and mortared for the past six months, and he thought, "All she had to worry about was whether the fucking Coke machine had Cokes in it." What he told her was, "Gee, that's tough," as he finished his paperwork to go home.

What was rattling Ken Cager's brain was that the Regular Army officer who was supposed to sign off on his property book just wouldn't make the trip to FOB Kalsu to get the job done. On Christmas Day he was fuming that the guy wouldn't come to complete the task, when mortar rounds started hitting the base. Here he was. Christmas. As far as he knew he was the last of the Mississippi Guard. Stuck in Kalsu, and getting mortared. And the Regular Army clowns wouldn't come and sign his papers. He thought to himself, "I've got to get out of here before I'm killed." So, he scanned the entire property book and had it sent to his counterpart. It was finally signed, allowing him to return home. But he still has a digital copy of that property book to this day, always wary that someone will come up and tell him something was missing from it in 2005.

Most of the other members of the 150th shipped home in waves, first flying to Germany, before landing in the United States, often in Maine, and then making their way to Camp Shelby for out-processing. Everywhere in the airports they were treated as homecoming heroes – there were flags waving, pats on the back, and nobody let you buy your own meal. It was plain that the United States had learned something from how it had treated its veterans in the wake of the Vietnam War. It sure was nice, but to everyone the goal was home and family. When at the airport in Maine, a passing civilian asked Stacey Ford if there was anything he could buy for him. Ford responded that he wanted a bottle of Scope mouthwash. When the man asked why, Ford responded that he had been away from home for a year and was going to see his wife for the first time in a damn long time that night. That was why he needed mouthwash. There was going to be some kissing.

READJUSTMENT

For most it was a quick out-processing at Camp Shelby before a break at home and then back to the Guard for any further service or deployments. Almost all the homecomings were full of joyous hugs and family welcomes. The Guard communities from Okolona to Lucedale turned out to give their sons and daughters a massive welcome home. But for nearly everyone, there were complications large and small in returning home. Ken Cager's mom hosted a welcome home feast for her son, with her specialty – fried chicken. Cager had craved that fried chicken for over a year and couldn't wait for it to hit his mouth. But he only ate a bit before he got sick – violently sick. His stomach had gotten "jacked up" from a year of eating Army food in Iraq, and the wonderful fried chicken just overwhelmed his system. He did make his excuses in time to reach the restroom; there was no way he was going to embarrass his mom.

For many the first sign of problems was startling at loud noises. Richard Rowland was asked by his wife Keltoum to get something from the hall closet. When he opened the door, an item came tumbling off the top shelf and clattered to the floor. Rowland "came unglued," throwing things everywhere and cursing loudly. Keltoum and their daughter Nadia gave him his space. In a short time, Rowland calmed down and tidied up the closet. The pair then asked him how he was, and he responded that he would be fine, but it was going to take him time to come to grips with the idea that he was home and not still "over there." Others had much the same story. For Chris Thomas the trigger was an afternoon class back in law school when a truck slammed a dumpster it was loading. Before he knew it he was under the desk, hoping that the teacher and the other students had not noticed, but of course they had. Sherman Hillhouse was at his civilian job when a load of pallets was dropped to the floor, sending him sprawling for cover. For Jamie Davis it was having to carry a weapon when he left the house; otherwise he felt naked and at risk.

For Dexter Thornton it was coming home to a wife and two young children. He had left for Iraq when the children were three years old and six weeks. So, he had never really experienced life with two children before. He had spent the last 18 months of his life planning things down to a "T," where even the slightest delay or mistake could mean death. But somehow getting his family to church on time seemed even more stressful and difficult than writing up a battalion-sized operation. There were so many variables and moving pieces. It had to grow on him that families don't work on detailed operations orders, and that a bit of chaos wasn't the end of the world. It was the love of his wife and the patience of his children that gave him the time to adjust to his new normal.

Many members of the 150th had difficulty driving once they returned home. For Richard Rowland it seemed perfectly natural to drive down the middle of Hardy Street to avoid IEDs. Neither oncoming traffic nor his family agreed. Sherman Hillhouse just couldn't keep his eyes on the road, constantly searching for roadside IEDs and rooftop snipers – something that had meant life or death only a few days before outside Firm Base 2 in Hit. Perhaps it was most dramatic for Kirk Dyer. He was passing an 18-wheeler on the highway when a car whizzed up behind him, tailgating him, before it cut into the right lane and then cut back into his lane and cut him off. The next thing he knew he had caught up to the offending vehicle and was running it off the road as his family was screaming at him. He came back to reality – no longer stuck in Iraq – and let the other driver back on the road before going his own way.

For many in the 150th the startles and constant hyper-alertness faded with time, but for many others the nightmares, fear of crowds, and other elements of Post-traumatic Stress Disorder (PTSD) became a part of their everyday lives. The Guard perhaps wasn't the most responsive institution to the needs of PTSD, but the disorder was no longer demonized as it had been in the immediate post-Vietnam era. Most subjects interviewed for this project have some level of government-rated PTSD, which did not necessarily mean an end to their Guard career. Indeed, many went on to serve out sterling careers while rated with PTSD. For others, it became a more dominant part of their everyday lives – and to some, PTSD would contribute to suicide. For Greg Wells, who had served as Trent Kelly's driver, there were some of the usual symptoms, including jumping at loud noises. But to him one change stood out. He had been a sports star, a high school All-American, and being with the crowd at football and basketball games was part of his DNA. But he no longer liked crowds; no longer enjoyed going to sporting events. He now preferred solitude. For Mike Beal, who had been platoon commander to Sean Cooley, Terrance Lee, and Larry Arnold, it meant years of counseling.

But no matter what he did, the guilt of losing those men never went away. The military does a good job of teaching responsibility. Officers like Beal are rewarded when positive outcomes happen. But that also means that when negative outcomes happen, when men are killed on your watch, it is your responsibility. Beal suffered greatly from headaches as well, and eventually was diagnosed with Traumatic Brain Injury (TBI) from the IED strike that had killed Arnold and Lee.

Medic Joe Smith, who had been present for most of the mass-casualty situations in Iraq, had ample trauma in his military past. And his homecoming was far from ideal. His wife had divorced him during the tour and had taken his two children to another state to live. So, Joe returned not to a home with familiar furniture and loving family members, but to a home that was stark and abandoned. He married again shortly thereafter, but that, too, was doomed to failure. Soon he was diagnosed with PTSD and put on disability, attending a three-month inpatient program with the Veterans Administration health care system. After receiving an honorable medical discharge from the Guard, Smith tried his hand at several jobs – correctional officer, bar bouncer, ambulance driver – all jobs that provided the adrenaline that he so needed. In 2009 he met Leah, a mental health nurse at a correctional institution. She loved him and understood him. The couple is still together and still deeply in love. She doesn't mind his nightmares and his talking to people who aren't there. They are part of his past in Iraq, but that past still has a grip on his present. And Leah is okay with that.

There were also a host of medical issues that stemmed from the 2005 tour – everything from tinnitus due to IED blasts to numerous health problems tied to being near burn pits or the explosion of hazardous materials. And such issues did not discriminate based on rank – Roy Robinson, the commander of the 150th, was diagnosed with serious heart issues after his return that were linked to the burning of hazardous waste, which nearly derailed his career.

Robinson knew that the men who had served under his command were having trouble, and he again thought outside the military box to provide what help he could. The National Guard was a family – still. And families take care of their own, no matter what. Roz Morris was in her office at Walter Reed Hospital in DC when the phone rang. It was Robinson. He had once asked her to break the mold and come help his soldiers in Iraq, and she had answered the call, forming a bond almost unique in that war. Now he wanted her to break the mold again and to come to Mississippi to rekindle her relationship with her beloved Mississippians. They needed her. But she protested that she was Regular Army; how was this going to happen? As he had in Iraq Robinson made calls, pulled strings, and twisted arms, and Roz Morris was sent on temporary duty to Mississippi to help the soldiers of the 150th deal with the issues that stemmed from their time together in Iraq. It was a balm to both the soldiers and to Roz Morris. PTSD is not something you medicate and it goes away. It is the memory of traumatic events – memories so strong that they sometimes stray into the waking world of the present. These were not things to be erased, but things to be confronted and to be dealt with carefully. PTSD remains a real issue in the 150th family, but for most it is manageable. And Roy Robinson and Roz Morris were key to that.

Another key factor for healing is that many of the 150th remained in the Guard. An important part of dealing with PTSD is to talk about those memories with the men and women who share and respect them. In the Guard those men and women are all around, friends who were there for the duration. And even for those who got out of the Guard after 2005, there remained the community. Lucedale, Quitman, Hattiesburg, Carthage, Houston, Okolona – these were communities of people with similar experiences and memories. They would always be there for their Guard brothers and sisters. Darrell Havard, a Guardsman born and raised in Lucedale, put the reality of the Guard well:

> We're family. We talk to each other once a week to check. We always see each other, and every time you see us hug, everybody thinks we're crazy. "What are you doing hugging?" But that's family. We're brothers. So we are always in touch, making sure everybody's all right, that once we got back everybody's doing okay. And if they need anything, they know that they can call or we can call them, and they will be there to help us.

IRAQI AFTERMATHS

After the 150th departed Iraq, its interpreters were reassigned. For Joseph that meant moving to the area around FOB Kalsu to work with a new infantry unit. He had built up nearly a year of trust with the

Mississippians and had gotten along with them well. They respected him, and he respected them. But his new unit was fresh to Iraq and looked at him with disdain and mistrust. One of his first missions with the new unit was a foot patrol through a populated and restive area. Joseph had heard from the other interpreters who had worked in the area longer that the route for the patrol was a hotbed for IEDs. And in one of the first homes they searched he was told that the way ahead was strewn with IEDs and to take great care. He passed on the information to his new commander, but it was met with derision. Probably a terrorist ploy. So, the patrol went on. A few steps further an American was killed by an IED, and another Iraqi interpreter lost his eyes to the same blast. Instead of understanding that he should have heeded Joseph's warning, the US commander trusted him even less, wondering if he could have been in on a plot against his troops.

Over the next weeks, Joseph continued gathering intelligence and giving what advice he could, but trust never developed as it had with the 150th. The new unit continued to think that Joseph had to be working for or with the bad guys. The suspicion and the risk just became too much to bear. These guys were going to get Joseph killed. They viewed him as some kind of traitor. And he knew that his own people branded him as a traitor as well. It was no longer worth it, so Joseph returned home and started a family, eventually having three children. He took a job teaching English in Iraqi schools, but his past never left him. He and his family tried hard to keep secret the fact that he had been an interpreter with the Americans, but somehow the word got out. The results varied from innocuous to potentially deadly. Some in his neighborhood contacted him for years afterwards, hoping that he would intercede with the Americans on their behalf. He would always respond that he had never been an interpreter with them; they were mistaken. Others warned him that people in the neighborhood were gunning for him, presuming that he was a spy for the Americans. He again responded that they were mistaken; he had never worked with the Americans. Even today, every night for Joseph is a fresh trauma, sleeping with a pistol under his pillow wondering if the door will break in and the shooting will begin.

Joseph had once believed the American promise that Iraq was going to be made a better place. Maybe one day it would become like Dubai – prosperous and peaceful. He worked hard for that dream. But it was not to be. Joseph cannot allow his teenage son to go to his soccer matches unattended; he has to be there and has to be armed. In the years after the war, chaos reigned in Iraq, not prosperity and peace. And echoes of that chaos remain. Joseph had hoped to live in an Iraq that the American presence had helped to heal. But now he hopes that there is some way that he and his family can immigrate to the United States. As Afghanistan was falling, he saw that many interpreters were evacuated from the country to be brought to America. He is wondering when and if that chance will ever come for him and his compatriots. They served; they died; they want a chance. And in Joseph's case, he would like to use that chance to get a Ph.D. in linguistics and perhaps teach at an American university in a country at peace.

OWESAT

In Anbar Province, the insurgents, especially those linked with al-Qaeda, were desperate to reverse the gains made by US forces during 2005. The result was the unleashing of a wave of terror, including assassinations and even the kidnap and torture of school children.[*] One of the most vulnerable places to recapture by the insurgents was Owesat. It no longer had American troops perched on its doorstep. It sat atop a critical supply route. And it had turned to support the Americans in the wake of the 150th's successes. These things could not be allowed to remain.

The Owesat leaders, though, decided to make a stand. Instead of knuckling under to an insurgent return, they accused the neighboring Fuhaylat tribe of harboring insurgents and attempted to marshal support against them. A wave of reprisal murders then rocked Owesat, as fighting broke out between the two tribes. Taking a stand to fight for their newfound freedom was a profoundly dangerous choice for Owesat, though. The insurgents had a force of some 200–300 fighters based in nearby Jurf al-Sakhar, something that the Owesat tribe could not hope to match. In a last-ditch effort to maintain their freedom, the leaders of Owesat raised and armed a 200-strong militia that was deputized by the Iraqi police. Records of what happened next are sparse, but

---

[*] Marine Corps Intelligence, *Study of the Insurgency in Anbar Province, Iraq*, Chapter 6, 18, 43.

the insurgents launched a bloody offensive against Owesat, eventually retaking the village and launching a wave of reprisals.* Owesat had fought for the freedom that the 150th had brought to the village, but it could not be maintained. The area fell once again under insurgent control, and what the Mississippians had accomplished was dashed.

THE PRICE OF FORGETFULNESS

During 2006 and 2007, the Marines and Multi-National Force/West made great strides in Anbar Province, especially in the populated areas along the Euphrates River further to the north and west of Owesat. A transition by the Marines to more counterinsurgent tactics, plus a rising abhorrence by the local populace for the deadly methods used by the insurgents, led to strong gains that would be the centerpiece of new US strategies as the war entered a new stage.† The area around Owesat, though, remained under insurgent control and distant from US interest at the time. On May 12, 2007, Specialist Alex Jimenez, Private Byron Fouty, and Joseph Anzack were kidnapped and killed in an ambush near Owesat. Anzack's body was found in the Euphrates the next day, but Jimenez and Fouty remained missing.‡ Insurgents from Owesat were the presumed culprits in the attack, and reprisals came quickly. Since the Marines had abandoned the area, and it was outside of Army control across the river, this corner of the Triangle of Death had once again become a lawless enclave. *Stars and Stripes* noted that, while the town had been raided in the past, there had never been a "permanent presence" there.§ Of course, there had been a "permanent presence" there, that of the 150th, but it had been forgotten.

The result was Operation *Marine Courageous*, in which 400 US and 150 Iraqi troops descended on Owesat to try to root out the insurgency and perhaps find the bodies of the missing soldiers. The fighting in and around Owesat lasted for a month and captured 47 presumed

---

*Marine Corps Intelligence, *Study of the Insurgency in Anbar Province, Iraq*, 120–122.
†Especially see Angel Rabasa et al., *From Insurgency to Stability: Volume II: Insights from Selected Case Studies* (Santa Monica, CA: RAND National Defense Research Institute, 2011).
‡Their bodies were found over a year later buried in Jurf al-Sakhar.
§Erik Slavin, "GIs Use Strategic Town as Base in Search for Missing Soldiers," *Stars and Stripes*, November 20, 2007.

insurgents. The commanders of the operation gushed that it was a "quintessential model" of counterinsurgency done right. Three sheiks met with US soldiers after the violent phase of the operation ended and asked for their support and continued presence, even offering to raise a local self-defense force to aid them. The new US force set up a patrol base in Owesat, sent out sniper teams into the desert, paid locals for contracting services, and ran MEDCAP missions.*

The operation in Owesat was such a stunning example of successful counterinsurgency in a previously unoccupied area that it even received coverage from a reporter from the *Los Angeles Times*. As US troops doled out aid to students in the local school – the same school that had two years before been adopted by the troops of the 150th – one of the new commanders told the reporter, "We're just trying to give them a taste of what could happen if they quit turning their heads and stop cooperating with al-Qaeda." One of the three local sheiks on hand reported, "I am tired, and everybody is tired. We don't want any enemies. We want to clear the area of bad people." And the doctors with the unit reported how proud they were to be part of "the first" medical mission to Owesat. They just knew if they showed the people there how committed the Americans were, things would change.† In January 2008, no less a person than General David Petraeus was on hand in the area to speak with local sheiks. As he walked with the sheik down the area's streets, he remarked, "It takes two hands to come together. If you extend a hand, someone might take it."‡

While the news from Owesat might not have registered deeply with the wider American public in 2007, it hit the Mississippians like a sledgehammer. All their fears had been realized. Dogwood had been closed, and Owesat had been left to its own devices after their departure. And the insurgency had returned – just like they had never been there. Just like Cooley, Lee, Arnold, and all the others had not paid for that chunk of desert with their lives. Paul Lyon was among many who kept up with the stories coming out of Owesat closely.

---

*Dale Andrade, *Surging South of Baghdad: The 3d Infantry Division and Task Force Marne in Iraq, 2007–2008* (Washington, DC: Center of Military History, 2010), 275–281.
†Ann Simmons, "In One Iraqi Village: A Taste of What Might Be," *Los Angeles Times*, December 24, 2007.
‡Andrade, *Surging South of Baghdad*, 285.

He contacted now General Roy Robinson and asked him if he could believe it. Robinson replied that it was just best to leave it alone. They weren't there anymore. There was nothing that they could do. Lyon responded, "Yes sir. I know. But it is still driving me crazy." Here were these guys in Owesat meeting with the same three sheiks, running the same kind of operations, adopting the same school, befriending the same children. And they were all saying that they were the first troops ever to be there or to do anything like this. These guys were being touted as a model of counterinsurgency for doing the exact same things that the Mississippians had done two years prior. It might have been even worse for Thomas Howell, who had been the executive officer in Alpha Company at Dogwood in 2005. He was at Balad Airbase on his second deployment to Iraq and read the story about the new operations in Owesat in *Stars and Stripes*. He was shocked that the National Guard deployment to eastern Anbar Province had seemingly been forgotten. What the Mississippians had done didn't seem to matter; perhaps it couldn't matter. Perhaps it didn't fit well in the grand narrative. So many had been killed or wounded during that deployment, and so much progress had been made. And that it was not even a footnote in history – that the American military itself seemed to have forgotten and cared so little – hurt. And it hurt deeply.

Sadly, it was not the end for Owesat; once again the Americans weren't there to stay, and the insurgents were not gone for good. The surge of US forces in Iraq and the advent of a more thoroughgoing counterinsurgency, which had its roots in Anbar Province, made the situation in the area better for a short period. But next came the slow US withdrawal, which quickly ended any US or Iraqi military presence in and around Owesat. As a result, the insurgents returned to take their revenge and to restore their rule. As Owesat and the surrounding areas once again became a thorn in the side of US and Iraqi forces, Operation *al-Sakar* was mounted in April 2009 to clear insurgents from the region. A blend of US and Iraqi forces hit Owesat in part to disrupt supply lines of munitions for the insurgency. The troops air-assaulted into Owesat as a show of force and began to round up suspected insurgents. The US and Iraqi forces also hoped to "build relationships with the local citizens of Owesat," and to show the locals that their needs could best be met by the coalition, which was a "positive influence they can trust to keep them safe." Then the troops gathered outside the local school to hand out backpacks and school supplies. Once again, the Mississippians looked on as the stories portrayed what was happening in Owesat as something new. It was the same old story stuck on repeat, like an old record that was scratched.

It was to be the last major coalition effort led into the region. Soon Operation *al-Sakar* was complete. The Americans and the Iraqi military went back to their bases, and the insurgents returned to dominate the people of Owesat, and the village slipped away from any news coverage. In undertaking my research for this book, I asked Joseph if there was any chance that any of the three sheiks of Owesat could possibly be reached for an interview. Joseph drew a deep breath and sighed. No. That would not be possible. Owesat had fought against insurgent domination too often. And, after al-Qaeda came and went, Owesat fell to the control of the even more lethal ISIS. The three sheiks were long since dead. In fact, he didn't think that there was anyone left in Owesat at all who could remember the time when the Mississippians were there.

THE GUARD LIFE

There were some who left the service after the 2005 deployment, but for the vast majority the National Guard was a career, even a way of life. For some, ongoing service in the Guard led to great things. Roy Robinson rose to the rank of Brigadier General and served as Assistant Adjutant General of the Guard in Mississippi. After that, he served as executive director of the National Guard Association of Mississippi and then as President of the National Guard Association of the United States. Trent Kelly, who served as S-3 at Dogwood for much of the deployment, also rose to the rank of Brigadier General and now serves as a US congressman. For most, though, in times of peace ongoing Guard service meant continuing with training cycles, promotions, responding to natural disasters, and transfers. But for nearly all of those who stayed in, remaining in the Guard also meant additional deployments. Most saw at least one more combat tour, to either Iraq or Afghanistan, and a second tour to Kuwait to serve as a regional response force in the event of an outbreak of major hostilities. In each case it meant being away from family for another year or more. And in some cases, it meant facing dangers even greater than those seen at FOB Dogwood in 2005. With transfers and promotions, many members of the 150th served with different units on their next deployments, defying generality in their story. However, the Lucedale unit stands as an example of what was to come.

Bravo Company of Lucedale was reassigned to become the 278th Mobility Augmentation Company, allowing it a more flexible role to serve as combat engineers attached to other units. In 2009 this meant deployment to Afghanistan to serve in a route clearance role for the American forces based there. Commanded by now Captain Marty Davis, the 278th served alongside the 101st Airborne Division in Gardez. Afghanistan in 2009 was a much more violent place than Iraq around FOB Dogwood in 2005. There was no question of winning over the population in the 278th's area. You could see the hatred in their eyes. The job of the 278th was to clear routes of IEDs for convoys along some of the most sensitive and contested roads in the troubled country. This time, though, the unit was equipped with specialist vehicles to find and destroy IEDs and vehicles designed to withstand IED blasts. When he saw the vehicles, Marty Davis couldn't help but marvel. These vehicles, including the Husky and the MRAP, were exactly what the 150th had been trying to jury-rig back at Dogwood in 2005. The Army had finally gotten it right. But Davis also couldn't help wondering how many lives would have been saved if the Guard had possessed such vehicles in Iraq. In Afghanistan in 2009, being part of a route clearance package meant that nearly every day the unit went out, it got blown up. There were more than 70 IED strikes on the unit during its deployment, along with 300 other IEDs found and destroyed. Nearly everyone got blown up at one time or another, but the vehicles and their occupants survived. Concussed. Tossed around. Scared shitless. But alive. Ready for another mission. And IED strikes were often followed by ground fire of all types, so leaving the vehicles was a death sentence. It was fix-what-you-could-from-inside and move on. For everyone on that deployment, and so many others like it, their time overseas couldn't end quickly enough.

Gary Kinsey kept up a very busy Guard and military career after the 2005 deployment. First, he held a leadership position at Mobilization Force Generation Installation Program's Operation Warrior Trainer at Camp Shelby, which brought in combat veterans from Iraq and

Afghanistan to give Guard soldiers who were headed to the war zone an unvarnished truth of what it was going to be like. Several members of Bravo Company, including Randall Jones and James McElroy, served with Kinsey in Operation Warrior Trainer. After that, Kinsey was on orders with the Army Reserve in Mustang, Oklahoma, to support a training mission. After several other deployments, including many in the Washington, DC area, Kinsey found himself in Kabul, Afghanistan, as the US military mission to the country ended in August 2021. He was working to evacuate US and Afghan civilians when he was wounded by a suicide bomber striking the Abbey Gate to the airfield on August 26.

Working with Kinsey during his time at Operation Warrior Trainer was James McElroy, whom everyone called Mac. From Searcy, Arkansas, Mac had joined the Marines fresh out of high school. After that stint was over, Mac still wanted to serve his country, but didn't know quite how to do it. He had just gotten a divorce and was at a loss. He had gotten to know Gary Kinsey and was even staying at Kinsey's house when Kinsey talked him into enlisting in the National Guard. Mac had moved to Mississippi by then, which meant that he wound up in the 150th in 2003. During training at Camp Shelby, he had become best friends with Randall Jones, who just loved Mac's sense of humor. Dude was constantly joking around, reminding Jones for all the world of Drew Carey. While at Camp Shelby, Mac was posted to Lieutenant Colonel Robinson's Personal Security Detachment (PSD). In Iraq, this meant serving under the command of Marshall Davis, who, along with his brother Marty, formed one of five sets of siblings in the unit. The PSD took part in battalion-level raids and the like, but mainly served as a constant quick reaction force in case of emergency. It was surmised that in this role the QRF logged as many miles on the dangerous roads of the Dogwood AO as any other part of the unit, but Mac was lucky enough that his PSD was never hit with an IED or saw any serious threat during its part of the tour. Mac had just lost his mother before the tour started, and he had been torn about going at all. On one hand, he missed his mother dearly and his family needed him. On the other hand, his buddies needed him. While in Iraq he kept up his smile, and kept people laughing, but those who knew him best wondered if he had ever put that internal tension behind him fully.

WARS DON'T END WITH THE PEACE TREATY

James McElroy/Randall Jones

Mac had remained in the Guard after 2005, and his life changed dramatically. He got married and the couple had a baby, and his father died of heart failure. When the time came for the 2009 deployment, Mac was in a very vulnerable place. Most of his family was gone, and his new wife and child needed him; and he needed them. But it was time to ship out again. Frankly, Mac wasn't sure if he could do it. His buddy Randall Jones sat him down and helped him through it all. This was Guard life. This is what they had signed on for and had to do. Mac also had severe back issues that required a powerful pain medicine. Just days before the deployment, he forgot where he was on his pain meds for the day and took too many, resulting in a trip to the hospital and then a mental health check. He convinced them that he was well enough, and then it was off to Afghanistan the next day.

To Jones and the rest of the 278th, Mac seemed fine on the Afghanistan deployment, noisy and violent as it was. But when Mac went home for leave in November, it all fell apart. Mac didn't feel able to go back to Afghanistan. He was having a panic attack. His wife, his son – they needed him. So, Mac didn't return to Afghanistan; instead, he was checked in for inpatient mental treatment in a facility in New Orleans. When Randall Jones got his own home leave, he went to check on his buddy, as did Gary Kinsey. The duo found Mac in bad shape. He was full of anxiety, drinking, and on a cocktail of medicines that the doctors had ordered. Kinsey and Jones couldn't even really tell if this was Mac. He seemed so listless and just not there. Jones got a bad feeling that the military was just trying to kind of make the problem of Mac go away rather than deal with it.

The Guard family in south Mississippi found itself in a real quandary. James McElroy was a Guard soldier, but he was not on full-time orders. So, he, like all Guardsmen and women, was expected to have a job in the real world to pay most of the bills. But the medications that Mac was on were so debilitating that he couldn't get or keep a job. Neither could his wife; she had to stay home to care for him. The family was nearly destitute, and there seemed no hope at all. For a Regular Army soldier there would be full-time Army pay in a case like this, but not in the Guard. For Mac to get paid, he had to go back on orders. Gary Kinsey knew that he had to do something, so he called the members of the 150th family. The right thing to do was to get Mac back on orders, and full-time pay, and to check him into a medical treatment facility to get him the help he needed. He was a serving member of the US military after all and a veteran of two combat tours. Again, in the Regular Army the next step was obvious – bases had medical facilities near to caring families. But the Guard did not. There were wonderful civilian medical facilities near to Mac, but none of those was an acceptable military option. The nearest military medical facility was at Fort Benning, Georgia. However, there Mac would be away from his support network. Mac would be vulnerable. But it was the least bad option.

At the same time Randall Jones was having both knee and back problems from his deployments. Tests on his back showed severe damage to two vertebrae due to IED detonations on his vehicle in Afghanistan. It was about the same time that his first wife told him that he was going to need to get some help, or they were through. Jones had come home from his deployments, but he had never really come home at all. Iraq and Afghanistan were still there as *the* defining points of his life and psyche. As a result, Jones was also sent to Fort Benning to deal with his health issues. Mac was in one barracks, and Jones was in the next. Not roommates but close enough to check on one another. And that is when Jones again noticed the impact Mac's meds were having on his behavior. One evening the duo went to the commissary to get some grub. Mac was acting a bit off, but it didn't seem too bad. The next morning Mac's wife called. What had they done the night before? Had they gone to a strip club? Mac had spent $250 that the family could ill afford. Jones went to check on Mac. There were pastries all over his room. He had bought $250 worth of the things without remembering it. Another night it was the same, but this time with chicken pot pies. Another night Jones found Mac asleep outside of his car, packed and ready to go somewhere. But he didn't know where. Jones reported to the base medical authorities that the meds were making Mac act unpredictably. Their response was that Mac himself or his doctors had to report such a thing.

With the problems duly reported, Jones left for a short fishing trip that was part of his own rehabilitation. He was only gone for a day before Mac's wife reached out. Mac was in jail. He had gotten into an accident and a fight outside of a McDonald's off base and had been arrested. Jones got on the next flight back to Fort Benning and couldn't believe that when he got there Mac was still in jail. Nobody had bailed him out. Sure, there needed to be justice, but an at-risk soldier in the general population of a county jail? Jones got to the jail and found that Mac had been assaulted and badly beaten while there. Mac told him that he had blacked out back on base and had woken up in the jail with people beating the shit out of him. Jones proceeded to go to Mac's platoon sergeant and, in his own words, "go apeshit on him," daring him to court-martial him for what he was saying. No military man in his right mind should have left Mac in that jail.

Two weeks later, now as vociferously on record as possible as to how the meds were impacting Mac, Jones went home for his anniversary. He was standing in the Walmart parking lot when his cellphone rang. It was Fort Benning. Mac was dead. Jones well and truly lost it. He told those damn paper pushers at Fort Benning that he was going to come back there and kill them. He had told them that something was going to happen to Mac, and they hadn't listened. As you might suspect, security met Jones at the gate of Fort Benning when he got back, and he was taken to counseling and had security most everywhere he went. Everyone was saying that Mac had intentionally overdosed and had committed suicide. But Jones never believed it. He and Mac had plans; and Mac didn't break plans. There was a nine-month investigation, but Jones did not believe the initial findings that Mac had died of what seemed to be an intentional overdose. He swears to this day that a doctor in charge of the investigation took him aside in confidence later and told him since he was the only one at Benning who had stuck by Mac's side that he deserved to know. Jones says that he saw for certain a report that it was a lethal drug interaction that had been obviously building over time that had killed Mac, not suicide. After pressing the matter, Mac's death was ruled accidental drug toxicity for treatment for injuries received in the line of duty.

Back home, Mac's close friend Gary Kinsey had to learn by telephone of his death. He had to ask twice to make sure that he had heard correctly. To this day, Kinsey can hardly believe it; it all seemed such a waste. Both he and Randall Jones showed up at Mac's house shortly after the casualty notification officers. Kinsey, Lyon, Jones, and so many more despaired of the situation that had unfolded. The only choice had been to send Mac away, but he had needed to be near home with his family support group. The Guard needed a better answer to such tragic situations. And Mac's example was not an isolated one; it was a wider problem for the Guard as a whole.

It had actually been Mac's three-year-old son Dane who had answered the door for the casualty officers that day. He ran for his mother, who didn't initially let the officers into the house. Alicia was stunned. Her hopes of the white picket fence and the perfect life with her husband were gone. But she and Dane worked hard at both their grief and their life together. At the time of writing, Mac's son, Dane, is a junior in high school and has increasingly difficult questions about how his life might have been different had his father not died. Dane has taken deeply to sports and is already one of the best players on his state champion high school baseball team. Before every game he visits his father's graveside and dedicates the game to him. Dane has also become a resource for friends who have undergone the loss of a loved one, offering them his counsel and his shoulder to cry on. It is through actions like these that he honors his father, and he hopes that the memory of James will never fade.

Randall Jones' own behavior and world began to crumble further after the loss of his friend. It was only months later that a new doctor who didn't know him at all quizzed him about his service. Upon hearing that he had been blown up more than once in Afghanistan, the doctor ordered Traumatic Brain Injury (TBI) tests on Jones. Sure enough, there it was. Now healing could begin. He received treatment for TBI for two years before his release from active duty and his eventual return home. His marriage had long since fallen apart, so he returned to an empty home and inhabited a dark place. A service dog provided by K9s for Warriors helped a great deal.* What helped him even more was getting involved with Mac's young son – especially taking the lad fishing. On their boat with the lines out, somehow everything seemed peaceful and okay. Then Jones got a crazy idea. He figured that there had to be more folks out there like Mac's son – so he started Mac's Place, taking children and their wounded warrior parents on hunting and fishing trips. Many of those trips wound up being to Pennsylvania, where Jones got involved with the Hunts for Healing Foundation in Laceyville. Founded by John and Mindy Piccotti, Hunts for Healing helps veterans bond and heal six at a time in the wilderness.† Jones had found his place in the world and his calling.

---

*Information on K9s for Warriors can be found at https://k9sforwarriors.org.
†Information on Hunts for Healing can be found at https://huntsforhealing.org.

Greg Fernandez/Chad Dauzat

Greg and Chad had been best friends since they began their training together in the 150th before the deployment to Iraq. Dauzat had been badly wounded in the arm by an IED strike in August 2005, and Fernandez had been shot in the neck by friendly fire in a convoy shortly thereafter. The two had met up in the hospital in Germany for a short time before Fernandez learned that he was headed to Walter Reed in DC, while Dauzat was to receive further treatment in a military hospital in Texas. Fernandez's mother got on the last flight out of Jackson as Katrina bore down on the city to go to her son's side at Walter Reed. Fernandez's flight from Germany to the United States had been agony. Someone had forgotten to send along his medical chart, so nobody on the aircraft knew what kind of medicines he could or should have. So, it was over 14 hours with no painkillers for Fernandez, who still had 25 staples in his neck, 52 staples in his leg, a chest tube, and severe wounds in both eyes. After the aircraft touched down, a chaplain made the rounds as the wounded were being hauled away, and when he asked Fernandez how he was doing, Fernandez used some words that chaplains perhaps don't often hear.

When Greg got to Walter Reed, he finally got some pain meds, and his parents, Betty and Frank, were there to greet him. Frank, who had worked in a factory in Grenada and then laid floors, saw his son lying there grimacing with tubes running every which way. Frank didn't know how to process that image, so he quickly stepped out of the room to compose himself. Betty had just enough time to tell Greg that she loved him before the pain meds blissfully put him to sleep. For the neck wound, even with his jugular being permanently cut off, it was a matter of painful healing. But Fernandez's eyes were another matter. A battery of eye surgeries began as Katrina struck home in Mississippi. There were shards of glass everywhere, and one of Fernandez's pupils had collapsed. So, the surgeries kept coming, which was made worse by the discovery of a gas bubble in his right eye. That meant that he had to lie only on his side with his head down to keep that gas bubble from becoming a worse problem. It was agony, and the drugs Fernandez was on gave him horrible nightmares. Nightmares of getting shot over and over.

Walter Reed was so crowded by the human cost of the war in Iraq that Fernandez was first moved to the cancer ward and then to Mologne

House for troops who no longer needed full-time care but who were still required to be nearby for surgeries and further treatment. Betty stayed with her son for a month, but his surgeries were so many and so complex, he would be a resident in Mologne House for another seven months. The most difficult surgeries were those to reconstruct his pupil and to suture in his lens. Fernandez took to always wearing sunglasses. Even the blinking red light on a VCR was enough to give him searing pain. After more surgeries than he can remember, Fernandez was finally sent home in 2006. Chad Dauzat had also been sent home from his hospital in Texas and the two hooked up often, especially in Oxford, Mississippi. They still loved to have a good time, and they shared experiences that anyone else could scarcely imagine. It brought them closer than ever.

With his eyes and the associated pain, Fernandez couldn't work anymore. Case in point: Fernandez was driving down the highway one day when he suddenly went blind in one of his eyes. The sutures holding his lens into place had given way, and his lens had tumbled backward into his eye. This meant yet more surgeries. For Chad Dauzat life was a bit different. He was fully cleared from his arm injury and joined the Army. The job that had begun in Iraq wasn't yet done, and he wanted to be in the war defending his country. Dauzat's new life involved two additional combat tours to Afghanistan where he was wounded again, necessitating another hospital stay. Whenever Chad was not on one of his stints overseas, he called Fernandez and the duo got together to drink and tell tall tales. Dauzat had been through two divorces and had married for a third time, and this one he was sure was going to stick. He had two children, Sophia and Jules. But, even though his life looked normal to outsiders, Chad let Fernandez know that he was having trouble with the past. Nightmares, flashbacks, anger management. While in a stay at Fort Gordon, he had been diagnosed with severe PTSD and had undergone treatment. But it got so bad that Dauzat attempted suicide by overdose but survived. Finally, Dauzat's wife couldn't take the strain anymore and left with the couple's child Jules. She later told Fernandez that Dauzat was at his wit's end because of constant headaches and nightmares. Dauzat told her that he was tired of hurting so much. So tired. Chad Dauzat killed himself on May 2, 2017.

In the research for this book, Dauzat's niece, Brittany Dauzat, wrote the following:

My Uncle Chad was an amazing uncle, son, brother, friend, and soldier. He saw and went through things that were so unimaginable, but still remained the person we knew and loved. He fought many demons alone, which is heartbreaking. The feeling of failing him is unbearable and will be something we will have to live with for the rest of our lives. I can only hope you can shine some light on how great he was, and people can get just a glimpse of how wonderful he was. We are proud of the man and soldier he was.

Greg Fernandez understands nightmares, PTSD, and pain. But even he couldn't imagine what it had been like for Dauzat. How bad must his pain have been? How tortured must his life have been? Fernandez misses his friend dearly and does what he can to keep his own demons at bay.

Chang Wong
In the hospital at Fort Sam Houston, Texas, Chang Wong had to come to grips with being a 20-year-old double amputee. He had lost both of his legs below the knees when his tank was hit by an IED in May 2005. Wong fell into a depression. What the hell was he going to do with his life with no legs? What was the use of going on just to be shackled to a wheelchair? There were several other amputees and double amputees on the ward with Wong. One was a Marine who had lost his legs below the knees, and both he and Wong were scheduled to get prostheses at the same time. The Marine could see the depression that tinged everything Wong did, so he took to pushing him. No way was a damn tanker going to learn how to walk again faster than a Marine! He pushed Wong; he prodded. And eventually, Wong decided to hell with it. He was going to beat that damn Marine. Wong also had another powerful motivator. His mom. At the beginning she showed him all the tenderness and care expected of a mother toward her wounded son. But about the time the Marine started pushing him, Wong's mother reached the end of her patience with his behavior. A motherly slap across the face also helped Wong to break free of his malaise. Chang Wong learned to walk again in near record time.

Then it was back to California, where Wong returned to school at Pasadena City College. It took him a while to get back into the academic swing of things, but with the help of Professor Christopher McCabe, Wong prospered. To Wong, the oddest part was that he sometimes got harsh looks when he parked in disabled parking, but then stepped out of the car. One hike up of his pants to show his prosthetic legs and those harsh looks went sheepishly away. McCabe and all of Wong's other professors were impressed with his ability and dignity. Other students were shaken by the smallest things, it seemed. But here was Chang Wong persevering, prospering, and never complaining.

Wong transferred to Cal State Fullerton and began to study marketing. While there he became a leading light in the student veteran organization, giving advice and support to other soldiers who were returning from war and adjusting to college life. By this time, Wong had several different prostheses. He had always enjoyed athletics. Why should being a double amputee stop that? He had different legs for running and for swimming. And soon he was a fixture on the running scene and in the university pool. Wong graduated from Cal State Fullerton with the hopes of working in marketing and becoming a member of the US paralympic team.*

Norris Galatas
Norris Galatas had been wounded by an IED strike in April 2005, tearing a hole in his buttock and doing significant internal damage. He had only been saved by the surreptitious presence of Hextend that amplified the volume of his blood, which had been purloined from the doctors back in Dogwood by medic Joe Smith. Galatas had then been on a carousel of major surgeries both in Germany and at Walter Reed. Even though he had been able to come home on a short leave in July 2005, Galatas kept having to make return visits to Walter Reed for additional procedures. It was especially the mesh in his abdomen, which was holding his guts in place, that continued to give Galatas real trouble. His final operation on

---

*The members of the 150th have lost touch with Chang Wong, and my efforts to locate and interview him did not bear fruit. That is why his story stops so abruptly. If any readers out there know of Chang Wong, I would love to get in touch with him so that I could learn more of his story.

his abdomen, a nine-hour affair, was not until October 2007. Lieutenant Colonel Robinson wrote to him in Walter Reed at the time to wish him well once again as he neared his 20th major surgical procedure since his wounding. Robinson could hardly believe it. Many who had been on the 2005 deployment with the 150th were making ready to deploy again, while Norris Galatas was still receiving complex medical treatment for his wounds suffered in that year. It wasn't until late January 2008 that Norris Galatas finally received his permanent release from Walter Reed. He was headed home for good. He had also made the decision to retire from the military. For some reason, though, even after all of that he carried only an 80 percent disability rating.

Physically unable to work, Galatas returned to his family land outside Meridian where he hoped to be able to spend some time taking care of his wife Janis, who had done so much to care for him over the past couple of years. Galatas took to tinkering with cars and taught himself the intricate and patient art of working on clocks and watches. Both pastimes were soothing to him, requiring quiet, concentration, and care. Perhaps it was the calm of working on such projects, but Galatas was not overly haunted by memories of the war or of his health issues after his wounding. He and Janis just kept ticking right along. It wasn't like he forgot Dogwood and Iraq. He remained very involved in unit functions and with the Wounded Warrior Program. So, Norris Galatas was certainly a valued member of the 150th family, but he worked hard to refuse to let the war define him in any way. He would much rather take care of the family horses than dwell on the past.

Sometimes, though, the past just came back in unexpected ways. One of Galatas' chief forms of relaxation was fishing. While at Walter Reed he had taken a class on the art of making bamboo fly rods and learned to tie his own flies. Again, both pastimes were soothing and fit well with Galatas' meticulous nature. On one special summer he had two major fishing trips scheduled with his buddies. It was going to be a summer to remember. On the first trip, the group was fishing from seated positions on the bank of a beautiful western river. When it came time to change fishing locations, Galatas got up and brushed off the seat of his pants. They were wet with blood. One of the other guys on the trip checked him out, bandaged him up, and told him to see a doctor when he got back home. Sure enough, the doctor said that, given his wounds and the shrapnel he still carried, he would be subject to abscesses on his rear end for years. A few stitches later, not enough for Galatas to call it a surgery, he was ready to go on fishing trip number two. His butt was still bandaged, so nothing could go wrong on their visit to the fishing holes of Tennessee. After the first day of fishing was over, Galatas changed his own dressing – he was a master at that by now. When the dressing came free there was a tiny *clang!* A piece of shrapnel had worked its way out of his butt and had dropped to the hotel's tile floor. It was the first piece, but shrapnel would continue to work its way out of his butt for years to come.

Although the past did come to revisit Norris Galatas in very tangible and often bloody ways, he and Janis had found happiness together in their quiet corner of the Mississippi countryside. Norris Galatas passed away on December 31, 2022, at the age of 60. His wife Janis works diligently to this day to keep his memory alive.

Larry Arnold
Robert Arnold was through talking with reporters. They had descended on his family like flies after the loss of his father had been compounded by the disaster that was Hurricane Katrina. The guys from *Esquire* were nice; he even kind of liked their story. But they all seemed like they were only interested in his father's death, not his life. The attention paid to Larry's life by his family and friends, though, had been gratifying. There had been so many visitors. But once the furor was over, the Arnold boys and their mother Melinda were left alone to come to terms with Larry's loss. Melinda put on a brave face. She attended the naming of the National Guard armory in Picayune in Larry's honor. Once the 150th returned from Iraq, they raised a flag next to Larry's gravesite. She attended that ceremony too, which has been reenacted every year since. Never did she let her real feelings show in front of others, but her children are sure that she never really got over Larry's loss. Her health began to deteriorate a few years later, and the boys remain convinced that her health spiral was linked to the loss of her husband and best friend.

Larry Jr. and James always carried their father's memory with them. But for Robert it was something more visceral. He had desperately wanted to return to serve out his time with the 150th in Iraq but had been refused. The Arnold family had already lost enough. That refusal, although he understood it completely, had impacted Robert almost like a physical blow. Instead of returning to Iraq, Robert went on orders at Camp Shelby in a job he didn't find fulfilling, and he felt that he had slipped through the cracks. Robert attended the ceremonies in his father's honor, but each one hit him that much harder with feelings of loss, guilt, despair, and depression. For the next two years, Robert felt lost and really couldn't make sense of the complex barrage of feelings. To this day he doesn't remember much about the two years that followed his father's death. He bounced around from job to job. Nothing seemed right.

In 2009, though, Robert's girlfriend gave birth to their son Lukan. For Robert it was like a candle being lit, lending its glow to his dark world. Robert was no longer living for himself. He had Lukan to care for. He knew that he had to get his act together. The first step was getting a steady job in security, which he has held ever since. He knew firsthand what losing a father was like. And he was damned if he was going to let his own son feel that same thing. Robert couldn't bring Larry back, but he could honor Larry's memory and life by being the best father he could be to Lukan. Robert would never say that he is at peace. The memories of past trauma still linger near the surface. But he has found his light, which helps to keep those memories at bay.

Robert McNail
Robert McNail was killed in February 2005 in an accident at FOB Iskandariyah. Once Mac's best friend, Jamie Davis, returned home, he never could quite bring himself to talk much with Mac's parents, Marvin and Linda, or Mac's fiancée, Denise. He attended the naming of the National Guard armory in Quitman for Mac and has been to many of the flag-raisings at his gravesite. But even at those events Davis couldn't talk to Mac's family. Davis somehow felt like he had let Mac down for not being with him that night at Iskandariyah. Maybe he could have done something. Maybe he could have saved him. In the immediate aftermath of Mac's passing, his parents and his fiancée had remained close. But even at the services in his honor everyone could see that the McNails were struggling with the loss of their son. In their grief they kept to themselves and shut off from most connection with Mac's comrades and friends. Nobody blamed them. What great cost is there in losing a son? The McNails even drew back from Denise. It was just a few weeks after his funeral that Marvin told Denise that

she needed to move on from them. Perhaps it was well meant; she was young and had a life to lead. But it jolted Denise nonetheless.

Denise tried to take their advice and move on. But her two children, Daniel and Sheridan, had come to look at Mac like a father and had constant questions about his absence. Denise also kept in close touch with Mac's brother, Bryan, and Mac's son Edward. So, moving on was much easier said than done. She couldn't stop visiting Mac's graveside every day; she just couldn't stop thinking of the future that they had been denied. She remained in close contact with many friends in the unit, including Jamie Davis and his wife Starla, who were still her best friends. And with Denise, Jamie finally began to open up and talk about the loss of his buddy. Together they talked through the dark times. Denise eventually fell in love again, married, and moved away. But it all came flooding right back when her son Daniel graduated from high school and told her that he wanted to join the military. That moment impacted her deeply, which Daniel was able to see. He told her that he knew what had happened to Mac, and how the influence of his loss had been felt in their family. But he still wanted to serve. Denise took some time to think about it, to come to grips with her feelings of loss once again. The next day she told Daniel that she supported his decision, and that Mac would have been proud of him.

Sean Cooley

Laura Cooley's parents had moved in with her following Sean's funeral. She protested that she wanted to be alone, but they weren't going to have it. She found that she desperately needed work; her routine kept her sane. Also, a family friend had just had a child that Laura was babysitting. That friend kindly offered to find another sitter, but Laura got so much out of having a baby around and having a little human to love and cuddle. Somehow that helped to lessen the void that Sean's loss had left in her life. The outpouring of love from the community and all of Sean's friends and admirers was overwhelming and comforting at the same time. She was there at the yearly flag-raising ceremonies on the anniversary of his death. There were so many, and still are so many, people at those events that it always reminds her of how her husband's memory was cherished and remains a living thing. But all that attention and all the well-wishes made it hard for her to move on – to move forward as Laura.

One of the main aspects of Laura's recovery was discovering the group TAPS – Tragedy Assistance Program for Survivors. A friend told Laura about TAPS three years after Sean's death, and, after some hemming and hawing, she gave it a try. Through TAPS Laura discovered that she wasn't alone. There was even a seminar for war widows with no children. Everywhere she looked, at the national and regional TAPS seminars, were people just like her. Wrestling with the same issues and dealing with the same reality. It was there that Laura first really opened up about loss and how that loss intersected with her life. The group's founder, Bonnie Carroll, had lost her own husband to war. With a new support group around her, Laura readied to face the future. Her past would always be there; Sean would always be there. But Laura Cooley finally realized that she had her own future.[*]

Laura founded the Sean M. Cooley Citizen Soldier Nursing Scholarship to help young nursing students follow in Sean's caring steps. Each year on the anniversary of Sean's death a 5k run is held in his honor to benefit the scholarship program.[†] Laura now works hard to curate Sean's memory and to ensure his legacy. A major part of that is the flag-raising at the small cemetery outside of Lucedale by Sean's graveside. Members of the 150th, veterans, and their families still turn out in large numbers for the solemn occasion. One who never missed the event was Jack Walker. Jack had been the gunner in Cooley's vehicle when it hit the IED that fateful day. Blown out of the gunner's hatch, Walker was injured and sent to Baghdad before being sent home. It was plain to all that Jack Walker had never quite come to terms with that day and with Sean's loss. He named one of his children after Sean. But whenever Jack attended the flag-raising, he was aloof. As the men and families stood around to talk, and later walked to the Cooleys' for a meal, Jack always stood off to the side. He didn't seem to want to socialize at all, lost in his world of thought. In 2022, Sean's flag-raising ceremony was delayed because of a freak ice storm in south Mississippi. But Jack Walker turned up, ceremony or no. And

[*]TAPS can be found at https://www.taps.org.
[†]If you would like more information on the Cooley Scholarship or perhaps would like to give, you can contact its leadership at seancooleyscholarship@gmail.com.

on February 3, the anniversary of Sean's death, Jack's car went off the road, killing him.

For Sean's parents, Jerry and Katherine, their son's loss still resonates deeply. They play gracious host to the events held in his honor and strongly appreciate all the well-wishes that continue to pour in, even decades later. They have been a rock in the unit, making sure to attend the funerals of the other men who were lost after Sean. If their experience in loss could in any way help those newly bereaved, they had to be there. One such experience took place over 12 years after Sean's loss, and the weeping parent asked if it ever got any easier. Jerry replied, "When we get to that point, I'll call you up and let you know." Though a smile is never far from his lips even in the worst of times, Jerry habitually wears sunglasses. One day a few years back, his tiny church got a new preacher. And that preacher just had to know why Jerry wore sunglasses in church. Jerry pointed to a stained-glass window in the church that bore Sean's name and said, "See that name? One day I'll tell you about it, and then you will understand why I wear sunglasses in church." Those sunglasses are Jerry's "safety blanket against the world."

I realized when I was collecting the oral histories that form the basis of this work that a conversation with Jerry and Katherine Cooley was greatly needed but was likely to be highly emotional. For that reason, I made sure that Paul Lyon, who led Bravo Company at Dogwood and was Sean's commander and friend, was there with me for support. In the Cooley home Sean's memory is tangible: alive. And as we spoke of their son, of his youthful antics, his teenage exuberance, the stories flowed out of Jerry and Katherine like someone had turned on a faucet. They were truly happy in his memory. But as we got closer to having to discuss that most difficult of events, Jerry had to excuse himself to make a pot of coffee. When he returned Lyon told him what Sean had meant to all the guys. How Sean was the glue that had held everyone together. It was plain that Jerry Cooley appreciated those sentiments. Then he looked at us and said, "But I would live under a bridge and eat out of a hubcap if I could just see Sean one more time."

Terrance Lee

After Terrance's funeral, the Lee family didn't have to cook for weeks. The community support was astounding and comforting. And as soon as the 150th returned from Iraq, the visits started from Terrance's friends and military colleagues. They held a beautiful flag-raising in his honor, and guys from the unit made speeches about how much Terrance had meant to everyone. The memories, though, were raw. Terrance had long been the shining light of the Lee family, and that light was just gone. And it hurt. Hurting the worst were Raemone and Terrance Jr., who simply couldn't understand why Daddy wasn't coming home. Stephanie also had to wrestle with the notion of when to tell Marchelle, her daughter with Terrance who had been born after his death, about her father. How old should a child be to be able to understand and process such news? Marchelle learned about her father at the age of five with a doctor showing her a film of *Sesame Street*'s Elmo dealing with the loss of his uncle, to help make her own loss more approachable.

It was four years later, in 2013, with Stephanie's oldest daughter Kamri in high school and Marchelle in elementary, that Tom Junod, the reporter from *Esquire* who had written a story on Stephanie after Katrina, received an email from Stephanie asking for prayers. She had been feeling unwell and had gone to her doctor.* They diagnosed her with stage 3 colon cancer and operated immediately. After surgery she was turned over to physicians at Keesler Air Force Base for further treatment. Just a few weeks later a CT scan revealed what the doctors had feared most; the cancer had already spread to her liver. They gave Stephanie their grim prognosis. She might have eight months to live if her body could withstand chemotherapy and perhaps six months if her body could not. At first Stephanie considered suicide for the second time in her young life. But then she decided that she was going to beat this damn thing. In her email to Junod she swore, "I will go back to college and get my degree. I will get a new and better job and become a success in my profession. I will see my girls grow to become women, and I will be a grandmother to my grandbabies one day. It's not fair. Marchelle won't lose both of her parents before she is 10. I won't let that happen."

---

*Much of the information in this section comes from a blend of interviews with the Lee family combined with Tom Junod's article "Mississippi Goddamn," which appeared in *Esquire* in November 2005 and the podcast "Mark Warren on the Odyssey of Stephanie Lee, 'Patient Zero,'" *Esquire Classic*, 2016, and Tom Junod's "The Death of a Friend: Stephanie Lee," *Esquire*, 2015.

For their part, the *Esquire* team of Mark Warren and Tom Junod crossed the journalistic barrier from reporters to friends. As luck would have it, they had just completed a series of stories on the cutting-edge cancer work of Eric Schadt, a computational biologist who advocated using big data mined from an individual's DNA and RNA to formulate customized treatments aimed at the individual's specific cancer. Schadt had just received a huge grant from business tycoon Carl Icahn and was teaming with Mount Sinai School of Medicine in New York to pioneer this new way to look at cancer. After receiving her email, Warren and Junod pulled every string that they could and got Stephanie Lee involved in the study at its inception. The first thing that Schadt needed was samples of Stephanie's tumor to sequence in his lab to see if it was treatable at all. Once genetically sequenced, the mountains of data produced would be cross-referenced against all the cancer databases worldwide to construct a picture with billions of connection points – all of which would intersect at Stephanie Lee.

Hundreds of scientists around the world immersed themselves into Stephanie's cancer and its genetic profile, which they eventually discovered to have 73 specific mutations that had caused the cells to run out of control – at least three of which were genetic and inherited. The work, as in any genetic modeling, was grueling and resulted in an unimaginable mountain of data points. With the information in hand, a Mount Sinai genetic biologist transplanted Stephanie's specific mutations into a fruit fly, which began to grow her exact cancer. Stephanie Lee was the fifth person in the world to have an organism bioengineered in such a manner. Now the team began to run tests on drugs of all types to see if any regimen attacked Stephanie's specific cancer.

In October 2013 a very weakened Stephanie visited New York to see what all the international fuss was about. Some drugs had proved very promising – with one actually curing one of Stephanie's flies totally. Dealing with 73 specific mutations was no small matter, but these first tests were VERY positive. However, Stephanie was at present too weak to receive the treatment, even if it did receive FDA approval. Stephanie needed time. And the doctors at Mount Sinai thought that they could give her the time. Surgeons developed a plan to gain Stephanie perhaps up to four years through an operation on her liver to remove the worst of the tumors, followed by more traditional modes of treatment. And

Schadt's team figured that those additional years would provide more than enough time for them to fully bioengineer a cure for Stephanie. Hope grew, and it began to look like Stephanie Lee might live long enough to hold her own grandchildren one day.

After the meetings at Mount Sinai, Stephanie toured the biomedical facility that had run her cancer's genome. It didn't look like a hospital at all. Hardware and giant computers everywhere, with genius-level-intellect geeks, formally termed bioinformatics scientists, hip deep in Stephanie's genome – something that they had been feverishly immersed in for months. It is one thing to work on mountains of data – it is another to hold a life in your hands. And these computer whizzes had devoted their talents to saving Stephanie Lee. Suddenly, with Stephanie's arrival, their work had more than just a name, and that name was walking into the room. As Stephanie walked around the room and shook hands, there was something of an amazed silence. This was Stephanie Lee. This was her. Several of the bioinformatics scientists broke down in tears as they met her – one, a hard-bitten Russian, could hardly bring himself to let her hands go.

Stephanie returned home with hope, which was sadly dashed. The surgery that was designed to give her the time she needed for a bioengineered miracle didn't work as planned, and conventional therapies couldn't extend her life long enough to allow miracles to happen. As the scientists put it, Stephanie's timeline had collapsed. Everyone in New York had redoubled their efforts to bend science and nature to their will, but the final breakthrough had not occurred in time. Stephanie visited them once again in the winter of 2014 so that her children could see New York and so that she could thank everyone for their efforts. She was so weak when she left that she had to be flown home by air ambulance.

Stephanie Lee passed away on February 4, 2015. At Mount Sinai the tests that began with Stephanie blossomed into a full 150-person clinical trial – and at least two of the women in that trial with young children of their own have seen their cancers go into complete remission based on treatments spearheaded by the team that worked with Stephanie Lee. Some of the brightest future treatments for cancer have come from this one Mississippi National Guard story.

After her mother's passing, Marchelle first went to live with her older sister Kamri before moving in to live with Anice Lee, as her father

Terrance Lee had done before her. And just like Terrance, Marchelle quickly became the apple of everyone's eyes. Marchelle was a straight A student in high school and was even working to get her collegiate associate degree while completing her high school work. Along the way Marchelle and her family received great solace and care from Gary Sinise's Snowball Express. Under the program's auspices, thousands of people just like Marchelle, Terrance Jr., and Raemone get together first in Dallas and then in Disney World to be kids and to enjoy life. They even get to march in the Disney parade. But it is also a place where the kids can talk to others who share the same experiences; a place where parents can talk and share their frustrations and joys. There was no way that the Lees could ever afford such a program, but the Gary Sinise Foundation paid for it all. Marchelle loved the entire experience, especially the Avatar ride. But deep down it was talking to other kids like her that meant the most. She has since "graduated" out of the Snowball Express, but it helped her come to grips with who she was and directed her toward a bright future.[*] The Guard is indeed a family, and a family takes care of its own. The National Guard Association of the United States (NGAUS) administers several scholarships for Guardsmen and women and their families. One such scholarship is the USAA Guardian Scholarship, which provides funds for the children of fallen Guard soldiers to attend college. When Roy Robinson, who had commanded the 150th in Iraq, was President of the National Guard Association, Marchelle Lee was awarded a Guardian Scholarship to help fund her college education. It was one of the brightest moments of Robinson's career as president of the association when he got word that one of his own Guard family had been chosen for the scholarship. Life was coming full circle.[†]

---

[*] Information on the Snowball Express can be found at https://www.garysinisefoundation.org/snowball-express.
[†] If you would like information on the Guardian Scholarship or perhaps would like to give to the scholarship, please see https://www.ngaus.org/membership/member-benefits/scholarships.

Afterword

TRADITION

Robert Munroe defined what it was to be a citizen soldier all those years ago when he and his sons strode forth from Buckman's Tavern and onto Lexington Green in 1775. John Parker and Munroe got the men lined up to face the oncoming British regulars. Parker hoped that the encounter would end without a fight, but nobody could say with any surety what the British would do. As the British formation gathered opposite the colonials, a British officer, probably John Pitcairn, yelled for the colonists to lay down their arms and to disperse. Parker still wanted the day to end without bloodshed and ordered his men to go home. However, there was confusion in the ranks. Some started for home, others not. And nobody gave up their arms. Suddenly a shot rang out. Nobody knows who fired first. But in a confused scene the colonial forces were scattered, and a few, notably including Robert Munroe, were killed. After Lexington the British moved on to Concord, where they received rather a rougher greeting, which was followed by a return march to Boston with British troops being harried by colonial irregulars. The colonial citizen soldiers had proven their mettle against the mighty British, portending a long war to come. One of the first casualties of that war, Robert Munroe, lies buried on Lexington Green.

Larry and Robert Arnold were the exemplars of the most American of military traditions when they departed as citizen soldiers to Iraq over two centuries later. Although now a superpower with gleaming, teeming modern cities, much of America's martial tradition remains focused on small towns and hamlets across the country that support local National Guard units and has done so for generations. Even in a military world dominated by tanks, missiles, and smart weapons, it is the enduring connection of the people to the military that defines the American way of war. Larry Arnold is buried outside of Lee's Chapel in Carriere, Mississippi. But, while standing there in the southern heat, a visitor could easily hearken back to Munroe's gravesite at Lexington Green.

The National Guard, America's citizen soldiers. Older than the country they serve, a building block of nationalism as envisioned by the Founding Fathers. This quintessentially American institution has been part of the fabric of the nation since its beginning and has been fundamental to the American way of war and way of life. But the Guard has lived in the historical shadows, all too often overlooked in the wider understanding of America and its wars. For most of America's history, the Guard was much larger and more integral to American doctrine and warmaking than the Regular Army. And the Guard also functioned in a home front role that law forbade to the Regular Army. From community mainstay, to family tradition, to storm relief, to political disturbance, to fighting in Guadalcanal and North Africa, the Guard was the fundamental nexus of the military and the people. In the post-Vietnam world, that nexus began to shift, toward a Guard that was more outwardly focused and kinetic, which transformed the military and its relationship to the people in ways that we are only beginning to understand.

The story of the National Guard in the 21st century is a key component to understanding perhaps the most crucial change ever to the way the United States prosecutes war. The long-term impacts of moving away from the true citizen soldier concept of war to reliance on a powerful, professional, standing military force will be debated by historians for decades to come. No force was more greatly impacted by that transformation than the National Guard. As a more kinetic and deployable force, the Guard trained at a higher tempo than ever in its history and served in combat overseas with a frequency that threatened to wear the institution down. As the wars in Iraq and Afghanistan wound down in 2013, National Guard Bureau Chief General Frank Grass informed Congress of the Guard's daunting task. Since the

September 11 terrorist attacks Guard soldiers had deployed more than 750,000 times to Iraq, Afghanistan, and elsewhere. This was in addition to the Guard's duty on the home front, which in 2012 alone resulted in more than 100 internal Guard deployments. Additionally, the Guard maintained the State Partnership Program in which Guard soldiers worked closely with the militaries of more than 65 foreign countries. When asked if the operational tempo threatened to wear out the Guard and its component communities, Grass responded that deployments needed to be more predictable going forward, with more guarantees of continued civilian employment, but he opined that it could be done.[*]

National Guard kinetic deployments have lessened dramatically since the conclusion of US involvement in Iraq and Afghanistan, but units still go abroad to serve as quick reaction forces, especially in Kuwait, along with service in other hotspots. And the Guard has only seen its domestic profile increase, with notable heavy use during the Covid crisis, in the January 2021 events in Washington, DC, and at the southern border with Mexico as part of the immigration issues there. This new, and seemingly ever-shifting, blend of Guard duties has resulted in a policy change dubbed "Guard 4.0" to continue to enhance Guard kinetic deployability alongside readiness for a potentially unprecedented level of home front deployments as well.[†]

Dogwood takes a microscope to but one Guard unit and its deployment to Iraq in 2005. However, hopefully the linkages are clear. In that year the National Guard was in the throes of negotiating the workings of the greatest ever change in its history. Things were fast changing, but the National Guard of *Dogwood* maintained its community purpose and its "Pals Battalions" feel of families and communities at war. Sean Cooley, Larry Arnold, Terrance Lee, Robert McNail, and all the rest could be imagined standing in lines on Lexington Green awaiting the Redcoats. The community send-offs to war, the welcome home, the community value placed on local veterans – all are links to an

---

[*]Jim Greenhill, "Guard Bureau Chief: National Guard Faces Challenges, Should Stay Operational," US Army, March 2013.
[†]Royce Locklear, "Army National Guard 4.0: A Transformation," Association of the United States Army, October 2022.

American military past that is still alive and well in the Guard, even as those links fade more and more among the Regular forces. On a kinetic and military institutional level, the 2005 deployment of the 150th carried all the hallmarks of a military that was finding its way to a new normal. The relationship between the Guard and the Regular Army has always been fraught – almost akin to a sibling rivalry. That warts-and-all relationship was certainly apparent in Iraq. Without the best equipment, without proper intelligence, without even knowing where it was headed, the 150th was given an unexpected mission in a place of unknown dangers. And as the Guard has so often done, the 150th thought outside of the box and got the job done in innovative ways. Perhaps Alpha Company executive officer Thomas Howell put it best by saying, "That is the way the Guard does things. We adapt and take on a new mission and roll with it." It all involved country boys solving problems any way they could, but paying a steep price. As was all too often the case, though, even after setting what would be a gold-standard version of successful counterinsurgency, what the 150th had done in Iraq was forgotten, leaving the area to be fought over again and again. It all left the brave men and women of the 150th wondering if what they had done was worth it or if anyone even cared.

How the National Guard fits into American military and social history is critical. How it will fit into America's military and social future is also critical even as Guard 4.0 navigates its course. *Dogwood* is a micro-history first step, using the 150th as a tight focus. To tell a human story like this one – a story of war and what it means to the men, women, and families who fight it – the focus must be narrow. The unit that is the subject of the book, though, had to be big enough to have a meaningful story, yet small enough to be relatable. And even in this telling of the story, only a minority of the men and women of the 150th were included. Otherwise, the book would have quickly spun out of control. I wish the book could have been more inclusive. Everyone in the 150th deserves to have their story told. The story of the wider 155th in Iraq in 2005 needs to be told. The story of the Mississippi Guard in its post-2005 deployments needs to be told. The stories of the other Guard units large and small deployed in the maelstrom that formed after 2001 need to be told. Hopefully *Dogwood* is just the first step in understanding the richness of the

Guard stories and sources that are out there and will spur others to tell those larger stories. Investigating how the Regular Army and the Guard coexist, or sometimes fail to, is also of key importance. Without these investigations and stories – without the bigger picture – the wider importance of the Guard will remain only poorly understood in an era in which the Guard will make up more and more of America's force for future conflicts. The Guard's story needs to be told; and I hope that *Dogwood* is only the beginning.

Cast of Characters

The list that follows is not meant as a comprehensive biography of members of the 150th but rather a snapshot of individuals whose stories featured significantly in the scope of this book.

Undaryl Allen – Natchez native; joined the Guard in high school in 2001. Served as a mechanic with the 1/155th at Iskandariyah. Family lived in Gulfport and lost everything in Katrina.

Larry Arnold – From rural Missouri; joined the Army after high school. Married to Melinda with children Larry Jr., Robert, and James. Served in the invasion of Iraq in 2003 with the 890th Engineer Battalion but was sent home for health reasons. Volunteered to go back to Iraq in 2005 and served alongside his son Robert. Killed in action on June 11, 2005.

Robert Arnold – Second son of Larry Arnold. Joined the Guard at 17 after the strikes on the World Trade Center. Transferred into the 150th during training at Camp Shelby. Was home on leave when his father was killed. His father's death was one of the formative experiences of his life. His son Lukan is now the centerpiece of his life.

Assim – Iraqi interpreter serving with Bravo Company. Was only 17 when he joined the troops of the 150th. Loved everything about America and Americans and hoped to study in the United States. Killed in action on June 11, 2005.

Bryan Barron – Served with the 155th. Native of Biloxi, Mississippi. Killed in action on May 23, 2005. Survived by his wife Amanda and daughter Haley.

Mike Beal – From New Hope near Carthage. Grew up on a farm and joined the Guard while still in high school. In 2005 served as a platoon leader in Bravo Company. Was on both the patrol where Sean Cooley was killed and the patrol where Terrance Lee, Larry Arnold, and Assim were killed.

Terrance Bloodsaw – From Walnut Grove in Leake County. Joined the Guard right out of high school in part to learn personal discipline. Served in the platoon of Alpha Company that remained stationed at Kalsu. Hit by IEDs twice during his service in Iraq.

Timothy Bolton – From Lucedale, home of Bravo Company. Was deployed to Operation *Desert Storm*. Served in Bravo Company in Iraq as a truck driver.

Durr Boyles – From Jackson and joined the National Guard in 1982. Served as the battalion commander of the 150th prior to its training at Camp Shelby in 2005, having built one of the best staffs in the state. During 2005 he served as executive officer of the 168th Engineers, which was heavily involved in the response to Hurricane Katrina. Rose to become the Adjutant General of the State of Mississippi.

Jerry Bratu – A police officer from Meridian. Served in charge of the headquarters staff with the 150th in Iraq in 2005. His experience with the police was invaluable to making decisions on how to strangle the insurgency, especially in Owesat.

Kevin Brown – Lieutenant in the 150th. Wounded in action on September 6, 2005.

Ken Cager – From Carthage, where his father worked on oil rigs and his mom ran a country store. Joined the Guard at 17 to earn money for college. Married to Audrey with two children, Richard and Phillip. In 2005 served as the commander of Alpha Company of the 150th. One of the final soldiers of the 150th in Iraq.

Leon Collins – From Booneville. Commander of the 155th Brigade Combat Team in Iraq in 2005. Later rose to become the Adjutant General of Mississippi.

Sean Cooley – From near Lucedale. Parents are Jerry and Katherine Cooley. Joined the Guard after a stint in the Navy. Was a trauma nurse at Singing River Hospital. Married to Laura Cooley. Was the glue that held Bravo Company together. Killed in action on February 3, 2005.

Chad Dauzat – From Thibodaux, Louisiana. Joined the Guard in 2004 influenced by the terrorist attacks of 9/11. Wounded in action on August 19, 2005. After recovery joined the Army and saw two more combat tours and was wounded again. Dauzat never got over the trauma of war and took his own life on May 2, 2017. Much of the information on Chad came from his niece, Brittany Dauzat.

Jamie Davis – From Stonewall. Joined the Guard right after high school as part of a family military tradition. Saw service in the Persian Gulf War. Best friends with Robert McNail. Was with the Assault and Obstacle Platoon during 2005, which was based at Iskandariyah.

Marshall Davis – From Lucedale. In 2005 served as the head of Lieutenant Colonel Robinson's Personal Security Detachment. Brother of Marty Davis.

Marty Davis – From Lucedale. Was a state highway patrolman and brought that unique skill set to the Guard. Served as a platoon leader in Bravo Company in Iraq in 2005. Led the 278th Mobility Augmentation Company in Afghanistan in 2009.

Jacob Dones – From Dimmitt, Texas. Served with the 2/11th ACR. Killed in action on October 20, 2005, in the city of Hit.

Christopher Dueitt – From rural Greene County. Joined the Guard after high school to find something better in life. Served with Bravo Company in Iraq in 2005.

Kirk Dyer – From Lucedale. Joined the Air Force before switching over to the Guard in 1993. Served with Bravo Company in Iraq in 2005.

Greg Fernandez – From Grenada. Joined the Guard in 2003 after working for his uncle's trucking company for many years. Joined the 150th during its training at Camp Shelby. Best friends with Chad Dauzat. Wounded in action on August 21, 2005.

Stacey Ford – From Buzzard Roost outside of Lucedale. Joined the Guard in part because he was in trouble with the law. Was wounded in the IED blast that killed Sean Cooley. Credits Roz Morris for saving his life after the incident.

Norris Galatas – Raised by his grandmother outside of Meridian. Joined the Guard right out of high school. Worked with the support platoon in Iraq in 2005. Wounded in action on April 19, 2005. Life was saved through the use of Hextend. His wife Janis played a huge role in his recovery and wrote a book about her experiences. Galatas had 20 major surgeries and was not released back to civilian life until October 2007. Galatas passed away in December 2022.

Mike Gilpin – Hattiesburg native. First joined the Army and served in Vietnam before switching to the Guard. Commanded the 150th in the 1990s for its switchover to combat engineers. In 2004 served as US Property and Fiscal Officer for Mississippi, which oversaw supply and care of soldiers at Camp Shelby prior to being sent to Iraq.

Russell Griffith – From the rural area outside Laurel. It was something of a family tradition to join the Guard for a brighter economic future in 1997. Served with the 150th in Iraq in 2005.

Joseph Hammonds – From Sand Hill. Joined the Guard aged 18. Was one of the primary witnesses to the wounding of Chang Wong, who was wounded in his tank on May 24, 2005.

Darrell Havard – From Lucedale. Had followed his father into the National Guard after he tired of college. Served with Bravo Company of the 150th in Iraq in 2005.

Sherman Hillhouse – From Okolona. Was won over to joining the Guard by a speaker at career day at his high school. Served with Charlie Company of the 150th in Iraq in 2005. Was part of the Charlie Company platoon that served in the city of Hit later in the deployment.

Brad Hollingsworth – From Tupelo. Went through ROTC at Mississippi State University and received his commission in 2002. Served as platoon leader and executive officer with Charlie Company in Iraq in 2005. Deployed back to Iraq in 2007 and to Kuwait in 2017 and 2022. Presently serves as Deputy G-5 for the state of Mississippi and as battalion commander of the 106th Support Battalion.

Thomas Howell – From Houston. Joined the Guard on the split option when he was still only 17. In Iraq in 2005 served as executive officer of Alpha Company of the 150th. He was the master scrounger of the unit, helping to bring supplies of all types into Dogwood, even hymnals for the chapel. Went on a second tour to Iraq in 2007.

Gary Huffman – A Mississippi State University graduate. Commander of the 2/114th Artillery in Iraq in 2005. Was wounded in action in Hit on November 25, 2005. Retired after 30 years of military service, with his last posting being as commander and senior military representative for the North Atlantic Treaty Organization Headquarters in Sarajevo, Bosnia.

Randall Jones – From Pascagoula. Served alongside his brother Ben Jones in the 150th. Best friends with James McElroy. Both also served in Afghanistan in 2009. After the death of James McElroy, Jones started Mac's Place to take children and their wounded warrior friends hunting and fishing. That program is now affiliated with the Hunts for Healing Foundation in Laceyville, Pennsylvania.

Joseph – Iraqi interpreter serving with Bravo Company. A Shia Muslim from Babylon. After serving with the 150th never found the acceptance again that he had achieved with the Mississippians. Resigned from his interpreter duties and returned home with his wife and family. Still lives in fear concerning his service with the Americans. Would like to relocate to the United States so that he and his family can find true freedom.

Kevin Kelly – From Union. Brother of Trent Kelly. Served with Alpha Company of the 150th in Iraq. His blog formed one of the most valuable sources for this book.

Trent Kelly – From Union. Brother of Kevin Kelly. Served as S-3 of the 150th before his transfer to FOB Kalsu to work with the training of Iraqi forces. Deployed in 2009 to Iraq in command of Task Force Knight of the 155th. In 2015 was first elected as US Congressman for the First District of Mississippi.

Gary Kinsey – From Gautier near the coast. Joined the Guard at 22 to work on helicopters. Shifted to the 150th in 2000. In 2005 served as executive officer of Bravo Company of the 150th in Iraq. Became a master scrounger, liberating all kinds of supplies from FOBs around Iraq. After 2005 served with the Mobilization Force Generation Installation Program's Operation Warrior Trainer at Camp Shelby. In 2021 was wounded during the American withdrawal from Afghanistan.

Jody Kyzar – From the tiny village of Sharon outside of Laurel. Joined the Guard in college in part to help pay off his student loans. In 2005 served as an NCO working in the personnel division of the 150th at Dogwood. In 2010 became a warrant officer and deployed to Afghanistan. Transferred to Jackson to become the officer personnel manager for the state. Then worked with the Warrant Officer Candidate Accession Program.

David Landrum – Served with Bravo Company of the 150th in Iraq. Wounded in action on June 11, 2005.

Terrance Lee – From Moss Point. Son of Dedrick Lee and Dinah. Was raised by his grandmother Anice Lee and her husband Robert Earl Lee along with his brother Darius. Married to Stephanie Carter. Children: Terrance Jr. and Raemone. Stephanie and Terrance had one child, Marchelle. Terrance served in Bravo Company of the 150th in Iraq and was renowned for his weightlifting and ability to repair any weapon. Killed in action on June 11, 2005. Stephanie gave birth to Marchelle during Hurricane Katrina. She passed away in 2015.

Tommy Little – From Aliceville, Alabama. Joined the Guard at 24 after working in the local cotton mill. Served with the 2/114th Artillery. Wounded in action on April 19, 2005. Died of his wounds on May 2, 2005. Wounded along with Little were Terrance Elizenberry, Melvin Gatewood, Wyman Jones, and Stephen Brooks.

Daron Lunsford – From Sardis. Had been a police officer and served a stint in the Army before joining the Guard in 2004. Served with the 1/155th. Killed in action on May 23, 2005. Survived by his wife Vangi and their daughter Paris-Audrey.

Paul Lyon – From Hattiesburg. Joined the Army after a stint at the University of Southern Mississippi. Commanded Bravo Company of the 150th during 2005. Married to Jane, who was active in the family organizations supporting the 150th. Children: Tamara, Tabatha, Victoria, and Kira. After the 2005 deployment also served in deployments to Afghanistan and Kuwait.

Douglas Mansfield – From Rocky Creek outside of Lucedale. Joined the Guard in part because he loved tanks. Served with Bravo Company of the 150th in Iraq. Served on the deployment to Afghanistan in 2009.

David Martian – From North Dakota. First served in the Army. Joined the Guard in part for college benefits to become a teacher. Transferred to the 2/114th Artillery to follow his wife Daniela who was relocating to Columbus for Air Force flight training. Served as commander of Alpha Battery of the 2/114th in 2005. After Iraq was deployed to Saudi Arabia several times. Presently serves as G-1 for the Mississippi National Guard.

Ellis Martin – Served with the 155th in 2005. Wounded in action on March 2, 2005.

Albert Matlock – From Carthage. Joined the Guard while still in high school. Served with Alpha Company. Blown up by an IED on September 6, 2005, but was uninjured and continued his bulldozing work.

Allen McDaniel – From Philadelphia. Joined the Guard just after high school and went into a career in law. In Iraq served as assistant S-3 of the 150th in 2005. Found that his job role moved increasingly toward contracting duties. Did yeoman work both in improving FOB Dogwood and in contracting outside of the FOB with Iraqi civilians. Now serves as State Judge Advocate and as Executive Director of the National Guard Association of Mississippi.

James McElroy – From Searcy, Arkansas. Known as "Mac." First joined the Marines fresh out of high school and then the Guard. Best friends with Gary Kinsey and Randall Jones. Served in the Personal Security Detachment for Lieutenant Colonel Robinson with the 150th in Iraq in 2005. Served on the Afghanistan deployment of 2009. Struggled with PTSD and died while receiving medical treatment at Fort Benning.

Robert McNail – From Meridian. Joined the Army right after high school. Saw service in the Persian Gulf War. Joined the Guard after the 9/11 terrorist attacks. Best friends with Jamie Davis. Was engaged to Denise Ahern. Served with the Assault and Obstacle Platoon of Bravo Company of the 150th in Iraq in 2005, based at Iskandariyah. Died in an accident at Iskandariyah on February 11, 2005.

Tucker McNeese – Raised in Hattiesburg. Followed his brother into the Guard in 1999 and later attended ROTC at the University of Southern Mississippi. Served as platoon leader of the Assault and Obstacle Platoon of Bravo Company in Iraq in 2005. Deployed with the 890th to Iraq in 2008 as executive officer of the Forward Support Company. Later brigade engineer for the 155th. In 2016 transferred into the Reserve.

Larry Mergenschroer – From Lucedale. Joined the Guard for its educational benefits. Served in the Persian Gulf War. Served with Bravo Company of the 150th in Iraq. Now works as a military family readiness specialist, helping Guard families in need.

Lowell Miller – From Flint, Michigan. Graduated from the Virginia Military Institute. Assigned to the 1/155th at Iskandariyah. Killed in action on August 31, 2005, by small-arms fire.

Reuben Ray Miller – Kellogg Brown and Root driver. Killed in action on May 12, 2005 while hauling a generator to FOB Dogwood.

Rosalyn Morris – From Chicago. Studied social work before joining the Army. Served several deployments across the world working with combat stress. Assigned to work with the 150th at Dogwood during the 2005 deployment. Was critical to the mental wellbeing of the unit. Was hit by an IED strike outside of Owesat, but not wounded. After the 2005 deployment she served in a number of ways, including at Walter Reed Hospital and in a Veterans Administration hospital in the emergency room.

Larry Odom – From Lucedale. Served in the Persian Gulf War. Was one of Sean Cooley's best friends. Served with Bravo Company of the 150th in Iraq.

Robert Oneto-Sikorski – From Bay St. Louis. Served with the 155th in Iraq in 2005. The mother of his children, Clare Rager, was also serving in Iraq at the time. Killed in action on October 31, 2005 by an IED strike. Was survived by his wife, Kristine, and his children, Robert, PJ, and Hannah.

Timothy Osbey – From Magnolia outside of McComb. Joined the Guard right after high school. Got married 11 days before shipping out. Served with the 155th in Iraq in 2005. Was killed in a vehicle accident on February 16, 2005.

Hap Palmer – From Meridian. Became an armor officer, then transferred to the 150th. Became battalion maintenance officer before training began at Camp Shelby in 2004. Kept a journal in Iraq, which was a fundamental source for this book. Was deployed to Afghanistan in 2009.

Saburant Parker – From Angie, Louisiana. Known as "Sabo." Had been a wrestler before his 16-year career in the Guard. Was serving with the 155th in Iraq in 2005. Killed in action on May 23, 2005. Survived by his wife Kitza and their children, Merissa and Sheliah.

Rickey Posey – From the rural countryside near Meridian. With two of his brothers already in the Guard, Rickey joined just out of high school. Retired just before the 150th was mobilized in 2004. During the 2005 deployment he worked with the Family Assistance Center, which helped Guard families during the deployment and with loss.

Robert Pugh – From Causeyville. Served as a medic with the 155th in Iraq in 2005. Killed in action on March 2, 2005. As he was dying he directed his attention to helping all of the other wounded around him.

Joseph Rahaim – From Crystal Springs. Served with the 155th in Iraq in 2005. Was killed in a vehicle accident on February 16, 2005.

Roy Robinson – From Meridian. Joined the Guard after a stint at the University of Southern Mississippi. Was moved to command of the 150th as it gathered at Camp Shelby in 2004. Oversaw the success of the 150th in pacifying its AO in Iraq in 2005. By his retirement in 2016 he had risen to be the Assistant Adjutant General. After retirement he served as President of the National Guard Association of the United States.

Richard Rowland – From Hattiesburg. Joined the Army after the Beirut bombing of 1983. Joined the Guard after the terrorist strikes of 9/11. Started at Camp Shelby in 2004 as leader of the support platoon. Married to Keltoum with one daughter, Nadia. In Iraq in 2005 first served in Charlie Company and then became a platoon leader in Bravo Company. Served another deployment to Iraq after 2005. Is now the deputy commander at Camp Shelby.

Joshua Russell – Served in the 890th Engineer Battalion and had taken part in Operation *Iraqi Freedom* in 2003. Was killed on August 29, 2005 while responding to Hurricane Katrina.

Bradley Sharp – From Wiggins. Joined the Guard shortly after high school. Served with Bravo Company of the 150th in Iraq in 2005. Was slated to drive the Humvee on the day that Sean Cooley died, but Cooley overruled him.

Joe Smith – From Meridian. Joined the Navy to see the world after high school. Joined the Guard after the terrorist attacks of 9/11. Served as a medic with Bravo Company of the 150th in Iraq in 2005. Was lightly wounded in the IED strike that killed Sean Cooley. Almost certainly saved the life of Norris Galatas by having Hextend to expand his remaining blood. Was also the medic on site for the loss of Arnold, Lee, and Assim. Struggled with PTSD after the 2005 deployment.

Jay Standley – From Oak Ridge, Louisiana. Had always wanted to be in the military and joined the Guard while in college. Was deployed to Bosnia. Was a platoon leader in Charlie Company of the 150th in Iraq. Late in the deployment Standley led a platoon of Charlie Company in the city of Hit. Was engaged in several deployments after 2005.

Chris Thomas – From Purvis. Joined the Guard on the split option while still in high school. His wife Kristi was pregnant when the 150th got mobilized. Served as commander of Charlie Company in Iraq in 2005. After Iraq served in a number of positions, including as commander of the 890th Engineer Battalion and regimental commander of the 154th Regional Training Institute. Is currently Director of Legislative Affairs and Economic Development for the Mississippi National Guard.

Dexter Thornton – From the Sunrise Community outside Carthage. Joined the Guard during his senior year in high school. Served as assistant S-3 in the 150th in Iraq in 2005. Served in Afghanistan in 2010 and in Iraq in 2018. Now serves as support operations officer for the 184th Sustainment Command.

George Trierweiler – From Gulfport. Joined the military at 18 because he was bored. Served with the 155th in Iraq during 2005.

Greg Tull – From Pocahontas, Iowa. Joined the Guard in high school in the wake of the 9/11 attacks. Served with Alpha Battery, 2/114th Artillery in Iraq in 2005. Killed in action on November 25, 2005.

Ricky Tyler – From Petal. Dropped out of high school at 17 and after two years of work decided to join the Guard in the wake of the 9/11 terrorist attacks. Served as chaplain's assistant before joining the 150th. Served as team leader in Bravo Company with the 150th in Iraq in 2005. Deployed again to Iraq in 2007. Later rose to platoon sergeant and first sergeant and saw a stint on brigade staff in Jackson.

Daniel Ryan Varnado – From Saucier. Joined the Guard following the 9/11 terrorist attacks. Served with the 155th in Iraq in 2005. Killed in action on May 23, 2005. Survived by his wife Sharon and his son Cannon.

Javier Villanueva – From Waco, Texas. Served with the 2/11th ACR in Iraq in 2005. Killed in action on November 24, 2005, in the city of Hit. Survived by his wife Felicia and daughter Taliyah.

John Voccio – From Brooklyn, New York. Joined the Army fresh out of high school. Served in the Persian Gulf War. Served with the 2/11th ACR alongside the 150th in Iraq in 2005.

Raymond Vreeland – From Meridian. His cousin talked him into joining the Guard. Served as a mechanic with the 150th in Iraq in 2005.

Jack Walker – From Hattiesburg. Served in Bravo Company of the 150th in Iraq in 2005. Was wounded in action on February 3, 2005, in the IED strike that killed Sean Cooley. Seemed haunted by that day for the rest of his life. Died in a car accident in 2022 on the anniversary of Sean Cooley's death.

Winston Walker – Medic with the 150th during 2005. Worked with both the Sean Cooley event and the Norris Galatas event.

Marcus Wallace – Born in Mobile and raised in Lucedale. Joined the military in 1998. Served in Bravo Company of the 150th in Iraq in 2005.

Greg Wells – From Madden, Mississippi. Grew up on a farm and was an All-American high school athlete. Joined the Guard in Junior College in 1986. Worked with Trent Kelly as his driver for much of his career. Served with the headquarters of the 150th in Iraq in 2005, often as Trent Kelly's driver. Retired from the Guard in 2007.

Chang Wong – From Malaysia and came to the US with his parents. Joined the Army to help pay for college. Served with the 2/11th ACR with the 150th in 2005. Wounded in action on May 24, 2005. Received his US citizenship while unconscious in the hospital in Germany. Went on to graduate from Cal State Fullerton with hopes of competing in the Paralympics.

Appendix

Weapons and armaments discovered and destroyed by the
150th during its year in Iraq.

Mortars (total): 2,007

57mm – 248	60mm – 660	70mm – 9	81mm – 49
82mm – 310	100mm – 56	120mm – 358	122mm – 317

Artillery (total): 386

84mm – 6	90mm – 2	106mm – 19	120mm – 40
125mm – 122	130mm – 123	152mm – 14	
155mm – 57	160mm – 3		

Miscellaneous rounds (total): 2,214

115mm – 3	60mm – 60	57mm AA – 393
37mm AA – 1677	20mm – 81	

Small-arms ammunition (total): 210 cases, 519 cans, 67,142 rds. loose

7.62 x 39 – 49 cases	13.5 cans	1,750 rds. loose
7.62 x 54 – 3 cases	10 cans	196 rds. loose
12.5mm – 0 cases	84 cans	60,000 rds. loose
12.7mm – 18 cases	8 cans	400 rds. loose
14.3mm – 6 cases	222 cans	
14.5mm – 46 cases	147 cans	3,400 rds. loose
.50 cal. – 88 cases	5 cans	
Unspecified – 0 cases	30 cans	1,396 rds. loose

RPGs: 633 rds., 47 RPG launchers

Type 69 – 28	PG-18 – 1	VG-9 – 15	OG-9 – 61	40mm OG-7 – 233
70mm PG-7 – 38	73mm PG-9 – 87	75mm APERS – 121		
85mm PG-7 – 49				

Rockets (total): 303

57mm – 14	80mm – 20	105mm – 5
107mm – 93	122mm – 171	

Other items

Milan French guided missiles – 4	Landmines – 26
AT-4 Sagger missiles – 20	SA-7s – 41
AK-47 rifles – 38	Hand/rifle grenades – 1,196
TNT blocks – 16	Suicide vests – 4
HE compound – 4,410lbs	Propellant – 1,990lbs
Ammonium nitrate – 2x 55-gallon drums	Detonators – 100
Time fuse – 24,010ft	Detonation cord – 7,202ft
Fuses (assorted types) – 1,629	M21 anti-tank mine – 1
Primers – 130	MICLIC man packs – 10
Propane tank IED (30lbs) – 1	Mortar tubes – 19
Rocket launchers – 2	AA guns – 9
CS grenade launcher – 2	RPG launcher – 11
Machine guns (unspecified) – 12	2.7mm machine guns – 2
Draganoff sniper rifle – 1	Shotgun – 1
9mm pistols – 4	7.9mm rifles – 9
M38/46 DSHK – 1	SPG-9s – 2
60mm recoilless rifle – 1	Misc. gun tubes – 2

Bibliography

ORAL INTERVIEWS

Extensive oral interviews with veterans of the 150th and their family members form the bedrock source for this work. The recordings of the interviews are now open to use by researchers and are housed in the Center of the Study of the National Guard (CSNG) at the University of Southern Mississippi. Written interviews are also open for research purposes and, along with copies of other relevant primary source material, are also housed in CSNG.

Interviews

150th Headquarters, Maintenance and Support, and home front: Roy Robinson (150th commander), Trent Kelly, Jody Kyzar, Norris Galatas, Mike Gilpin, Allen McDaniel, Rosalyn Morris, Hap Palmer, Rickey Posey, James Scarborough, Joe Smith, Alicia Thornton (wife of James McElroy), Greg Wells.

Alpha Company: Ken Cager (commander), Terrance Bloodsaw, Russell Griffith, Thomas Howell, Annie Lockhart, Albert Matlock, Eddie Smith, Dexter Thornton.

Bravo Company: Paul Lyon (commander), Larry Arnold Junior, Robert Arnold (sons of Larry Arnold Senior), Mike Beal, Timothy Bolton, Jerry Cooley, Katherine Cooley, Laura Cooley (parents and wife of Sean Cooley), Marty Davis, Christopher Dueitt, Kirk Dyer, Stacey Ford, Joseph Hammonds, Darrell Havard, Javanian Jones, Randall Jones, Gary Kinsey, Robert Lagrone, Anice Lee, Dinah Lee, Darius Lee, Marchelle Lee (Terrance Lee's family), Douglas Mansfield, Larry Mergenschroer, Larry Odom, Bradley Sharp, Ricky Tyler, Marcus Wallace.

Charlie Company: Chris Thomas (commander), Brittany Dauzat (Chad Dauzat's niece), Greg Fernandez, Sherman Hillhouse, Brad Hollingsworth, Richard Rowland, Jay Standley, Raymond Vreeland.

Others: A&O Platoon, Denise Ahern (fiancée of Robert McNail), Jamie Davis, James Tucker McNeese. Interpreter, Joseph. 2nd Battalion, 12th Cavalry, John Voccio (commander). Alpha Battery, 2nd Battalion, 114th Field Artillery, David Martian (commander). 155th Brigade Combat Team, Undaryl Allen, Edward Anderson, Corey Bell, Dwight Blackman, Jeffrey Cornett, Mandie Curtis, Gene Dufrene, Jason Frazure, Shaun James, Ryan McMillan, George Trierweiler.

PERSONAL PAPERS

Several 150th veterans have been kind enough to share their personal papers (including letters, diaries, pictures, notebooks, and writings) with the author, a collection that forms a major source for this work. The papers (some of which are restricted by agreement with the donor) are now housed in CSNG.
Kevin Kelly, Alpha Company. Jody Kyzar, Headquarters. Paul Lyon, Bravo Company. Rosalyn Morris, Headquarters. Allen McDaniel, Headquarters. Hap Palmer, Headquarters. Jay Standley, Charlie Company. Chris Thomas, Charlie Company.

PERSONAL PRIMARY SOURCES

Two members of the 150th have published books regarding their experiences that were critical sources:
Galatas, Janis. *A Soldier's Courage* (Booksurge, 2007).
Talley, Dan. *The Stan* (CreateSpace, 2016).

PUBLISHED PRIMARY SOURCE MATERIAL

Krepinevich, Andrew. *The War in Iraq: An Interim Assessment* (Washington, DC: Center for Strategic and Budgetary Assessments, 2005).
Marine Corps Intelligence. *Study of the Insurgency in Anbar Province Iraq* (Carlisle, PA: US Army War College, 2007).
Mississippi Legislature. Senate Concurrent Resolution No. 504. Regular Session, 2006.
The National Security Strategy of the United States of America (Washington, DC: The White House, 2006).
Todd, Lin. *Iraq Tribal Study – Al-Anbar Governorate: The Albu Fahd Tribe, The Albu Mahal Tribe, and the Albu Issa Tribe* (Washington, DC: Department of Defense, 2006).

U.S. Army Field Manual (FM) 3-0, *Operations* (Washington, DC: Department of the Army, 2001).

PRIMARY SOURCE MEDIA COVERAGE

Belth, Alex. "Mark Warren on the Odyssey of Stephanie Lee, 'Patient Zero.'" *Esquire Classic Podcast*, 2016.

"Bleak Mood at Black Watch Base in Wilderness of Mud: Camp Dogwood Deaths Increase Tension of Night Rocket Attacks." *The Guardian*, November 5, 2004.

Bostrom, Majsan. "Soldier Laid to Rest." *Wilmington Star News*, May 22, 2005.

"Bryan Edward Barron Obituary." *Times Picayune*, May 30, 2005.

Carolio, Russell and Mike Wagner. "Deadly Price Paid for Humvee Armor Used to Protect Vehicles." *Dayton Daily News,* June 19, 2006.

"Cavalry Moves in on Insurgents Near Euphrates." *Defense Visual Information Distribution Service*, January 18, 2005.

"Congressman Taylor Back in Mississippi After Visiting Troops Overseas." WLOX, April 4, 2005.

"Travis Cooper." Honor the Fallen. militarytimes.com, July 16, 2005.

Elkins, Ashley. "Four Mississippi Soldiers, Another from Alabama Injured in Iraq." *Daily Journal*, April 19, 2005.

Fallen Heroes Project.

"Family Loses Home to Katrina, Son to War." EastValley.com, November 3, 2005.

Flannigan, Allison. "IA, Rakkasans Find Caches in Owesat, Yusufiyah." U.S. Central Command, March 3, 2008.

Greenhill, Jim. "Guard Bureau Chief: National Guard Faces Challenges, Should Stay Operational." U.S. Army, March 2013.

Hill, William. "Honor is Their Strength." *Defense Visual Information Distribution Service*, November 29, 2016.

"'In That Moment, He Chose to Act': JECC Reserve Director is Decorated for Heroism and Sacrifice in Afghanistan," Joint Enabling Capabilities Command, February 23, 2023.

"Iraqi Forces Arrest 220 Suspects in Al Qaeda Raid." *World News*, October 31, 2008.

Junod, Tom. "Mississippi Goddamn." *Esquire*, November 2005.

Junod, Tom. "The Death of a Friend: Stephanie Lee." *Esquire*, February 2015.

Kulo, Warren. "Stephanie Lee: A Story of Unspeakable Tragedy, Remarkable Courage, and Hope." Gulflive.com, January 25, 2014.

Lancaster, John. "Mississippi Citizen-Soldiers Refusing to Fade Away." *Washington Post*, January 1992.

Lloyd, Evan. "Iron Brigade and Iraqi Army Commando Battalion Secures Owesat in Operation Al-Sakar." *Defense Visual Information Distribution Service,* April 17, 2009.

"Local Fallen Soldier Honored at Memorial Garden Dedication." WLOX, May 22, 2009.

"Local Soldier Injured: Convoy Attacked by Suicide Bomber." *Tuscaloosa News*, April 21, 2005.

Locklear, Royce. "Army National Guard 4.0: A Transformation." Association of the United States Army, October 2022.

"Lucedale Mourns Loss of Sgt. Cooley." WLOX, February 6, 2005.

"Audrey Daron Lunsford Obituary." Legacy.com.

Mason, Kevin. "Iowa History Daily: November 25, Sergeant Gregory Tull." *Notes on Iowa*, November 25, 2005.

"Lowell Miller." Honor the Fallen. militarytimes.com, August 31, 2005.

"Lowell Miller." The National Gold Star Family Registry, August 31, 2005.

"Mississippi Soldiers Receive Purple Hearts." WLBT, August 21, 2005.

Murray, Ben. "Unauthorized Medical Device Keeps Soldier Alive." *Stars and Stripes*, June 15, 2005.

"Operation Marine Courageous." Institute for the Study of War.

"Joseph A. Rahaim." *Fallen Heroes of Operation Iraqi Freedom*, https://www.fallenheroesmemorial.com/oif/profiles/rahaimjosepha.html.

Roan, Shari. "Science Quickens Its Steps." *Los Angeles Times*, March 9, 2006.

Robinson, Roy. "I Came Home Wounded." *The Hill*, June 19, 2017.

"Saburant Parker Obituary." Legacy.com.

"Scorpions Brigade (SWAT 'Al Hillah') – Special Weapons and Tactics," Corpi D' Elite.net.

Self, Jane. "Fallen Warrior: Longtime National Guardsman Couldn't Leave the Job He Loved to the Public." *Tuscaloosanews.com*, July 9, 2006.

Simmons, Ann. "In One Iraqi Village: A Taste of What Might Be." *Los Angeles Times*, December 24, 2007.

Slavin, Erik. "GIs Use Strategic Town as Base in Search for Missing Soldiers." *Stars and Stripes*, November 20, 2007.

"Top US General Tracks 'Rat Lines' in Iraqi Villages." *Taipei Times*, January 9, 2008.

"Gregory Tull." Honor the Fallen. militarytimes.com, November 25, 2005.

"U.S., Iraqi Forces Launch Strike." *Associated Press*, November 16, 2007.

"Danny Varnado Obituary." *Sun Herald*, June 1, 2005.

"Javier Villanueva." Fallen Heroes Project, November 24, 2005, https://www.fallenheroesproject.org/post/javier-antonio-villanueva.

"Javier Villanueva Obituary." Legacy.com.

Warren, Mark and Jom Junod. "Patient Zero." *Esquire*, November 2013.

Weiss, Caleb. "Islamic State Continues to Advance in Iraq's Anbar Province." *Long War Journal*, February 24, 2015.

"Who is Kataib Hezbollah, the Group Blamed for Killing US Troops." *Reuters*, January 2024.

"Wounded Warriors Fight Back Through Paralympics." Menstuff.

SECONDARY SOURCES

Andrade, Dale. *Surging South of Baghdad: The 3d Infantry Division and Task Force Marne in Iraq, 2007–2008* (Washington, DC: Center of Military History, 2010).

Avant, Deborah. *Political Institutions and Military Change: Lessons from Peripheral Wars* (Ithaca, NY: Cornell University Press, 1994).

Baker, James and Lee Hamilton, Co-Chairs. *The Iraq Study Group Report* (New York: Vintage Books, 2006).

Beckett, Ian F. W. *Modern Insurgencies and Counter-Insurgencies: Guerrillas and their Opponents since 1750* (New York: Routledge, 2001).

Bremer, L. Paul III, with Malcolm McConnell. *My Year in Iraq, The Struggle to Build a Future of Hope* (New York: Simon & Schuster, 2006).

Castaneda Laura et al. *Deployment Experiences of Guard and Reserve Families: Implications for Support and Retention* (Santa Monica, CA: RAND National Defense Research Institute, 2008).

Cottam, Martha and Joe W. Huseby. *Confronting al Qaeda: The Sunni Awakening and American Strategy in al Anbar* (Washington, DC: Rowan and Littlefield, 2016).

Doubler, Michael. *I Am the Guard; A History of the Army National Guard, 1636–2000* (Washington, DC: Army National Guard, 2001).

Doubler, Michael. *The National Guard and the War on Terror: Operation Iraqi Freedom* (Washington, DC: Army National Guard, 2008).

Estes, Kenneth. *U.S. Marines in Iraq, 2004–2005: Into the Fray* (Washington, DC: History Division, United States Marine Corps, 2011).

Frederick, Jim. *Black Hearts: One Platoon's Descent into Madness in Iraq's Triangle of Death* (New York: Broadway, 2010).

Hashim, Ahmed. *Insurgency and Counter-Insurgency in Iraq* (Ithaca, NY: Cornell University Press, 2006).

Hashim, Ahmed. "Iraq's Sunni Insurgency." *The Adelphi Papers*, Volume 48, Issue 402, 2008.

Haskell, Bob. "The Guard Surge in Iraq." *National Guard Magazine*, March 2014.

Jones, Franklin. *Domestic and Expeditionary Readiness in the Twenty-First Century: Maintaining an Operationalized Army National Guard* (Fort Leavenworth, KS: School of Advanced Military Studies, 2012).

Komer, Robert. *Bureaucracy at War: U.S. Performance in the Vietnam Conflict* (Boulder, CO: Westview Press, 1986).

Lynch, Michael and William Stover. "A Turbulent Transition: The Army National Guard and Army Reserve's Movement to an Operational Reserve," *Journal of Political and Military Sociology* (Summer 2008).

McGrath, John. *Between the Rivers: Combat Action in Iraq, 2003–2005* (Fort Leavenworth, KS: Combat Studies Institute Press, 2013).

Minear, Larry. *The US Citizen-Soldier and the Global War on Terror: The National Guard Experience* (Feinstein International Center, Tufts University, 2007).

Neumann, Brian, editor. *The US. Army in the World War I Era* (Washington, DC: Center of Military History, 2017).

O'Neill, Bard. *Insurgency and Terrorism: From Revolution to the Apocalypse* (Washington, DC: Potomac Books, 2005).

Pirnie, Bruce and Edward O'Connell. *Counterinsurgency in Iraq (2003–2006)* (Santa Monica, CA: RAND National Defense Research Institute, 2008).

Posen, Barry. *The Sources of Military Doctrine: France, Britain, and Germany Between the World Wars* (Ithaca, NY: Cornell University Press, 2014).

Rabasa, Angel et al. *From Insurgency to Stability: Volume II: Insights from Selected Case Studies* (Santa Monica, CA: RAND National Defense Research Institute, 2011).

Rayburn, Colonel Joel and Colonel Frank Sobchak, editors. *The U.S. Army in the Iraq War, Volume 1: Invasion, Insurgency, Civil War, 2003–2006* (Carlisle, PA: United States Army War College Press, 2019).

Ricks, Thomas. *The Gamble: General David Petraeus and the American Military Adventure in Iraq, 2006–2008* (New York: The Penguin Press, 2009).

Rosen, Stephen. *Winning the Next War: Innovation and the Modern Military* (Ithaca, NY: Cornell University Press, 1994).

Russell, James. *The United States Counterinsurgency Campaign in Iraq, 2005–2007* (Dissertation; King's College, London, 2009).

Shultz, Richard. *The Marines Take Anbar: The Four Year Fight Against al Qaeda* (Annapolis: Naval Institute Press, 2013).

Zelner, Kyle. *A Rabble in Arms: Massachusetts Towns and Militiamen during King Phillip's War* (New York: New York University Press, 2010).

Acknowledgments

First and forever foremost I would like to thank the soldiers and families of the Mississippi National Guard for welcoming me into their community. No project like this can ever take shape without the trust and forbearance of the men and women who are chronicled in the story that became this book. Soldiers and their families have shared their stories with me, allowing me into their world to see their highs and lows. They have opened up about some of the most difficult moments in their lives and they have entrusted me to treat those moments with care. These men and women deserve to have their stories told in the most accurate and sensitive way possible. And I can only hope that my meager words do them justice.

The research and preparation for this project was especially wide ranging and has resulted in a great debt to a host of people who have aided my work. Paul Lyon has long been my best of friends, and I long ago decided that I wanted to write a book about the unit he served in during the war in Iraq. Ever since that decision, he has been there with me every step of the way, helping introduce me to people, aiding in interviews, reading the manuscript, and even giving me extra mulligans at golf. This is as much Paul's project as it is mine. Also at my side during this whole book adventure was Kevin Greene, colleague, friend, and guitar player extraordinaire. Without his friendship and aid, especially in the myriad oral histories that make up this project, it could not have been done. Also of tremendous help in every way imaginable has been Brigadier General (ret.) Roy Robinson. As commander of the 150th in Iraq, getting to know his story and having his support in this project was key in every way.

And all three, Paul, Kevin, and Roy, were fundamental to the idea of this book also spawning the notion of founding the Center for the Study of the National Guard at the University of Southern Mississippi, to ensure that more Guard stories like this one can be collected and told. The National Guard lacks a comprehensive archive to house and chronicle its history. The Center for the Study of the National Guard plans to serve that purpose, and this first book from its collections stands as testament to what it can become.

During my work on this project, I have received tremendous levels of support from the University of Southern Mississippi. At the pinnacle, President Joe Paul and Provost Lance Nail have been key in their unflagging support. Vice President for Research Kelly Lucas and her predecessor in that position Gordon Cannon also deserve my profuse thanks for their support. Dean of the College of Arts and Sciences Chris Winstead, Director of the School of Humanities Matt Casey, and USM Foundation Executive Director Stace Mercier have also been instrumental in supporting this project. I was fortunate to receive the General Buford "Buff" Blount Professorship in Military History as I neared the completion of this project, which allowed me the time to research and write that I needed to get the job done. Thus, my thanks to General Buff Blount for his founding and support of that wonderful opportunity.

I am fortunate to be part of the Dale Center for the Study of War and Society at Southern Miss, which has provided me support, funding, camaraderie, and advice throughout this project. Beverly Dale, the chief benefactor of the Dale Center, is a pal and an unwavering supporter of everything the Center and I do. My debt to her runs deep in all ways. My colleagues in the Dale Center, Kyle Zelner, Heather Stur, Kevin Greene, Ken Swope, Douglas Bristol, Bafu Mocheregwa, Katya Maslakowski, and Laura Mammina, all are deserving of my thanks. My thanks also go to a couple of Dale Center members and pals who have moved on, Susannah Ural and Allison Abra. There are also several students in the Dale Center who have been helpful to my research, especially in helping with oral histories: Bearington Curtis, Daniel Driss, Sarah Hogue, Justin Major, Christian Singletary, and Brian Washam.

With so much of this book being based on oral histories of the soldiers and families of the 150th, I owe a deep debt of gratitude to the Center for Oral History and Cultural Heritage at Southern Miss. The folks there are true professionals, and their collections are unmatched. Thus my thanks go to Kevin Greene, Ross Walton, Stephanie DeArmey, and Isabel Loya for all that they have done, from having to put up with my lack of organizational skills, to having to transcribe so many interviews. And my thanks also go out to the Center for Digital Humanities here at Southern Miss for its support of this project, especially the work of Maeve Losen. Also the great folks at the Center of Military History certainly deserve my thanks: Jon Hoffman, Nicholas Schlosser, and Shane Story. Also I wish to thank Major General (ret.) Jeff Hammond and the good folks at the Center for Military Veterans, Service Members, and Families at Southern Miss for their support not only of this project but also of our student veteran population.

I also owe a deep debt of gratitude to many within the National Guard who helped me far beyond being a part of this story. Congressman and Major General Trent Kelly and Major General Durr Boyles have been unflagging in their support of this project and have also been main supporters of the Center for the Study of the National Guard. Dennis Clark, Chief of the National Guard Bureau History Office, has also been there every step of the way and has offered everything from his historical wisdom to his support and advice regarding the Guard Center. Kandi Murphy, the command historian for the National Guard in Mississippi, and her predecessor Andy Thaggard have also been instrumental in my research for this project.

I am blessed to have a wonderful publishing team at Osprey/ Bloomsbury who always take my projects and make them better. I would like to thank Editorial Director Marcus Cowper for once again taking a chance on me and for listening to me dream aloud at so many wonderful dinners. Thanks also to Publisher Kate Moore for again reading my work with such care and giving me thoughtful advice. My thanks also to Managing Editor Gemma Gardner for all of her help and to my excellent copy editor Julie Frederick. My thanks as always to my great literary agent Jeff Gerecke for making everything on the business end run like clockwork.

I have accumulated many debts in the wider historical world as I wended my way through this book. I presented aspects of my research to the Society for Military History; the Gulf South History and Humanities Conference; the Ways of War, Ways of Peace conference at the University of Alabama in association with the Centre for Army Leadership, Royal Military Academy, Sandhurst; the Mississippi Department of Archives and History; and at the Institute of Historical Research and the War Studies Department of King's College London. For those opportunities and the wonderful feedback I received I would like to thank Lesley Gordon, Lloyd Clark, Chris Goodwin, Rebecca Tuuri, and William Philpott. Broader thanks go to historians who have talked me through this project in a number of ways: Sean McKnight, Gary Sheffield, Hayley Hasik, Rob Thompson, Jim Willbanks, Glenn Robins, Tommy Lofton, John Young, Steve Hopper, and to a young historian who will outshine me in every way – Abigail Wiest.

In closing, my most profound thanks are, as always, reserved for my wonderful family. Without their support and forbearance none of what I do would be possible. First – my lady wife Jill Wiest who is our rock. And to my great kiddos – Abigail, Luke, and Wyatt. It has been the ride of my life watching y'all blossom into such fine adults. I owe this all to you.

Dedication

This book is dedicated to all the soldiers of the US National Guard who have served their country during the War on Terror. More specifically, this book is dedicated to those members of the 155th Brigade Combat Team and its affiliated units who were unable to return home after the deployment to Iraq in 2005.

Sean Cooley, 150th Engineer Battalion, February 3, 2005
Robert McNail, 150th Engineer Battalion, February 11, 2005
Timothy Osbey, 1/155th Infantry Battalion, February 16, 2005
Joseph Rahaim, 1/155th Infantry Battalion, February 16, 2005
Robert Pugh, 1/155th Infantry Battalion, March 2, 2005
Casey Laware, 2/11th Cavalry, April 5, 2005
Tyler Dickens, 2/11th Cavalry, April 12, 2005
Kevin Prince, 2/11th Cavalry, April 23, 2005
Stephen Frank, 2/11th Cavalry, April 29, 2005
Ralph Hartling, 2/11th Cavalry, April 29, 2005
Tommy Little, 2/114th Field Artillery, May 2, 2005
Reuben Ray Miller, Civilian Contractor, May 12, 2005
John Smith, 2/11th Cavalry, May 12, 2005
Bryan Barron, 1/155th Infantry Battalion, May 23, 2005
Audrey Daron Lunsford, 1/155th Infantry Battalion, May 23, 2005
Saburant Parker, 1/155th Infantry Battalion, May 23, 2005
Daniel Varnado, 1/155th Infantry Battalion, May 23, 2005
Mark Maida, 2/11th Cavalry, May 26, 2005
Larry Arnold, 150th Engineer Battalion, June 11, 2005
Assim, Iraqi Interpreter, June 11, 2005

Terrance Lee, 150th Engineer Battalion, June 11, 2005
Travis Cooper, 2/114th Field Artillery, July 16, 2005
Carl Carroll, Civilian Contractor, August 20, 2005
Gregory Fester, 490th Civil Affairs, August 30, 2005
Lowell Miller, 1/155th Infantry Battalion, August 31, 2005
Jacob Dones, 2/11th Cavalry, October 20, 2005
Robert Oneto-Sikorski, 1/155th Infantry Battalion, October 31, 2005
Javier Villanueva, 2/11th Cavalry, November 24, 2005
Gregory Tull, 2/114th Field Artillery, November 25, 2005
Milton Rivera-Vargas, 1/296th Infantry Battalion, December 8, 2005

Index